GOLDEN BOYS

GOLDEN BOYS

BOYS

The Top 50 Manitoba Hockey Players Of All Time

TY DILELLO

GREAT PLAINS
PUBLICATIONS

Great Plains Publications
233 Garfield Street
Winnipeg, MB R3G 2M1
www.greatplains.mb.ca

Great Plains Publications gratefully acknowledges the financial support
provided for its publishing program by the Government of Canada through
the Canada Book Fund; the Canada Council for the Arts; the Province of
Manitoba through the Book Publishing Tax Credit and the Book Publisher
Marketing Assistance Program; and the Manitoba Arts Council.

Design & Typography by Relish New Brand Experience
Printed in Canada by Friesens

LIBRARY AND ARCHIVES CANADA CATALOGUING IN PUBLICATION

Dilello, Ty, author
    Golden boys : the top 50 Manitoba hockey players of all time / Ty Dilello.

Issued in print and electronic formats.
ISBN 978-1-927855-82-9 (softcover).--ISBN 978-1-927855-83-6 (EPUB).--
ISBN 978-1-927855-84-3 (Kindle)

    1. Hockey players--Manitoba--Biography. I. Title.

GV848.5.AID54 2017   796.96209227127   C2017-902874-X
                                     C2017-902875-8

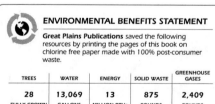

ENVIRONMENTAL BENEFITS STATEMENT

Great Plains Publications saved the following
resources by printing the pages of this book on
chlorine free paper made with 100% post-consumer
waste.

TREES	WATER	ENERGY	SOLID WASTE	GREENHOUSE GASES
28	13,069	13	875	2,409
FULLY GROWN	GALLONS	MILLION BTUs	POUNDS	POUNDS

Environmental impact estimates were made using the Environmental Paper Network
Paper Calculator 3.2. For more information visit www.papercalculator.org.

Canadä

FSC
www.fsc.org
MIX
Paper from
responsible sources
FSC® C016245

For Roy and Iris

CONTENTS

INTRODUCTION

A lot of writers tell some cool story here in the introduction of how their idea for a book came to them in some unique way. Unfortunately, I don't have some startling tale to tell, but here it goes anyway.

In the summer of 2016 I had just finished my last book and was looking to do a new project in conjunction with the 100th anniversary of the National Hockey League. I toyed around with some ideas for a few weeks but eventually came to the conclusion that I wanted to do something that had to do with my home province because of how much hockey is connected with the people here.

Our province and Winnipeg especially played such a big role in the history of hockey. In the late 1890's and early 1900's, the Winnipeg Victorias won three Stanley Cups. They were the first western Canadian city to make legitimate strides in the hockey world. In 1920, the Winnipeg Falcons won the first ever Olympic gold medal in ice hockey.

I basically wanted to write a hockey book that was interesting enough that my mom would read it, because she barely opened any of my last three books. I remembered watching a Top 50 Playoff Goals VHS featuring Ron MacLean and Dick Irvin Jr. over and over again when I was kid, so I kind of used that idea and from there, quickly came up with the Top 50 Manitoba Hockey Players of All Time. I got to interview Dick Irvin Jr. for this book because his dad is very high on the list, which was quite the surreal moment in itself because like most kids, I grew up listening to Irvin on Hockey Night in Canada.

Looking back, I really got to talk to a lot of amazing people while writing this book. Every person I interviewed, I have nothing but great things to say about. I tried to interview at least one person for every chapter, whether it be the player himself, family member, friend, teammate, etc. For example, Ted Harris, who is in his 80's now and is well-known to be very reclusive and unresponsive to media requests was just a total sweetheart with me. I also got to visit Chuck Gardiner's niece at her home and she was kind enough to let me go through scrapbooks and photo albums of Chuck that the family had kept after all these years. I actually got to hold Gardiner's Hall of Fame medal in my hand. For a hockey history buff like me that's a moment I'll never forget.

My research for this book was really quite endless. I went very deep into internet databases, news archives, army papers, etc., to find everything I possibly could on each player. I watched old NHL games from as early as the 1920's to get a better sense of earlier eras of the sport. I even went as far as buying a one-day subscription to an Omaha newspaper archive just so I could attempt to get some quotes from the late Mud Bruneteau. I became extremely enthralled with this project and for the past year it's all I've really thought about. If you were to look at my laptop at any point over the last year, you'd notice I'd always have at least twenty tabs open on Google Chrome, all relating to this book. Let's just say that I'm very relieved it's all over with now and I can sit back and enjoy the finished product with you.

It ended up becoming extremely hard once I got to the second half or so of the book to try and contain each player's chapter to 3,000 words or less. I wanted to include unique stories of each player's upbringing, not just the usual info you could find after a quick Google search, in writing these 50 mini-biographies.

The criteria for making this Top 50 list was pretty simple—you had to start playing hockey as a kid in Manitoba. Players from Kenora were also considered for this list based on the town's proximity to Manitoba and isolation from the rest of Ontario. As the great Manitoba sportswriter Vince Leah once said, "Kenora has always owned a valued corner of the Manitoba hockey scene."

When it was all said and done, the final tally of the Top 50 Manitoba Hockey Players of All-Time were 24 forwards, 20 defencemen, and 6 goalies. I consulted with many other writers, historians, hockey players, coaches, and everyone I could to help make this list as accurate as possible. I didn't want to just give my sole opinion on who I thought the Top 50 are since most people are probably going to think 'what the hell does a 24-year-old know about hockey?'

Here's a brief lesson about the two early indoor arenas in Winnipeg that over half of the players on this list played at. Trust me, they get mentioned plenty throughout this book because if you grew up between the 1910's and 1950's there's a high probability you played at some point at either Shea's Amphitheatre or the Olympic Rink. Both are extremely important in our province's hockey history. The Amphitheatre was located on the site of where the Great-West Life Building on Osborne presently sits. A 5,000-seat arena, it was for a long time the only artificial ice surface between Toronto and Vancouver. The Olympic Rink is now an apartment building called Olympic Towers at the corner of Church Avenue and Charles Street in the North End.

I have to say that it was extremely tough making the final call on some of the players at the tail-end of the list. There were about 10-15 other guys that could have been included, but like I said, some very tough calls were made. I guess part of the interest in this book is that it's going to spark debates on who should be on the list and "this guy should be higher than so and so."

At the end of the day, however, the point of this book is that we are celebrating fifty world-class hockey players that came from Manitoba, many of whom have passed away and long since been forgotten because practically everyone on the list played before the internet was around. Heck, lots played before television was invented! This is my way of educating the younger generations in remembering the legends of the past who came from these parts.

What I would have given to be at the very first Winnipeg Jets game in the NHL in 1979. Not for the game, but for what happened before the game. The Jets had invited all of Manitoba's living Hockey Hall of Fame players in a special pre-game ceremony. Name by name, legends came out on to the ice like Harry Oliver, Andy Bathgate, Black Jack Stewart, Babe Pratt, Art Coulter, Bill Mosienko and Bryan Hextall. To me that just seems like the most surreal and coolest thing ever, but sadly I wasn't alive for that.

I sincerely hope that you enjoy this book.

50
MURRAY BANNERMAN

tarting off our Top 50 Manitoba Hockey Players of All Time countdown at number fifty is goaltender Murray Bannerman, or just simply "BANNERMAN!" if you were a Chicago Blackhawks fan in the 1980's.

Pat Foley's call on Murray Bannerman making a two-pad stack breakaway save on the Minnesota North Stars in the 1985 Norris Division Finals was one of the more memorable Blackhawks moments of the 1980's. To this day, long-time Chicago Blackhawks play-by-play announcer Pat Foley still gets asked to reprise that call more than any other call he's made over the years. The original video of the "BANNERMAN!" call can be found on YouTube for those wondering what the heck I'm talking about.

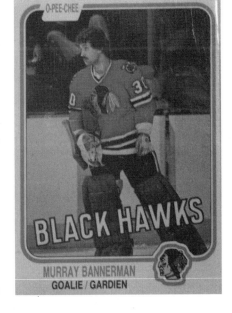

Born in Fort Francis, Ontario, a town of nearly 8,000 in northwestern Ontario that is located on the international border adjacent to International Falls, MN., Bannerman moved to Winnipeg at a young age and grew up in the St. James area, not too far from the Assiniboia Downs racetrack. It was in Winnipeg that Murray honed his skills on the outdoor rink at Crestview Community Club that was just a block from his house.

"As a kid growing up in Winnipeg, it was just something you did," said Bannerman. "You had long cold winters. I learned to skate shortly after I had learned to walk so it just seemed like the natural thing to do. The local community club was a block from my house and my dad was involved in the youth hockey program there."

It wasn't long before Bannerman found his way between the pipes and started tending goal for his local community club. He was primarily a stand-up goalie early on, "My style was pretty typical of most goalies in that era. You stood up more than you went down and positioning was very important, playing the angle and relying on what happens. Playing in that era, not many goalies went down often, and those who did were considered floppers—but my style was more of standing up and reacting to the shot."

Murray progressed enough through the ranks of junior hockey in Winnipeg that he was playing in the Manitoba Junior Hockey League as a fifteen-year-old for his neighbourhood St. James Canadians. He played a season and a half for St. James before moving on to play in the Western Canadian Junior Hockey League (WCJHL) for the Winnipeg Clubs for another season and a half.

Bannerman had a breakthrough year when he was eighteen years old. He started the 1975-76 season back in the MJHL playing for the Assiniboine Park Monarchs, but after a strong start in his first eight games of the year, he jumped at an offer to join the Victoria Cougars of the WCJHL. It was in Victoria that Bannerman continued his strong play and began to attract attention from NHL scouts.

"I started playing in the MJHL at fourteen years of age. Including my time with Victoria, I actually played six years of junior hockey," Bannerman recalls. "My last couple of years with Victoria is when I first started thinking that I had a realistic shot at the NHL. We had a pretty decent team and as far as my play went, it was supposedly one of the best in the league, so at that point in time I thought I had at least a chance to play pro."

After his second season with Victoria, Murray was drafted to both the NHL and the WHA. The Vancouver Canucks selected him with the 58th overall pick at the 1977 NHL Entry Draft, while the Winnipeg Jets picked him with the 88th overall pick at their respective draft that year. Bannerman chose the NHL route and signed with Vancouver. They assigned him to the Fort Wayne Komets of the old International Hockey League (IHL), where he spent the 1977-78 season. He was called up briefly to the Canucks during the season and made his NHL debut, playing in one period of one game. It would be the only appearance that Murray would ever make in a Vancouver Canucks uniform.

Soon after his NHL debut, Murray was dealt to the Chicago Blackhawks where he would spend the next two seasons developing with their AHL affiliate, the New Brunswick Hawks. For the 1980-81 season, Murray would become a full-time NHLer for the first time. He earned a permanent spot on the Blackhawks roster out of training camp, and would now be backing up the legendary and future Hockey Hall of Famer Tony Esposito, with whom Murray would learn a great deal about goaltending the next couple of seasons.

"It was good and bad playing behind Tony. It was difficult my first year because Tony was so good and he played all the time so I didn't get a lot of opportunities to play. Having said that, I had the chance to watch from the bench one of the best goalies in the NHL so you could learn a lot from that. You can learn about his preparation and everything that went into being how he is on the ice, so playing alongside him was definitely a wonderful learning experience," Bannerman recalls. "Just to have a chance to learn from somebody with that type of ability and everything that Tony brought to the game was a definite benefit for me. Later, we got to the point where I started to play a little more and obviously that's why I was there; I wanted to play. I just didn't want to be a guy sitting on the bench watching the games, so it was a good thing for me in that point of time when I started to play more."

It was a lot of watching and not much playing for Murray in his first couple of years in Chicago. He played fifteen games the first year and then twenty-nine the following season. It was then in the 1982 Stanley Cup Playoffs (his second season) where Bannerman first made a name for himself in the NHL when his strong play lifted the Blackhawks to a first-round series win over the heavily favoured Minnesota North Stars who were the Stanley Cup finalists the year before. After Murray's playoff performance that year, he was now the man in Chicago and was playing the same amount of games, if not more than Tony Esposito.

Bannerman talks about that playoff run in 1982, "That was probably the biggest high of my career. It was the first year I really got to play and contribute in the playoffs. We ended up playing the North Stars in the first round and they were a huge favourite. They finished way ahead of us in the standing and we ended up beating them!"

Terry Ruskowski, a teammate of Murray's in Chicago, recalls that, "Murray was a guy that started off as a really good goaltender. He was in the shadow of (Tony) Esposito for a number of years, but when it was his time to play, he played, and he played very, very well."

Bannerman would go on to put up four consecutive 20-plus win seasons in Chicago and was considered to be one of the league's top goalies during his prime, appearing in the 1983 and 1984 NHL All-Star game. The pinnacle of Murray's career came in the 1984-85 season, where he helped the Blackhawks get to the Conference Finals, sweeping the Bruins and defeating the North Stars in six games. They fell to the eventual Stanley Cup champ Edmonton Oilers in six games, a dynasty squad that won five Stanley Cup's between 1984 and 1990. For Bannerman, that 1985 run to the Conference Finals would be the closest he would ever get to the Stanley Cup.

To hockey fans today, Bannerman might be best known for that scary looking mask he wore when he played for Chicago. *The Hockey News* might have said it best when they were ranking the scariest masks of all-time a few years back by calling it, "A Native-American motif that looks alien-creepy in a Japanese doll sort of way."

"The design of the mask was for that era unique in that guys have different things. Really what I wanted was something that was reflective of the Indian Head; something that was kind of a unique logo, so when I had it made, that's what I wanted it to reflect. I think one of the things that makes it more memorable is that I still wore that when guys were switching to the mask with the cage built in. I was probably one of the last NHL goalies to wear that type of mask so I think that added to it being memorable," said Bannerman with a smile. "I tried to switch to the mask with the cage built in to it. It was a hard switch for me because I found it heavy and it was almost uncomfortable, plus the bars in front of your eyes was somewhat distracting. I think that when you play your whole life as a goalie with a mask that pretty much sits right on your face, you have that visibility with nothing in front of your eyes. It was a difficult adjustment for me to try and switch to something else."

After seven seasons with Chicago, Murray was sent to Saginaw of the IHL early in the 1987-88 season. He would quit professional hockey shortly after. During his career, he played in 289 NHL games, recording 116 wins and 8 shutouts.

Since his retirement from hockey, Murray has kept himself busy working for a number of different companies. "I've been in sales are far as work goes. Things like the material handling business and recycling business. And I've been in the transportation industry for the last seven years. I also spend a lot of time in youth hockey. I spent the last 18 years either coaching or being a hockey director for different organizations," said Bannerman. "Right now, I work for a Canadian company called Traffic Tech and they're actually based out of Montreal. We have a US division which I'm the vice president of sales for. It's an interesting industry."

Looking back on his eight-year NHL career, Bannerman only has one regret. "I regret that we never won a Stanley Cup because that's the ultimate goal. We had some pretty good teams in the early to mid 80's. The unfortunate thing for us is that Edmonton always had a pretty good team. We always lost to them in the playoffs so maybe it was just a matter of timing. I believed we had a great collection of talent in Chicago, but we just could never get over that hump against Edmonton."

CHICO RESCH SAYS

I liked him as a goalie and I liked his mask a lot, it was great. With Murray, you think about success in sports and how it's all about timing. When he went to the Blackhawks, they had come out of some dark times in the 1970's towards the end of Tony Esposito's career when they weren't very good. Bobby Hull had left, Stan Mikita was old—so Murray was there when the Hawks started their rebuild and he was good.

The thing with Murray is he had some flamboyancy to his game, but he was pretty consistent. He was kind of like me in that he wasn't that great of a goalie, but he found a way to be consistent. At that point in Chicago's development, he was an important part of that club's resurgence. As a goalie, you sometimes think 'Oh, you can find some holes on this guy or that guy,' and I never felt that way about Murray. You were always going to have to make nice plays and take good shots to beat him.

49
GORD LANE

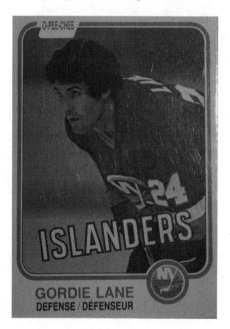

O-PEE-CHEE

GORDIE LANE
DEFENSE / DEFENSEUR

Anyone who wins four consecutive Stanley Cups in their career automatically qualifies themselves for this Top 50 list. That's why you're now going to be reading about Brandon native Gord Lane, a name that you might not be familiar with, but was an integral piece of the New York Islanders dynasty squad of the early 1980's that won four straight Stanley Cups and nineteen consecutive playoff series, the latter a record which will likely never be broken.

It's been said that every championship team needs that one player to do the little things that may go unnoticed, but certainly not unappreciated. Gord Lane was the defender the Islanders needed to help bring greatness to Long Island.

"The big thing about our hockey club is that everyone brought a little something different to the table. Gordie Lane was an individual who came along to the Isles just before I did, and he was a very steady defenceman. He was a smart guy on the ice who made simple plays," recalls former teammate Butch Goring. "If you ask Billy Smith who his favourite defenceman was on the Islanders, I'm pretty sure he's going to tell you it was Gordie Lane because he played a similar game to Billy in many ways despite playing different positions!"

Gord Lane was born in Brandon on March 31, 1953. "Growing up there in Brandon in the fifties and sixties was something else," Gord recalls. "Our television had one channel, so we mostly played outside as kids. Anybody who grows up there understands that you go play hockey from the time you can walk, that's just what you do, and I was no different."

Always an aggressive defensive-defenceman, Gord played his minor and junior hockey in Brandon, and by the time he was seventeen he was playing for his hometown Brandon Wheat Kings of the Western Hockey League (WHL). Despite playing two years with the Wheat Kings and another with the New Westminster Bruins, Lane never thought he had a realistic chance at the NHL until after his junior career was over with and he'd been drafted in the ninth round (134th overall) by the Pittsburgh Penguins at the 1973 NHL Entry Draft.

"I never really thought about the NHL. It was just something that played out after junior hockey," said Lane. "I was a ninth-round pick because I was always just an average junior hockey player. The only reason I was even picked is because I was a physical player. I was tough, and in those days, that was part of the game and you had to have that physical presence. I was not a skills player at that stage."

After being drafted by the Penguins, Lane signed a minor-league deal that saw him spend the 1973-74 season with the International Hockey League's (IHL) Fort Wayne Komets. After a season with Fort Wayne he was traded to the Dayton Gems, a farm team of the Washington Capitals. Gord would win a Turner Cup with Dayton in 1975-76, and was then finally promoted full-time to the Capitals the following season.

Gord talks about his jump to the NHL: "I was in the minors playing with Dayton for a couple of seasons and Tom McVie was my coach there. Tommy helped me a lot and I was able to develop my skills outside of just physical play. Tommy was eventually called up to coach the Capitals around Christmas of 1975, and then the following season, he called up six of us who had played for him in Dayton and I was one of them. I was fortunate to stay on with the Capitals after that. They were not a good hockey team back then, being new to the league and all. It was very challenging just to be competitive at times, but overall I liked playing in Washington a great deal."

Lane went on to play parts of five seasons in a Washington Capitals uniform before being traded to the New York Islanders on December 7, 1979 for forward Mike Kaszycki. "I think the initial thought after I was traded was that I was going to New York and living in the big city, and to be honest I wasn't really excited about it. When I got there, however, I realized we weren't in New York City, but a little bit out there in Long Island which was a little different and nice," said Lane. "As far as now being on a contender, I knew it was a good hockey team when I was traded to the Islanders. They had good hockey players and such, but I think up until that stage, they were in the mix, but they weren't the Montreal Canadiens."

As soon as Lane joined the club, he made his presence known on the ice, and his strong play didn't go unnoticed. New York Islanders head coach Al Arbour was a stay-at-home defenceman as well in his playing days, so there was a great appreciation that Al had for Gordie's game.

"Gordie's thing was that he was a real tough son of a gun. He would pound you and was a very physical guy to play with in the corners and in front of the net. He was never afraid to fight and was always such a tremendous team player," said former Isles teammate Butch Goring. "Gordie fit in like a glove. Everything that Isles GM Bill Torrey did, he seemed to always get the right guy at the right time in the right spot, and Gordie was always just a really, really good guy for us."

With Lane's tough play and strong defence, he helped the Islanders win four straight Stanley Cups (1980, 1981, 1982, 1983). They are the last NHL team to win four consecutive Cups, and as stated previously, their record of winning nineteen playoff series in a row is a record that will most likely stand the test of time. When Gord won his first Stanley Cup in 1980, he became the first former Washington Capitals player to have his name engraved on the Cup.

Gord talks about his success on Long Island, "You just kind of fall into it when you become a part of the organization. It was nice because you felt like you were a productive member of the hockey club and that gave us some satisfaction. We always strived to be the best we possibly could in all our hockey situations, and that was a pretty satisfying feeling coming from where I started in the game to what I did with the Islanders."

A fifth consecutive Stanley Cup might have been in the cards had it not been for some untimely injuries during the Isles playoff run in 1984. Gord was injured and missed almost all of the playoffs that year. His presence was especially missed in the Cup finals, as the Oilers skated past the tired, battered, and undermanned Islanders in five games to win their first Stanley Cup, ending the incredible run that Long Island had been on. They say that all good things eventually must come to an end, and that held true for Gord Lane and the New York Islanders. Since 1984, the franchise has failed to make it back to the Stanley Cup finals.

Lane spent another couple seasons with the Islanders before closing out his career in the American League. He retired from the game in 1987 at the age of 34. When it was all said and done, Lane played 540 games in the NHL, scoring 19 goals and 113 points over the course of 10 seasons, while also accumulating 1,228 minutes in penalties.

Over the years, Lane has been credited by different people in the hockey world as being the Islanders most effective defender during their Stanley Cup years. Gord has nothing but good memories when looking back today at his former career, "Certainly just making an NHL roster was amazing," said Gord with a smile. "Being a core hockey player on a Stanley Cup dynasty team is tops for me though. Winning the four Stanley Cups with the Islanders was just an incredible feeling."

After his retirement from hockey in 1987, Lane went back to school and earned himself an undergraduate degree in construction management and then went on to start up Next Shift Enterprises, a multi-venture business run by, and employing, retired and current hockey players with the purpose of helping them make the transition from hockey into the business world. In addition to that, Gord started a highly successful Maryland-based construction company that he still runs today at the age of 63.

In regard to how much Gord comes back these days to his hometown, he said, "I come back to Brandon twice a year now. I come up in the summer and then again in the fall around October. I try and stay away from there from November through March!"

CHICO RESCH SAYS

A dynasty team is made up of many, many components. And one of them back then was a tough kind of "I don't know what this guy might do" player. Gordie was that way. Skill-wise he was driven, ferocious and fearless. What Gordie could do is he defended real well. You could defend differently in those days. A two-hander wasn't called by the refs, a stick between the legs wasn't called. Gordo was an average skater at best, but the rest of his game was refined to play on the edge of what the rules allowed back in that day. He gave us an edge where he could fight when he had to, and was certainly mean enough to put people on their heels if they started to monkey around physically.

Gordie was smart. When I think of prairie people I think of farmers and Gordie was kind of like a farmer, where if they had a problem on the farm and they had to fix it themselves, they didn't hire someone to do it like today. He could figure things out.

He seemed to always make a pretty nice first pass. His shot was a goalie friendly shot and he didn't score many goals, but he could make that good first pass. He was exactly what we needed. From a coaching standpoint, Al Arbour really liked him. He was low maintenance. I won't say he was an Al Arbour, but out of all our defencemen he was the closest to our coach in being the 5-6th defencemen who knew his role, so I think Al appreciated that.

I sat next to Gordie in the dressing room and I remember he would always bring me M&M's. He had a speech impediment, stuttering a little bit. But he would sing, and when he sang there was no stutter. It was very enjoyable to play with Gordie. He liked to laugh and have a good time, and then when it was time to get the job done, he was there, no questions asked. You knew he would be there when you needed him.

48
BILL JUZDA

oronto Maple Leafs' general manager Conn Smythe might have said it
best that Bill Juzda had "guts to burn, and gave every ounce, every game."
Bill Juzda was arguably the hardest-hitting player of the 1940's. A stay-
at-home defenceman who didn't take part in much offence, Bill made sure he
never lost control of the puck when it was in his team's end. Juzda's philosophy
was that if you have the puck on your stick,
then you should never be giving it away.

A multi-sport athlete, Bill was so
good at hitting people as a halfback in
football that the Winnipeg Blue Bombers
tried hard to acquire his services but failed
since the CFL couldn't pay him the same
kind of money that he could make in
hockey playing in the National Hockey
League.

Bill had a few different colourful nick-
names that went with the tough customer
role he had on the ice during his playing
career, such as The Beast, Bouncing Bill,
and The Honest Brakeman. The last one
was a reference to his summertime job he
had working on the railway.

Bill was born in Winnipeg on October 29, 1920. The son of Ukrainian
immigrants from the province of Galicia, then controlled by the Austro-
Hungarian empire, Juzda grew up during the Depression in the city's North
End in the area known today as Point Douglas. Early on it was clear that the
5'9" Bill Juzda was a natural athlete, excelling at every sport he played. He was
a star on the football field and soccer pitch, and held his high school's shotput

record for more than four decades. Amazingly, Bill didn't even start skating or playing organized hockey until he was well into high school.

Bill's son, Stuart, recalls his father's beginnings into the game of hockey, "The junior team in his area, the Elmwood Maple Leafs, were a late entry into the city league. All the other kids who were playing hockey at that time in the city had already been scouted and taken by the other teams, so the person who was starting up the Elmwood team went around to different high schools in Winnipeg and asked the Phys Ed teachers who the best athletes at their school were who didn't already play hockey. My father played football, he had never skated or played hockey prior to this person approaching his school's gym teacher. I don't even think he owned skates since his family was so poor at the time."

That was Bill's introduction to organized hockey. He played a season with Elmwood and enjoyed his new sport a great deal. It turned out that he was also pretty good at it. Enough so that he was asked to join the Kenora Thistles of the Manitoba Junior Hockey League (MJHL) for the 1939-40 season, where he played a big role in getting Kenora to the 1940 Memorial Cup final in Winnipeg at the old Amphitheatre. Although Kenora ultimately fell to the Oshawa Generals three games to one, Bill's strong play and sturdiness on the blueline was noticed by several NHL teams.

The very next season Juzda made his NHL debut with the New York Rangers, which is incredible considering he had only been playing hockey for two years. I guess this proved just how much of a natural athlete Bill was. "He went to the Rangers right away because the war was on I guess," remarked Stuart. "What had happened is a number of the league's players went into the service all around the same time, so the teams had to quickly stock up their squads. There were more opportunities for younger guys like my dad to get into the league."

Bill ended up going into the service himself in 1942. He joined the Royal Canadian Air Force and was a pilot during World War II. When the war ended, he rejoined the New York Rangers despite some heavy competition for roster spots. "My father said that in those years after the war (1946/1947), the NHL was extremely competitive because you had players who went off to the war like himself who were coming back and wanted to get back into the game," said Stuart. "And then you had the younger fellows who had come up and wanted to keep their jobs. It made the league very competitive."

When Bill Juzda was a member of the New York Rangers he was involved in possibly one of the greatest fights of all time. It came on March 16th, 1947 against the Montreal Canadiens. A bench-clearing brawl broke out late in the game, and everyone who was dressed that game was on the ice participating. There were a total of fifteen fights over the course of only a couple minutes.

Hockey historian Stan Fischler recalls Juzda's role in that famous brawl, "Maurice 'Rocket' Richard broke his stick over Juzda's head, snapping the shaft in two. Juzda arose slowly, like a Frankenstein monster, and tackled Richard, bringing him down violently. Juzda then excused himself from Richard, picked up a stray stick and poleaxed Buddy O'Connor, breaking his jaw."

This was just a chapter in the long-standing on-ice feud between Maurice Richard and Bill Juzda. Their continuing war over the years resulted in Bill being known as Richard's "Anglo Nemesis". On one particular night, Juzda hit Richard so hard that the Plexiglas shattered. Plexiglas was new to the league back then, and no one thought it could be broken.

A good example of Richard's long-standing feud with Juzda comes from this excerpt from Dave Bidini's eulogy of fellow writer James Duplacey in the December 16, 2015 edition of *The Globe & Mail*:

> In my book The Best Game You Can Name, *Mr. Duplacey recalled the time he set Rocket Richard straight on a memorable moment in hockey history. Mr. Richard and Hockey Hall of Fame president Scotty Morrison were discussing the famous Turofsky brothers' photograph that captured the moment the Rocket's skate shattered the new (and supposedly unbreakable) Plexiglas at Maple Leaf Gardens, in 1949.*
>
> *That picture, which ran in newspapers across the country, shows the Rocket falling to the ice amid a shower of glass while Maple Leafs left winger Vic Lynn looked on. Mr. Richard confessed to not being sure who had shoved him into the glass that night and Mr. Morrison asked Mr. Duplacey if he could shed some light on the matter. Mr. Duplacey had just been researching the episode and told The Rocket that the guilty party was defenceman Bill Juzda.*
>
> *"The words hadn't even left my lips," Mr. Duplacey said, "when the Rocket erupted, shouting and swearing, 'Juzda! Juzda! I hate that guy. I hate Bill Juzda! I hate that dirty, little ….' His eyes turned from pieces of black coal to blazing fireballs. Suddenly, it was as if the Rocket was back on the ice on that night, reliving the moment and ready to do damage to anyone he saw who might even remotely remind him of Bill Juzda."*

Rocket Richard wasn't the only star player in the league that Juzda fought. Bill was known never to have backed down from anybody on the ice. He had a couple notable tussles with Mr. Hockey himself, Gordie Howe. Their first fight, Bill took a good punch from Gordie before eventually picking Howe up and slamming him to the ice. In their rematch fight a few months later, Juzda wrestled the bigger Howe to a draw.

Juzda was eventually traded to the Toronto Maple Leafs for the 1948-49 season. Sometimes it's all about timing in hockey, and for Juzda that proved to be the case as he won his first Stanley Cup in his first season with the Maple Leafs. He would go on to win a second Stanley Cup with Toronto in 1951. By the end of the following 1951-52 season, Bill Juzda had played his last NHL game.

"He was playing with Pittsburgh in the American League, and at the same time was working on a contract with the Detroit Red Wings. He was trying to get his release from Toronto but Conn Smythe wouldn't allow it or even trade him to another team," said Stuart. "They didn't really do well by the players in those days, you were basically a serf. Once you signed your C-Form contract, you had to basically abide by whatever you were given."

Not wanting to be a part of that system any longer, Juzda returned home to Manitoba and suited up for the Winnipeg Maroons of the local senior league for a number of years, in addition to some stints for teams in Brandon, Pine Falls, and Warroad, Minnesota. While playing for the Winnipeg Maroons, he got to play in the Allan Cup numerous times, and on one occasion, Juzda and the Maroons went on a tour of Czechoslovakia, where veterans there still refer to a bone-rattling bodycheck as a "Juzda".

Bill officially retired from hockey in 1963, although he played old-timers hockey well into his 70's. His NHL totals were 68 points in 398 National Hockey League games. Juzda's two Stanley Cups in 1949 and 1951 were of course the big highlights of his nine-year NHL career. A two-time NHL All-Star (1948 and 1949), Bill only had 398 penalty minutes in his entire career, matching his career games number, which paints a picture that although Juzda was a very physical player, he played a pretty clean game.

After Juzda's hockey playing ended, he continued his work as an engineer with the Canadian Pacific Railway (CPR). He also stayed in the game by coaching local hockey from midget all the way up to senior. From the St. Boniface Seals junior team to the senior Winnipeg Maroons, Bill played a big role in developing many of the city's aspiring young hockey players for a number of decades.

Bill passed away at the age of 87 on February 17, 2008 in a Winnipeg nursing home from complications related to cancer. Juzda is remembered today not only as a two-time Stanley Cup champion with the Toronto Maple Leafs, but as a man who gave a lot back to the city he hailed from in regard to his coaching and mentoring in the game of hockey long after his own play-ing career ended. Today, Juzda is an "Honoured Member" of the Manitoba Hockey Hall of Fame. He was also inducted into the Manitoba Sports Hall of Fame and Museum in 1992.

"He was always a very modest guy in everything he did," said Stuart. "The city wanted to name a street after him in East Kildonan, and he refused. 'Why me?'"

47
DON RALEIGH

Don Raleigh very well might be the only National Hockey League player to ever have his poetry reviewed by *The New York Times*. The Renaissance Man of the New York Rangers in the 1940's and 1950's, his nickname "Bones" stayed with him his entire life, as did his skinny body weight of 145 pounds.

Being so skinny, one would speculate that Raleigh was susceptible to get hurt often on the ice, and that he wouldn't be able to last in the NHL. "I knew how to collapse my body so that when guys hit me, I didn't get hurt," Raleigh told John Halligan and John Kreiser in the 2006 oral history *Game of My Life: New York Rangers*.

Bones went on to be a star and captain of the New York Rangers during his ten-season NHL career. He proved that despite not being the biggest or strongest player on the ice, his big heart and competitive juices more than made up for it. And because of that, Raleigh succeeded at the world's highest level of hockey.

Born in Kenora, Ontario on June 27, 1926, Don and his family moved to Winnipeg when he was just a young boy. Don grew up in the East Kildonan/Elmwood area and attended East Kildonan Collegiate, which is now Lord Wolseley School on Henderson Highway. He was elected Student President for the 1942/1943 school year. Now, he was playing hockey for his school team as well as Vince Leah's Excelsior A championship teams. Believe it or not, the very next season, Don was making his National Hockey League debut.

The 1943-44 New York Rangers had a fair bit of trouble replacing players who had gone off to fight in World War II. They ended up calling up Bones, who was just a hotshot seventeen-year-old from Winnipeg. The Rangers were so depleted that they even dressed coach Frank Boucher, who was 26 years Don's senior at the age of 43. Bones suffered a broken jaw fifteen games into his NHL career, but still became the youngest full-time NHLer in league history. He scored two goals and two assists in that four-game stint. The next year he returned to junior hockey with the Winnipeg Monarchs, making him the first player to ever play in the NHL and then return to playing in the junior ranks.

The next season, Raleigh was playing for six different teams at the same time! Local hockey historian Ted "Dutch" Holland relays the story, "Well, Bones and Wally Hergesheimer were the best forwards on the Winnipeg Monarchs in 1944-45. One day they both decided that they'd go to Brandon and make a few bucks—and by a few bucks I mean twenty bucks a week if they're lucky. So, they left the Monarchs and it's kind of ironic that the two top scorers left the team since the Monarchs went on to win the Memorial Cup in 1946.

"Bones went out to Brandon because he was still junior age and he played for the MJHL's Brandon Elks and led the league in scoring. At this time, he attended classes at Brandon College and played for their hockey team, as well as the University of Manitoba's team since they were in separate leagues. He was just getting out of the army as well so he was still with the army team too!

"On Sunday nights, a lot of these guys (including Bones) would drive in from other various towns to Winnipeg because they had this Catholic League going on that night. It was pretty good hockey because a lot of these guys were playing juniors or seniors, but they liked that Sunday night league because they liked to have a good time. Bones' team in the Catholic Hockey League was St. Mary's/St. Alphonsus. The sixth team was Raleigh playing senior hockey for the Winnipeg Reo Flyers, so it's safe to say he got in a lot of hockey that season!"

Skip ahead a few years and with the war over, the Rangers were dying for Bones to turn pro because their roster still wasn't as strong as it was pre-World War II. Don would admit he wasn't in a big rush to turn pro, but ended up finally joining the Rangers partway through the 1947-48 season. He scored 33 points in 52 games, and impressed the league with his quickness and stick-handling skills. Opposing players often complained that they couldn't take the puck off his stick.

Long-time hockey historian Stan Fischler recalls how Don got the nickname that stuck with him his whole life. "Raleigh got his nickname from the *New York Journal-American*—American hockey writer Barney Kremenko. As it happened, Kremenko won some money at Belmont race track betting on a horse named Bag of Bones. That night, Raleigh had a big game and Kremenko decided to call him after his winning horse, shortening it simply to 'Bones'."

Raleigh was known for being streaky and scoring in bunches. During the 1950 Stanley Cup Finals against the Detroit Red Wings, Bones scored the overtime winner in both game four and game five, making him the first player to score back-to-back overtime goals in the Stanley Cup finals. Detroit rallied to win game six, setting the stage for a one game winner-take-all to decide the Stanley Cup. Game 7 was an absolute thriller. It went to overtime, of course, and legend has it that Raleigh ringed one off the crossbar in the first overtime. The game trickled into a second overtime, and right after the Rangers had a good chance to score, Detroit's Pete Babando fired a backhand on net that beat a screened Chuck Rayner at 8:30 of the second overtime to win the Stanley Cup. To this day, it's only the second time in the history of the Stanley Cup Finals that a game 7 was decided in overtime. The other instance came a few years later in the 1954 Stanley Cup Finals when Detroit's Tony Leswick scored at 4:29 of the first overtime to win the Cup over the Montreal Canadiens.

Unfortunately for Bones, that would be the closest he would ever get to hoisting the Stanley Cup.

Despite never winning a Cup, Don enjoyed a successful ten-year NHL career, all with the New York Rangers. His strong leadership skills led to him being the Rangers captain from 1953 to 1955. Bones played in two NHL All-Star Games (1951 and 1954), and in the 1951-52 season he scored 61 points, which was fourth best in the league after Gordie Howe, Ted Lindsay and Elmer Lach. In 535 career NHL games, Don scored 101 goals, 219 assists for a total of 320 points with only 96 penalty minutes.

Raleigh was one of the inaugural inductees into the Manitoba Hockey Hall of Fame, as well as an honoured member of the Manitoba Sports Hockey Hall of Fame. In addition, Don is also a member of Brandon University's Hockey Hall of Fame. He was a co-wearer of the New York Rangers #7 jersey that has now been retired at Madison Square Garden.

Don will always be known to his former Rangers teammates as a Renaissance Man. His hobbies included stamp collecting, war history, gardening, astronomy, poetry and classical music. In a *New York Times* article from a few years back, Rangers legend Harry Howell recalled how Bones loved the opera.

"An older hockey player is going to see the opera; it really didn't sound right," Howell said. "But he always enjoyed that kind of stuff. He helped us all grow up."

In the same article, hockey historian Stan Fischler said, "Bones Raleigh was the quintessential antihero. He was an intellectual; he would write poetry on the Staten Island Ferry."

During his time in New York he would often visit various Manhattan clubs to see musicians perform. On one occasion, Bones organized his team for an off-day tour of the Ford plant in Detroit. In the offseason, he would spend his summers checking out old US Civil War battlefields.

After his hockey career ended, Raleigh returned to Winnipeg and entered the insurance field, eventually owning his own agency. Bones stayed very active in Winnipeg all throughout the rest of his life. He served on a number of different boards including the Manitoba Hockey Foundation, the Misericordia Hospital Foundation, the Lions Club of Winnipeg, the Lions Housing Foundation, the Winnipeg Winter Club, and Rainbow Stage.

Bones also established bursaries at the University of Brandon, as well as establishing the Raleigh Family Mozart Scholarships at the Manitoba Arts Festivals to express his love of Mozart's music. He was also the chairman of the #6 (Jim Whitecross) Air Cadet Squadron Sponsoring Committee, on behalf of the Lions Club of Winnipeg.

Later in life, Bones spent a lot of hours on the tennis court and in the summer could often be found at his family cottage at Sandy Hook. One of his biggest passions late in life was his role as the long-time chairman and president of the Lindsay Street Garden Club, a victory garden that had been once used to produce food for troops in World War II. If weeding hadn't been done in your plot, you received a polite but firm call from Bones. Ted "Dutch" Holland remembers a friend of his once getting such a phone call from Mr. Raleigh, "Bones called him one night and said 'I wanna talk to you about the weeds in your garden." This guy was a hockey fan and starts saying, 'Oh you're Bones Raleigh from the New York Rangers!' Bones snapped back at him, 'Never mind the hockey, I'm interested in the weeds young man!' Bones was always funny like that."

"We always got a chuckle out of Bones," Holland said. "He'd whip out his hockey card that he carried in his wallet at a moment's notice. I think he carried it around with him all the time. He kind of liked to let people know about one particular night with the Rangers where he scored a bunch of goals."

Towards the end, Bones moved to Kingston to be with his son, Jack, who is a family physician in Ontario. Don passed away on August 21, 2012 at the age of 86. Don's son Jack recalls how his dad still had his hockey skills decades after his career ended, "Even when my dad was well into his 50's, he liked to go down to the corner rink, and everyone there would ask, 'Who's this old geezer?' And he'd take the puck away, skate circles around them, and never give it back."

46
MIKE RIDLEY

W hen I was conducting interviews early on for this book, I asked players like Butch Goring, Gord Lane, and James Patrick which Manitobans that had played in their time period would make their top 50 list. The first player that each guy mentioned was Mike Ridley and what a great career he had had in Washington. So, with endorsements like that, it was hard to keep a player of Ridley's calibre off of this Top 50 list.

Mike Ridley was a crafty and productive scorer in the National Hockey League for much of his career. He's a player who made the most of the skill and talent he had, and persevered through very long odds to become one of the premier scoring centremen in Washington Capitals history.

He's also a prime example of how scouts can sometimes be very wrong about a player. Despite being passed over at several NHL entry drafts, Ridley walked into an NHL training camp on an invitation, promptly won a spot on the team, and went on to have quite the successful National Hockey League career.

Ridley is still well known in Manitoba hockey circles for his breakout record-breaking season while playing for the St. Boniface Saints in 1982-83 when he scored 91 goals and 100 assists for 191 points in 48 games.

Mike Ridley was born in Winnipeg on July 8th, 1963. He grew up in the Windsor Park neighbourhood and spent countless hours on the outdoor rinks at Winakwa Community Club during Winnipeg's cold winter months. He played his minor hockey for various Winakwa teams at nearby Maginot Arena.

"What else are you going to do in the winter?" Ridley asked with a smile. "I played lots of different sports growing up and hockey was kind of that number one sport we all played in the winter. I don't remember any big decision to get into hockey, it just happened. My dad coached a little bit early on when I played here and there, but that was it."

Growing up in Windsor Park, the NHL seemed very far away from Ridley. "There was never any thought that I could play in the NHL one day. My friends, street neighbours, people from school would all play around on the ice all the time, but there was a zero percent chance we thought that one day one of us could play in the NHL for a living."

Ridley's junior hockey days can be defined by persevering through some terrible injuries as well as overcoming being cut by several junior teams. When he was eleven and twelve years old it was obvious he was one of the more skilled players in the St. Boniface area, being one of the leading scorers on the AAA team. At thirteen, he was playing street hockey one afternoon with his friends at the Bonivital Pool parking lot when he got into a scrap with one of his pals and ended up breaking his pinky finger. Having been the leading scorer on the St. Boniface Saints AAA team the past two years, he still made the team despite having a cast on his arm. There was a new coach and Mike didn't exactly get along with him. The coach moved Ridley from centre to wing before cutting him just six games into the year. When Mike was cut, AA teams in Winnipeg were already formed so his only option was to play single A hockey for a local Winakwa team.

The following year, Ridley tried out for the St. Boniface Saints AAA fourteen-year-old team and was cut again, so this time he spent the year playing AA hockey. At fifteen, he was finally back playing AAA again. At the time that was the highest level of junior hockey. "I remember my sixth game with the team," Ridley recalled. "We had a game at Maginot Arena and one of the opposing players James Patrick, who went on to a great NHL career, caught me accidently at the knee. Our trainer Daryl "Rosie" Steen checked it out after the game and said it was just a charley horse, but it turned out the bone in front of my knee was cracked and there was a hollow spot (cyst) in my bone so I ended up having to miss the whole year. They had to do surgery on me that summer. I remember going to the hospital and finally having the surgery where they took bone from my hip, cleaned out the hollow spot bellow my knee, and put the bone from my hip into there to promote new bone growth which eventually worked, but I missed my whole season."

Mike came back and spent his sixteenth year with the AAA Saints. The next year he was cut from the MJHL team, but he practised with them throughout the year and spent the season playing juvenile hockey. He was called-up to the MJHL squad and promptly broke his collarbone, so he missed most of that year as well. When he was eighteen he played his first full year with the MJHL's St Boniface Saints, but it was the following year when Ridley exploded onto the scene. He scored 91 goals and 100 assists for 191 points in 48 games. Ridley shattered the scoring records in the MJHL previously set by Bobby Clarke in the late 1960's, and still holds the record today. An award bearing his name, The Mike Ridley Trophy, is given out every year to the player who leads the MJHL in scoring during the regular season.

"It's one of the big things that I'm proud of about my hockey career. I don't know what happened that got my game to a new level. I was always a good athlete and was always a smart player in hockey and other sports. I grew a little bit that year, matured a little, and had some really good linemates. Our team was also pretty good, but besides those reasons I can't really explain it. All of the sudden it was like playing was easy. I had to work hard and push myself of course, but everything seemed to go well and I was scoring three or four points a game."

After that season, Mike fielded a couple of calls from some American colleges about potential scholarships. He was then in his first year at the University of Winnipeg and the problem was that the University of Winnipeg happened to have a team in Canadian college hockey so because of that he would have had to be redshirted to go to the States and play hockey. For an American team to take him on, they would have to sit him out for a year and pay him for the scholarship. Instead, he decided to play two years of hockey with the University of Manitoba Bisons squad.

"Playing university hockey was the only route available for me to keep playing hockey," Mike recalled. "It was either quit hockey and get a job or I could keep playing hockey at university while going to school and getting scholarship money."

After two years with the Bisons, Ridley accepted a tryout to go to a New York Rangers rookie camp at the beginning of the 1985-86 season. Mike clearly made a big impression at the camp because the Rangers ended up signing him as a free agent and he made his NHL debut on opening night.

A monumental step from playing university hockey just a few months prior. Ridley ended up leading the Rangers in scoring his rookie year with 65 points and was named to the NHL's All-Rookie Team. Not too bad at all from the 22-year-old university student, who'd had no expectations when he first went into the Rangers training camp.

Mike talks about the transition of going from Winnipeg to living in New York City as a young man away from home for the first time, "Nowadays they have people that take care of you, but back then it was basically 'Here's a real estate agent, find a place to live.' I ended up renting a place with goalie Terry Kleisinger and that lasted about two or three weeks before he was sent down to the minors. So, I was by myself, renting the top floor of a house in Rye, New York which is about thirty minutes north of the city. I had a rental car to drive myself down every day, no one helped me out. I had to buy my own cutlery, dishes and everything. Today they make sure that the rookies are well taken care of, but I'm happy to say that I managed to tough it out. My wife, who was my girlfriend at the time, was living in Winnipeg. Everything I knew was back in Winnipeg. I was still enrolled in school back in Winnipeg because I wasn't planning on making the Rangers since it was just a tryout. There was a thousand times I probably thought about quitting and going home. If I could have snapped my fingers and been home in Winnipeg playing for the Bisons and going to school, I would have done it a thousand times at least. Obviously, I knew I was playing in the NHL and to pick up and quit would be stupid and out of the question, but I really did miss being home in Winnipeg a great deal."

After a season and a half as the leading scorer in the Big Apple, Ridley was shockingly traded to the Washington Capitals in a New Year's Day deal on January 1st, 1987. He was dealt along with Kelly Miller and Bob Crawford for Bobby Carpenter and a second-round pick. The deal caught Mike by surprise, but he made the best of it and joined his new team in Washington. He went to the playoffs with them that year and was involved in one of the longest and most remembered hockey games of all time. It went down on April 18th, 1987. Ridley's Capitals were up against the New York Islanders in Game 7 of the Patrick Division Semifinals at the Capital Centre in Landover, Maryland. The Islanders eventually won the game 3-2 in a fourth overtime. It is a game that is simply known today as the Easter Epic and it's so notable because it is the longest Game 7 in the history of the Stanley Cup Playoffs.

Mike recalls the Easter Epic that went well into the early hours of April 19th: "Well for me it was a tough time because my grandfather in Thunder

Bay had a heart attack and I only found out right before the game. After we lost, and because the game went so long, I flew out on no sleep to Thunder Bay, and he passed away. I was playing with a heavy heart that game, but the game just went on and on and on. There wasn't an end in sight. The goalies were outstanding in Kelly Hrudey and Bob Mason. I've seen clips of the game here and there over the years, but I don't remember much about it. A lot of games from my career I can remember vividly, but that game is hard to remember because I was so exhausted. The biggest thing today is people will tell me that they remember that game from my career. Friends of my age, they were younger people and they were watching the game, and then it was time to go out. In Winnipeg, it was an hour behind of the East Coast. So, they're watching it and they'd go out and were watching it at the bar or at a social. They couldn't believe the game was still going on so late into the night. They figured it was just a replay of it and not the actual game. People still tell me about that today so it's kind of neat that way."

Ridley went on to spend eight seasons in a Capitals uniform. Looking back, he has fond memories of his time in Washington DC. Today, he still ranks in the top ten on the Capitals all-time scoring list. "I enjoyed living there a great deal. It wasn't much of a hockey town at the time, but now I think it is. The Redskins of the NFL are always number one there," Ridley said. "We didn't get a lot of the attention that the Canadian teams did back in the day. We would see our local sports reporters in Washington at the beginning of the season and then at the start of playoffs. That was it. Friends of mine in Winnipeg only saw me play a few times a year when we were playing Toronto or Montreal. The channel CKND-TV would show the highlights of the Canadian teams and then my friends would only see the Washington score, no highlights."

Late in Ridley's career, he moved on from Washington and spent the last few years of his career playing in Canada with the Toronto Maple Leafs and Vancouver Canucks. "It was kind of bittersweet because I had a back problem for the last couple of seasons. I have no idea where it came about, and if there was the medical care they have now in the league, I would have probably played a lot longer. I was traded to Toronto and then was traded to Vancouver a year later. My first season in Vancouver I had surgery on my back, and to be honest, I really could never play at close to 100% those last three or four seasons. Even today, there isn't a day that goes by where I don't know that I have a back problem. I've tried to work on it and fix it, but it is an ongoing problem. If

I could go back and do it over again, I'd like my back injury erased and see what I could have done without it because I really feel I could play with the best of 'em when I was feeling healthy. I never claimed to be a number one centreman, even though I had to play against guys like Lemieux, Gretzky, Sakic, Yzerman, and a lot of times I outplayed them with the help of my linemates Kelly Miller and either Dino Ciccarelli or Mike Gartner."

Mike retired from the NHL after the 1996-97 season. He had a short four game stint with the IHL's Manitoba Moose the following season, but after another injury, he decided to hang up the skates for good. When it was all said and done, Ridley had scored 292 goals and 466 assists for 758 points in 866 career NHL games. Nearly a point per game player during his career, Mike's best season offensively came in the 1988-89 NHL campaign where he tallied 41 goals and 89 points, both career highs. That season he got to play in his first and only NHL All-Star Game of his career.

"We moved back to Winnipeg after my career ended. Later I was with Home Run Sports and I'm still an owner today, but more of a silent owner. From 2000-2004 I was working at the store doing this and that, but I'm not a salesman type of guy and I'm not really a people person: it wasn't really for me. When we moved to Kelowna I was doing some hockey academies and coaching my kids here. I'm just an old guy now. Retired. I do projects around the house. We have a ski place at Big White that we go up to in the winter. I go on a couple of golf trips in the winter. Other than that, I'm not up to too much!"

These days, Mike doesn't get back to Winnipeg all that often. He calls Kelowna home now and enjoys his golf and his once a week hockey league. Looking back on everything, Ridley didn't mind playing out of the spotlight during his career. That was just fine for him. "I just did the best I could when I played. I understand that I didn't come up as a first-round draft pick. The way I played wasn't really flashy or fast, I wasn't a huge goal scorer or much of a fighter, so I fully understand how I flew under the radar, which was fine with me. I don't have any problems with it. I always laugh when I meet people, whether it was in Winnipeg when I first retired or in Kelowna when I'm at the Kelowna Golf Course. There's a bunch of guys that come up to me and tell me what my stats were in the NHL. 'Did you know that you scored 41 goals in one season?' That stuff kind of makes me laugh because they don't really know me since I played in Washington at a time when there was no internet, no twenty-four-hour sports station playing replays of games. So, I take pride when people my age will come up and say to me, 'Hey, you were a good player!'"

45
MEL HILL

The Boston Bruins coach in the 1930's and 1940's was a man by the name of Art Ross. One of the premier defencemen of his era, Art always considered his first Stanley Cup win with Kenora in 1907 to be his greatest thrill in hockey. His second greatest thrill? Being front and center for Mel Hill's three overtime winners in the 1939 Stanley Cup playoffs.

This just begs the question: Who is Mel Hill?

Mel Hill may not have been the biggest superstar in the NHL in his day, and he'd be the first person to tell you that. But he will always be remembered in the folklore of hockey history for his NHL record of three overtime goals in the same playoff series. That's why he's forever known as simply "Sudden Death" Mel Hill.

"I was a basic, unspectacular player who usually performed well when it counted, but I just happened to get super-

MANITOBA SPORTS HALL OF FAME

hot in that series with New York," said Hill. "It wasn't an easy tag to carry the rest of my career. It seemed like I was expected to be the hero in every playoff game from that moment on. The name 'Sudden Death' was easier to live with after I retired."

Mel Hill was born on February 15, 1914 in Glenboro, a small town about an hour southeast of Brandon. His parents came over to Manitoba from England shortly before he was born, and as a youngster, Mel started playing hockey on the local outdoor rink in Glenboro.

Shortly after he started attending school, however, his family left Glenboro and moved to Saskatoon. Mel remembered his childhood as being from a typical poor family that worked hard. He later said that he got a lot of his fun from hockey and listening to the radio. To help supplement his family's income, Hill worked at a series of odd job throughout the early parts of his life. For example, one summer he worked in Regina cleaning bricks when the old Crystal Brewery there was being dismantled.

It was in Saskatoon that Hill's prowess in hockey went noticed by reporters and scouts. He wasn't just a one trick pony, however. A multi-sport athlete of sorts, Mel also played baseball and some competitive soccer on the left wing for the Saskatoon Legion in the late 1930's. He was selected to play on several Saskatchewan all-star teams that went up against the touring Islington Corinthians from England in 1938 and the Scottish F.A. team in 1939.

Hill played junior hockey as an eighteen and nineteen-year-old in the early 1930's for the Saskatoon Tigers and Wesleys of the Saskatoon City League. Somebody watching one of his games one night must have liked what he saw, because Hill left Saskatoon for the 1934-35 season and moved to northern Ontario where he played with the Sudbury Cub Wolves Jr. team of the Nickel Belt Hockey League.

At the beginning of the 1934-35 season, Mel attended the New York Rangers training camp in Winnipeg at the old Amphitheatre. Rangers manager Lester Patrick got a good look at Hill over the course of the camp, but ultimately let him loose because as Lester said he was "too frail for big time hockey." Hill later recalled, "I was 5'10" and weighed about 140 pounds at that camp and Lester Patrick told me, 'You're too small, son. You might last the 50 games, but you'll never survive the playoffs. You'd better go back to the farm.'"

What a mistake that would turn out to be for Lester Patrick.

After his first season in Sudbury, Mel got a job working in the Frood Mine and played hockey for the Sudbury Frood Miners/Tigers. One day when Mel was working in the mine, a stope collapsed about 100 yards from him and four men were killed. He later said that incident changed his outlook on life and it helped him persevere in the sport of hockey.

In the 1936-37 season, he scored a league-leading eighteen goals in fifteen games. He was the main reason why his Sudbury squad went on to win the Allan Cup that year, defeating North Battleford Beavers three games to two for national senior hockey supremacy.

The Boston Bruins caught wind of Hill's senior hockey exploits and quickly signed him as a free agent on October 26th, 1937. At the time of the signing, *Globe and Mail* writer Vern DeGeer was calling him "the swift-moving sharpshooter who waves a flaming torch," while Saskatoon sportscaster Lloyd Saunders recalled that, "Hill had one hell of a shot and it was so accurate too."

It wasn't straight to the National Hockey League by any means for Hill. His first professional hockey season was spent primarily with the Providence Reds of the AHL. Hill did make his NHL debut that season however, appearing in six games.

The 1938-39 season was Mel's rookie NHL campaign. It was also his best season in the league. He scored twenty points during the regular season, but it would be his performance in the playoffs that would make this season his career highlight.

Mel Hill's hockey career can be defined by his heroics in the 1939 Stanley Cup Playoffs. In the semifinals against Lester Patrick's New York Rangers, Hill scored three overtime winners. It's a record that has stood the test of time. No player in the history of the National Hockey League has ever scored three overtime goals in the same series.

Lester Patrick at the time was probably thinking to himself, "Oops!" I guess even the greatest of hockey minds can be wrong about a player occasionally.

Game 1 of the series went three overtimes, in fact it was only thirty-five seconds away from a fourth overtime when Hill struck the winning goal. It was 1:10 in the morning when Bruins centre Bill Cowley skated swiftly along the boards into the Rangers zone and centered a high pass directly in front of Dave Kerr's goal. It was then that 23-year-old rookie Mel Hill skated in and batted the puck clean past Kerr and into the side of the Rangers goal. The Bruins bench swarmed Hill without showing any signs of fatigue from the marathon game and practically carried him to the dressing room to celebrate the win.

Two nights later, it was more of the same as once again the Bill Cowley, Roy Conacher, Mel Hill line produced the overtime winner to give the Bruins a two-game lead in the series. Mel scored the overtime winner at the 8:24 mark of the first overtime on another fantastic play by Cowley who jumped the Rangers forwards, and when they came tearing in on him, he swiftly passed the puck over to Hill, who was coming in at full flight and he proceeded to take the puck and rifle it through the legs of Bert Gardiner, a rookie goalie recalled from Philadelphia to replace the injured Dave Kerr. It was almost a mirror replica of the Hill's overtime winner in Game One.

Boston won Game Three as well to take a commanding three games to zero lead in the series, but the Rangers fought back. They won three straight games to set the stage for a pivotal Game 7 at the Boston Garden. The game became a high drama affair and after three of periods of play, the teams were locked in a 1-1 stalemate. Once again, overtime was needed. Still nothing. A second overtime came and passed as well.

The game extended into the wee hours of the next morning into triple overtime where a familiar hero got the winner for the partisan Boston crowd. Eight minutes into the third overtime period at 12:40 am, Hill took a pass from Bill Cowley, who himself received a nice pass from Roy Conacher and let go a blistering shot from fifteen feet out that beat Rangers goalie Bert Gardiner to send the Bruins crowd into hysterics.

"It was around eight minutes of the third overtime," Hill remembered. "Cowley fed me a pass from behind the net and I was right on top of Rangers goalie Bert Gardiner. I held the puck for a second then flipped it up into the net on the short side. The fans went wild and it was a tremendous thrill to win a series for my team. "

With that triple overtime winner in Game Seven, Boston advanced to the Stanley Cup where they met the Toronto Maple Leafs. Boston continued the roll they were on and quickly blasted the Maple Leafs in five games to win the Stanley Cup. Bruins rookie goalie Frank Brimsek, otherwise known as "Mr. Zero," held the Maple Leafs to just six goals in the five-game series.

In the Cup final, Hill picked up where he left off and assisted on both of Roy Conacher's goals in a Game Four victory. He then opened the scoring in the cup clinching Game Five that the Bruins won 3-1. It capped off quite the rookie season for Hill. He had twenty points during the regular season and scored nine in the playoffs, including six goals. The Stanley Cup was the cherry on top on a fantastic rookie season. Also, the Conn Smythe Trophy for playoff MVP wasn't around yet, but had it been, Mel would have been right in line to win the award along with teammates Bill Cowley and Frank Brimsek.

Hill credited a lot of his success with the Bruins during that playoff run to his four teammates that lived with him in a big suburban Brookline, Massachusetts rooming home. He also had high praise for Bill Cowley, the centre who gave him the passes for all three overtime goals.

"The Krauts (Schmidt, Bauer, Dumart) lived together last winter and they asked Roy Conacher and me to come live at the house when Art Ross made us regulars this season," Hill explained. "We clicked right away, and soon we were talking, eating and sleeping hockey. None of us can sleep until three or four o'clock in the morning after a game, so everybody gathers in one of the room and sometimes we play cards for a while to take the edge off. But mostly we just talk over the games, figuring out what we should have done in such and such a case."

To put things into perspective a little bit, Mel's salary that season was only $3,000. He got a bonus of $2,000 for winning the Stanley Cup and an extra $1,000 for his overtime heroics. Simply put, salaries weren't anywhere near what they are today.

Hill spent two more seasons with the Bruins after that dream rookie year. He would go on to win another Stanley Cup with the Bruins in 1941. During the summers, he would return home to Saskatoon to see his family and friends. He was a little bit of a celebrity you could say back home. After all, he was Sudden Death Mel Hill! And he had a lasting impact on one particular young player who would go onto be one of, if not the greatest player in the history of our fine sport.

Gordie Howe was a young hockey prodigy, a star in the local Saskatoon junior hockey scene. There were lots of great players in the NHL that Gordie could have idolized, but when he was growing up, he aspired to be like "Sudden Death" Mel Hill.

"There was a great name in hockey by the name of Mel Hill," Gordie recalled. "When I was a young fellow about nine years of age, he used to drive by our house in a great big convertible, sitting proud as a peacock, and that was a professional hockey player. I used to dream that maybe one day that could be me."

Howe also had fond memories of the time that Mel spotted him shooting tin cans on the rink in the schoolyard one summer night, stopped and went over to him, and advised him on how to get more power on his shot. Gordie then said that he didn't stop practising that night until his mom came out and got him. He was forever grateful for the advice from Mel, because that shot that Gordie worked on became one of the most lethal in the National Hockey League, accounting for 801 goals in a career that spanned 26 seasons (plus six in the WHA).

Mel was traded to the Brooklyn Americans for cash on June 27, 1941. He played one season in Brooklyn, scoring 37 points. During the offseason, the franchise folded and Mel was entered into the dispersal draft where he was picked up by the Toronto Maple Leafs.

Hill's best season points-wise came in 1942-43 when he scored 42 points in 49 games. Two seasons later, in 1945 with the Leafs, Mel won his third and final Stanley Cup, defeating the Detroit Red Wings in a seven game Stanley Cup final.

After one more year in the NHL, Mel was sent to the minors where he closed off his professional career with the AHL's Pittsburgh Hornets. He came back to Saskatchewan for good after that and played some senior hockey with the Regina Caps, losing an Allan Cup final in 1949.

Hill officially retired from hockey in 1952. He finished with 198 points in 324 NHL games over nine seasons. A utility player for most of his career, Mel was always a threat when it mattered most. His overtime record is proof of that.

After his hockey career was done he returned to Saskatchewan and got into the soft drink business, owning Mel Hill Beverages in Regina until 1970, when he and his wife Jean retired to a farm in the Fort Qu'Appelle area. "I was happy being a businessman," Mel recalled. "I had my own soft-drink plant and I did all right for myself, but I always feel sorry for the fellows from our time who got out of the game and haven't got a nickel today. When you think about what we made and then you see guys holding out for an extra hundred thousand, well, that's sad. But nothing in this life is easy."

Mel passed away in Fort Qu'Appelle on April 11, 1996, a little over a month after his wife Jean died. He was 82 years old.

In an old *Globe and Mail* article I found that had covered Mel in his later years, he said, "I've achieved every ambition in life I ever had. My wife and I have the land now, and our four children are grown. And hey, if I didn't score those goals back then, nobody would know I'm alive."

To this day, every time a Boston Bruins playoff game heads to overtime, "Sudden Death" Mel Hill gets mentioned and people remember his exploits in the 1939 playoffs. And that itself is a pretty cool thing for someone that was supposed to be too small and frail to even play in the National Hockey League.

44
GARY BERGMAN

Gary Bergman will always be best remembered for his heroics in the 1972 Summit Series.

"He was one of the biggest surprises in terms of contribution that we had," said coach Harry Sinden in retrospect. "We felt he could be a regular member of the team but his contribution exceeded that. He was a terrific member of the team, and well respected."

From the website 1972SummitSeries.com, it gives a fairly accurate description of Bergman as an NHL player. "From 1964 through 1976, Gary Bergman established himself as one of the NHL's steadiest defensive defencemen. Reliable though never fancy, Bergman was a fantastic shot blocker who was never underestimated by his peers and teammates."

Gary Gunnar Bergman was born in Kenora, Ontario, on October 7, 1938. A natural athlete growing up, Bergman played many sports in addition to hockey, such as rowing, curling, and football. He was a very talented football player to the point where the Winnipeg Blue Bombers offered him a spot on their roster in 1959. He declined, hoping to make it in hockey instead.

Bergman's father, Gunnar, was of Swedish descent and he himself had played hockey as a youngster. When the time was right, Gunnar passed on the game to his son when Gary was about three years old. Young Gary took to the ice on the outdoor ponds of Kenora and later excelled in the local junior hockey ranks as a budding defenceman.

Wanting the chance to try and make a run at a professional hockey career, Gary moved from Kenora to Winnipeg at the age of twenty to join the Winnipeg Braves of the MJHL. It turned out to be a successful move for him as the Braves won the Memorial Cup in 1958-59. In the playoffs, Bergman exploded for 24 points in 24 playoff games.

Former Winnipeg Braves teammate and ex-NHLer Bob Leiter recalls Bergman and the Braves. "We had a good team. Bergman was the big guy on defence. We had Ted Green and the captain Wayne Larkin who was real good and looked after everyone to do their job. Everything went really well that year."

The Montreal Canadiens owned the rights to Gary Bergman, but at the time were stacked on the blueline, as they were just coming off their five consecutive Stanley Cup's in the late 1950's. They had no room for Gary on their team so as a result, he was sent to the minors and stayed there for four seasons.

Gary bounced around for various teams in the Montreal AHL farm system including the Buffalo Bisons, Cleveland Barons, and Quebec Aces. His strong play in the minors did not go unnoticed as he ended up getting claimed in the 1964 intra-league draft by the Detroit Red Wings. For the 1964-65 season, Bergman made his NHL debut with Detroit and proved to be a stabilizing force on the Red Wings blueline.

In his second NHL season, Gary would have his deepest playoff run of his career when his Red Wings lost to the Montreal Canadiens in six games in the 1966 Stanley Cup Finals. Surprisingly though, he would only play in one other playoff series after that for the rest of his career.

Gary's career would be defined by his performance in the 1972 Canada vs. Russia Summit Series. Initially it was a surprise that Bergman was even selected for the team. In an interview years later, Gary recalled the day that Team Canada head coach and manager Harry Sinden called him to deliver the good news. "Harry called me Sunday morning. Janie and the kids and I were just going out the door to church, and I had to stop. Janie was saying, 'Would you get off the damn phone, we have to get to church.' It was Harry Sinden on the phone asking me if I'd be part of the team."

During the Summit Series, Bergman was the perfect defensive partner for Brad Park. A great scoring defenceman, Park liked to take the puck and attack the opposing goal, so that meant that someone like Gary had to fall back and be careful of Russians on the counter-attack. That role seemed to suit Bergman just fine.

"We hit it off really good for guys who didn't know each other very well," said Brad Park. "Right away I realized what a classy guy he was in how he handled himself on and off the ice, and what a great competitor he was. He had a lot of confidence in his ability and wasn't worried about how he was going to play. He just went out and played. He was as solid a defenceman as has ever played the game."

Bergman's physical presence on the ice quickly made life uncomfortable for the Russians. In Mike Leonetti's book *Titans of '72: Team Canada's Summit Series Heroes*, he writes,

> It was clear that Bergman was getting under the skin of some of the Russian players when he had a battle with Boris Mikhailov behind the Team Canada net late in the seventh game of the series. It ended with both players getting major penalties and the Russian player kicking Bergman more than once. The bold defenceman made all sorts of threatening gestures to more than one Russian player in the games in Moscow and he absolutely frightened one of the penalty box attendants at the Luzhniki Arena! However, the penalty he took in the seventh game made it a four-on-four situation on the ice and Paul Henderson was able to use that to his advantage to score his best game-winning goal of the series. Bergman was on the ice when Yvan Cournoyer scored to tie the eighth game 5-5 in the second half of the third period.

"From my perspective, he was one of the great unsung heroes of that series," Paul Henderson told *The Canadian Press*. "He just played incredible hockey."

Gary played all eight games of the series for Team Canada. Although he didn't score any goals, he had three assists, thirteen penalty minutes, and was a +5 on the tournament. Bergman would later say that winning that series was the best moment of his hockey career.

"As we skated off the ice after the last game, I stopped for one more look around the old barn," Gary said. "I realized that never in my life would I be prouder or have more respect for a group of men than I did at that moment."

After eleven seasons with the Red Wings, he finished his career playing his last few seasons with the Minnesota North Stars and Kansas City Scouts. Gary retired after the 1975-76 season. He played 838 NHL games and scored 68 goals and 299 assists for a total of 367 points, with 1249 penalty minutes.

Bob Leiter recalls his friend and former teammate, "He was a really great guy, treated everybody the same. I really liked him. As a player, he was an amazing defenceman, definitely one of the better defencemen in the NHL at that time."

After his retirement from hockey, Bergman stayed in the Detroit area and resided for the rest of his life in West Bloomfield, Michigan. Gary passed away on December 8th, 2000 after an eight-month battle with cancer. He was 62.

The great Bobby Orr might have said it best when asked about Bergman's contributions as a fellow defenceman by simply saying, "He was a rock."

He certainly was.

CHICO RESCH SAYS

Gary played on Team Canada in 1972 so that tells you all you need to know. In terms of his game, he was always a defenceman that never had enough offence to wow people so he never got the recognition that an offensive defenceman got.

He was very mobile on the ice and had a flow to his game where he could skate with you and knew how to defend really well, blocking shots constantly. Bergman got caught in the minds of the Red Wings with the WHA when Gordie Howe left. Gary wasn't in a stable situation near the end of his career.

He'd be the type of guy that could have played on a dynasty team with the right role. He was on that 1972 Summit Series squad because he was the best at what he did and that's why he was chosen.

43
MUD BRUNETEAU

Modere "Mud" Bruneteau was a solid two-way player during much of the 1930's and 1940's. He was the first player in NHL history to win the Stanley Cup in each of his first two seasons in the league, but more importantly is forever remembered for ending the longest overtime in the history of the National Hockey League.

Even today when the odd Stanley Cup playoff game creeps into triple overtime, the tale of Mud Bruneteau and the NHL's longest game gets told once again to a newer audience.

"That one goal was really nothing special, just like others I've scored," Mud later recalled. "But people never forgot it. They remembered me as the guy who ended hockey's longest game."

Despite being known for his 1936 overtime heroics, Mud carved out a very solid career for himself with three 20-plus goal seasons and was a member of three Stanley Cup winning teams in Detroit.

Modere Bruneteau was born in Winnipeg on November 28, 1914. He was the middle child of three hockey-playing brothers. John being the oldest by quite a bit, and Ed was five years younger than Modere.

Modere and his brothers went to Ecole Provencher, a Catholic school in St. Boniface. It was early on in his schooling that one of his teachers, an Englishman by the name of Brother George, had trouble pronouncing "Modere" so he started calling him "Mud" instead and it would go on to stick for the rest of his life.

The house that the Bruneteau boys grew up in was directly behind Provencher School and right next to the rink that the school flooded every winter. It was there that the Bruneteau brothers spent countless hours skating and developing their skills. Modere and Ed would even go to great lengths to improve their shooting strength by firing brass weights with their sticks on a regular basis.

Mud played two years of junior hockey for the Winnipeg Knights of Columbus and then followed that up with a season with the legendary Winnipeg Falcons senior club. While playing hockey in Winnipeg, Bruneteau also worked as a grains commissions clerk at the local Grain Exchange office and was employed by none-other than Detroit Red Wings owner James Norris.

In the fall of 1932, Mud travelled to the Red Wings training camp with his buddy Turk Broda and another pal. The rink they were supposed to be skating at was closed when they arrived, so they pooled their money and found out they had just enough cash on them for one room at a second-rate hotel. They flipped for the double bed; Mud lost and slept in the bathtub.

He returned to Winnipeg after the camp, but ended up signing with the Red Wings a few years later and they assigned him to their Detroit Olympics farm club in the old International Hockey League (IHL).

After a year and a half in the minors, Mud made his debut as a 21-year-old rookie with the Detroit Red Wings during the 1935-36 season. Rarely getting on the ice during the regular season, he scored just two goals in twenty-four games.

It would be the first game of the playoffs, however, where the legend of Mud Bruneteau was born.

The night in question was March 24, 1936 at 8:30pm local. Game one of the best-of-five semifinal series between the Montreal Maroons and Detroit Red Wings at the fabled Montreal Forum.

It would be a night where the goaltenders would steal the show. Normie Smith was in goal for the Red Wings goalie, while Lorne Chabot tended the Maroons goal.

The teams battled hard and after regulation the score was still tied 0-0, which meant that sudden-death overtime was needed.

The first overtime came and went without a goal, as did the second extra frame. The crowd started to get restless. One hundred minutes of action and still not a goal in sight. The players were dealing with worsening ice conditions since there was no such thing as a Zamboni in those days.

The clock struck midnight and that's about the time when triple overtime got underway. The crowd cheered loudly, hoping to ignite their Maroons to score the winning goal, but it was all for naught as the third overtime finished without a goal.

Bruneteau later recalled that he and his teammates were given brandy and orange juice during the intermissions to keep their stamina up.

The fourth and fifth overtime periods provided some great action on both ends of the ice, but both Normie Smith and Lorne Chabot fought valiantly to keep the puck out of the net.

By the time that the sixth overtime began, the ice was very badly chopped up and players could barely skate properly on it. At the 4:46 mark of the sixth overtime, the teams had broken the longest NHL game record set previously by the Toronto Maple Leafs and Boston Bruins. By now, it was past 2 am and most people in the crowd were fighting to stay awake because they didn't want to miss the game-winning goal if it was ever scored.

Both teams were fatigued to the extreme. All of the veterans' legs were dead and it was up to the coaches to let the players with the most stamina play. And that meant the inexperienced players who had ridden the bench for much of the game. Enter Mud Bruneteau. At 21 years of age he was the youngest player on the ice that night.

Red Wings coach Jack Adams later recalled, "The game settled into an endurance test, hour after hour. One o'clock came, and then 2 am, and by now the ice was a chopped brutal mess. At 2:25, I looked along our bench for the strongest legs and I scrambled the lines to send out Syd Howe, Hec Kilrea, and Mud Bruneteau."

Legendary hockey author Stan Fischler wrote that, "As a rookie on a loaded first-place club, Bruneteau saw very little action during the season and scored only two goals while achieving no assists for a grand total of two points. But he was young, and at the twelve minute mark of the ninth period, Mud Bruneteau was in a lot better shape than most of his teammates or opponents."

Mud took off with the puck from his own team's zone and passed it to Kilrea, who dashed up the ice. Challenging the Montreal defence, Kilrea faked a return pass before sliding it across the blueline. Bruneteau cut behind the defense where he found Kilrea's pass and shot the bobbling puck into the net.

"Thank god," Bruneteau later recalled. "Chabot fell down as I drove it in the net. It was the funniest thing. The puck just stuck there in the twine and didn't fall on the ice."

There was a bit of a dispute when the goal judge failed to flash the red light, but referee Nels Stewart intervened. "You're bloody right it's a goal!" Stewart barked, and put up his hand to signal the goal. The longest game in the history of the National Hockey League was finally finished after 116 minutes and 30 seconds of overtime.

A game of world-class goaltending, Detroit's Normie Smith turned aside all 90 shots he faced, while his counterpart Lorne Chabot made 67 saves.

Stan Fischler wrote in his book *Behind the Net: 101 Incredible Hockey Stories* that, "There was a wild, capering anticlimax. Bruneteau's sweater was removed, not delicately, by his relieved associates. One fan thrust a $20 bill on Bruneteau as he left the ice. Other exuberants reached for their wallets."

"There I was with my stick under one arm and my gloves under another," Bruneteau said laughing. "I grabbed money in every direction!"

When he got to the Detroit dressing room, Mud tossed the money onto a rubbing table. "Count it," he told his teams trainer, "and split it for the gang." It came out to $22 for each member of the Wings, coach Jack Adams, the trainer, and even the stick boy. That was a lot of money in the Great Depression!

When Bruneteau finally got back to his room at Montreal's Windsor Hotel it was nearly 5 am. He was about to undress and get into bed for the night after a beer celebration with his team when there came a knock at the door. Mud was a little startled perhaps when the visitor was none other than Lorne Chabot, the goalie he had beaten to end the marathon game just a few hours prior.

"Sorry to bother you, kid," Chabot said, "but you forgot something when you left the rink." Then he handed Mud a puck. "Maybe you'd like to have this souvenir of the goal you scored."

That puck now sits firmly for display at the Hockey Hall of Fame in Toronto.

Just 36 hours later, Normie Smith shut out the Maroons again, this time minus the six overtimes. Detroit won game three as well to sweep the Montreal Maroons and advance to the Stanley Cup finals where they met up with the Toronto Maple Leafs. In another best-of-five series, Detroit took it to the Leafs and beat them three games to one to win their first ever Stanley Cup. Not too bad of an ending for the 21-year-old rookie Mud Bruneteau.

The next year Detroit repeated as Stanley Cup champions, becoming the first American club to do so. With two Stanley Cup's in his first two NHL seasons, Mud was living the good life in Motown. In the early 1940's, he eventually took on a more offensive role as he played right wing on a top line with Syd Howe and Carl Liscombe.

In the 1943 Stanley Cup playoffs, Mud scored the first ever playoff hat trick by a Red Wing and his club eventually would go on to win the Cup that year as well. The next season, 1943-44, he set a personal scoring high with 35 goals and 53 points, and also served as the team's co-captain alongside Flash Hollett. This was around the time that Mud's younger brother Ed joined the team, and the brothers became teammates in the National Hockey League for a few seasons.

Eventually as Mud got older, his role on the team started to lessen and he was sent to the minors where he was asked to be the player-coach of the United States Hockey League's (USHL) Omaha Knights.

After some time as the player-coach of the Omaha Knights, Mud formally retired from hockey and switched his attention to coaching during the 1947-48 season. Bruneteau ended his career with 277 points in 411 NHL games over eleven seasons, all in a Detroit Red Wings uniform. He won three Stanley Cups (1936, 1937, 1943) and is forever known for ending the longest game in National Hockey League history.

Mud was handpicked by Red Wings boss Jack Adams to coach and nurture the club's farm team in Omaha. It was there that he became the first professional coach of Terry Sawchuk. A solid communicator, Bruneteau mentored Sawchuk and taught him what he could about playing pro hockey. Terry would later credit Mud for his quick development in the minors.

The Hockey News recognized Mud's strong coaching when they named him the 1951 Coach of the Year, selecting him over all six coaches in the NHL. That just goes to show that Mud was certainly good enough to have coached in the NHL, but at a time when there were only six teams in the league, jobs were limited.

Motto McLean, who played four seasons under Bruneteau called him a "master psychologist who how to get the most out of his talent. He was hard but fair. We played together and we partied together. He never liked guys to go off in twos and threes by themselves."

Under Bruneteau's coaching, the Omaha Knights won three regular-season titles and one playoff championship in 1951.

Mud stayed in Omaha, Nebraska when his coaching career ended because he said that the schools for his kids were better in Omaha than Detroit. So, Mud settled in Omaha where he owned and operated Bruneteau's Bar & Grill for many years. He also owned a bar for many years back in his hometown of St. Boniface alongside the Red River.

Besides hockey, Mud always had another very strong passion in life. Fishing. Ever since he first signed with the Red Wings he would come home to Manitoba in the spring and go fishing until the season started up in the fall.

When Mud was playing in the NHL with a young family, his Canadian trips would only last two or three weeks, but once he was through with coaching and retired from his bar, he would head north as soon as the ice had melted to his paradise, Lake Athapapuskow, a gorgeous and scenic body of water just south of Flin Flon in northern Manitoba.

That's where you could find Mud Bruneteau in the summer months and he loved to tell old hockey or fishing stories to anyone that wanted to listen.

Mud Bruneteau passed away on April 15, 1982 at the age of 67. He had spent his last year living in beautiful South Padre Island, Texas and he passed away in Houston while undergoing cancer treatments for his hairy cell leukemia.

When Bruneteau first signed with the Red Wings he was given a $200 bonus that his father wanted him to give it back because he felt that his son hadn't done anything to earn it. This was of course before Mud scored the marathon game winner in 1936.

His rookie salary was $2,500 for the season and his biggest Stanley Cup bonus was for $700. Bruneteau played long before there was big money to be made in the NHL, but still he felt no hardship about that. "Sure, I don't have a lot of money," said Mud. "But I've been able to do all the things in life I wanted to do. I played hockey in the NHL, I raised a wonderful family and I've done a lot of fishing and hunting. You can't ask for a whole lot more."

42

ALEXANDER STEEN

A few years ago, ESPN did a poll asking players throughout the National Hockey League who their choice for the league's most underrated player was. When ESPN announced their find- ings, they gave the claim of NHL's most underrated player to Alexander Steen of the St. Louis Blues. It hardly came as a surprise to most as Alex has quietly put up solid numbers for years. In fact, he's consistently been a top 10 left winger in the league throughout his career.

St. Louis Blues head coach Ken Hitchcock has always been one of the first guys to sing Alex's praises, going on record and saying that he's the best player on a Blues roster that includes world-class sniper Vladimir Tarasenko.

"Well he's always been underrated because he does all the little things that you appreciate but I think more than anything he's a complete player. There's not many like him left," Hitchcock said. "Steen has the rare combination of hockey sense and competitiveness. His hockey sense is through the roof. He's obviously his father's son. As a coach, there's a lot of things that go on during the game and when you look back at it on the tape, you see all the little things that take you years to teach that he does naturally: angles, stick positioning, feet positioning, being able to read, trap two forecheckers. And then he's a fierce competitor, it's a great quality. It's what makes him a special player. I've said this before, to me he's a lock to win the Selke Trophy (the award given to the league's top defensive forward) one day."

Alexander Steen was born in Winnipeg on March 1, 1984 to Swedish parents, Thomas and Mona, who had come over to Winnipeg just three years prior as father Thomas was playing in the NHL for the Winnipeg Jets. Thomas Steen went on to be one of the most beloved Winnipeg Jets of all-time and spent his entire NHL career in Winnipeg, posting 264 goals and 553 assists (817 points) in 950 career games.

Alex wasn't just born in Winnipeg, he lived there for the first twelve years of his life. He then lived in Germany for three years while his dad was finishing his pro career there, and then moved to Sweden, where he currently resides in the offseason. Because of his parents' background, Alex holds both a Canadian and Swedish passport and early on in his own hockey career, Alex made the choice of representing Sweden in international competition.

One could certainly argue whether or not Alex should qualify for the Manitoba Top 50 list since he's chosen to represent a different country internationally, but the criteria is very straightforward. You had to develop your skills as a youngster in Manitoba. And Alex certainly did that, spending most of his youth playing outdoor minor hockey in Winnipeg.

Now say what you want, but I think at the end of the day, Alex's upbringing was just about as Canadian as it gets. The Steen family home in St. James backed onto a man-made lake and Thomas put up big floodlights during the winter so Alex and his friends could play there at night. Alex and his pals would shovel off a patch of ice and play on it for hours at a time.

Alex has certainly been crazy about hockey ever since he was two years old.

"When I was a little kid I didn't have anything else but a little plastic stick with a Jets logo and a ball," Alex recalled. "I didn't have any G.I. Joes or anything like that."

Just a few short years later he was playing his first organized minor hockey game at River Heights Arena, and it was very evident early on that Alex was exceptionally talented at the sport. In minor hockey one year he helped the Assiniboine Park Rangers win a city championship.

It also didn't hurt that while he was growing up, his dad was one of the biggest stars on the Winnipeg Jets. Alex's childhood was spent hanging out all the time with Jets players in the locker room.

Randy Carlyle had a son that was the same age. Andy Murray, the assistant coach had a son the same age, and they all used to come down to the dressing room and hang out with the players. At the time it was a normal, everyday kind of thing to them, but looking back on it, Alex realizes how lucky he was.

"Growing up around the room the guys were awesome. I got to come in and run around whenever I wanted. I played mini sticks and stuff, it was just a blast," said Alex. "There's a lot of stuff about that time that was unbelievable. I always remember the certain smells of the Winnipeg Arena. When you first walked in, it smelled like popcorn and when you got to the room it reeked of sweat. The boys were always loose in there and thought it was awesome that I was around, even though I was probably a nuisance. It was pretty special."

On a daily basis Alex would hang out with the likes of Alexei Zhamnov, Teemu Selanne and Teppo Numminen. He'd fire shots with his mini-stick at Bryan Marchment, who was always willing to play goal, and clown around with resident tough-guy Tie Domi. On Alex's tenth birthday, Domi got him a brand-new pair of CCM pump skates.

"I went to practice with my dad that day and when I got home, Tie had left the pump skates on my bed," Steen recalled. "I loved those skates. I wore them until I grew out of them."

Domi also went to see Alex play in minor hockey games a few times with Thomas and was blown away even back then by young Alex. "He was unbelievable," recalls Domi. "It was scary how good he was."

Little did Domi know at the time that he would go on to be teammates with young Alex in the NHL a decade or so later with the Toronto Maple Leafs.

Everything in life seemed to be going great for Alex. That is until it became confirmed that his beloved Winnipeg Jets were leaving town. Alex was only eleven years old when it happened, and no one was more devastated by it than he was.

"I was young and didn't understand the business side of it. That was my whole world, my whole life was leaving," Alex recalls. "I didn't know what I was going to do with my time. I was pissed off and angry, but mostly just upset. It was tough. The organization and the team became a part of the family basically and at that young age to have it taken from you, it was tough."

Alex was so against the team moving, that he even resorted to ask his dad if they had enough money to buy the Jets a new arena so the team would stay.

"The deal could get done still. They only need 7-8 million dollars," said an eleven-year-old Alex. "We have that don't we?"

Thomas said that if he did, he'd fix the whole problem in a heartbeat.

"Can we buy the arena?" chuckled Alex today. "I didn't have much comprehension for how much money that was. I was so upset I just wanted them to stay in any possible way, so I brought it up with my old man and asked can't we buy this team a new arena?"

On May 6th, 1995, Alex, Thomas, and the rest of the Steen family gathered onto the Winnipeg Arena ice as the Jets permanently retired Thomas's number 25 into the rafters. It marked the first time a European-trained player received that honour from an NHL team, and he became just the second Jet after Bobby Hull to have his number retired.

It was a very emotional day for everybody in the building that day.

"There's a lot of stuff from that day that I still remember," recalls Alex. "It's one of those experiences where you remember everything that was going on. Your feelings, the music that was playing, the smells. All your senses were firing and you had so many mixed emotions. You were happy and excited that they were honouring your dad, but at the same time you couldn't let this feeling go that the team was leaving and you're losing a part of yourself almost. I think you see the emotion on my dad as he's rambling in his speech, that really gets to me too. How appreciated and respected he was. And how much of himself he put into the team, the organization, and the city. When he came on to the ice and to see everybody react the way they did even though it was a sad day, it was something really special."

With the Jets leaving town, an aging Thomas Steen decided to take up an opportunity to finish his career in Germany. He spent his final three seasons playing with the Frankfurt Lions and Berlin Polar Bears. During this time, the Steen family kept a home in the Lindenwoods area of Winnipeg.

Alexander Steen remembers showing up for his first day of school in Berlin as a 12-year-old kid from Winnipeg who didn't know a word of German. "I didn't know anything," said Alex. "They just threw me into a room, closed the door and told me, 'You have to learn German.'"

While the junior hockey programs in Germany weren't in the same ballpark as Canada, Alex still thrived on the ice. And for Thomas, he got to fulfill the dream of skating alongside his talented son during an exhibition game with the Berlin Polar Bears.

When Alex was fifteen, he went to Sweden to further develop his hockey skills by playing with top club Frolunda for five seasons, split between their junior and men's team. During this time, Alex represented Sweden at a World U18 Tournament, as well as back-to-back World Juniors in 2003 and 2004.

Alex became one of the most sought out Swedish prospects at the 2002 NHL Entry Draft, and without hesitation, the Toronto Maple Leafs scooped him up with their first-round pick (24th overall). After the NHL lockout season of 2004-05, Steen made his debut with the Maple Leafs on October 5th, 2005 during their season opener against the Ottawa Senators.

Alex recalls his first game as one of the best experiences of his hockey career, "My first game with the Leafs will always be special because it was my first game in the NHL. It was also my first battle of Ontario and it was the first NHL game since the lockout so the fans of Toronto were really pumped that the game was back on the ice. The atmosphere in the Air Canada Centre was incredible."

Overall it was a solid rookie campaign for Steen as he put up 45 points. Alex played two more seasons after that, before being traded to the St Louis Blues on November 24th, 2008 along with Carlo Colaiacovo for Lee Stempniak. Looking back on it now, it's probably one of the all-time worst trades the Leafs have ever made.

Alex joined the Blues and was given a fresh start. That's all he needed to excel, as he started to score more and more every season. "When I was in Toronto there was a lot of 'he's just a checker' and that bothered me," said Steen. "I wanted to prove that I was more."

Over the past five years, Steen has become of the best two-way players in the league. Averaging over 60 points a season, Steen combines a scoring touch with the grittiness that he probably picked up from all the days and nights playing outdoor hockey in Winnipeg.

Alex's dad Thomas knows all too well the pressures of playing in the National Hockey League. "It's hard because he had a father who played in the NHL so he's been hearing stuff his whole life, and I told him early on just to let it go in one ear and then out the other. You're your own person and you gotta do this on your own. You don't have to copy what I did, you are your own person. And I think he does that really well, but of course he's influenced in his style of play because it's very much like mine.

"I watch almost every game since he started in Toronto. In his first season, I got to about 35 games because I'd fly into Toronto all the time for business and I'd always stay an extra day instead of going home so I could watch Alex play. Now that he's in St. Louis though, I mainly just watch on television because it's much tougher to fly there than it is to Toronto."

While his father, a former city councillor resides his Winnipeg today, Alex only returns to his birthplace a few times during the offseason to visit family and friends. He's also the owner of Great Big Adventure, a gigantic indoor amusement park off Kenaston Boulevard near The Golf Dome. Alex put up one million dollars of his own money to see through the construction of a top-notch indoor play centre for children in his hometown.

"I'll always have roots in Canada; there's no doubt. Winnipeg will always be dear to my heart. Obviously growing up there was something very special that I don't take lightly."

Right now, in 2017, Alex plays on a very strong St. Louis Blues squad. With a couple of deep playoff runs over the past few seasons, Alex will be looking to one-up his dad a little bit by perhaps winning the first Stanley Cup in the Steen family.

If Alex does win the Stanley Cup one day, the only debate in the Steen household in the days following the victory is if he's going to have his day with the Cup back home in Winnipeg or in Sweden.

Let's hope it's Winnipeg!

41
GLEN HARMON

Glen Harmon was everything you wanted in a defenceman. At 5'8" and 165 pounds, Glen's stocky frame was put to good use as he could crunch opposing players with some of the league's most physical bodychecks. Mixed in with solid positioning, strong defensive play, and the offensive skills required to support his forwards on a nightly basis, Glen was a speedy skater who could carry the puck up himself or send it to his teammates with perfect passes.

"He was really fast for a defenceman," recalled Habs teammate Howard Riopelle. "He could carry it out and headman the puck, too. That's the big thing, getting it out of your end."

Harmon could also score when it was needed. A high-scoring defenceman of his time, he was one of the first masters of the slapshot, a good decade before Bernie "Boom Boom" Geoffrion started claiming it as his own invention.

Harmon could have no doubt been a Hall of Famer, but he was the third defenceman behind Ken Reardon and Emile "Butch" Bouchard on a star-studded Montreal Canadiens lineup. On any other team in the league, Glen would have been a top-pairing defenceman and would have gotten the credit that he definitely deserved.

The *Montreal Gazette* used to praise Harmon on a nightly basis when talking about the positives of their city's team: "The underrated Harmon moves fast enough to cover up his mistakes and even those of his teammates, and if there is a defenceman in the league who can come out of his own end-zone with the puck faster than Glen, then we haven't seen him."

Glen Harmon was born on January 2, 1921 in Holland, a small town in south-central Manitoba. It was in Holland where Glen, the son of a barber, had his hockey beginnings. He learned how to play the game on local ponds, thanks to other kids that passed down their outgrown skates. When Glen was a teenager, his family moved to Winnipeg and bought a house on Sherbrook Street. He attended nearby Gordon Bell High School and played for their hockey team.

Harmon also played with the East Kildonan Bisons for a season and won the Winnipeg and District Midget league title and the W.J. Holmes Trophy. The next year he moved on and joined the Brandon Elks for the 1938-39 campaign. That year the Elks got all the way to the Memorial Cup western final where they fell to the Edmonton Athletic Club Roamers three games to one. His coach in Brandon was a former NHLer by the name of Jimmy Creighton who would go on to become the mayor of Brandon. The pair would stay friends throughout their lives.

Harmon got another crack at the Memorial Cup during the 1940-41 campaign when he joined a very strong Winnipeg Rangers club for his final year of junior hockey. At the time, the Rangers were coached by former Montreal Maroons star Baldy Northcott, and it was under his coaching that Harmon really came into his own at defence.

"Mr. Northcott had definite ideas," said Earl Fast, one of Glen's teammates on the Rangers. "He wanted us to play a particular way. I guess now you'd call it a defensive style. The wingers had to stay on their wing. They just patrolled up and down the boards, not the way they play nowadays with all five players all over the ice all of the time."

Led by Harmon on the blueline, the Rangers won their league championship and then overcame the Saskatoon Quakers in a barnburner seven-game western final. This sent them out east to play in the best-of-five Memorial Cup final against the very powerful Montreal Royals squad.

It was a highly contested, back and forth type series, but in the end, Winnipeg edged Montreal 7-4 in the fifth and decisive game to win the Memorial Cup. The general manager of the Montreal Canadiens, Tommy Gorman, must have liked what he saw in Harmon while watching him play in the finals because just weeks after Glen's Memorial Cup triumph, the Canadiens claimed him in an Intra-League Draft.

Harmon was assigned to the Montreal Senior Canadiens of the Quebec Senior Hockey League where he first became teammates with the great Maurice "Rocket" Richard. After a year and a half of senior hockey, Glen made the jump to the NHL in 1942-43 with the Habs and even though he only skated in 27 games that season, Harmon was the runner-up for the Calder Trophy as the NHL's top rookie with his nine goals and fourteen points.

The following season, Harmon played his role on a very powerful Canadiens squad that lost just five regular season games all year. Under coach Dick Irvin, the Habs rolled over their opponents, finishing twenty-five points ahead of the second-place Detroit Red Wings. In the playoffs, it was more of the same as the Habs blasted Toronto four games to one, and then swept the Red Wings to win the Stanley Cup and end a thirteen-year-Cup drought in the process.

Harmon would win his second Stanley Cup in 1946 when his Montreal Canadiens defeated the Boston Bruins three games to one in the Cup finals. During his time, Glen was one of the most effective players in the league, leading all NHL defencemen in goals for a number of years.

Throughout the league, Harmon garnished high praise for his play. Red Wings coach Jack Adams said once that, "Harmon has put plenty of life into Montreal. He's travelling all the time. He's got speed to burn. He clears pretty well, is shifty, and seems to give the team more pep than they ever had early on in the season."

Montreal general manager Tommy Gorman chimed in by saying, "You know the most underrated player on the team? Glen Harmon! Boy, he's a dandy. He always gets a goal when it's badly needed, like the tying one in Toronto on Saturday. And he has been on the ice for only sixteen goals scored against the club all season!"

During his playing career and life after hockey, Glen used to try and get back to Winnipeg to visit family as often as possible. He even drove there for his honeymoon. When his kids were young, Glen would drive the family to Winnipeg every summer in his station wagon to visit his mom and other family.

The most well-known Glen Harmon story that gets told today has to do with a bet regarding a fancy hat. You see, Harmon's wife used to own a trendy hat shop in Montreal's West End called Juliette's that he would work at during the offseason. And during the 1947-48 season, teammate Butch Bouchard's wife took a shine to one of the store's higher-end hats. After she decided to buy it, Glen arranged for it to be brought to the Habs dressing room, but when it arrived, he warned Bouchard that it was very expensive and told him to take a peek at the price tag.

"I'll tell you what I'll do," said Harmon. "If you score two goals tonight it's yours for nothing!"

Since Bouchard had scored only four goals the previous year it seemed like a pretty safe bet for him. Of course, Bouchard got hot and scored the only two goals that evening for the Canadiens. And just like that the hat was his.

The 1950-51 season was Harmon's last in the National Hockey League. He would go on to spend four years playing senior hockey with the Montreal Royals. Harmon retired at the conclusion of the 1953-54 season at the age of 34. He finished with 146 points in 452 NHL games over nine seasons. Some of his top accomplishments include being named a Second Team NHL All Star in 1945 and 1949 and his two NHL All-Star Game appearances (1949 and 1950). Glen won the Stanley Cup twice with the Canadiens (1944 and 1946) over the course of his career and was consistently one of the league's top scoring defencemen in his time.

After he retired from hockey, Harmon was offered a refereeing gig but he wasn't interested. Instead, he stayed involved with the sport by playing a big role in the starting up of a pension fund for retired NHL players. He made his living after hockey in the car business. Harmon worked for Doyle Motors in Verdun for a little bit and then spent 31 years with Parkway Motors, a major Montreal GM dealership, eventually becoming the fleet manager. Glen was even the top salesman in Canada one year. He was so popular that he often had people waiting so they could buy from him!

After retiring from Parkway Motors, Glen settled in the Toronto area where he lived out his remaining years. He wanted to keep busy so he tried driving a school bus for a while and then drove the courtesy car at a dealership in Mississauga for a few years.

Glen Harmon passed away on March 9, 2007 at the age of 86 in Mississauga, Ontario after a lengthy struggle with Alzheimer's. "Everyone loved our father," recalled Glen's daughter, Gloria. "All of our friends growing up thought he was the nicest, funniest father around. People loved to sit with him and hear all his stories about growing up in Manitoba, playing hockey, and living and loving life. He always had a smile on his face. He was a very honest, hardworking man who always cared about his family first."

The final word on Glen comes from one of his old Habs teammates: "I remember one time, we had a bad first period," recalled Howard Riopelle.

"Glen had been on a couple times. The first time he was going pretty good and the next time it wasn't going so good. He was waiting for his turn to come up again when Irvin came up behind him and quietly said, 'I'd like you to let the other line go ahead on the next shift because you looked a little tired out there. Just stay here and rest a bit.' I'll tell you, when he went out the next time, Glen was really going."

40
JAMES PATRICK

Fact: No Manitoban has played more career NHL games than James Patrick. The journeyman defenceman from St. James played in 1,280 NHL games in a career that spanned over three decades. He also ranks 30th all-time in career NHL points for a defenceman at 639. As underrated as James was during his playing career, for me at least, he was an obvious Top 50 choice right from the start.

"He's good enough that I can't screw him up," proclaimed his Rangers coach Herb Brooks, who is best known for guiding a group of American college kids to the 1980 Olympic gold medal, highlighted by their famous triumph over the Soviet Union that is simply known today as the Miracle on Ice. Herb always had high praise for his defensive stalwart who preferred to stay in the background, out of the spotlight, and play a support role for his club.

Andrew Podnieks' 2003 book *Players: The Ultimate A-Z Guide of Everyone Who Has Ever Played In the NHL* said that, "Patrick combined speed with skill and defensive maturity beyond his years. He moved the puck extremely well and was durable year to year. Patrick's longevity and consistent performance has left an indelible impression on the game and the Canadian national program."

James Patrick was born in Winnipeg on June 14, 1963. Sports were always going to play a big role in Patrick's life it seemed. His father Stephen Patrick is a Winnipeg Blue Bombers legend of the 1950's and 1960's, and his brother Steve Jr (two years older than James) also went on to play in the National Hockey League.

"I think I just did what every other kid did growing up at that time," James said. "My brother started skating around three or four years old. We lived on the schoolyard since they used to flood an ice patch right behind Bruce Middle School."

James and his brother would put their skates on at the back door of their house, and from there it was just a one-hundred-yard walk or so to the Bruce Middle School ice patch. They would walk to Woodhaven Community Club on weekends and go skating there all day long. "I pretty much grew up at Woodhaven," James said. "I started playing house league there when I was six and just moved up through the minor hockey ranks from there over the years."

James grew up idolizing the likes of prolific Swedish scorers Ulf Nilsson and Anders Hedberg of the WHA's Winnipeg Jets. He also got really good at hockey really quickly. James was known as not only the best defenceman around, but also one of the smoothest skaters in all of Winnipeg for his age. At fourteen, James was already playing with the MJHL's St. James Canadiens. A few years later he left home to play midget hockey in Saskatchewan with the Notre Dame Hounds, a boarding school in Wilcox, SK., known for developing NHL talent. The next year (1980-81) he was playing in the SJHL for the Prince Albert Raiders. It was a big step, but Patrick sought out the college hockey route, getting an education while still playing the game he loved. And he couldn't do that if he played major junior hockey in the WHL, so Patrick went and played Tier II for a season with Prince Albert.

It was during that year in Prince Albert that James first thought that he could potentially play hockey for a living. "Well like every kid when you're seven, eight or nine years old it was a dream of mine. It was always my dream," Patrick said. "Maybe when I was seventeen playing Tier II junior hockey in Prince Albert—I had no idea it was even my draft year. Halfway through the year someone told me I was ranked to go in the first round of the NHL Entry Draft. I had no idea it was my draft year until that point. I was playing Tier II because I was going to go play college the following year, but by the end of the year I was told I was going to be a first round draft pick. Some teams started interviewing me over the phone and I guess maybe that's when I thought it was possible."

James went 9th overall to the New York Rangers at the 1981 NHL Entry

Draft. "It was a huge thrill," he said. "It wasn't exactly a dream come true since I hadn't made the NHL yet, but still to be associated with the Rangers and to be a first round pick of theirs, I was overjoyed. I remember my teammates in Prince Albert were also really excited for me. Bob Lowes, my closest friend at the time, and Dave Tippett, I remember them both being really happy for me. I was just overjoyed."

After being drafted, Patrick fulfilled his college commitment and spent two years at the University of North Dakota. His first year there, they won the NCAA Championships. It was another big thrill for James in the early goings of his career. "It was great, I had a great time in college. I left home when I was fifteen and went to Notre Dame and played midget hockey there, and then the next year I played Tier II in Prince Albert. So then playing college hockey was just continuing on that path I guess. I went to North Dakota for two years and had a real good coach in John 'Gino' Gasparini. It was amazing right from the start because in my first year there we won the NCAA Championships. We had a lot of great players on the team who later played in the NHL. Guys like Troy Murray, Craig Ludwig, Phil Sykes, Dave Tippett, and both of our goalies Jon Casey and Darren Jensen all played in the NHL later on.

"Overall it was a great experience, a great place to go to school and have a social life, and play great hockey. The whole experience was really just fantastic. I didn't know what I was getting into, college life in the United States living on campus. We ended up winning it all which was just a huge thrill for me and my team, I just loved the time I spent there in North Dakota."

While playing college at North Dakota, Patrick also got the call on multiple occasions to represent the Canadian National Team at a variety of world-class tournaments. He suited up for his country at two World Junior championships (1982 and 1983), the 1983 World Men's Championship, and at the 1984 Sarajevo Winter Olympics. The big accomplishment in those tournaments was winning a gold medal at the 1982 World Juniors. More remarkably, Patrick did all of this before playing a single game in the National Hockey League.

"The year when I was eighteen, they started up the national junior program. I don't think they had it for a few years prior, but they started it up again. The first year with that we won the World Juniors which was an awesome experience. Some of the games were in Winnipeg, but the Americans also hosted it in Minnesota and the final was actually in Rochester, MN.

"I got to play in the World Championships and Olympics before I played in the NHL because back then the Olympics was all amateurs, so our team was mostly made up of 18-20-year-olds. A couple of us played with the NHLers at the Worlds in 1983 and then played in the 1984 Sarajevo Olympics, which I know wasn't considered a big deal to most young Canadians at the time. But when I came to Notre Dame as a fifteen-year-old, I was coached by a former Olympian in Barry MacKenzie who kind of planted that seed that being an Olympian is something special. Since then it was something I had wanted to do, and I guess to be an Olympian is something to be proud of.

"The Olympics itself was really disappointing. We really wanted to medal, that was our goal, but we ended up losing the bronze medal game. We weren't in the same league as the Russians, they beat us 4-0 and we couldn't have played a better game. It was devastating to lose that bronze medal game because it was a long year leading up to it. We started in August and the Olympics were at the end of February. We trained a lot in that time, being on the ice twice a day until almost Christmas. It wasn't always fun but we were pushing for that goal of playing at the Olympics and winning a medal. It's just disappointing. We were tied 0-0 with Sweden with ten minutes left and we lost the game 2-0. It could have gone either way, but we didn't get it done so it still stings."

After the Olympics, it was off to the NHL for James as he reported right to the New York Rangers to close out the 1983-84 season. Another remarkable thing about Patrick's career is that because he played college hockey and was on the Canadian National Team, he never had to play a game in the minor leagues. In fact, for his whole career he didn't play a single game in the minor leagues.

James joined the New York Rangers and actually scored his first goal on a feed from his idol Anders Hedberg. It was something that Patrick had likely played out thousands of times on the outdoor rinks of St. James, but for it to happen for real in the NHL must have been something truly special. "I think I was just young and naive. I was excited just to be playing in the NHL, it didn't matter where. My dream since I was a young kid finally came true to play in the NHL. I got to play on the Rangers with Anders Hedberg who was a huge idol of mine when I was twelve in Winnipeg. And I got to play for Herb Brooks for a year and a half which was really interesting and enjoyable. I got to develop my career and play with some great players like Brian Leetch, John Vanbiesbrouck, Mark Messier, Marcel Dionne, and Guy Lafleur who was another idol of mine."

Patrick became an impact player right away in the Big Apple. A force on the blueline, James also got into a fair bit of offence with his most productive season coming in 1991-92 when he scored 71 points. Perhaps his best season overall, however, was the 1987-88 campaign. It began with James being called upon to play for Team Canada at the 1987 Canada Cup. For those who don't remember, the 1987 Canada Cup was the tournament where Gretzky fed Lemieux for that historic goal in the final minute of the final game against the Soviet Union to win the Canada Cup. Patrick went on to have a strong season with New York and despite his club not making the playoffs that year, he finished the season as the Rangers best defenceman and was named Team MVP for his efforts.

"At the start of my NHL career, I was just trying to get better as a player. Later, when I got established, you wanted to try and have some success with your team. And in New York we certainly had some ups and downs. We won the President's Trophy, went to the semifinals a few times, but that was really it. I loved playing there and living in the big city. Coming from Winnipeg, maybe I was naive or whatever but I certainly wasn't overwhelmed by the big city. Most of the players lived a little out of the city in Westchester where we practised, and over the years I learned to love the city and what it had to offer. At the end of the day I'm very lucky to say that I played for that franchise. I think being from anywhere in Canada, you appreciate just getting to the NHL and playing in any city, so that's the way I looked at my whole career. I enjoyed every city I played in. Just to be able to play in the league was a dream come true. I was able to play in the league for a long time, but I have to say it went by very quickly!"

After eleven seasons with the Rangers, James was dealt to the Hartford Whalers where he spent most of the 1993-94 season before being shipped once again, this time to the Calgary Flames late in the year. James spent five years in Calgary, and then signed with the Buffalo Sabres as a free agent at the conclusion of the 1997-98 season. Patrick would play the last six years of his career in Buffalo and spent a lot of that time mentoring some of the younger defencemen on the team. He announced his retirement from the NHL on September 8th, 2005 at the age of 42 after 21 seasons.

When it was all said and done he finished with 639 points in 1280 career games. Despite playing in the league for so long, Patrick usually managed to stay out of the spotlight. The underrated role he seemed to have in the NHL never really affected him all that much, he claims. In fact, he couldn't really care less about the subject. "I don't really even think about it. I think as a player I had certain skills. For a number of years, I thought I was close to being a top-level player. I was top ten in scoring for defencemen a few times, so I know where I stand as a player. Later on, I was a depth player, veteran, dependable two-way defenceman. Certainly, my years in Buffalo was a good fit for that as we had a lot of young guys and I was an older presence around them.

"As far as being underrated and underappreciated, I know I competed hard as a player. I know my teammates respected me and my talent. I came to the rink every day happy to be there. One of the things as a coach now I try to pass on to the players is 'try to get better every day.' Every day you come to the rink and think what can I do to get better. I know that's how I approached my career."

After his career ended, James immediately fell into coaching. He was teammates with Lindy Ruff in the late 80's with the Rangers and then played for him in Buffalo. Lindy eventually asked James to be an assistant coach in Buffalo, and then later in Dallas where the two are currently coaching together.

Patrick talks about what led him down the coaching route following his career. "If you would have asked me halfway through my career, it wasn't something I would have thought about doing. When I ended up going to Buffalo, certainly my last four or five years there they had a lot of young defencemen, and almost every time a young guy was called up he'd end up playing with me. Guys like Henrik Tallinder, Brian Campbell, Dmitri Kalinin, Jay McKee come to mind. I played a lot of hockey with those guys towards the end, so I certainly became more of a mentor.

"I was still able to contribute, that was still my number one focus—what can I do for the team. But it just became natural for me to help. If my teammates could play better then it helps everyone. I saw different teammates, I saw guys who were insecure with young guys coming up and taking their jobs. They would go out of their way to undermine them. I was the opposite of that, I wanted to help everyone out as best as I could. At that stage of my career I knew where I stood as a player.

"I remember playing with Brian Campbell and we played a lot together, and pretty much after every shift he would ask me questions, should I have done that or this. We had a lot of dialogue on the bench during the game and also after the game we would talk, so we became real close. And I think those type of relationships pushed me into the coaching direction. I was fortunate that I played with Lindy Ruff in New York for three years, and then I played for him in Buffalo for six years. I think he saw that in me, so when my career was done he got me to come in as a skills development coach and it kind of spiralled from there to then being his assistant coach with Dallas."

James Patrick's Manitoba All-Time Rankings:

1. Jonathan Toews
2. Terry Sawchuk
3. Theo Fleury
4. Bobby Clarke
5. Andy Bathgate

CHICO RESCH SAYS

I love James, what a nice guy. I liked his dad a lot when I was growing up as a Saskatchewan Roughriders fan even though he was a football player on the rival Winnipeg Blue Bombers. I had his football card and kept it. As much as I liked James, I was in more awe and respected his father.

James looked good and skated pretty well on the ice. He could move the puck well; lateral movement was good. He was the right height and was mobile and could manoeuvre around pretty well. James brought some offence too. Occasionally he'd sneak in and score a goal.

He was sort of a transition player from when the game went from really strict defensive stuff, you could get away with a lot of stuff like grabbing, slashing, hooking, tripping. He kind of bridged that new movement of a little less defensive restrictions.

James was just a terrific guy. He could be an MLA of an area if he ever decided to try and get into the Manitoba government. He was just kind of brought up in the sports world with his dad, and he knew right away how to represent himself and his team. It shows when he went into coaching after his playing career ended because he was universally liked by everyone. He just represented everything well, an ambassador you might say.

39
TED HARRIS

Not many hockey players who played for the notorious Eddie Shore can say that they liked him while playing for him. Winnipeg native Ted Harris is one of the notable exceptions to that claim. Shore mentored Harris while he played in the AHL for many years, and played an instrumental role in getting Ted to the NHL where he went on to have an amazing career winning five Stanley Cups.

"Ted Harris was a throwback defenceman to the days when crunching body checks were more vogue than in contemporary hockey," recalls hockey historian Stan Fischler.

In the April 17, 1969 issue of *The Phoenix*, there was a very accurate description of Harris as a hockey player that read, "Hockey fans look at Ted Harris, the burly defenceman with the Montreal Canadiens and say, 'look at him, he was born talented.' Opposing NHL Players look at Ted Harris and gush respect for this rough and tumble and talented rearguard. But, five years ago people weren't so free in flinging compliments his way. That was when Harris was performing in the shadow of other Habs stars. Then, things started to swing for Harris. He developed confidence and painted his performances with skill and polish and toughness. He emerged from under a cloak of relative obscurity into an area of leadership and now is regarded as one of the Canadiens best defencemen. He certainly is their most consistent performer."

Ted Harris was born in Winnipeg on July 18, 1936. He grew up in a house on Jamison Avenue in the East Kildonan/Elmwood part of town. Ted began his hockey career at the age of six, a curious youngster on the outdoor rinks of what is now Bronx Park Community Centre. He also played lacrosse at nearby Kelvin Community Centre.

"I used to walk about three quarters of a mile to the Bronx Park rink," Harris said. "Lots of time when me and my friends would get there, the damn rink would be covered in snow so we'd have to shovel it before we could practice or play."

When Ted was eleven, he played as a goaltender for his junior high school team. He moved onto playing as a defenceman a few years later when he joined the bantam hockey ranks for his local Elmwood Bantam Terriers squad at Bronx Park. Despite being a defenceman, Harris was a consistent goal scorer and usually one of, if not the best player on the ice. A few years later he was a power defenceman, playing three seasons with the MJHL's Winnipeg Monarchs, who played their home games out of the old Amphitheatre that once stood where The Great-West Life Assurance Company building currently is on Osborne Street. While playing with the Monarchs, Ted funded his hockey dream by working for a local telephone company in Winnipeg.

"When I first got out of high school in the early 1950's, I worked with MTS," recalls Harris. "I used to be what they call a line station installer. I'd put phones in the houses and also many times I'd be up a telephone pole when it was thirty below."

Childhood friend and Monarchs teammate Len Morrow recalls one wild night at the Amphitheatre. "We were playing the Fort William Canadiens one night in the playoffs, and the dressing rooms at the Amphitheatre were downstairs below the ice surface. You had to walk in your skates down a flight of stairs just to get to the dressing room," says Morrow. "Of course, the trainer is the person who has the key to the dressing room, and he's the last to get down the stairs. So, while we're waiting, the coach of Fort William, Mickey Hennessey, a little wee guy is standing there near us and starts to berate Teddy Harris, who is standing at 6'2", probably 6'5" on skates. Hennessey was just giving him hell, until Teddy punches him. All hell broke loose and a huge fight started! It was just a pile of errors that started the fight, but you were in close quarters down there so that kind of thing would happen from time to time."

While playing for the Monarchs, Harris received some attention for his strong play from NHL scouts who wanted to sign him to the C-form that was such a common theme back in those days. "After I finished playing juniors with the Monarchs, I signed a C-form with the Toronto Maple Leafs. The day I signed it, someone from the Montreal Canadiens organization came to my door, I didn't even know they were interested. When I told him I'd already signed the C-form with Toronto, he just turned around and walked out. He said, 'I can't talk to you then,'" recalls Harris. "It's funny since as life went on, I ended up with Montreal. It's crazy how things work out."

In 1955, Ted's Monarchs won the MJHL's Turnbull Cup. He was named a First-Team All-Star for his efforts that year. The following year, Harris turned pro with the notorious Eddie Shore and his Springfield Indians. In his first few years with Springfield, Harris was loaned out to the EHL's Philadelphia Ramblers and WHL's Victoria Cougars. He returned to Springfield full-time for the 1959-60 season, and spent four full seasons learning the game from Shore.

Known as an extremely tough person to get along with, Eddie took a liking to Harris because I think he saw a lot of himself as a player in Teddy. Harris talked about the role of his mentor. "Shore taught me how to play the man and the puck. I figure he made me more versatile," Harris said. "He's the one that got me to the NHL. I was a late developer and Shore gave me a chance to play and worked with me every day. Nobody else would even have bothered."

Of course, Shore was a very tough guy to play for. "He was one tough son of a bitch as a coach. One of the things about him was 'Eddie Shore Time'. He'd tell you to be at the bus for 8am if we were heading out on a road trip, and if you weren't there a quarter to eight you'd miss the bus because he left fifteen minutes early. We always made sure to be there nice and early so we didn't get left behind," said Harris with a hearty chuckle. "He used to stand on the boards during practice and he'd call you over and say, 'Mr. Harris, what the hell do you think you're doing?' and you had to stand there and listen. But let me tell you, he sure taught you the game, that's for damn sure."

Harris ended up winning three straight AHL championships with the Springfield Indians (1960 to 1962). In June of 1963, Ted was traded to the Montreal Canadiens, who were the first NHL team to take a chance on him. He made his debut the following 1963-64 season, playing in four games, while spending most of the year with the Cleveland Barons of the American League. He was selected as a First-Team All-Star defenceman that year and won the Eddie Shore Award as the AHL's top blueliner. Oh, and he also won the league championships that year, making it four championships in five years.

Championships would be a common theme in Ted's career if you haven't already noticed.

Ted made the Montreal Canadiens out of training camp for the 1964-65 season. He never played in the minor leagues again for the rest of his career. Harris' physical presence was immediately recognized by the league. He was a force to be reckoned with on the ice, and opposing forwards had to think twice before they tried to get by Harris, because more often than not he would send them flying to the ice.

"When I first went to Montreal, they had gotten the crap beaten out of them on the ice, so the year I joined them, they got John Ferguson and myself. Between the two of us, we gave everyone a little more stability and I think that's what we needed to win."

Known as one of the most powerful checkers in the league, he was also considered one of the top three fighters along with John Ferguson and Orland Kurtenbach. Harris and Kurtenbach had themselves two classic one-on-one tilts one year in which each took a decision. In regard to being such a physical player during his career, Harris said, "I just did what I thought I had to do at that time. You weren't out there to be a goon, it was just about playing the game and trying to help your team be successful."

In a past issue of *The Globe and Mail*, the legendary Bobby Orr recalls his first NHL fight being against Harris. "My first fight was against Ted Harris of the Montreal Canadiens. He wanted to see what I was made of—that happens to every rookie. If you answer the challenge, you will have the respect of both your teammates and your opponents."

Being on such a powerhouse Montreal Canadiens team, Ted might have had an idea that success was in his future. But in sports and like with anything, there is always uncertainty. Ted shined and played his part with his very strong play and solid defending in helping lead Montreal to Stanley Cups in 1965, 1966, 1968 and 1969. It was the height of his career and it was certainly a major high for any hockey player to win four Stanley Cups in five years.

One story that Ted shared with me from his Montreal days was about the first and only time in his life where he tried the sport of curling. Being from Winnipeg he knew all about the game growing up, but was always too busy with hockey and other sports to give it a try. "I remember our coach Toe Blake loved to curl. During the playoffs every year they would take us up to the mountains in northern Montreal, and one night, Toe said 'Let's go curling!' So, we put together a couple of teams from the guys and he got ice for us to curl, and we went and curled. My damn arms were so sore from sweeping with those brooms that the next day I could barely shoot the puck!"

Eventually, as we all know, all good things have to come to an end, and for Ted it was no different. He was left unprotected in the spring of 1970 for the intra-league draft and was claimed by the Minnesota North Stars. He would go on to serve as the team captain in Minnesota for the next four seasons.

He then spent a brief stint with both the Detroit Red Wings and St. Louis Blues, before the Philadelphia Flyers took a chance on him for the 1974-75 season. Ted's experience and sturdy play proved key as the Flyers repeated as Stanley Cup champions. For Harris, it would mark the fifth and final time he would hoist the Stanley Cup.

It was the perfect ending to Ted's career as he retired shortly after winning that final Cup. He was nearly forty years old after all. In the end, Ted spent twelve seasons in the National Hockey League. He finished with 198 points in 788 NHL games. In addition to his five Stanley Cups he also played in five NHL All-Star Games (1965, 1967, 1969, 1971, 1972). Add that up with exactly 1000 career penalty minutes and it was an absolutely stellar career for the man who came up from a very modest background in the Elmwood neighbourhood of Winnipeg.

Ted went back to Minnesota after his career and coached the North Stars for two and a half years. After that stint coaching in Minnesota, he decided to move back to Philadelphia where he found himself managing a place called Conroy's Corner paint store in Westmont, New Jersey. At the age of 80, Harris moved to Lilydale, Minnesota to be closer to his kids that live in and around the Minneapolis area.

"I lost my wife five years ago. Both of my kids live here in Minnesota so being 80 years old now, it's good to be back so close with family. I don't get back to Winnipeg all that much anymore, but I still have my sister and a few nieces that live there. It seems like every time I go back to Winnipeg it's always forty-two below outside!"

Looking back on everything, Ted only has fond memories of the sport that was so good to him for a career that spanned three decades. He claims his first Stanley Cup he won with Montreal stands out the most in his career because his team overcame a lot of critics who thought they didn't have it in them. At the end of the day, Ted just loved playing hockey. It's as simple as that.

"I was lucky. I think in eighteen years of professional hockey, I won nine championships, which is kind of nice. You have to be fortunate and you have to be at the right place at the right time, but I was very happy with how my career went. I never made much money, but I sure enjoyed playing the game."

CHICO RESCH SAYS

What you liked about Teddy was that his face told you that he got involved in the physical play. He had that crooked nose if you look at his old pictures. His nose was a big curve, I can still see it today in my mind. It was well earned I'm sure.

Ted in some ways he was a bigger, larger, earlier version of Gordie Lane. He did all the little things playing on a really good Montreal Canadiens team, and then the not so good Minnesota North Stars where I saw him play. Steady Teddy all the time, but he'd step up and get involved, blocking shots left and right, and was very physical.

He could play for any team, great teams or bad teams, it didn't matter. He was the kind of guy that teams thought if you could get Teddy Harris you would always be upgrading your team. Of course, he wasn't a number one or two defenceman. He was a number four, five kind of defenceman on the depth chart. One of the best of his era which wasn't bad. Those guys don't get much recognition, but they should. They have a huge influence in your team winning.

38
CULLY WILSON

C ully Wilson was one of the earliest bad boys of professional hockey. The best example that I can give was in 1919 when he was banned from the Pacific Coast Hockey Association (PCHA) after a vicious stick attack that ended up breaking the jaw of Vancouver Millionaires' Mickey MacKay. Another time came in the 1924 playoffs when he levelled Montreal Canadiens legend Howie Morenz with a vicious cross-check that tore ligaments in Morenz's shoulder and chipped his collarbone. No penalty was assessed on the play, however, as it was allegedly a clean check!

That's not to say that Wilson was merely a goon on the ice. He finished in the top ten for league scoring numerous times during his career after all! One of the smaller players at 5'8", Wilson did what he had to do in order to give his team the best chance at winning in every game he played. If that meant crossing a certain line, he'd cross it in a heartbeat and worry about the potential consequences later.

The 1999 book *Ultimate Hockey* states that Cully was "the Left Coast's answer to Joe Hall. Wilson was a mean, moon-faced goblin of a man who specialized in running star players." In that book, he was voted as both the dirtiest, and the most hated player of the 1910's.

Another great historical hockey book called *Trails of the Stanley Cup* said, "Fiery is a great word to describe Cully. One of the bad men of hockey, who although he was an excellent player, always seemed to be embroiled in fisticuffs or stick swinging duels—he didn't back away from the biggest players in the game."

I love this quote from *Trails of the Stanley Cup* when they're talking about that infamous 1919 Stanley Cup Final that ended up being cancelled because of the influenza outbreak. "Joe Hall and Cully Wilson kept the game nicely spiced with their rough play. Hall was picking on (Jack) Walker while Wilson, as usual, took on everybody."

Despite all the rough play that Wilson was involved with, he was also a notable scorer. The Legends of Hockey website attests to that, saying, "He (Cully) was a talented goal scorer who attained success in the PCHA, NHA, minors and senior leagues."

So when I first started putting names together for this book, Cully Wilson was one of the players I immediately thought of to include in the Top 50. I understand that most of you reading this book right now may not have even heard the name Cully Wilson until now, but rest assured that he is truly one of the forgotten heroes of the early professional hockey days.

Wes Wilson and Elma (Wilson) Kozub grew up in Vidir, a small hamlet just north of Arborg. Cully was their great-uncle, and their grandfather Albert (Cully's brother) lived in Vidir as well and often told his grandkids stories about Cully's exploits in pro hockey. Later on, Elma started researching her family tree and did a very thorough job of it. After Wes read what Elma had found on Cully, it sparked memories of his grandfather telling those stories about Cully, and so Wes began researching his great-uncle, and he also started to write an article about Cully's life.

Wes wrote Cully's biography in 2005 for *Lögberg-Heimskringla*, a Manitoba-based newspaper that serves the North American Icelandic community. I was blown away when I first stumbled upon the article while researching Cully myself. Everything I was looking for was right there in front of me. There was nothing I could have possibly added that would have been new material.

I called up Wes to get permission to use what he wrote about Cully for this book, and he was just a pleasure to talk to. Wes was more than happy to regale me with stories about his great-uncle. He told me about how he actually met Cully once on a family road-trip to Seattle when he was ten years old. Wes also said how he had a strong assumption that Cully had a deep hatred for the Montreal Canadiens throughout his career, despite him playing eleven games for the Canadiens in the 1920-21 NHL season.

I kind of wish that all of the players who made this Top 50 list and played in the older eras had relatives that did this kind of thorough research and made it available online. It would have made my job a little easier! Nonetheless, here is the fascinating story of Cully Wilson's life as told by Wes Wilson and Elma Kozub.

Karl Wilhons Erlendson was born in Winnipeg on June 5th, 1892 to Sigurdur Erlendson and Metonia Indridsdottir. Like many newcomers to Canada at the time, Icelanders experienced problems fitting in because of language and customs. Sigurdur understood this early on and decided to change his surname. Adopting an English-sounding name like Wilson was more likely to offer advantages in a job market not always friendly to immigrants. Their children, five sons and three daughters, all grew up adopting the Wilson name. For Karl, he quickly became Carol "Cully" Wilson.

Cully grew up on Home Street in what was then known as Winnipeg's Icelandic "West End." From an early age, he showed a natural talent and passion for skating, and ultimately hockey. Although not confirmed, it's almost a certainty that Cully was noticed early on and nurtured by some of the players that made up the two-tier Icelandic league in Winnipeg at the time—the Vikings and the Falcons.

Both of these teams were made up entirely of Icelanders. In the beginning, they were shunned by the elite Winnipeg City League and weren't allowed to compete. Not being allowed to compete only made the Icelanders more determined to play the sport they loved, so they formed their own league that included teams from Selkirk, Portage la Prairie, and Winnipeg's AAA League. At times adversity and alienation can provoke greatness, and out of that situation a hockey powerhouse grew. [You'll read more about this in the chapters coming up on Slim Halderson and Frank Frederickson of the Winnipeg Falcons.]

The first record of Cully's hockey playing days comes in 1909 when he started playing for the local Vikings as a seventeen-year-old. The next season he started with the Winnipeg Falcons, but his talents soon brought him to the attention of the Kenora Thistles, who had won the Stanley Cup in 1907 in a matchup against the Montreal Wanderers. To this day, Kenora, Ontario retains the distinction of being the smallest town to ever host a Stanley Cup winner. There he played for a portion of the year before finishing off the season with the famed Winnipeg Monarchs.

The Monarchs were the elite Winnipeg team at the time, and for the young Icelander it was a validation of his emerging abilities as a player.

Cully went back to the Falcons for the 1911 season, but the pro scouts were out and about on the Prairies, and he'd been noticed. It was time to move on.

Cully officially joined the pro ranks in 1912 when he signed with the Toronto Blueshirts. They belonged to the National Hockey Association, an eastern league that included the Montreal Canadiens, Montreal Wanderers, Ottawa Senators, and Quebec Bulldogs. The NHA was Canada's recognized professional league at the time and teams competed for the Stanley Cup. Wilson scored 12 goals in 19 games in debut, and although the Blueshirts did well during the season, the Quebec Bulldogs won the Cup.

For 21-year-old Cully, the next season was a dream come true. The Blueshirts finished at the top of the standings along with the Canadiens. Neither team had ever competed for the championship before and spirits were high as the series opened in Montreal. The Canadiens had a power-house team that included Newsy Lalonde and the legendary Georges Vezina in goal, and Montreal came away with a 2-0 home ice victory. The teams then travelled to Toronto for game two and the first Stanley Cup final game ever played on artificial ice at the Arena Gardens. On March 14th, 1914, the Blueshirts whipped the Canadiens 6-0, taking the NHA and Stanley Cup championship based on the two-game total point series.

After that series ended, Wilson and the Blueshirts had to take on the PCHA champion Victoria Aristocrats for the Stanley Cup in a best-of-five series. It was a historic matchup for a number of reasons. Not only was it the first time the top teams from the two leagues met, but it also began a process that would include PCHA teams competing against the NHA for the Stanley Cup (like in baseball with the World Series). It was also the start of an east-west rivalry that helped spread hockey's popularity across the country and into the United States.

These were exciting times for the sport. Hockey was evolving, and Cully was in the thick of it.

During the next season, the Blueshirts struggled and ended up in fourth place with an 8-12 record. On the scoring front, though, it was a great year for Cully, who led the team with 22 goals. He also amassed an incredible 138 minutes in penalties that year, which is quite a feat considering the teams only played a 20-game schedule back in those days. That stat right there should start to give you an idea of what kind of player Cully was.

The 1914-15 season was Cully's last with the Blueshirts. In three years with the team, he had a respectable 43 goals to his credit and had also gained notoriety in another area. Cully's hard-hitting style and penchant for a good mix-up had earned him a total of 216 minutes in the penalty box. He was quickly gaining a reputation as the bad boy of hockey.

Out on the West Coast, the Patrick brothers were introducing hockey to a whole new audience. At various times, the Pacific Coast Hockey Association included teams from Victoria, Vancouver, New Westminster, Spokane, Washington, and Portland, Oregon. But in 1915, a brand new team was added that would make hockey history.

With the Seattle Metropolitans, the Patricks were determined to make hockey a success in the west, and they began raiding the eastern NHA of its best players. The Toronto Blueshirts were a favourite target, and in 1915 Cully found himself in Seattle along with four other Blueshirt players that included fellow forwards Bernie Morris (a Manitoban) and Frank Foyston, and goalie Harry "Hap" Holmes. Moving to the West Coast proved to be one of the most important decisions Cully ever made. In spite of where hockey took him in following years, Seattle would be home for the rest of his life.

The Seattle Metropolitans debuted on home ice on December 8th, 1915 beating Victoria by a score of 3-2. Cully's debut with the team was noted when the reporter added, "It was a real fight all the way. Cully Wilson, the energetic right wing of Seattle, is the Johnny Evers (Boston Red Sox baseball player) of hockey, for every time there is trouble he is there or thereabouts. He a little fellow but is built all in a bundle. He is a fast skater and absolutely fearless in a mix-up and the way he went crashing into the big fellows on the Victoria team had the crowd yipping with delight and yelling his name."

It's also worth noting that during that game, Cully became the first player in Seattle franchise history to be penalized and the first to be ejected.

Cully enjoyed four exciting years with the Metropolitans that included winning his second Stanley Cup in 1917 against the Montreal Canadiens. As always, there's an interesting story behind the story. Although the two leagues had already agreed to compete for the Stanley Cup, some of the movers and shakers in the NHA were disturbed by the addition of an American team. What if the NHA were to actually lose to a team south of the border? By the time the Metropolitans and Montreal were set to meet for the Cup in 1917, the uproar and mistrust were so great that Seattle wouldn't take on the Canadiens without a formal written acceptance. Simply put, the Mets wanted a guarantee that if they won the series, the Cup would be sent south of the border. In fact, the series started without the Cup and it didn't arrive in Seattle until three months after the playoff was over, and only after a $500 bond was put up for its safe return.

The first game of the 1917 playoff saw Seattle lose 8-4 to the Habs. In an amazing turnaround, Seattle fought back, allowing only three goals in the next three games to win the series and Lord Stanley's Cup.

As Cully and the rest of the Metropolitans entered the 1917-18 season, a new organization was formed to oversee professional hockey. The National Hockey League (NHL) replaced the east's old NHA but continued to include the PCHA in competition for the Stanley Cup. Once again it looked like Seattle was going to have another shot at the Cup, but their hopes were dashed in the final game of the season when the Vancouver Millionaires beat them 1-0. Vancouver then headed east to meet the Toronto Arenas (formerly the Blueshirts), but lost the series.

As the 1918-19 season progressed, the Seattle Metropolitans enjoyed a successful season and ended up on top of the PCHA standings. Once again, they would compete for the Stanley Cup against the Montreal Canadiens. This series would prove to be both historic and tragic as it was the only time in the Stanley Cup's history (until the 2004-05 lockout) that no team was awarded the Cup. The cause was the dreaded Spanish flu pandemic that had affected many parts of the world and was brought to North America in part by soldiers returning from the Great War.

As the championship series opened, Harry Holmes was invincible in the Seattle net, and the Mets blanked Montreal 7-0. But Montreal fought back in the second game to tie the series. Unimpressed, Seattle trounced the Canadiens in game three by a score of 7-2. Game four, a 0-0 draw, was brutally tough on the teams as they fought it out for 80 minutes. Seattle came very close to possibly winning the Cup when at the end of the first period, Cully took a pass and fired the puck past goalie Georges Vezina. But he was a half-second late as the whistle had already blown to end the period.

Montreal tied it up again in game five but the effects of the fast-paced and tremendously physical series had taken its toll on both teams. A good number of players were nursing painful injuries, and as the game progressed some fell to the ice from weakness and exhaustion.

In a 1975 story about the ill-fated series, Royal Brougham of the Seattle Post-Intelligencer described the incredible difficulties the players were experiencing. Cully's physical state was typical. "Cully Wilson, like many players of that era, who had a body built of scrap iron and a never-give-up spirit, limped to the bench and hung helpless over the railing. He was carried to the locker room incoherently protesting that he was able to continue. Manager Pete Muldoon looked for a replacement but there was no one. The bench was empty."

Within hours, the Spanish flu spread quickly and hit the Canadiens particularly hard. Montreal's stalwart man on defense, "Bad" Joe Hall [a fellow Manitoban that you'll learn more about later in the book], developed a dangerously high fever of 106. As the virus advanced to members of the Metropolitans, it soon became apparent that neither team would have enough men to play a final game. The Seattle Board of Health stepped in and it was decided that the series would end. Sadly, "Bad" Joe Hall died a few days later.

Prior to the tragic final with Montreal, Cully had gotten into serious trouble with the PCHA. During a regular season against the Vancouver Millionaires, Cully and Vancouver forward Mickey MacKay whacked furiously away at the puck for possession. Sticks were everywhere, and Cully's connected with MacKay's face so hard that it fractured the young star's jaw. The injury put MacKay out for the rest of the season, and Cully was immediately suspended by league president Frank Patrick. That created an uproar with the Seattle players, who vowed they wouldn't step on the ice for another game without Cully. Patrick relented, somewhat. He fined Cully fifty dollars and allowed him to finish the season. After that, Patrick suspended him from the PCHA.

The Metropolitans felt they were unfairly penalized more than other teams, and that Cully was a favourite target. The support he had from his teammates was evident in a Seattle Times article at the time of the incident. "To a man they are all agreed that Cully Wilson is the most abused player in hockey today. Every player of each opposing team is out to do something to get him off the ice. He is playing the best and cleanest *hockey he has ever played. He is a little dervish on skates when he is in action and they don't want him out there."*

After the aborted series with Montreal, it was over for Cully in Seattle. In his four years with the Metropolitans, Cully had been a solid contributor to the team's success and a fan favourite. He scored 52 goals, 8 of them in one PCHA All-Star game alone, and assisted on 23 others. On the penalty side, he chalked up a hefty 198 minutes in 68 games. The camaraderie and friendship he enjoyed with his teammates coupled with the fierce loyalty of the fans had made his four years in Seattle one of the happiest times in his career.

Cully headed back east to Toronto and immediately signed a contract with his old team. A lot had changed in four years. The Blueshirts had briefly become the Toronto Arenas in a controversial ownership showdown as the NHL was being formed. Then after the NHL took control of the NHA in 1917, the team had been renamed the Toronto St. Patricks.

The 1919-20 season with the St. Pats was a bonafide success. Cully scored 20 goals in 23 games and had six assists to his credit. He also served 86 minutes in penalties. It was obvious that even with all the trouble he'd gotten into the season before, he wasn't about to change his rough-and-tumble style. What happened the following season didn't do anything to change his temperament either.

On January 21st, 1921, Toronto made a deal to loan Cully to the Montreal Canadiens. What was behind this decision is unknown. In any case, Cully was very upset and felt slighted by his team. However, he reported to the Canadiens, scored six goals for them, and when recalled by Toronto three weeks later, refused to join the team. As a result, Toronto suspended him for the remainder of the 1920-21. Strangely, through all of this, Cully remained under the control of the Canadiens, and just before the start of the 1921-22 season he was one of five players involved in the NHL's first multi-player trade. Cully and two other Montreal players went to Hamilton in exchange for the Tigers' Sprague Cleghorn and Billy Coutu.

The Hamilton Tigers were essentially the old Quebec Bulldogs team who had been relocated and renamed by the NHL. Cully spent two seasons with the Tigers; but the new team floundered at the bottom of the standings. During his second year, Cully made the NHL's top ten scoring list, but was unhappy and had hopes of returning out west to play. Hamilton gave him the opportunity when they traded him to the Calgary Tigers of the Western Canada Hockey League at the start of the 1923 season.

It proved to be a very eventful year all around. The WCHL had an interlocking schedule with the Pacific Coast Hockey Association who agreed to officially reinstate Cully after the Mickey MacKay incident four years earlier. With that problem resolved, Cully seemed revitalized and went on to score 16 goals with 17 assists, and established a WCHL record when he scored three goals in 61 seconds during a regular league game. By the end of the season, Calgary was at the top of the WCHL standings and had won the right to compete for the Stanley Cup in one of the most convoluted playoff formats in pro hockey's ever-evolving history. Once again, Cully would face off against the NHL champion Montreal Canadiens.

The Habs travelled west with a typically strong team that included rookie Howie Morenz. They beat Calgary, then headed to the coast where they overwhelmed the PCHA's top team, the Vancouver Maroons. It was a very strange playoff indeed. The Tigers would compete under the WCHL banner for one more year before the team was relegated to semi-professional status in the Western Hockey League. Cully played with Calgary for three full seasons. In that time, he scored a respectable 41 goals and, not surprisingly, accumulated 120 minutes in the penalty box.

Although he was now in his early thirties, Cully remained fearless on the ice. For a man who barely weighed one hundred and fifty pounds, he had proven himself in a decade of pro hockey to be one of the toughest and scrappiest players to ever play the game. But that doesn't tell the whole story. Cully was also one of the fastest and most adept skaters of his era, and although his fisticuffs and stick-swinging duels made the headlines, and he wouldn't back down from any of the biggest players, his goals and assists won many a game.

Throughout his career, sports reporters loved describing Cully's exploits on the ice. If you were a hometown reporter, the slant was mostly positive, no matter what the infraction. But out-of-town reporters weren't always so sympathetic to the feisty Icelander. Here's an example. This poem was written by a sports reporter for the Edmonton Journal and published on February 27th, 1924 when Cully was playing in his first season with the Calgary Tigers.

Cully The Carver!

It's always struck me kind of queer that accidents abound,
and men get sliced from toe to ear when Cully is around.
It can't be that he's bold or rough, the Tigers ne'er were that.
And yet we always find such stuff wherever Wilson's at.
It's funny when upon home ice his stick so soft and meek,
is knocked aside and takes a slice from some poor beggar's cheek.
It's funny too when harmlessly he's catting all about.
He slips, shoots out a sudden knee, and lays a fellow out.
These accidents are funny things,
they're most of them "repeats."
Yet little Cully never swings upon Iron Duke Keats.
And little Cully is not loved in other leagues he's known,
for from them he's been gently shoved—Cowtown loves him alone.
We don't despise a man who's tough and let the whole world know,
we don't despise a man who's rough if he will stand the show.
We like a man who smiles and sticks despite each razzing yell.
But God we'll never like those tricks that Cully knows so well.

Whether one looks at this poem as good press or bad, it proved to be better than no press at all. Cully took a solid hip check with the ode but it endeared him to the Calgary hometown fans more than ever.

After his third season with the Tigers, Cully decided to move on. He wanted another shot at the pros and he found it in the Windy City. The NHL had been looking further afield for a new franchise and decided to base it in Chicago. When the 1926-27 season opened, Cully was a member of the brand new Black Hawks. Unfortunately, it was a disappointing year for Cully with only 8 goals and 4 assists. It would be his last year in the NHL, but it wasn't the end of his career in hockey.

In 1927, at the age of 35, Chicago traded Cully to the St. Paul Saints of the American Hockey Association (AHA). He spent three years with the Saints, the last two as both a player and Head Coach. In 1930, he split the season between the San Francisco Tigers of the Cal-Pro League and the Duluth Hornets of the AHA. The 1931-32 season with the Kansas City Pla-Mors would be Cully's last. At age 40, it was time to hang up the skates.

When all was said and done, Cully Wilson enjoyed a storied career in hockey. Starting in 1909 with the Winnipeg Vikings to his retirement *in 1932 with the Kansas City Pla-Mors, he devoted 23 years of his life to the game. Although he was never a candidate for the Hockey Hall of Fame, Cully's accomplishments were considerable. He had the unique opportunity to play professional hockey during its formative years in North America and he witnessed and was part of many firsts in the game. He also had the honour of playing alongside some of the greatest legends of the game.*

Although Cully was widely renowned for an aggressive style that put him in the record books as the most penalized NHL player during the 1919-20 season, he also made two top ten scoring leader lists. The first was in 1919-20 with the Toronto St. Pats and the second in 1922-23 with the Hamilton Tigers. Best of all, there were two Stanley Cups.

Cully had always maintained a home in Seattle, and during many off-seasons he worked for Northwest Steamship Lines. After leaving the game, he worked as an Embarking Checker for the company until his retirement. Cully took great pride in his home and yard, and over the years he became a skilled amateur horticulturist. The hands that laid many an opponent low in the heat of the game not sculptured beautiful backyard gardens. Roses were his specialty.

Carol "Cully" Wilson passed away on July 6th, 1962 at the age of 70 and is buried in Seattle. After his death, his wife Violet donated his skates to the City of Seattle. At the time of her donation she said, "You might be interested in my husband's skates. He played for the Metropolitans in 1917." Violet Wilson was justly proud of her husband's accomplishments—and so are we.

—Wes Wilson and Elma Kozub

37
PETE STEMKOWSKI

Pete Stemkowski was exactly the type of player you wanted on your team. The fun-loving, quick-witted, laidback Stemmer went about his business night in and night out and had a solid fourteen-year NHL career that was highlighted by the 1967 Stanley Cup, which still lives in folklore to this day as the last Cup that the Toronto Maple Leafs have won. Pete said, "I think the biggest thrill for any athlete at any level is to win the championship, so having that one Stanley Cup is probably the biggest thrill of my NHL career."

Hall of Fame goaltender Ed Giacomin recalls his Rangers teammate as a calming influence on the team through high-pressure situations, "Stemkowski knows how to do it. He always knew how to break the stress in the dressing room, he knew how to get you relaxed. He'd ask before a game, 'Who's in goal tonight?' And after our coach said 'Eddie,' he'd say 'Oh, we can play wide open tonight— Eddie's in goal.' Stemmer would really get the dressing room going. He was a comic, very quick with his answers and was a very witty type of individual."

During Pete's days in the NHL, he had a routine that he stuck to on game-days as best as he could. Stemmer would eat at 1pm, and then forced whatever roommate he had at the time to watch *General Hospital* with him at 3pm. Then at 3:30, they would sleep until 5pm. After downing a cup of tea, it was off to the rink for Stemkowski. Once in the locker room, Pete was always the jokester on the team, loosening up the guys before they set out to do battle.

Pete Stemkowski was born in Winnipeg on August 25, 1943 to parents of Polish descent. He came up through humble beginnings in the city's North and West End. " When I was really young we lived at 111 Lusted Avenue in the North End, and I don't know how I can remember that because we probably moved out of there when I was five years old, but I remember 111 Lusted Avenue for whatever reason," Stemkowski said. "We then moved to 798 William Avenue which was really close to the General Hospital (now Health Sciences Centre). That's where I spent all of my youth until I left for Toronto to play with the Marlies. So, until then we lived in the West End, and growing up I always went to the West End Memorial Community Club (now Burton Cummings Community Club). That's where I started playing hockey."

In his mid-70's today, Pete still has great memories of his childhood hockey days in Winnipeg. "I guess Winnipeg and Manitoba has a lot to be proud of regarding some of the guys they put in the NHL. I had played for the Monarchs and had some great memories growing up at West End Memorials. Playing peewee in -20 below zero, walking home in your skates and there would be the old hot stove there. People always ask about why do they call it 'The Hot Stove,' and it's because there was a shack with a hot stove inside. That's where you went to heat up between periods of playing outdoor games. We never complained about the weather because we didn't know any better."

When asked about when he first got the idea in his head that he could one day maybe play the sport he loves for a living, Stemmer said, "It never crossed my mind. I played for fun, loved the game right from the start. I played for a team and they said 'Hey, you're not bad, maybe you should play for that team.' Then I'd go to the other team and they said, 'You're good, you should go over there.' Finally, when I was sixteen they told me that I was good enough to play junior and that the Winnipeg Monarchs wanted me to play. So, I played for them, but believe me, it was never in the back of my mind even that I wanted to play in the NHL. I just showed up and played hockey. I was a young, carefree kind of guy in high school, looked at girls and what now, and didn't really take hockey seriously until about seventeen when the Toronto Maple Leafs decided to give me a call and told me that I was good enough to move to Toronto and play for the Marlboros, one of the better junior teams in Southern Ontario. At first, I was very hesitant, not wanting to go, and actually a lot of other people didn't expect me to go I guess. I eventually thought you know what, I got all these people doubting me, so what the heck I might as well try it. I said no at first, and then in the spur of the moment I said, 'to hell with it, I'm going.' So, I told my folks and the girl I was seeing at the time, and I took off and went to Toronto and the rest is history."

Pete played for the Marlboros the first year but tore his knee cartilage early on and went back to Winnipeg in December. He never expected them to invite him back the next year, but they did and Stemkowski ended up winning a Memorial Cup. Right then and there the Maple Leafs signed him to a pro contract. "At no point before that did I ever put my head on a pillow at night and think 'God, I wanna play in the NHL one day,'" Pete recalled. "It just kind of happened."

Stemkowski started off in the AHL and that's where he learned how to be a professional hockey player. In the beginning his teammates really didn't converse with him until he proved himself. In fact, Pete told me that when he first arrived in Rochester, his first roommate didn't say a single word to him the whole three days they were roomed together.

Eventually the team warmed up to him and everything went along great. He even got some help one day from teammate Al Arbour (Yes, the same Al Arbour who coached the Islanders dynasty). Pete recalls, "I had a car and got a ticket one day and I walked into the locker room in Rochester. I looked sad and disappointed I guess and Al asked, 'What's the matter?' I was only making $5,500 dollars back then and I told him I got a ticket. He said, 'give the ticket to me' and I never heard from him about it after that. I guess he took care of it, but for all I know there could be a warrant for me about that ticket out in Rochester."

Stemkowski came home to Winnipeg after his first pro season and claimed he felt like the richest man in Winnipeg since he was making $7,000 a year. It was in his second pro season, however, that he was finally called up to the NHL for good. "I was called up and down from the Americans to the Maple Leafs in the first season. The second year I started in Rochester and was tied for the scoring lead after fifteen games or something so they called me up and I pretty much stuck with the Toronto Maple Leafs after that."

Playing for the Leafs in the 1960's, Pete became that big body presence up the middle who would often go to the net and cause havoc. He's probably best known for the pivotal role he played for Toronto in their 1967 Stanley Cup triumph, scoring twelve points in twelve playoff games. In fact, it was his line that scored the Stanley Cup winning goal.

Pete talks about that Stanley Cup run, "It's really funny because during January/February of that year we went on a ten-game losing streak, and one day we were told that Punch Imlach was hospitalized from exhaustion. I think he had a mild heart attack but we weren't quite sure. King Clancy was going to take over as coach until Imlach returned. It was a big contrast because Imlach was the tyrant—he yelled and screamed, cracked a whip, and would keep you out there for two hours at practice. Clancy was the happy-go-lucky Irishman, so if we had a problem with Punch we could go to King and say 'What's wrong with Punch? Why is he acting like this?'

"Anyhow, Joe Crozier was down in Rochester at the time and we thought he'd be the guy to get the call when Imlach was away, but no they put King Clancy in charge. I always remember the first practice with him and he's trying to figure out what line rushes to do, and he just kind of made them up. He says, "Stemkowski, center. (Bob) Pulford, you go over to the left side and (Jim) Pappin you on the right side. I think those guys looked at each other and thought, 'Oh, we gotta play with the kid?' Pulford was always a center and now he's on the left wing. The practices were always 1.5-2 hours with Imlach and now they were only half an hour with King. He went right to Club Med as far as practices were concerned, but our line that he put together started to click. I went into corners and started knocking guys down while Pappin went wide and got the puck, and Pulford was a pretty good guy in front of the net. The three of us just really connected well and carried the team into the playoffs.

"One of the big things I'll always remember is my line scored the Cup winning goal. It's been fifty years since the Leafs have won the Stanley Cup, and it was Pulford, Pappin and Stemkowski that got that goal on Gump Worsley and the Montreal Canadiens to win it. The funny thing about it all is that we came back to training camp the next year in Peterborough and the coach didn't put us together. The line was done, we never played together again."

Winning the Stanley Cup was a major thrill for Stemkowski, and when asked about it, he'll tell you that it was the best moment of his hockey career. "You go to a parade, sit in a car and be driven around. I came back to Winnipeg that summer and high school kids would stop me and ask how I was doing. You know something, we won the Stanley Cup that year, and that makes us the best hockey team in the world for one year technically. I'm very proud of that. We came close a couple times with the Rangers after that, getting to the finals, but I never reached the promise land again."

In March of 1968, less than a year after winning the Cup, Stemkowski was shipped to Detroit as a throw-in of the big Frank Mahovlich trade. "Things weren't really working well after the expansion," Stemkowski explains. "We had different guys coming up because we lost some players with the expansion. I was having a bit of a rough time putting up points. The trade itself came as a bit of a shock, I think it was early March when I got the call that I'd been traded to the Detroit Red Wings with Frank Mahovlich and Garry Unger. It was a change since playing with the Toronto Maple Leafs, you're on *Hockey Night in Canada* and people all over the country are watching you on Wednesday and Saturdays. Suddenly I was off to Detroit which wasn't a big market at the time so that was disappointing, but the fact that I had two guys coming with me was nice, and I ended up becoming good friends with Garry."

Stemkowski did pretty well for himself in Detroit all things considered with back-to-back 20 plus goal seasons. He got to play on the top lines regularly as the Red Wings were not a strong team back in those days. "Well I played in Detroit for a couple of years and did alright," Pete explains. "We had a guy named Ned Harkness as our coach. He was from Cornell University so he was a real college kind of coach. Everything was raw, blue blazer, grey slacks and hair cut. We had Alex Delvecchio and Gordie Howe on the team so it was a real veteran-type squad over there and we kind of did it our way. There was a clash between the coaches and players, and I don't think Ned liked me too much. He used to blow the whistle in practices like the college guys do and I think I did it one day and didn't realize that he was standing right behind me. So, I ended up getting traded on Halloween night. Sid Abel called me as I was leaving my apartment in Dearborn, Michigan and said I'd been traded to the New York Rangers. That's where my life kind of unfolded. I ended up in New York where I found a girl, got married and had kids. I still call New York home to this day, so I always think of Sid Abel and if he had told me I was going somewhere else like Chicago or Boston that my life would have been much different than it is today."

Pete joined the New York Rangers in 1970. A fan favourite from the moment he arrived at Madison Square Garden, Stemkowski played six strong seasons in New York and came very close to winning the Cup on three occasions. He had his highest scoring season in 1973-74 when he put up 70 points.

His biggest moment in a Rangers uniform without a doubt came on April 29th, 1971 where he scored one of the most important goals in New York Rangers history. His tally in triple overtime of Game 6 of the Stanley Cup playoff semifinals at Madison Square Garden forced a decisive seventh game against the Blackhawks back at Chicago Stadium. The clip of the goal can be found on YouTube, but unfortunately as it turns out it was not meant to be as the Rangers lost Game 7, ending their hopes of winning a Stanley Cup that season.

Stemmer talks about the goal, "Tim Horton got the assist, that was his last point ever in a Rangers uniform. I wish it would have been a series winner but it wasn't. The goal itself was really exciting, but we went into Chicago a few days later for Game 7 and lost unfortunately. The thing about that one is people still come up to me and tell me what they were doing, that it was a school night and they had their transistor radios in bed listening to the game, so I'm flattered that it's a memory that people still hold and bring it up to me."

At the end of his career, Pete was traded to the Los Angeles Kings where he played his last NHL season. He retired after the 1978-79 season with 967 career NHL games under his belt in which he scored 206 goals and 349 assists for 555 points. When you look at his accomplishments, you think of the Stanley Cup and Memorial Cup he won. He also played in the 1968 NHL All-Star Game.

Pete talks about life after hockey, and how he spent time living on both the East and West Coast when his playing career was done. "Well I spent eight years in California working with the San Jose Sharks. Nowadays I do some work for the Rangers—radio and public/alumni appearances mainly for them. There's also this junior team starting up on Long Beach this year so I'm doing some work for them since I'm out living on Long Island. I live four houses from the Atlantic Ocean, in fact I was in the Atlantic Ocean today. I got up this morning, walked down and jumped in the ocean. New York isn't all cement, big buildings and lots of traffic. There are beaches and that's where I spend some time during the summers. I'm in my 70's now so I'm kind of settling down and doing things a little slower than I used to."

Despite being so far away from Winnipeg today, Pete's never forgotten his hometown. It's been a few years now since he's been back, but Stemkowski still gets very nostalgic when talking about Winnipeg.

"I miss Winnipeg big time! I wanna go to Juniors. I wanna go to some of these old places I used to go to and hang out at. Places like Polo Park, Salisbury House, Rae and Jerry's Steakhouse and Smitty's. I'd always stay at the Viscount Gort when I was in town over the years. That'd be my home base. Nowadays I don't know how many friends I have that are still there, but my family has now passed on from Winnipeg. There's this one guy who keeps in touch with me and lets me know what the older guys are up to, but I'd love to come back to my hometown and visit sometime soon!"

CHICO RESCH SAYS

I loved the Stemmer. I played against him and he'd always be yapping at me saying "Oh you're lucky Chico!" He was a Rangers player and did some media stuff after his career. He was a "don't judge a book by its cover" kind of player.

Stemmer wasn't smooth, explosive or dynamic offensively, but he would be like a poor man's version of Phil Esposito. If Phil was a 10/10 in how he scored goals, Pete would be a 7 where he's not going to wow people and you're not going to notice him until he's got his hands in the air after he's tipped one by you or lifted a rebound. Pete around the net was really smart and he'd just show up at the right time.

He had a personality like Butch Goring. Guys like him try to lure you in, trying to make you think that they're not really into the game, and then the play is on and they score on you and they're chuckling. Those guys are hard to figure out. Don't try to figure them out on first impression because there's two games going on. He'd say something like "Oh, good check! I gotta keep my head up next time!" Pete was having fun while playing the game, but at the same time he was trying to get you off your game by relaxing.

No one ever wanted to two-hand Pete because he's such a nice guy. No one really disliked him in the league. He's just enjoyable to be around. Coaches might have thought that he's not being serious enough, but he was. It was just a different style of playing.

He was big, lanky and awkward at times, but when he had his hands and feet going to set up or shoot a puck, he was a threat.

36
BLAINE STOUGHTON

Blaine Stoughton was the type of hockey player who liked to enjoy himself and have a good time, while at the same time competing at the highest level of the sport. He was never the hardest working player or the most the physical guy on the ice. Nor was he known for a strong defensive game. What he was good at was scoring goals. Blaine seemed to have that natural goal scoring ability that can't be taught.

Stoughton wasn't nicknamed "Stash" just for his classic Fu Manchu moustache. It was also for his ability of stashing pucks into the net routinely. Blaine topped the fifty-goal plateau twice in the NHL and once in the WHA. He scored 196 goals over a four-season period of 1979-80 to 1982-83, which ranks fourth, only behind hockey legends Wayne Gretzky, Mike Bossy, and Marcel Dionne.

He didn't get the recognition he probably deserved because he didn't play in a big-city market. *Sports Illustrated* once called him hockey's anonymous goal scorer. In fact, when Gordie Howe and Blaine were teammates in Hartford, Gordie used to say when asked how it was like being famous in Hartford, that more people knew who Blaine's wife was than Blaine or even himself. You'll read why that was very soon.

Blaine Stoughton was a player that I was aware of early on in life. I had collected a few of his hockey cards when I was a kid because of his connection to my family. My grandpa Roy was the superintendent of Tasker Enterprises—a construction company based out of Winnipeg that operated in Manitoba, Saskatchewan, and North Dakota. They built a lot of the highways here in Manitoba and Stoughton's parents worked for Roy. Blaine's mom was a cook and his father operated a grader machine. My mom also was friends with Blaine's youngest sister growing up, so I always thought that was kind of neat.

Blaine Stoughton was born on March 13, 1953 in Gilbert Plains, a small farming community just west of Dauphin that didn't even have a traffic light until Blaine was fourteen. It was in Gilbert Plains that Blaine had his hockey beginnings. He was introduced to sports early on in life as his father was the town's recreation director. "I grew up in a humble background. My parents weren't that well off but we had everything that we needed," said Stoughton "Like most Canadians, we played baseball in the summer and hockey all winter—indoors and outdoors. I was very fortunate that way living in rural Manitoba and getting all the ice time I wanted."

Playing every day on the outdoor rink near his house was vital in Blaine's quick development as a hockey player. When he was ten years old, he'd be playing pick-up hockey every day with sixteen and seventeen-year-olds. His talent was evident at an early age, and because of this he started playing for the MJHL's Dauphin Kings at the ripe age of fourteen. He was also a notable baseball player around this time, winning two Western Canadian championships for his hometown Gilbert Plains Bantam team as a first baseman and pitcher. Blaine's father, Mel, who was just recently inducted into the Manitoba Baseball Hall of Fame in 2016, was the coach.

"I started playing with Dauphin when I was fourteen and back then the Memorial Cup was played by the Tier II junior leagues, not the WHL/OHL/QMJHL we see today. My second year in Dauphin, we got to the finals of Western Canada and lost a heartbreaker in the seventh game. We were lucky getting that far because we had Butch Goring join our team late in the season since he was originally playing for Winnipeg, but was having issues with the team owner so he came and played for us. Our team was really good and I was fortunate to get experience playing at the MJHL level."

After spending a couple seasons in Dauphin, it was time for Blaine to continue his progression through the ranks of junior hockey. Now as a 16-year-old, Stoughton moved up to northern Manitoba to play with the legendary Flin Flon Bombers of the WHL.

"When I was sixteen I went to Flin Flon to play with the Bombers. They always had great teams in the WHL with the likes of Bobby Clarke and Reggie Leach playing for them. I ended up playing four years with the Bombers and at the time when you're there as a young kid, you don't realize it's not the greatest place to play in the world, but I always enjoyed it. I was kept out of trouble being up north and I had a very demanding coach in Pat Ginnell. I was always playing with good players like Chuck Arnason and Gene Carr so I kind of thought I was ready for the NHL when I graduated from the junior ranks, but I really wasn't ready quite yet as I found out the next year."

Blaine was a first round draft pick of the Pittsburgh Penguins (7th overall) at the 1973 NHL Entry Draft. He failed to make the Penguins out of training camp so he spent the first half of the year with the AHL's Hershey Bears. After the Christmas break, Blaine was called up to the big club and spent the rest of the year with Pittsburgh. At the start of the next season, Blaine drove from Dauphin to St. Catharines, Ontario for the Penguins training camp, only to realize upon arriving at the team hotel that he had been traded.

"I remember driving down there and the whole way I couldn't get any radio stations so I just listened to music the whole time. I pulled into St. Catharines at the hotel and some of the players were in the lobby looking at me funny so I went to the front desk and when they said I didn't have a room, I originally thought another player was playing a practical joke on me or something. But then the trainer comes by and says, 'I sent all your sticks to Toronto.' He then told me to go to the GM's room, and finally then did I find out I'd been traded to the Maple Leafs."

Stoughton spent two seasons with the Maple Leafs and it was in Toronto that he realized he wasn't strong enough to compete in the NHL at the level he would have liked. He was also having contract issues with notorious Toronto GM Harold Ballard, which also played a part in why Blaine bolted for the WHA in time for the 1976-77 season.

A few things changed when Blaine joined the WHA's Cincinnati Stingers. First, he met a Playboy Bunny named Cindy who he later married. It was funny because Blaine's linemates that year were also dating Bunnies, so they of course became known as the "The Bunny Line." In an old *Sports Illustrated* article back in the early 1980's that featured Blaine, it tells a funny story about the players' girlfriends and dealing with loudmouth fans. "One year in the playoffs all three of us went to a game in Indianapolis wearing our boyfriends' uniform tops with names and numbers on the back," Cindy said. "We were jumping around and cheering, getting a lot of attention as you might expect.

A lot of the fans started yelling at us, 'Hey, fuck the Stingers!' I looked back at them and said, 'We do and it's great!'"

It was in that first season with Cincinnati that Blaine also changed as a hockey player and it showed. He exploded for 52 goals and 52 assists for 104 points in the 1976-77 WHA season. "I was always one of those guys who worked his hardest on the ice during games, but after the games I liked to have fun," Blaine said with a smile. "When I met my future wife, I started staying in more and began lifting weights. I never lifted a weight in my life until I was 25/26 years old."

Blaine spent a season and a half in Cincinnati, followed by parts of two seasons with the Indianapolis Racers before the franchise eventually folded. He ended up joining the WHA's New England Whalers, which later became the Hartford Whalers after they were one of four cities (Hartford, Edmonton, Quebec City, Winnipeg) to merge with the NHL when the WHA closed up shop for good after the 1978-79 season.

Back in the NHL with Hartford, Stoughton quickly burst onto the scene. Playing on the "Bash, Dash and Stash" line with Mike Rogers and Pat Boutette, he scored 56 goals and 44 assists for 100 points, leading the NHL in goals that 1979-80 season. Blaine scored 43 the next year, followed by another fifty-plus goal season of 52, and then he scored another 45 in 1982-83. He was a very dangerous player once he got into the offensive zone and was known for his incredibly quick release of the puck that seemed to fool almost every goalie in the league at one point or another.

But playing in Hartford, his strong scoring prowess went greatly unnoticed. However, playing in anonymity most of the time despite being one of the top goal scorers in the National Hockey League was something that never really bothered Blaine. "It's kind of out of your control. It bothered my wife more than me actually," said Stoughton. "In hindsight, it kind of hurt my career I guess. If you play in a big city, it kind of does more for you once your career is over. It is what it is though and I have some lifelong friends in Hartford so I can't complain."

When Blaine got to Hartford, he may have cooled down with the partying a little bit, but that certainly didn't stop him from having fun. For example, this hilarious story after the season finale one year in Chicago: "I got back to the hotel at around 5am because the bus was leaving to go to the airport at 6am, and I figured I didn't want to go to sleep because I'd miss the bus," said Stoughton. "So, what I did is I went upstairs and grabbed my luggage and then came back outside and just sat on the stairs in front of the hotel. I used to smoke back then too, and I guess after a while I fell asleep. At about 5:30, our coach Larry Pleau comes outside and sees me sleeping with a cigarette butt hanging out of my mouth and yells 'There's my fuckin' fifty goal scorer!' I've known Larry for years and every time I see him we always laugh about that story."

There was also that time in Buffalo when Blaine was awarded a penalty shot with ten seconds remaining in the game and the score tied. "Our interim coach John Cunniff was really nervous, pacing around on the bench. And I was just kind of leaning on the boards, joking around with my teammates, waiting for the referee to signal me to go shoot. So, I said to the coach, 'Hey Cunny, why are you walking around all nervous? I'm the one taking the shot not you!' He quickly shoots back, 'Will you be serious here for once Blaine?' I said, 'I'll bet you five bucks that I'll call the shot where it's going to go.' He was getting frustrated at me so I said, 'I'll bet you ten bucks that I'll score going low stick side.' Normally I go five-hole on a penalty shot, but I knew Buffalo's goalie (Doug Soetaert) liked closing the five-hole immediately after a shot. So, when I went in there and shot, he closed his five-hole like I thought, leaving about six inches open on the low stick side and it went right in the net. I went back to the bench and Cunny's just shaking his head. He had to pay me right in the dressing room after the game!"

Jordy Douglas was a born and raised Winnipegger. Growing up a block from the old Winnipeg Arena in St. James, he used to sneak in regularly to watch the WHA's Winnipeg Jets practice. When he became a professional hockey player himself, he was given the option of signing with either Winnipeg or New England (Hartford) of the WHA. There wasn't much mystery to the Jets since he'd seen them so much over the years, so he went to New England instead. It was there that he met Blaine Stoughton for the first time. Five years younger than Blaine, Jordy had heard stories of him up in Flin Flon since they both played their junior hockey for the Bombers. Blaine and Jordy were teammates in Hartford for four seasons, and the two have since stayed friends over the years.

"I'm proud to say that Blaine was a model of efficiencies. In fact, he was the most efficient hockey player I ever played with. What I mean by that is Blaine never did any more work than he absolutely had to!" chuckled Jordy. "We'd be at training camp and everyone would be bag-skated up and down at the end of practice. Those were one and a half hour up-tempo practices and we'd come off the ice soaking wet, and he'd be asking where to hang up the dry underwear. He was just a model of efficiencies. What do I need to do to play my game but not exert myself any more than I have to.

"But man could he score goals. Blaine Stoughton would have scored a shitload more goals if he only had one-year contracts instead of multi-year deals—then he'd have to produce every year. His best year was when he was ready to negotiate, and he scored a bucketful. He was just a natural goal scorer. That Bash, Dash and Stash line was very successful in Hartford. You had Pat Boutette at left wing who would get the puck out of the corner and dig it around and do the grunt work. Mike Rogers was a quick, skilled passer of the puck. He was a centreman that had a ton of points as well. Blaine Stoughton at right wing was the mailman. He delivered it. He put the puck in the net when you didn't think there was an opportunity to put the puck in the net. The man could score goals, that's what he did. He was incredibly gifted, but he was also the type of player who'd say, 'you don't get your name in the paper for assists.' So, his attitude was to score goals, that's how you get your name in the paper. He's a character, there's no denying that."

After that stretch in Hartford it was off to the Rangers where Blaine spent the final season of his NHL career before eventually retiring in 1985. He didn't exactly see eye to eye for the most part with Rangers coach Herb Brooks. But the two are forever a part of this legendary story, told by Whalers historian Bruce Berlet: "Blaine used to drive back and forth from New York to Hartford every day, and one morning he was sitting in the driveway reading the paper when Brooks arrived about 8:30 am. Stoughton and Brooks hadn't had any one-on-one chats, so Stoughton got into Brooks' car and the two started talking. Ten minutes later, a limousine pulls up, the door opens, loud music blares, marijuana smoke fills the air and out step Cher, Cheryl Tiegs and Carol Alt. 'You should have seen the look on Herb's face,' Stoughton said.

"Then came the clincher. The next three people out of the car are Rangers stars Barry Beck, Ron Duguay and Ron Greschner. 'Herb's face was just white,' Stoughton said, howling. 'He was used to coaching junior kids and telling them what to do, and these guys are loaded. They hadn't been to bed yet. They had been to Studio 54 all night and came right there to the rink in a limo. That was one of the funniest things I've ever seen. Herbie didn't know what the heck to do.'"

Stoughton left the NHL as one of the best pure goal scorers of his time. "When I was on a breakaway, in my mind I always thought that the goalie has no chance," said Blaine. "One time a reporter asked me who do I think the best goalie in the NHL is? And I said, 'As far as I'm concerned, none of them.'"

Blaine's career totals when it was all said and done were 258 goals and 449 points in 526 NHL games. Add that up with another 179 points in 219 WHA games, and it was a very solid career by anyone's standards. His top personal accolades include leading the NHL in goals once, and playing in the 1982 NHL All-Star Game. He and Bobby Hull are the only two players to score fifty goals in both the NHL and the World Hockey Association, and Blaine also holds the record for the most goals (56) with a first-year expansion NHL team. Not too shabby for a guy who didn't like to work hard in practice.

After his career ended, Blaine got his mortgage license and worked a little while residing in Boca Raton, Florida. In 1987, a few years after Blaine had retired, he was approached by long-time friend Gary Davidson of Brandon, to come and play in northern Italy for the team that he coached because his one import player was injured a week before the season started. So, Blaine briefly came out of retirement to play with Asiago HC in the Italian League, which turned out to be quite the memorable experience for Blaine and his family. "My wife and I really enjoyed it over there. Everyone treated you like Gretzky, you didn't pay for meals or anything. As a family, it was a great experience for us. I recommend it to anybody at the end of your career to go and play in Italy. I couldn't speak the language but I always played cards with those Italians after games, and I quickly picked up on the swear words playing cards I'll tell you that!"

Stoughton and his family returned to Boca Raton after his stint in Italy ended. He owned and operated a sports bar in Boca Raton for a little while before moving on to Cincinnati where he got into coaching. Blaine started as an assistant coach with the Cincinnati Cyclones of the East Coast and International Hockey League's, and then later became an assistant coach to former Whalers teammate and current Chicago Blackhawks head coach Joel Quenneville of the AHL's Springfield Indians. After that, Blaine and a buddy purchased the Austin Ice Bats of the WPHL (Western Professional Hockey League). He became the team's general manager for the four years he was a franchise owner, and even became the head coach for a while. Stoughton remarked how they were fairly successful, drawing about five thousand fans a game in Austin. After selling the team, Blaine moved back to Cincinnati and has coached several teams over the years, including the University of Cincinnati hockey club.

Through it all, Stoughton has never forgotten his roots and still spends about five weeks of the year back home in the Dauphin/Gilbert Plains area "I come home for three weeks in the summer and one other time in the spring. I like to curl when I'm home. They always have a bunch of bonspiels on back-to-back weekends so I like to play one in Dauphin one weekend and then one in Gilbert Plains the next weekend or something like that."

Very underrated during his career, Blaine made the most of it and enjoyed success as one of the most prolific snipers of the early 1980's despite playing in a low-market city like Hartford for the peak of his career. "I didn't like practice too much, I just wanted to play! I was blessed with that natural ability as a goal scorer. I don't think you can teach that."

To close off this chapter, I think it's appropriate that I include one more hilarious Blaine Stoughton story. Jordy Douglas recalls an outdoor alumni game in Hartford a few years back that Blaine "suited up" for. "The last time I saw Blaine was about six years ago. Ray Neufeld and myself went down to Hartford and played in an outdoor game. We were invited because the Connecticut Whale of the AHL were owned at the time by Howard Baldwin and his son Howard Jr, and they were hosting a Whalers festival. They had an outdoor rink at this football stadium, and had hockey players at all levels skating on the ice over the period of a few days with the culmination being two games on Saturday. The Hartford Whalers alumni against the Boston Bruins alumni, followed by the Connecticut Whale and the Providence Bruins of the AHL.

"So, we get there to play on the Saturday and they had put our line together. It was a Flin Flon line since all of us played for the Bombers at one point. I played centre, with Ray on one side and Blaine on the other. Blaine hadn't been on the ice very much lately so he comes out to play and he basically put on all his gear except his shin pads and shoulder pads. He says it will slow him down, and he's telling us, 'well I'm not going anywhere near the puck and I'm not backchecking.' And we're looking at him all funny and I said to him, 'Are you fucking kidding me! You played in the NHL for ten years and you never backchecked—what's the difference!?" That's how Blaine played that alumni game. No shin pads, no shoulder pads. Minimal gear because he wanted to be a little faster as he got older. Who does that? Blaine Stoughton does!"

CHICO RESCH SAYS

Blaine kind of lived up to his name. He wasn't a Bobby Hull or a Guy Lafleur, but he sure could snap those pucks into the net. As a goalie you were left thinking "How the heck did he score that? He didn't do anything that special." But he just had this really quick, deceptive release. That's why they always say you can't teach goal scoring I guess. Some people have it and some don't. And Blaine had it.

He was just kind of nonchalant on the ice, you didn't notice him. I don't want to say he was camouflaged, but you didn't notice him because he wasn't a corner man or a blow-through-the-neutral-zone-with-speed type of forward. Blaine and Butchie Goring would have been a good pair I think. When Blaine would get the puck in a scoring zone, as a goalie you'd think "Uh oh! This isn't good!" And then he'd snap it into the net.

Blaine was the type of shooter that if you stopped him, you'd say to yourself "Good save." Whereas if it's a guy that's not a big-time threat you're thinking, "Yeah I should have had that one no problem." You'd kind of expect to stop certain players, but with guys like Blaine you'd kind of mentally pat yourself on the back if you stopped them.

Everything about Blaine was sort of hard to identify except for his shot and his ability to score, and that would jump out at you and get in your face. I have a vision of him, it's not really anything identifiable in terms of this or that, it's kind of like a reed blowing in the breeze until he got the puck and then it was always "Uh oh, this is trouble." And it usually was.

35
SUGAR JIM HENRY

Perseverance is a pretty good word to describe Jim Henry's career in the big leagues. After coming into the NHL with the New York Rangers in 1941-42 and leading the league in wins during his rookie season, Henry

went into the army for World War II and when the war ended, he had lost his starting job. Stuck behind hockey legends Chuck Rayner, Frank Brimsek and Terry Sawchuk on various NHL team depth charts, Sugar Jim overcame numerous stints in the minors and even a two-goalie carousel in New York before he finally took over the reins of the Bruins net in 1951.

Sugar Jim Henry might be the only hockey player in the history of the NHL that's more famous for a photo he's in than his career itself. Long-time *Montreal Gazette* writer Dave Stubbs called it "hockey's most compelling photo." The famous shot of Sugar Jim and Maurice "Rocket" Richard shaking hands after Richard scored what is known as "The Unconscious Goal" or "The Goal of the Century."

The photo is forever immortalized in our sport's history as depicting the true toughness that was required to be successful in the game back then. Sugar Jim with his face puffy and both eyes blackened, and Richard who was also black-eyed and blood-streaked from being knocked unconscious in the first period, scored the overtime winner on Henry in Game 7 of the Stanley Cup semifinals that sent Montreal to the Cup finals.

Samuel James Henry was born in Winnipeg on October 23, 1920. Growing up in the Weston area of the city, Henry got his "Sugar" nickname because he was always in the neighbour's sugar bowl as a toddler. Later, when Henry got into hockey, he made his own first goalie glove by taking a first baseman's mitt and putting the cuff of another glove on the top and then getting a shoemaker to sew it on for him.

Jim started off his junior hockey days with the Winnipeg Lombards in 1937. He then spent two years with the Brandon Elks that was highlighted by a trip to the Western Canadian final (Abbott Cup) in 1939. When talking about some of the most outstanding single-game goaltending performances in our province's history, famous Manitoba hockey writer and historian Vince Leah mentioned in his book that Sugar Jim Henry's magnificent performance in the third game of the Western junior final between the Brandon Elks and Edmonton A.C. was right up there with the all-time greats. Jim shut out the Albertans 5-0 for Brandon's only victory in the series.

After his junior hockey was behind him, Sugar Jim played senior hockey in the Saskatchewan league for the Regina Rangers during the 1940-41 season. It turned out to be a fantastic year for Henry as his team won the Allan Cup, overcoming an 0-2-1 series deficit in the final to defeat the Sydney Millionaires in six games.

The NHL's New York Rangers caught wind of the whiz-kid in Regina and Brandon and quickly got him to come out to the Big Apple and play for the big club. The 5'9" Henry made his NHL debut during the 1941-42 season and played every minute of every game for the Rangers that year, leading the league in wins with 29. At the beginning of that rookie season, Sugar Jim tried wearing an excessively long belly pad that touched the ice every time he dropped to his knees, blocking the five-hole. The league eventually stopped allowing him to wear the belly pad when they saw for themselves just how much of the five-hole it covered up.

It was a terrific rookie year for Henry and although his first-place Rangers fell in the semifinals to the eventual Stanley Cup-winning Toronto Maple Leafs in six games, it seemed that Sugar Jim had shown just about everyone that he was going to be one of the top goalies in the NHL for many years to come. Unfortunately, it didn't exactly work out like that. The onset of World War II saw Henry enlist in the Canadian Army. Despite the war, Henry continued to play hockey for various Army/Navy teams in Ottawa, Calgary and Red Deer. He won his second Allan Cup with the Ottawa Commandoes in 1943.

When the war ended, Sugar Jim was no longer the starting goalie of the Rangers. Instead he shared the duties with Chuck Rayner, a terrific goaltender in his own right, and the two would form the first "two-goalie" rotation in NHL history. Rangers head coach Frank Boucher would alternate them game by game and sometimes period by period. He even went as far as changing them shift by shift on occasion as he was changing the team's defencemen. As odd as the pairing was, the two of them would go on to become lifelong friends. "We weren't crazy about that system," recalled Chuck Rayner in an interview a few years before his death in 2002. "But we were roommates and best friends, so we lived with it."

The Rayner/Henry tandem went on for three seasons with Sugar Jim also seeing action in the minors during this time. Eventually it was evident that the duo was becoming inefficient constantly switching up the two, and as a result Henry was traded to the Chicago Black Hawks on October 7, 1948 for Emile "The Cat" Francis and Alex Kaleta.

Henry went on to play all sixty games for Chicago in the 1948-49 season, but was then traded to Detroit during the offseason since the Black Hawks had acquired the legendary Frank Brimsek. Sugar Jim never got to play a game for the Red Wings—instead he toiled in the minors for the two years he was in their organization because the club was staking their future on the young Terry Sawchuk.

The big break for Sugar Jim came on September 28, 1951 when he was sold to the Boston Bruins. He almost never made it to Boston, however, as during that offseason he was severely burned in a shed fire. After hearing from doctors that he'd never play hockey again, Henry proved them all wrong when he appeared in Boston for training camp, and the rest, as they say, is history, as Sugar Jim would go on to play the next 210 games for the Bruins franchise.

Henry's first season in Boston he was simply spectacular, proving any doubters wrong that he may have had. He was so impressive in goal that he finished third in voting for the Hart Trophy behind Gordie Howe and Elmer Lach. In the 1952 playoffs, Boston met the heavily favoured Montreal Canadiens in the semifinals and my oh my what a series it was. After going down 0-2, Boston rallied to win the next three games including an overtime game at the Montreal Forum. The Canadiens rallied themselves to win Game 6 at the Boston Garden in double overtime, which set the stage for a dramatic Game 7 back at the Forum. Sugar Jim arrived in Montreal for Game 7 with two black eyes and a broken nose, suffered in Game 6. He spent the day with his trainer, who applied hot and cold towels to his eyes to reduce the swelling. "Yes, I had two great shiners," Henry recalled. "I could hardly see."

The story goes that after being knocked unconscious in the first period and carried off the ice, a woozy Rocket Richard returned in the final minutes of the game and told Coach Dick Irvin he could play, so Irvin relented and put him in. "The Rocket crossed the centre line in full flight, shifted past the left-winger checking him, crossed our blueline and skated towards the corner with Bruins defenceman Bill Quackenbush draped all over him. The Rocket used the tremendous strength of his arms to beat him and, being a left-handed shot and, the great player he was, he cut in front of the net and put the puck past me to score the winning goal," said Sugar Jim. "I felt bad of course, because he had just eliminated us from the playoffs, but I had to congratulate The Rocket because it was one of the greatest goals I had ever seen and it was no shame being beat by such a player."

Sugar Jim always had a lot of respect for Maurice Richard. A few seasons earlier when he was playing against him at the Forum, he actually saved Richard from a potential serious injury. Maurice was dumped by a Bruins defenceman deep in Bruins territory and he slid full-speed toward Henry's nearly immovable goal as the nets then were firmly anchored to the ice. "It just occurred to me that I couldn't let Maurice crash into the goalpost—he would have broken his leg, or worse," recalled Henry in a past interview with Dave Stubbs. "So, I slid out and let his body hit mine, to protect him. He got up and thanked me, as did a few others on the ice. It was the greatest ovation I ever received in Montreal."

The next season saw Henry continue his fine form. In the 1953 playoffs, he was vital in Boston pulling off one of the great playoff upsets of the Original Six era. With Henry playing like Frank Brimsek once did for the Bruins ten years prior, Boston shocked the defending Stanley Cup champ Detroit Red Wings in six games, holding Gordie Howe, who had 49 goals in the regular season, to just two goals in the series. Detroit's coach Tommy Ivan felt that Sugar Jim was the difference-maker in the series, outmatching the legend Terry Sawchuk himself. Ivan said at the time that Henry was "the player who hurt us the most."

Unfortunately, the Bruins' luck ran out in the Stanley Cup Finals as they once again faltered at the hands of the Montreal Canadiens who were seen as the Bruins' biggest nemesis of the 1950's. Montreal won the series in five games on Elmer Lach's overtime winner in Game 5. In Henry's four seasons with the Bruins, his club went up against the legendary Montreal Canadiens in the playoffs each and every year, and despite the fact that the Bruins lost every single series to them, the pinnacle of Sugar Jim's career is his playoff performances in those years because he was just simply outstanding. He rose to the occasion of the moment and will always be known as a solid playoff netminder.

An ironman of sorts, Sugar Jim started every game for the Bruins between the 1951-52 and 1953-54 seasons. But Henry's time in the NHL ended abruptly when he was hit just below the eye by a shot from Montreal Canadiens forward Baldy MacKay in the 1955 Stanley Cup playoffs. "The cheek was shattered and is still all wired up, my sight still isn't perfect and all the nerves in the lid are shot," said Sugar Jim back in a 1988 interview. The funny thing is that shot from Baldy MacKay came in the second period of a double overtime game, and it was Henry that stayed in goal for the remainder of the game and performed valiantly while in immense pain. Afterwards he had to go through a three-hour operation, and although the procedure was considered a success, that was the end of Sugar Jim's days in the NHL.

He then went into coaching while still playing for various minor and senior league teams in Sault Ste. Marie, Winnipeg, Warroad and St. Paul before fully retiring from the sport in 1960. Sugar Jim left the game with a record of 161-173-70 in 406 career NHL games. He was named to the NHL Second All-Star Team in 1952 and played in his one and only NHL All-Star Game that same year.

When Sugar Jim retired from hockey, he and his good buddy Chuck Rayner opened a tourist resort called "Hockey Haven" in Kenora, a very successful operation they owned and ran for over twenty years. He also helped run an auto dealership in Winnipeg. In addition to that, Sugar Jim also owned a farm in Plumas where he raised purebred Hereford cattle.

In his later years, Henry lived on Lodge Avenue in St. James, right near his buddy Bobby Chrystal, a fellow former NHLer. "I got to know Sugar Jim after our hockey careers were over and we became real good pals," said Chrystal. "I spent a lot of time with Jim. He had lost his wife, so mine would make us lunch some days and then we'd go over to his place to catch the Monday Night Football or whatever hockey game was on. We were also hunting buddies. We did that for years together and when he passed away, I stopped hunting.

"We used to have a breakfast club on Thursday mornings at Salisbury House on Ellice Avenue with guys that used to play hockey. There were six or eight of us and it was guys like Jim Henry, Billy Robinson, Doug Lewis and myself, and we'd keep up our friendship that way."

Sugar Jim Henry passed away on January 22, 2004 in Winnipeg at the age of 83 from heart failure.

As for the Rocket and Sugar Jim, the last time the two saw each other was in the spring of 1999 at a sports memorabilia show in Boston, where they spent a couple of hours signing hockey cards sitting side by side. During the signing, Henry scolded Richard not just for the goal, but for having scored it on his wedding anniversary, an occasion he may have initially forgotten in the heat of the Stanley Cup playoffs.

34
HALDOR "SLIM" HALDERSON

The Winnipeg Falcons are quite possibly the greatest rags to riches story in the history of hockey. The Falcons were in tough right from their beginnings in our sport. They were made up solely of Icelandic immigrants not allowed to play on other teams. The strong discrimination against them didn't stop them from playing the sport they loved, and excelling at it. It also didn't stop them from signing up to fight for their new country in World War I. When they returned, the team got back together and promptly won the Allan Cup and the 1920 Olympic gold medal in the first-ever Olympics that featured ice hockey as a discipline.

One of the key players in the Falcons' success was a tall, lanky man by the name of Haldor "Slim" Halderson. He got his nickname "Slim" and "The Human Hockey Stick" because of his slender 6'4", 165-pound frame. Also known as "String Bean," "the Big Fellow," "the Elongated One," Slim was like a Zdeno Chara of the 1920's. He used a very long stick and was often accused of illegal hits to the head because of his size.

In Kevin Allen and Bob Duff's book *100 Things Red Wings Fan Should Know & Do Before They Die*, it states that, "Halderson was reported to be a wizard with the puck and a brilliant combination player, a stellar defenceman, shrewd and competent and equipped with great hockey sense. A clever all-around player with exceptional stick-handling skills, he was a very good playmaker. Slim was deceptively fast, and many were fooled by his size. His loose-limbed skating style looked awkward, but he gained speed in a few strides and was difficult to stop."

Slim was the first player in history, along with his Falcons teammate Frank Fredrickson, to win both an Olympic gold medal (1920) and the Stanley Cup (1925). A popular player in his day, Slim always seemed to get an ovation from the crowd every time he stepped onto the ice.

Slim Halderson was born on January 7, 1898 in Winnipeg. The son of Icelanders who had emigrated to Canada, Slim grew up in the West End of Winnipeg in the section that was known as "Little Iceland" and played his junior hockey with the Young Men's Lutheran Club of the local church league.

Slim and his fellow Icelanders grew up battling kids from other nationalities, and held their own in pickup hockey games on the Assiniboine River. The river was considered to be a boundary between Little Iceland on the north and the Anglophone community in the River and Osborne area.

To get a proper sense of what Slim and his teammates went through to reach the pinnacle of our sport, you really have to tell the complete story of him and his fellow Icelanders' to really understand the big picture.

Basically, in the late 1800's, lots of native Icelanders flocked to the Winnipeg area when a volcanic eruption in Iceland made farming extremely difficult. Most of the Icelanders lived in small single-storey houses or overcrowded duplexes and tenements in the poor part of Winnipeg called the West End, which was then known as "Little Iceland" because it was mainly Icelandic people residing there.

The center of Little Iceland was the corner of Victor Street and Sargent Avenue; the latter being known as Goolie Crescent. The word "Goolie" was a racial slur in those days towards Icelanders in Winnipeg. The meaning of it isn't confirmed but some theories are that it was slang for "Ghouls" because of the death-white complexion of arriving Icelanders. Another one is it was just how the Icelanders pronounced the word "Goalie" when they were playing hockey at the outdoor rinks.

The Icelanders' modest homes were packed with grandparents, parents, and children living together, sometimes in a single room heated by a wood stove and lit by a coal oil lamp. It maybe wasn't the most ideal living quarters, but despite hardship, poverty and discrimination, the Icelandic community continued to grow in large numbers.

One of the biggest activities Icelanders did for leisure in Winnipeg was hockey. Icelanders had been playing together and against each other for many years and had been organizing themselves into hockey teams since 1897. The historic Winnipeg Falcons originated with the Icelandic Hockey League. The Icelandic Athletic Club (IAC) and the Vikings Club would play a series of games each year to determine the top Icelandic team in the city. It was quite the rivalry as each team came from a different part of the West End. The Vikings were the north end club who resided in the neighbourhood of Jemima Street (Elgin Avenue), while the IAC was the south end club from the wide-open province to the west of Sherbrook Street in the neighbourhood of Nellie Street (Ellice Avenue).

Before the 1908-09 season, the two teams decided to bury the hatchet and amalgamate to wage a joint war against the other leagues. They met at a meeting hall in the home of Sam Johnson on Portage Avenue West. Emil Goodman, a former hockey player, came up with the name Falcons. It was symbolic as the Falcon was the national bird of Iceland.

For the next ten years the Falcon Hockey Club sponsored intermediate and senior clubs. Their greatest battles, however, were fought off the ice as they tried to gain admittance into the prestigious city league. The Icelanders' efforts before World War I weren't successful so they were forced to go their own way.

When World War I came about, the Falcons didn't hesitate. In the spring of 1916, almost all of the Falcons enlisted in the Canadian Army to go to war in Europe. They did this despite being bullied for years by fellow Canadians who didn't like their Icelandic background. When they enlisted, it wasn't something like "if we go fight in the War, they will finally accept us." They enlisted because it was just the right thing to do. The Falcons were Canadians and they wanted to protect their country's freedom. As historian Norman Leach said, "It wasn't bravado and it wasn't showing off. It was just the right thing to do."

After training for a year in Winnipeg and Camp Hughes, they left by train to Halifax where they were shipped to England in April 1917. Slim stayed somewhat sharp by playing in a number of games with the Winnipeg Ypres of the Winnipeg Military Hockey League. Two of the Falcons (Frank Thorsteinson and George Cumbers) ultimately lost their lives fighting for their country, but the rest had returned home by May 1919, a solid two years since the Falcons had played a game of hockey or even skated for that matter.

Of course, when the war ended, the Falcons were still treated as outsiders when they got back to Winnipeg from fighting for their country. They wanted to get back into hockey and talked about the revival of a Manitoba Senior Hockey League (MSHL). There were lots of great hockey players in Winnipeg, but there weren't a lot of available rinks to play at. The historic Auditorium Rink was closed during the war, which left the Amphitheatre as the only option for senior hockey games.

The teams were made up of the old guard Victorias, Winnipegs, and Monarchs, along with the outsiders like the Winnipeg Falcons, Brandon, Selkirk Fishermen, and Portage la Prairie. The old guard teams continued to control hockey in the city like they had previously before the war.

The Falcons were almost pushed out of any possible league. The Vics, Monarchs, and 'Pegs all secured ice time at the Amphitheatre but the Falcons couldn't. They were given the ultimatum to secure ice for games or else they were not allowed into the MSHL league. The other Winnipeg clubs did nothing to help them out.

"The feeling of admitting Falcons to senior company is not as friendly as it should be," wrote the *Winnipeg Tribune*. "There is no reason why the Falcons should not be given the same support in their efforts to revive their club as it has been given Winnipegs or Vics. The Falcons have done a great deal for hockey."

The Falcons eventually complied with the wishes of the senior officers and secured ice time for games and practices at the much smaller Arena Rink. They thought they had followed all of the Winnipeg hockey moguls' requirements that had been laid out. But of course, a day after the Falcons announced their success, the Vics, 'Pegs, and Monarchs formed their own league, the Winnipeg Senior Hockey League (WSHL). They didn't want to play in the same league as the other four clubs that year. They said that Selkirk and Brandon could join the following year, but not the Falcons or Portage.

The MSHL included the Winnipeg Falcons, Selkirk Fishermen, and Brandon. Portage la Prairie was left out again. The league wanted to play at the Amphitheatre, not the Arena Rink, because of the greater spectator accommodation.

Winnipeg was now home to two senior leagues with a total of six teams. That brought on the next problem. The Amphitheatre rink manager said his rink could not accommodate the two leagues, especially if the Allan Cup playoffs started in the last week of February. He issued an ultimatum that a single league was the only one he could handle at the rink and that a five-team league was the only possible solution.

The three WSHL clubs agreed with the Amphitheatre manager and wanted to talk with Brandon and Selkirk to form a single league. They didn't want the Falcons or Portage. Brandon and Selkirk both went on record saying that they would not break faith with the Falcons.

This argument over senior hockey lasted half a month. On one side were the three Winnipeg clubs and the Amphitheatre Rink against the Falcons, Selkirk, and Brandon. Caught in the middle were the hockey supporters who quickly sided with the underdog Falcons.

This strong public opinion forced the rink manager to change his five-team single-league ultimatum. He agreed to allow both the Winnipeg and Manitoba leagues to play at his rink. The off-ice war was over.

That 1919-20 season would prove to be quite the historic year for Manitoba hockey, thanks in part to the Winnipeg Falcons. They won their league championships and the provincial championship via a dramatic 6-5 double overtime win over the Selkirk Fisherman, in which they rallied from a 5-1 deficit during the game. The sudden-death goal was scored by none other than Slim Halderson.

This sent the Falcons to the Western Canadian championship where they easily defeated the Fort William Maple Leafs 9-1 and 7-2, putting them in the Allan Cup finals against the University of Toronto, who had been heavily favoured by most as the best senior team in hockey. If the Falcons were the underdogs, they certainly didn't show it as they trounced Toronto by a wide 11-5 margin in a two-game total goals series.

The Winnipeg Falcons had won the Allan Cup, a title emblematic of ama-teur-team superiority in Canada. Their reward was going right from Toronto to Antwerp, Belgium to represent Canada at the 1920 Summer Olympics. The weeklong ocean journey from Saint John, New Brunswick, to Liverpool, England cost about $10,000, and it was paid for by Allan Cup receipts and donations from the government of Manitoba and the city of Winnipeg. It was an uneventful crossing of the Atlantic for the most part aboard the *S.S. Melita* for Canada's eight-man team, which included seven players of Icelandic descent and six members who were returning to Europe after having fought in World War I.

The ship's carpenter on the *S.S. Melita* carved two dozen sticks from "rough" wood the team had obtained in Montreal—these were the only sticks the Falcons used in the Olympics. Once they got to England, a second travel leg then took the team from Dover to Ostend, Belgium, for the Olympic Games.

Canada was considered the huge favourite in a format that saw six play-ers and a free-ranging rover play two 20-minute halves with substitutions not permitted. An injury would require the opponent to remove a player to keep the sides even, at least in number. The draw format was the "Bergvall" system of elimination, an interesting knockout bracket that set up the medal-round games, with "Canadian rules" in place. The regulations had been written by highly respected Falcons manager and hockey pioneer William Hewitt, the father of future hockey broadcast legend Foster Hewitt, and featured four goal judges among a host of other off-ice officials.

The matches were played on a surface that was roughly 170 feet long by 65 feet wide but appeared smaller with seven players per side. The games featured well-heeled spectators eating and drinking extravagantly at rinkside while an orchestra played throughout.

During the Olympics, Slim roomed with Frank Frederickson, and their hotel room became the hang-spot for the Falcons at night. Halderson never smoked, unlike most of his teammates, so when they tried to light up a smoke in the room, Slim would tell them, "Sorry, this is a non-smoking room. You must go somewhere else to do that!"

Canada defeated Czechoslovakia in their opening game 15-0, with Halderson scoring seven of the goals. After watching Canada's first game and seeing how hard players like Halderson could shoot the puck, Swedish netminder Seth Howander sought out extra padding to further protect himself from the bullet shots of the Canadian shooters.

The Americans gave Canada a tough game but couldn't score on Falcons goalie Wally Byron as the Canadians were victorious 2-0, setting them up with a gold medal game date with Sweden. Halderson scored the first-ever goal in an Olympic final just over a minute in. He added another in the third period as Canada won 12-1 to win the gold medal.

It should be noted that the one goal Sweden scored was a bit of a set-up. Showing a lot of sportsmanship and class, the Falcons basically let the Swedes score a goal. Immediately after the goal, the Swedes said, "Thank you" to the Canadians. It was a gentlemen's game in those days and the Falcons were as gentlemanly as hockey players came.

The parade that the city of Winnipeg held for the Falcons when they returned home from their Olympic triumph was really something else. They were driven down Portage Avenue and Main Street, eventually getting to City Hall where they were each presented with a gold medallion to match the gold medals they received in Antwerp.

After the 1920 Olympics, word got out that Frank Frederickson was one of the best players in the game. Lester Patrick quickly got in touch with him upon the Falcons returning home, and by the 1920-21 season, Frederickson was out west playing for the Victoria Aristocrats of the Pacific Coast Hockey

Association (PCHA). Eventually, Patrick started looking for more talented players to bolster his roster and Frank suggested picking up Halderson, who had played the season following the Olympics with the Saskatoon Crescents in the Saskatchewan senior league. So, Lester got in contact with Slim and soon after he was joining his old pal Frank Frederickson in Victoria.

At the time of Slim going out to Victoria he had been playing both forward and defence, but Lester saw him practice and told Slim that he was going to make him the best defenceman there ever was. Patrick took him under his wing and coached his defensive game, and Slim played solid defence for the rest of his career. Slim scored his first goal in his first game as a professional. It also proved to be the game winner in a 4-1 win for Victoria over the Seattle Metropolitans.

After Slim's first season with the Aristocrats, Victoria changed its team name to the Cougars. In 1924-25, Halderson's fourth campaign with the club, they won the league championship and hosted the Stanley Cup Final against the Montreal Canadiens. Led by the Icelandic pair of Frederickson and Halderson, the Victoria Cougars won the best-of-five series three games to one, outscoring the Montreal side 16-8.

When Victoria won the Stanley Cup in 1925, it was the last time a team from outside the NHL hoisted the Cup. After losing the Stanley Cup final the following season to the Montreal Maroons in four games, the Victoria franchise was then sold to a group of owners in Detroit for the sum of $100,000 and the team became known as the Detroit Cougars.

Now playing in the National Hockey League for the first time in his career, Slim scored the first ever goal for the Detroit Cougars (Red Wings) franchise on November 20th, 1926 in a 4-1 loss to the Pittsburgh Pirates.

Midway through the Detroit Cougars inaugural NHL season, things weren't going particularly well, and so on January 7th, 1927, Halderson was shipped off to the Toronto St. Patricks (Maple Leafs) for winger Pete Bellefeuille. Slim played the rest of the season with Toronto, but that one season would mark his only in the National Hockey League.

That certainly didn't mean that it was the end of Slim's hockey career. He continued playing pro hockey for another decade after that in either the Canadian-American Hockey Association (CAHA) or the American Hockey Association (AHA) with teams based in Quebec, Newark, Kansas City, Duluth, Wichita and Tulsa.

Halderson's longevity in the sport should be noted because when he finally retired from pro hockey in 1937, he had played the most pro hockey games (656) than anyone had in the history of the sport up to that point in time. He was recognized a few years after his retirement in 1932 when he was named to an All-Star Canadian Olympic team selected by the *Winnipeg Tribune*.

When Halderson retired from hockey, he first got a job at a local bar. From there a liquor salesman saw him working one day and recognized him and got him working in one of the liquor stores in Winnipeg. After that he worked in accounting at the main office of the Manitoba Liquor Control Commission on McGillivray Boulevard until he retired at age 65.

Viola Perkins, Slim's first of five kids, was born in Detroit in 1927 while he was playing for the Cougars. She's the only one of Slim's five children that is still alive today, and at ninety years old, she's still very sharp at remembering her father's hockey exploits.

"My mom and dad got married in April 1923, and after that, mother went with dad everywhere when he was playing hockey. He always wanted her with him," remembers Viola. "So my early years were spent on the road where Dad was playing professional hockey. When I got to the age of going to school, mother and the kids had to stay home in Winnipeg and Dad would be gone in the fall and we didn't see him till the spring."

In the mid 1920's, Slim bought a new house on 1014 Dominion Street in the new part of the West End that was opening up. Falcons teammate Frank Frederickson lived on Dominion Street as well and the two families would often socialize at one of their houses.

"Sargent Park was right at the corner of where we lived and they had tennis courts," recalls Viola. "Dad used to go down there to play tennis because you have to run around a lot and it kept his legs in shape. I remember going with him and sitting on the bench while he played. He always managed to find someone to play with him when we went to the courts.

"I always enjoyed being the daughter of a hockey player. As a kid, I used to go with my mom and watch his practices. It was exciting for a little girl in those days. When he retired from hockey we used to go to games at the old Amphitheatre and the people working the gates would always wave him in. He never had to pay because they all knew who he was from winning with the Falcons. We always got a box seat and it was a really good time."

Slim Halderson passed away on August 1, 1965 at the age of 67 from a heart attack. "Dad loved his candy. He had a sweet tooth," recalled Viola. "He always had to have his dessert with lunch and supper, and he'd always say his usual 'What's for dinner, Mom?' when he came to the dining room table. On the day he died, he came to the table, said his catchphrase, and then collapsed on the table. His heart gave out. He was rushed to the hospital but there was nothing they could do, he was already gone."

Halderson's funeral was at First Lutheran Church on Victor Street. Because he was so well known in the community, his funeral was attended by many of Winnipeg's elite and they gave him a nice police motorcycle escort from the church to the cemetery.

Slim and his fellow Winnipeg Falcons are still remembered today with a display inside the MTS Centre, as well as a large mural portrait of the 1920 team at the corner of Portage Avenue and Furby Street, in the heart of the West End where the Falcons first took to hockey over a hundred years ago.

33
TED GREEN

When Boston general manager Lynn Patrick was looking for a successor to respected tough guy Fern Flaman, he spotted young Ted Green who was playing with the WHL's Winnipeg Warriors. In June of 1960 Patrick took the opportunity to draft Green in an intra-league draft. He knew right there and then that Green would go on to lead his Bruins blueline for years to come.

"Pound for pound, Ted Green was the toughest of the post-World War II Bruins and—with the exception of Eddie Shore—the meanest player to ever don the black, gold, and white," said hockey historian Stan Fischler. "Like the immortal Shore, Green would do anything to win a hockey game. Anything. And he learned very early in his hockey career that shortcomings in the realm of skill could be compensated for by brute force."

"I had one philosophy," Green recalled, "and that was this—the corners were mine. Any man who tried to take a corner away from me was stealing from me. I get mad when a man tries to steal from me."

As you'll read about very shortly, Ted Green was a champion at every level of his hockey career, but he will forever be linked not with his championships, but with on-ice violence and the infamous stick-swinging incident with Wayne Maki that almost resulted in his death.

Ted Green was born in Eriksdale on March 23, 1940. Shortly after birth, his family moved to the Norwood area of Winnipeg. Ted's family home was a stone's throw from the old Canada Packers plant on Marion Street. Growing up, Ted played his hockey on the outdoor rinks of Norwood Falcons Community Club.

From an early age Ted was playing for minor hockey teams based out of Norwood including the St. Boniface Optimist Falcons. He played junior hockey with the St. Boniface Canadiens, which made him property of the big-league squad in Montreal.

Years later when Green got inducted into the Manitoba Sports Hall of Fame, one of the people he thanked in his speech for getting him to where he is today was fellow Manitoba Top 50 player Bill Juzda. "He would come out to the Olympic Rink in full uniform, show us the art of hip checking. It was always easier for me to elbow check than hip check, but it's a lost art today," said Green. "The big thing, however, I learned from Bill Juzda was timing and awareness on the ice. That's something that stuck with me for my entire hockey career."

At 5'11" and 185 pounds, Ted wasn't the biggest guy out on the ice, but he certainly was one of, if not the toughest player out there. Green joined the Winnipeg Braves during the 1958-59 season and they would go on to win the Memorial Cup, defeating the Peterborough Petes four games to one.

"A month after the Memorial Cup win, I was drafted by the Montreal Canadiens. That was good and bad news for me because I was happy to be drafted, but I was not a Montreal fan. I probably got that from my mother," Ted recalled in his Manitoba Sports Hall of Fame induction speech. "When I went to Montreal's training camp in the fall that year, I was very impressed. The first guy I met there was Ab McDonald, and there's not a nicer person on this green earth than Ab.

"It was awe-inspiring for me as a teenager to be playing with and against, being in the same room, same bus, same train as Rocket Richard and his brother the Pocket Rocket and the Vest Pocket Rocket, Claude Richard. Boom Boom Geoffrion who took all my mail money on a trip from Montreal to Chicoutimi. Jacques Plante, Jean Beliveau. And the guy I admired the most in my career, Doug Harvey.

"I got called up to Frank Selke's office at the end of camp and he gave me royal hell for knocking the three Richard brothers on their rear end in an intrasquad game. He then complimented me on my training camp and wanted me to go back to Winnipeg to play junior hockey, and I ended up playing for Jack Perrin's Winnipeg Warriors and made the awesome amount of $4,500 dollars. I went right out and bought myself a Lada."

Ted skated with the Winnipeg Warriors of the minor pro Western Hockey League during the 1959-60 season. The Canadiens seemed to be unimpressed with the fact that Ted decided to play minor pro instead of going back to juniors so they left him unprotected in the 1960 intra-league draft and he was promptly claimed by the Boston Bruins.

By the 1961-62 season, Green was a regular on the Bruins roster. Although Boston wasn't the best team in the league by any stretch in those days, Ted was a force to be reckoned with at the blueline, and word quickly spread through the league that Green was not someone to be taken lightly on the ice.

"My wife didn't like my reputation anymore than I did. I remember once early in our marriage she asked me why I played so hard," recalled Green. "'Look,' I told her, 'they expect this of me right now. This is the only way I'm going to stay up. If I don't knock people down, which is what fans expect me to do, I don't keep my job. I'm learning. The more I learn, the more they'll depend on my ability instead of my roughness. Right now, I'm the team policeman. If somebody gets hit, it's up to me to go after the guy. This helps attract attention to the Bruins, because we're not winning.'"

Green's strong play was one of the reasons why Boston came out from the basement of the NHL to becoming a powerhouse in the late 1960's. Although a big part of that came from the emergence of Bobby Orr, Bruins coach Harry Sinden said at the time that Green was the stand-alone leader of the Bruins locker room and was always the guy to get the team going when it needed a boost.

Ted's play didn't go unnoticed by the league as he was named to the NHL Second All-Star team in 1969 and skated in the 1965 and 1969 NHL All-Star Game. Averaging more than 100 penalty minutes and thirty points a season during the 1960's, there might have not been a better player in the league than Ted Green at knowing his role on the team and sticking to it every night.

"One thing in my favour—when you played the way I did then—was reputation. Players on the other teams knew that I was going to get them," Green said. "They had to be thinking about it. I got a lesson from Leo Boivin. He'd crack an arm when they tried to get around him. That was my style."

Going into the 1969-70 season, Green was coming off the best campaign of his career the year prior and was looking to produce even more for his club going forward. The hockey gods had other ideas however, as on September 21, 1969, in an exhibition game in Ottawa against the St. Louis Blues, Green was involved in an infamous stick-swinging incident with Blues forward Wayne Maki that really brought forward some concessions regarding player safety in the game of hockey.

Ted wrote about the incident years later in his autobiography *High Stick*. He said that he had never clashed with Wayne Maki in the past and wasn't concerned about him when stepped on the ice that night in Ottawa.

"As I trapped the puck behind the net the kid hit me from behind, and I got a little ticked off, as I always do when that happens. But my first obligation was to clear the puck. I kicked it with my skate to my stick and shot it out around the boards to our right wing. Then I turned to take care of the guy who hit me.

"By that time, we had both moved in front and a little to the left of our net. I reached out with my gloved left hand and shot Maki in the face. He went down by the side of the net. Figuring that was the end of that, I turned away, but then Maki speared me.

"Where at first I had just been annoyed, now I was sore as hell, and I hit Maki with my stick just below the shoulder at the biceps, knocking him off balance and, I think, down on one knee."

To this day, Ted doesn't remember what happened next. But that's just because Maki's retaliatory blow almost killed him.

As soon as Green turned away, Maki hit him right smack over the head with his stick. With no helmet, Ted fell to the ice. The result was a fractured skull and at the very least, a mild form of brain damage. Some of his teammates came right away to his aid, while others went and laid a severe beating on Maki.

Author Brad Schultz wrote that, "The sight of Green trying to get off the ice, his legs buckled and his face contorted in pain, made Blues' broadcaster Dan Kelly almost physically ill. Even as he was carried from the ice and speaking almost unintelligibly, Green wanted to go after Maki to finish the fight. To keep him away from the enraged Bruins, Maki was eventually hustled off the ice and watched the rest of the game in street clothes. The league later suspended him for 30 games."

When Green arrived at the local hospital, the severity of his injury was finally recognized and he asked for the last rites of the church. Ted had lost his speech and was realizing that the end may very well be on its way.

"I cried," Green later wrote in his book, "because my head hurt, and I cried because I didn't know if I was going to die when I wanted so badly to live, and I cried when I thought of my wife, Pat, and my kids and my parents and my brothers."

The neurosurgeon doctor on-call that fateful night was a guy named

Michael Richard, a passionate Montreal fan. Knowing very well who Ted Green was, Dr. Richard worked on Green for two and a half hours, saving his life.

"He hated the Boston Bruins and he hated my guts. His wife was a Bruins fan and was sort of like me, an English person," said a laughing Green. "Over the course of three operations and a year of rehab. Michael and his wife became good friends with me and my wife. And the third operation was minor, he just prepared the hole in my skull to receive the acrylic plate. After the operation, I was in my room recovering and Mike comes bouncing in saying 'Green I fixed your wagon and I finally got even with you.' I said, 'What the hell are you talking about Mike!' He said, 'When you were out on my table, I wrote 'Yay, Montreal' on your plate."

Green didn't return to action that season, but when the Bruins went on to win the Cup that year, he was given a full share of the playoff money and had his name engraved on the Stanley Cup.

Ted returned the following 1970-71 season with the metal plate intact, and skated in all the Bruins' 78 games that year. The next year, Green and his Bruins won their second Stanley Cup in three years.

Ted Green was at the top of the hockey world and was now a highly sought out free agent. This was also around the time where the WHA was gaining traction, and Green jumped at the big money that the league had to offer, signing with Boston's cross-town rivals, the New England Whalers. He became the team's first captain and led them to the WHA's inaugural championship.

After three years with the Whalers, Ted would come home to Winnipeg and play the last four seasons of his career with the WHA's Winnipeg Jets. He won two more AVCO Cups in that time with the Jets. When it was all said and done, he won a Memorial Cup, two Stanley Cups and three AVCO Cups.

Green ended his playing career in 1979 with 254 points and 1029 penalty minutes in 620 NHL games. In the WHA he put up 180 points and 304 penalty minutes in 452 games. He ranks 17th all-time in games played in the WHA.

After his retirement from hockey, Ted stayed in Winnipeg and decided that he wanted to explore coaching and see if that was something he'd be good at. Ted and his brother Tony took up an offer to coach the Carman Beavers senior squad of the South Eastern Manitoba Hockey League for the 1980-81 season. Ted proved to be a pretty darn good coach as he led the squad to both the league and provincial championship. They won 44 out of 49 games, and by the end of it, Ted realized that coaching was something he wanted to do going forward.

Green went from the Carman Beavers to the Edmonton Oilers of the NHL where he served for many years as an assistant coach under close friend and former teammate Glen Sather. He won five more cups during that stretch (1984, 1985, 1987, 1988, 1990), and was later named head coach of the Oilers in 1991. Despite the fact that the Oilers dynasty years were now behind them, he still led the team to the Conference Finals in 1992.

Ted later followed Glen Sather to the New York Rangers in the early 2000's and spent three years working again as an assistant coach. Since then, Green returned to Alberta where he is currently living.

"It's a matter of being lucky," said Ted when asked about all the success he had in his career. "I was lucky being in the right place at the right time with the right players in the right time of their careers to have been on all those successful teams."

And in case you were wondering, Ted never had any hard feelings toward Maki following the incident. Always quick to make a joke, Ted laughs about the injury and claims it helps his golf game because the weight of the steel plate in his head forces him to keep his head down, but the bad part is he can't play in the rain because he is a human lightning rod.

32
ANDY HEBENTON

Andy Hebenton was hockey's original Iron Man. He never missed a game, seldom missed a shift, and rarely took penalties. "Nobody works harder or complains less," said his old Rangers general manager Muzz Patrick. Hebenton found his place in the NHL and was widely respected as a persistent right winger with a left-hand shot, a steady professional who played the game as he understood it, without shoving and grabbing and clutching an opponent.

An article from *The Globe and Mail* featured Andy in 1966 talked about his athletic anonymity despite being a key player for the New York Rangers over the course of eight seasons. "Many hockey players in the National Hockey League live in a spectacular obscurity. They may last in the big time a long time, but they are inconspicuous even when their skills are adequate. Andy Hebenton, on the edge of fame, is the kind of player who autograph hounds don't recognize or pester. He survives within the dimensions of the game, and dwells in secrecy once he leaves the rink."

During his 27 years in the pros, including nine seasons in the NHL, Andy's motto was relatively simple: "The tough guys never bothered me so I might as well stay out of their way and play my game." Recalling a moment when Hebenton decided he was better off scoring goals, he said "Just before I got traded to the New York Rangers, I played against a tough guy and he

MANITOBA HOCKEY HALL OF FAME

told me 'You better stick to your game because you're not a very good fighter.' So, then I stuck to playing hockey."

A true gentleman on and off the ice, Hebenton was recognized as the most gentlemanly player in his league on seven occasions. With the NHL's New York Rangers, he won the Lady Byng Trophy in 1957, and then he won the Fred J. Hume Cup in the WHL for the Portland Buckaroos six times (1964, 1970, 1971, 1972, 1973, 1974).

Andy Hebenton was born in Winnipeg on October 3, 1929 in Winnipeg. Growing up on Valour Road in the West End not too far from where the Polo Park Racetrack was (now Polo Park Shopping Centre), Andy began skating at four years old on a makeshift backyard rink at his house with an old pair of skates his dad brought home for him one day.

Being in Winnipeg, Andy watched his dad get up every morning and walk quite a distance to work in -40 temperatures. "I used to think he was crazy," recalled Andy. "It must have made an impression, though. When I started school, I did the same thing."

Hebenton played his minor hockey at Isaac Brock Community Centre and went to Isaac Brock School. A great skater, he was a member of a school team that won the junior high boys relay one year. "When I was still a young kid, I took up working in construction and I think that helped my legs and everything else," Andy recalled. "It made my arms a little stronger. Doing that kind of work in the summer time instead of playing a lot of golf helped a lot."

By the time he got to high school at Daniel McIntyre Collegiate, Hebenton was an all-around athlete. In addition to his prowess on the hockey rink, Andy was also a great football and lacrosse player, and was an excellent swimmer to boot.

Known as "Spud" because of his lifelong love for potatoes, Andy signed a C-Form binding him to the Montreal Canadiens as a junior so he played his junior hockey with the St. Boniface and Winnipeg Canadiens respectively. Turning pro in the 1949-50 season, Hebenton played with the Cincinnati Mohawks and Montreal Royals, both of whom were affiliated with the Montreal Canadiens.

Unfortunately, Andy would never get to play a game with the Canadiens. He tore some ligaments in his right knee that first pro season and the Habs felt that he would have chronic knee problems so they let him go.

Not deterred at all by what the Canadiens thought, Hebenton went out to the west coast and played with the Victoria Cougars of the Pacific Coast

Hockey League (PCHL) and Western Hockey League (WHL) for five seasons. It was in Victoria that Andy learned the ropes of being a pro hockey player, so when the NHL's New York Rangers bought his rights in 1955, he was ready right from the get-go to make an impact in the heyday of the Original Six.

The 5'9", 185-pound Andy Hebenton joined the Rangers in time for the 1955-56 NHL debut at age 26 and finished with 38 points in his rookie season. His best NHL season points-wise came a few years later when he scored 62 points in 1958-59.

After eight seasons with the Rangers, Andy was claimed via the waiver draft by the Boston Bruins where he would go on to play his final season in the NHL in 1963-64. His rights were then sold to the WHL's Portland Buckaroos and he would play in Portland for the rest of his career, minus a two-year stint with the Victoria Maple Leafs.

Andy was very disappointed at first when he was demoted to Portland. He needed one more season in the NHL to be eligible for the pension given to all players who had completed ten or more seasons in the league. However upset he must have felt about it, he kept it on the inside as he reported to Portland right away, scored 74 points that season and was the major reason why his Buckaroos won the league championship.

The number one thing about Andy Hebenton that is still remembered and talked about is his incredible Iron Man streak in the game of hockey. Andy would miss a couple of games with Victoria in the early 1950's when he had his appendix removed, and then another couple after he got married in 1952. After that he would go on his streak of playing in 1,064 consecutive professional games over the course of sixteen seasons. Included in that was 630 consecutive NHL games, in which he never missed a game during his nine years in the NHL. The NHL streak ended when the Boston Bruins sent him to the minors in 1964.

"I was lucky, but I also played hurt a few times. In those days, there was always somebody ready to take your place." Andy said. "The closest I'd come to missing a game was after one night in New York when I got slashed over my left eye for two stitches, and the next night we had to play in Montreal," The eye was shut tighter than the slot in a piggy bank, but eye-drops reduced the swelling enough to let him play the game.

The streak finally ended early into the 1967 season when Andy had to return to Winnipeg suddenly for his father's funeral. He then went on another streak that lasted until he retired from the sport in 1975. Jack Evans, a former defenceman who played NHL while Andy was with the Rangers was interviewed by *Sports Illustrated* back in 1967 and was asked about how Andy managed to play all those games in a row.

"He says he's been lucky," said Evans. "He says he's managed to escape a lot of injuries other guys got. Well, hell, I know Andy and I know some of the guys he played with up there. They said there were nights he should have quit—just like everybody else—but that he went out and played anyway. They also say nobody's ever goin' to do what he's done again."

Andy's longevity in hockey was recognized in 1966 when his club, the WHL's Victoria Maple Leafs held an "Andy Hebenton Night" to celebrate his Iron Man streak in professional hockey. Between the second and third period of a league game with Seattle, Andy was given plenty of gifts totalling around $6,000. Victoria fans contributed $1,007, a dollar for every game in his prolonged streak. The NHL kicked in $652 for his 652 straight games there. The Montreal Canadiens and the New York Rangers coughed up $100 each. He was also given a colour TV set, a brand-new set of golf clubs, a liquor cabinet, and 365 loaves of bread, a year's supply from a Victoria bakery.

The microphone was handed to Andy after they were finished presenting him with all of the stuff. "Thank you," he shyly said over the public-address system. "Thank you for recognizing my durability, but I really don't deserve all of this."

Andy retired from hockey in 1975 when he was 45 years old. The injury bug finally caught up with him as he suffered a separated shoulder when falling into the boards in Portland, effectively ending his hockey career. When he called it quits he had played in a remarkable 26 pro seasons. Only Gordie Howe has played more professional hockey than Hebenton in the entire history of our sport.

Hebenton finished with 391 points in 690 NHL games, in addition to his 869 points in 934 WHL games. He played in the 1960 NHL All Star Game, and was a First Team All-Star twice in the WHL and a three-time Second Team All-Star as well. To this day he holds the record for the longest streak without missing a game in professional hockey. At 1,062 consecutive games, it's a record that most likely will never going to be touched.

To give you a better understanding of how gentlemanly Andy was on the ice, over the course of his nine NHL seasons, he averaged only nine penalty minutes a year. And although he never did win a Stanley Cup he was certainly on his fair share of championship teams. He won the PCHL Championship with the Victoria Cougars in 1951, and won the WHL Championships in back-to-back campaigns with the Portland Buckaroos and Victoria Maple Leafs respectively (1965 and 1966).

Former NHLer Bob Chrystal grew up on Ashburn Street, just one block away from Andy, and the two played some minor hockey together during their childhood at Isaac Brock. He said that, "Andy was very much like Gordie Howe as a hockey player except that he didn't have Howe's roughness since he actually won the Lady Byng Memorial Trophy one year."

Andy stayed in Portland, Oregon after his playing days were done and operated a cement business (patio and driveway cement) there for many years. He also enjoyed the fact that he could spend more time on his golf game once he retired from hockey. Now at 87 years old, Andy still lives in Portland, not too far from his daughter Terry.

"I'm proud of what I accomplished in the NHL as far as the consecutive game streak is concerned," said Hebenton. "I did it as a member of the old six-team NHL. I had to be doing something right to have lasted that long because there weren't as many jobs available in the NHL back then as there are today."

31
ERIC NESTERENKO

How many former NHL players do you know that have also worked as a disc jockey, a stockbroker, a travel broker, a freelance writer, a university professor, and a ski instructor at some point in their life? I only know of one, and that's Eric Nesterenko, who is my pick for the most interesting person ever to play in the National Hockey League. Oh, and did I mention that Eric also took up odd jobs like driving a loader and diesel Cat in the Arctic. He has also acted, playing the father in the great hockey movie *Youngblood*.

That's a lot of jobs for anybody, but especially for someone who spent over twenty seasons playing in the NHL as one of the league's more dominant right wingers. Nesterenko recalls, "I did all of those, tried them out and every one of them was fun. When I was in Chicago I made decent money, but always thought I needed more so I worked these summer jobs. It was fun doing all those things."

The book *Players: The Ultimate A-Z Guide of Everyone Who Has Ever Played in the NHL* might have said it best in that, "Eric was a player that could do everything well. He scored, played physical, stickhandled nicely, and backchecked."

Eric Nesterenko was born in Flin Flon on October 31, 1933. Flin Flon is and always has been a mining hub. Located on the border of Manitoba and Saskatchewan, with most of the town being in Manitoba territory, Flin Flon was founded back in 1927 by the Hudson Bay Mining and Smelting Company to mine the large copper and zinc ore resources that were in that area. Flin Flon got its town name from the lead character in an old novel called The Sunless City by J.E. Preston Muddock. The main character in that book was Josiah Flintabbatey Flonatin, and from that, the name was shortened and the town became Flin Flon.

"Hockey was an indelible part of the culture in Flin Flon. I lived across the street from an outdoor complex run by the mine (Hudson Bay Mining and Smelting), which had four hockey rinks and a gigantic pleasure skating rink. It was great because winters in Flin Flon back then were at least five months," said Nesterenko. "So, every day after school, every night after supper and all-day Saturday/Sunday, we skated and/or played hockey. We always tried to get a game going and our de facto coaches were the older players. We'd get a game going and they'd allow us to play with them. We were forced to pass the puck because the players were bigger, faster, and stronger than us. You learn some of the basic aspects of the game without formal coaching, which I find is really interesting. I think a lot of kids nowadays are over-coached at an early age. They won't let the kids play and learn some of the basics on their own."

Eric goes on to talk about his childhood in Flin Flon, "My father was a skater and always bought me decent skates. Also, when I started to play he got me my first hockey stick and puck to play with. My dad worked for the mine as a chemist. He knew six languages, and was a very smart man. My parents were from Ukraine but were political refugees who escaped the Russian Revolution and moved to Canada. I loved growing up in Flin Flon. I played in Winnipeg in the 1950s and I went back up to Flin Flon for a visit for four days in July one year. When I was a kid it seemed like a very large place, but when I went as a grown-up, it really was just a small town.

"They had a senior team in Flin Flon and my dad used to take me to watch the games sometimes," Eric said. "When I lived there, it was a covered arena with natural ice. It had a roof, but it was minus 30 below outside and maybe zero inside. The lobby was heated and so were the dressing rooms at least. They also had pipes running underneath the seats. But the outdoor rinks are where I played mostly growing up. The rinks were part of a big operation run by the mine, and I think there were other outdoor rinks in town, but the thing I remember mainly was that the mine ran the recreational complex, and it was called Jubilee Park."

Nesterenko was a good hockey player back in Flin Flon for a youngster, but when he and his family moved to Ontario, his hockey career really took off. "When I was ten years old, we moved to Toronto. The first formal team I played for was a peewee team and it was an elite team in Toronto, and when

I was playing there I realized that I could play with all these guys that were formally coached. In fact, I could play better than most kids there. In Toronto, there was a league called the OHA and when I was 15 years old I ended up playing Junior B hockey, and the next year I was playing Junior A with the Toronto Marlboros. That's when I realized that I probably had some talent, since I was one of the top scorers in the league."

From the Marlboros, it was on to the NHL for Nesterenko. The Leafs brought him in as an eighteen-year-old for one game during the 1951-52 season. The next season, Eric became more of a fixture for the Maple Leafs, playing in 35 games. Nesterenko recalls the experience of his early NHL days: "They decided to bring me up because in those days you could play three games in the NHL and still maintain your so-called amateur status—although we all get paid to play major junior hockey. We actually made quite a bit of money playing junior. I remember my first game during my first real season in the league because I scored two goals and an assist. Jean Beliveau was brought in by Montreal at the same time, and when I got the goals against Boston, I got a lot of local publicity. Conn Smythe figured he might get some free publicity for the team if he brought me in as an eighteen-year-old, and to be honest I really wasn't ready for the NHL and that was a big mistake. I've resented Toronto ever since. I actually quit hockey when I got sold to Chicago, but they kept after me to play so I only played weekend games for the Blackhawks since I was going to school at the University of Toronto. I did that for my first two years with Chicago, and after that they wouldn't let me do that anymore, I'd have to join the team full-time. At least I got two years of college, and those years I did that, I had some of my best years as a player where I just travelled to the games by myself and then afterwards, I'd fly back to Toronto and go to school, as well as workout with the university team. I'm probably the only guy to ever to do that in the history of the league so looking back, it seems crazy that an NHL team let someone play only part-time."

Nesterenko would go on to have a lot of great moments in his career, although none really compare to his one and only Stanley Cup championship with the Blackhawks in 1961. Eric remembers that season vividly, "It was a great year. Our big stars were young and emerging players like Stan Mikita, Bobby Hull and some others. We were a good team and in the last twenty games of the regular season, we won eighteen of them. We then beat Montreal and Detroit in the playoffs. It was only a six-team league in those days and everyone kind of knew each other. There were no bad players. Sure, some were better than others, but everyone was good. Our Blackhawks could have won, or should have won an additional two or three Stanley Cups. The worst one we lost was in the seventh game against Montreal in 1971. That was just heartbreaking."

Eric forged out a reputation in the league as a shadow, hounding the top scorers in the league like Gordie Howe, Johnny Bucyk and Frank Mahovlich. Nesterenko accepted the thankless job without complaint and became quite proficient in this line of work. His long reach helped him to check and his use of his elbows kept the opposition on alert at all times.

Eric goes on to talk about the Blackhawk squad that has been very successful in recent years, "The current Chicago Blackhawks are a really well-run organization with those three Stanley Cups in six years. They have a promotion called the Blackhawk Convention in town. They've had eight of them in the last eight years. It's in the middle of summer and it's an amazing time! Thirty thousand people showed up at a fifteen-hundred-room hotel in Chicago. It was quite the event to say the least."

Nesterenko spent 16 seasons with the Blackhawks and was one of the team's key contributors throughout the years. Despite his long tenure with the club, Eric never considered himself to be one of the leaders on the squad. "I don't know if I was ever a leader. I was probably one of the people that helped develop the culture of the team. We were a very good team defensively and had some real good offensive players. Plus, we had Glenn Hall who was an instigator of the defensive style of play. Bill Hay was another good contributor. We were just a mature team that really liked each other, and I think I always had a place on the team, although I probably wasn't a leader. I think that being a leader is overrated anyway!"

When it was all said and done, Eric retired after 1219 NHL games in which he scored 574 points. He played in two NHL All-Star Games (1961, 1965) and of course has that one Stanley Cup ring that he won in 1961. It was a great career by any players standards, and for Eric, he left the game when he felt the time was right. When he retired he was one of the few players in the history of the NHL that had skated in over twenty seasons. "My career was so long ago; the whole thing seems like a blur. Overall, I think it was a great way to live and it was very exciting too, every day. I was fortunate not to get hurt much since I tended to stay out of trouble. For the first three quarters of my career, I enjoyed the travel to New York and Boston. And Montreal was a magical place. It was an interesting way to live and in the end, I decided to retire because I was tired of living in hotel rooms. I also didn't really enjoy flying. When my hockey career was over, I quickly realized that I was an adrenaline junkie, and the afterlife of playing was basically really dull for a

while, so I found some things to do. I think that's the problem with pro athletes that played a long time, when they retire, life can be boring unless they
really have a plan to make the transition to regular life."

After he retired from the game, Eric moved to Vail, Colorado and became
a ski instructor. He talks about that decision to go all rocky mountain high
and go to Colorado, "I've been in Vail for 35 years. I ended up seeing a psych-
iatrist and he kept asking what did I really like to do with my time? What gave
me some excitement that I got from playing hockey? When I quit hockey, I
went to Switzerland and worked as a coach in Lausanne. While I was there I
picked up on this little activity called skiing and, right from the beginning, it
gave me that thrill. It occurred to me that I really liked skiing and my psych-
iatrist told me why don't I make a life out of it. It's not a very big life, but it
certainly has given me an awful lot of pleasure."

Of all things in the world and all the cool jobs that Eric worked throughout his life, it was skiing that gave Nesterenko the biggest thrill since he left
the hockey world. Now at 83 years old, Eric still goes at it on the ski slopes.
When I talked to him for this book he gave me an open offer if I ever wanted
to come to Vail and go skiing with him. An offer that I'd be stupid not to
take up at some point!

"I still ski. I skied 120 days last year. I worked about 15, only part time
since I only have a couple clients left that aren't dead, or have quit skiing. I
only have two or three that are left and the company allows me to teach on a
part-time basis. I still love to ski and Vail itself is such a nice place to live. The
contrast to living in Vail to Chicago is startling. Small town living to the big
bustling city, and I realized that I like the small town living very much. Vail
is a very sophisticated place. We have a great culture here and people come
from all over the world. I've been here long enough and people do recognize
me, but there are lots of people here who are much bigger celebrities than I
ever was. And it really is a live and let live town. People don't bother you, they
really don't, and I like that. However, during the Blackhawks run in 2015,
people were coming up to me so that was kind of fun!

"The coach of the Blackhawks, Joel Quenneville, has a place here in Vail,
and when the Olympics were going on in 2014, he had a two-week break. So,
he phoned me up and we went skiing together and had some real nice conversa-
tions. I really liked his philosophy. He lets his players play and doesn't over-coach.
They're really well organized and he really supports the idea that players get to
know each other and support each other. Plus, the management is really smart
because they're willing to spend money to win and buy good players."

30
WALLY STANOWSKI

There weren't many faster skaters in the 1940's than Wally Stanowski. Known as the Whirling Dervish, Wally was a speedy and clever defensive defenceman who always took care of the business in his own zone rather than taking part in the offense.

When asked about the top speedster on the Toronto defence in the 1940's, Boston Bruins legend Milt Schmidt said that, "I would say as far as skating is concerned, in my opinion, Stanowski was the fastest skater."

Toronto Maple Leafs boss at the time, Conn Smythe, went even further, recalling, "Wally plays defence as though he was swivelled at the hips. He skates sweepingly with legs spread out. You can rock him but he is harder to knock down than Joe Lewis."

Wally Stanowski was born in Winnipeg on April 28, 1919. The son of a blacksmith, Wally grew up in East Kildonan. The first pair of skates he owned were female skates. Eventually his mother bought him a pair for $2.95 brand new. They were size nine

skates even though that young Wally's feet were only a size five at the time. He was supposed to grow into them!

Wally had a friend growing up whose house backed onto an open-air hockey rink. A small cabin was built by the hockey rink to keep the kids warm. The boards were two and a half feet high, with snow built up even higher than that. It was there while playing with his friends that Wally started to love the game of hockey.

Stanowski's father would have preferred him to be a blacksmith as opposed to a hockey player, but Wally was determined to make it happen in the sport that he loved. Wally was a big fan of the Bruins tough, rugged defenceman Eddie Shore so maybe that's why young Wally took a liking to that position.

Looking back on Wally's early hockey days, a crazy fact is that five members of his East Kildonan juvenile team eventually made the NHL. That's something that would be unheard of today. The five who made the NHL were Alf Pike, Billy Reay, Terry Reardon, Johnny McCreedy and Wally.

As a junior, Wally initially tried out for the Winnipeg Monarchs but failed to make the team. Instead he joined his local East Kildonan Bisons for a season, before making the St. Boniface Seals MJHL club the following year. While a member of the Seals, Wally was placed on the NHL's New York Americans negotiation list and attended the team's 1938 training camp in Calgary.

As a prelude of things to come in Wally's career, his St. Boniface Seals won the 1938 Memorial Cup. In a best-of-five series at Toronto's Maple Leaf Gardens, the Seals defeated the Oshawa Generals three games to two to claim the trophy.

Something interesting that very few people know about is that before the fifth and final game in the series, Wally was approached by gamblers to throw the game.

"I got this letter that was slipped under my hotel door. It stated that they would give me $100 to throw the game," remembered Wally. "It also said that (teammate) Billy Reay was to get $50. If I was going to accept the deal I was instructed that during the warm-up to skate behind the net and bend over, pretending I was lacing my skates up."

Wally didn't give the letter a second thought. He handed it to his coach right away and then set his focus for the game at hand. During the warm-up, he thought about lacing up his skates behind the net as a gag but decided against it. That night St. Boniface blew Oshawa out of the water 7-1 to win the Memorial Cup.

There wasn't much celebration the night of the big Memorial Cup win. It was during the peak of the Depression and no one really had all that much money so the team just played a dice game in their hotel rooms before taking the train home to Winnipeg the next day.

Since the Memorial Cup was in Toronto, of course the Maple Leafs were scouting all the players and the club was so impressed with Wally handling things on the Seals blueline, that Leafs boss Conn Smythe made a deal with the New York Americans for his rights.

Wally's first pro contract earned him $1,500 playing with Syracuse and $3,000 with the Maple Leafs, minus the $30 deduction for his team jersey. People might scoff at those numbers today, but back then it was a lot of money.

Wally didn't make the Leafs right away. He spent his first pro season in the minors with the Syracuse Stars. His Syracuse team had too many defencemen at the time so Wally started at left wing. Later on, several teammates went out with injuries during the year and before long Stanowski was back playing on defence.

The following 1939-40 season was when Stanowski broke in with the Toronto Maple Leafs. He skated in twenty-seven games that year and scored nine points. His first defence partner with the Leafs was a guy by the name of Rudolph "Bingo" Kampman and the pair of them had some chemistry that made them a force to be reckoned with on the Leafs blueline, with Wally being the take-charge guy.

"I was the one with the Leafs that if a puck came into our zone and I could get hold of it, they couldn't stop me from getting it out of our zone," Wally once recalled in an interview with the *Society for International Hockey Research*.

Wally wasn't too fond of his first coach with the Maple Leafs who was a guy by the name of Dick Irvin (another Manitoba Top 50 player). "He never taught me a thing," Wally recalled. "I thought well here (in the NHL) I'll learn something, but no. John McCormick backed me up too by saying Dick Irvin was the worst coach he ever played for."

The Leafs brought in a new coach for the 1940-41 season named Hap Day. Wally liked Hap a little better saying "Hap was very good. He got instructions from Smythe, but he did a lot of good things on his own."

There would be no sophomore slump for Stanowski as he had a fantastic 1940-41 campaign, scoring 21 points in 47 games. At the end of the season he was named an NHL First Team All-Star. It would be the only time in his career that he would receive that honour.

Let's skip ahead to the 1942 Stanley Cup Finals where Wally was front and center for possibly the greatest comeback in sports history. His Toronto Maple Leafs were down three games to zero to the Detroit Red Wings and had their tails between their legs. It wasn't pretty, but what happened next was truly remarkable. The Leafs managed to rattle off four straight wins to win the coveted Lord Stanley's Cup.

Now, just how on earth did the Leafs pull off such an historic comeback? Maybe the Red Wings got a little too cocky and assured of themselves when they started planning a Stanley Cup party after winning just the first game in the series. Maybe it had a little bit to do with Hap Day shaking up his team and benching a few of its star players. And maybe the team got fired up after an emotional letter written by a fourteen-year-old girl was read before one of the games, pleading the team not to give up. Conn Smythe and Hap Day also tried every trick in the book to motivate their team. They played up the newspaper reports of their demise, saying the team was toast and told the team's staff to criticize them in public. It's hard to pick an exact moment, but a perfect storm brewed, and at the end of it, the Toronto Maple Leafs were the Stanley Cup champs. For Wally, it would be his first of four Cups, and without a doubt the most memorable for him.

It was an historic series that is still very much remembered to this day. Not only was it the first Stanley Cup final to go seven games, but it was the first time that a team in any NHL playoff series came back from three games to win the series. It's only happened three times since the Leafs 1942 triumph and none of the other times happened in a Stanley Cup final.

Just a few days after winning that miraculous 1942 Stanley Cup, Wally and his Leafs teammate Pete Langelle returned to Winnipeg to serve in World War II. And with that his NHL career was put on hold for two and a half years. Stanowski joined the Royal Canadian Air Force (RCAF) wanting to be a pilot, but during the initial testing, they had found out that Wally was colour-blind so there was no way that he could be a pilot. Instead he became a physical training instructor and was stationed in Brandon, Winnipeg and later Trenton, Ontario during the war.

During the war, Wally played some hockey with the Winnipeg RCAF team and competed in Allan Cup playdowns. Stanowski later recalled that he enjoyed playing for the RCAF team because he got to take hockey a little less seriously than the rigors of playing in the NHL, while still staying in top physical shape for his return to the NHL following the war.

When the war ended, Wally returned to the Toronto Maple Leafs and continued right where he left off, winning Stanley Cups in 1945, 1947 and 1948. It was during the 1947-48 season that the Whirling Dervish earned his nickname. It had been a tough year for Wally as he had mainly been sitting on the bench as ordered by owner Conn Smythe because Wally had his wife join him at the team hotel during training camp and was in defiance of a no-sex edict from Smythe.

Well on the fateful night at the Boston Garden, legendary Bruins goalie Frank Brimsek took a puck to the face and had to be sent to the locker room for repairs. In those days teams didn't carry a backup goalie so play was halted while the goalie got treated.

Seeing the break in play as a chance for Stanowski to warm up since he hadn't seen any ice time in the game yet, Leafs coach Hap Day ordered him to get on the ice.

"I was embarrassed," Wally recalled. "So, I just skated in front of the bench a little."

"Not like that," cried Hap Day. "Get out there and go hard. Let's see some real skating."

Maybe Day should have been more specific because with that instruction, Wally went out to center ice and proceeded to break out into a full figure skating routine, doing all sorts of spins and twirls. The organist saw what was going on and gave Wally some music to skate to as the shocked crowd joined in and clapped along.

"I could see Smythe sitting in the stands, mad as hell," Wally said. "But the crowd loved it. I skated back to the bench, backwards on one skate, with the other one foot up behind me. My leg touched the boards so I knew I was there. When I turned around to look for Hap, I couldn't see him. He had his head below the boards. He was laughing like hell but didn't want Smythe to see him."

Wally had played his last game in a Leafs uniform when he won the 1948 Stanley Cup. Conn Smythe had stopped giving Wally much ice time so he wanted a way out and a chance to play on a different team.

"I told a Toronto reporter of my intention to quit hockey and go into business on my own. He was the only one I told. My wife didn't even know," Stanowski recalled. "I knew the reporter would take that information up to Smythe. He was a tattletale and he would get a favour from Smythe."

Just like a hunter, Wally waited patiently for his trap to work.

It worked as the reporter went right to Smythe and told him of Wally's intentions. Smythe didn't want to lose Wally for nothing so he dealt him to the New York Rangers.

Wally went on to spend the final three years of his NHL career with the Rangers. The last two seasons he was unfortunately hampered with knee injuries that hurt his usual production on the team. For the 1951-52 campaign, he would play the final year of his hockey career in the AHL with the Cincinnati Mohawks.

The legendary New York Rangers coach Emile Francis once told a funny story to hockey historian Jim Amodeo that involved Wally, Ivan Irwin and

Jean-Paul Denis when the four of them roomed together while playing in the AHL with Cincinnati. It was the night before a game and Wally was injured so he wasn't playing. He was rubbing it in to his roommates that he was going to a pub while the others had to go to bed to get their rest. Well, unknown to Wally, Ivan Irwin had planted an exploding device in Wally's vehicle. Emile Francis heard the loud bang noise as he slept in their apartment and later recalled that, "Wally came out of that car and he looked 100 years old."

Wally's hockey career came to an abrupt end one night with the Mohawks. What had happened is he caught an edge on a penny some fan had thrown on the ice and he crashed hard into the boards feet first, badly breaking one of his legs in the process. That would be it for Wally.

Stanowski retired with 111 points in 428 NHL games over ten seasons. A winner at every level he played, Wally won an MJHL and Memorial Cup championship in 1938, and then went on to win four Stanley Cup's with the Toronto Maple Leafs in 1942, 1945, 1947 and 1948 respectively. Wally was also named to the NHL First All-Star Team in 1941 and he played in the 1947 NHL All-Star Game.

After his career was over, Wally stayed in the Toronto area and sold heavy construction equipment. In his later years he was a regular at a monthly NHL old-timers luncheon in Markham where retired players would gather and retell old stories.

Wally Stanowski passed away on June 28, 2015 at the age of 96. He was the second-oldest living NHL player at the time of his death after Milt Schmidt. Wally had been in declining health with lung problems that were complicated in the last few days of his life by a fall at his home.

Through all the success he had in the sport, Wally's fondest hockey memory was simply making the NHL and getting to compete at the highest level.

"In anything you do, you should like it," Wally would say. "If you don't like something than you shouldn't do it. And I loved hockey. We would have played for nothing because we loved the game so much."

29
AB MCDONALD

Ab McDonald is one of those rare NHLers who is just universally liked, plain and simple. I don't think there's ever been a bigger ambassador for the sport of hockey in Manitoba than Ab.

"I love Ab McDonald," says Jordy Douglas. "He's such a classy guy that I consider him to be the Jean Beliveau of Manitoba. Everyone knows how revered Jean Beliveau was in the province of Quebec and that's how Ab McDonald is here in Manitoba. People can judge his hockey stats all they want, but as a person he's second to none. Just a fabulous man that I have so much respect for."

Ab McDonald did everything a hockey player should. A solid playmaker of his day whose lanky frame made it difficult for opposing defencemen to push him off the puck, Ab is in rare company for winning four Stanley Cups in his first four seasons in the National Hockey League.

Ab McDonald was born in Winnipeg on February 18, 1936. He grew up in the working-class neighbourhood of Weston and played his minor hockey out of the local Weston Community Club. "Back then you played hockey day and night," Ab recalled. "We played playground hockey up until twelve years of age at the old rinks of Weston, Sherburn, Notre Dame, Old Exhibition and West Kildonan. Most of the rinks didn't even have boards because it was just playground hockey. Only Notre Dame had boards and they were only six inches high!"

When Ab was thirteen he started playing community club hockey for Weston. There weren't enough boys in his area for a team that year so in order to play that season they had to pick up some kids from other areas of town that no one wanted.

In 1952-53, Ab made his junior hockey debut at sixteen with the St. Boniface Canadiens of the MJHL, while at the same time attending classes at Daniel McIntyre Collegiate. He broke in as a right winger with a left-handed shot who scored 50 points in his first season with the club. That year his St. Boniface team won the Abbott Cup over the Lethbridge Native Sons which made them Western Canadian champs. They would go on to play in the Memorial Cup final, but lost the to the Barrie Flyers four games to one in a series that was held at both Shea's Amphitheatre in Winnipeg and at the Wheat City Arena in Brandon.

The next year McDonald put up 58 points which was tops in the league as his St. Boniface Canadiens defended their MJHL title, but fell in the Western Canadian semi to the Fort William Canadiens.

Eventually the Montreal Canadiens wanted Ab to come a little closer to them so they could see him on a more regular basis. Ab headed east to join the St. Catharines Teepees of the OHA in time for the 1954-55 season. He kept up his scoring ways in St. Catharines, promptly putting up 73 and 80 points in his two seasons with the Teepees.

This was around the time when Ab started realizing he might have a shot at an NHL career, "Everyone wanted to play in the NHL and win the Stanley Cup. That was the big thing for everyone growing up in Winnipeg. When I was fifteen and sixteen I was playing with kids two years older than me with St. Boniface, and in St. Catharines when I was one of the better scorers in the league, that was when I first had an idea that I could one day play in the National Hockey League."

Ab started his pro career with the Rochester Americans of the AHL. He spent two seasons there before being called up to the Montreal Canadiens in the 1958 playoffs where he played two games in Montreal's run to the Cup that spring.

The next season, McDonald was a full-time NHLer with the Canadiens, replacing Bert Olmstead who had been traded to Toronto. He enjoyed more success with Montreal as they won five straight Cups from 1956 to 1960. Ab was a part of the 1958, 1959, 1960 Stanley Cup winning teams.

Talking about what it was like to start his NHL career with Cup after

Cup, "It's kind of nice!" Ab chuckled. "To get to the NHL and play with the Montreal Canadiens, the best team in the league at that time was quite an experience. It was a little overwhelming at times but I certainly learned a lot about the game of hockey by playing in Montreal."

Ab went on to say, "It was good to be on a club like Montreal that knew how to win. Learning how to win doesn't happen overnight, but the other players were very helpful. If you lost a game, no one was too pleased about it. Even if you won a game 4-1, it was all about how did they score that one goal against you. That's what makes a good team and that's what we had in Montreal. Everybody took a little of the blame, so I was very fortunate to go to Montreal."

After Ab's third Stanley Cup, Montreal shipped him to the Chicago Blackhawks on June 7, 1960 in a deal that sent Bob Courcy, Reggie Fleming and Cecil Hoekstra along with him in return for Bob Bailey, Lorne Ferguson, Terry Gray, Glen Skov and the rights to Danny Lewicki.

McDonald took to his new club instantly and won a Stanley Cup in 1961 with the Blackhawks. In doing so, he accomplished the incredibly rare feat of winning the Stanley Cup in each of his first four NHL seasons.

"I played juniors in St. Catharines with Bobby Hull and other future Hawks teammates like Moose Vasko and others which made it feel like a homecoming going to Chicago since I knew so many of the players that were there. They had a great junior club for the years I was there and while I was playing for St. Catharines about twelve of us ended up making the NHL."

Ab spent four seasons with the Chicago Blackhawks. For him, it was a good change of scenery from playing with Montreal where he was primarily a fourth line player. With Chicago, he excelled on their first or second line, and his point totals reflected that.

"I got to play with Stan Mikita and Kenny Wharram on 'the Scooter Line' for four years and that was really great," said McDonald. "We had good chemistry and did very well. Working well together, it was easy to play the game when they know what you're going to do and vice versa."

After his time in Chicago, Ab spent a few years playing with both the Boston Bruins and later the Detroit Red Wings. He also spent some time in the AHL and CPHL between the years of 1964 and 1967.

All would change, however, when the NHL expanded from six to twelve teams in 1967. That meant there were a lot more jobs available in the league and Ab became one of the beneficiaries of expansion. He was selected by the

Pittsburgh Penguins at the 1967 Expansion Draft and went on to become the first captain in Penguins history.

McDonald scored 43 points that year for Pittsburgh in a season where they ended up missing the playoffs by a mere two points. Ab was dealt in the offseason to the St. Louis Blues, which was a blessing because St. Louis was by far the best of the expansion teams early on, losing the Stanley Cup final in 1968, 1969 and 1970. McDonald was on the Blues team for the two runs to the Cup final in 1969 and 1970 where they fell in four straight to Montreal and Boston respectively.

"All of the expansion teams were so close in getting into the playoffs and everyone could compete amongst the other expansion teams. I played in Pittsburgh the first year and then went to St. Louis," Ab recalled. "One of the reasons I went there is because Scotty Bowman was there and I knew him from Montreal. He got as many Montreal or former Montreal players as he could get his hands on when he took over the Blues because he knew people that came from the Montreal system and they knew how to win. Because of that, we had a few real good years in St. Louis. Scotty was an innovator and we got along really well, in fact we still do. When I go to Chicago I see him and we get together and have a good chat or two. It was good for me going to St. Louis since I had played with some of the guys back in Montreal like Red Berenson, Jean-Guy Talbot and Phil Goyette. It made it easier having people you could talk to and hang out with from the start, and I think it helped along the way to making us a successful team."

After another brief stint with the Detroit Red Wings in 1971-72, it was a homecoming for Ab when he decided to come back to Winnipeg and spend the final two seasons of his career with the Winnipeg Jets of the newly-formed World Hockey Association (WHA). He was the first ever captain of the Winnipeg Jets and led them to the AVCO Cup final in the first year of the WHA.

"It was really great to be able to come home," Ab recalled. "I always thought during my career that it'd be really nice if pro hockey was in Winnipeg and I could go and play in my hometown. When the WHA came about and Winnipeg was going to be included in the league, it was at the point where I was getting towards the end of my career, so when I was asked to play here it was a no-brainer. It was something I always wanted to do and we had a pretty good club the few years I played in Winnipeg before I retired. If it wasn't for the WHA Jets, we might not have the team here today."

Ab retired after the 1973-74 season. The 15-year NHL veteran finished with 430 points in 762 NHL games. The highlight of his career being the four straight Stanley Cups at the beginning of his career. It should also be noted that he played in five NHL All-Star games (1958, 1959, 1961, 1969, 1970) and on five different occasions was in the top-10 for All Star voting at left wing.

A true Winnipegger through thick and thin, Ab has stayed in Winnipeg his whole life. He spent a few years coaching the MJHL's Portage Terriers and also owned an equipment rental business for a number of years.

While he was in the NHL, Ab had a home in St. Vital that he would rent out during the season and return to in the summer. In 1967, Ab and his wife Pat moved into their St. James bungalow that they still live in today. That's fifty years for those keeping track at home!

Ab is 81 years old now and is still very active in the hockey community with no signs of slowing down, attending Jets games and every Manitoba Hockey Hall of Fame induction ceremony since they started up over thirty years ago.

He's an incredible human being. A one of a kind person that just so happens to be Manitoba's biggest hockey's ambassador. And with that, I raise my glass to Ab McDonald!

28
JIMMY THOMSON

Jimmy Thomson is about as underrated as it gets when discussing the great all-time defencemen of our sport. He has become a forgotten hero of the 1940's and 1950's Toronto Maple Leafs.

Howie Meeker is the last surviving member of the 1947 Toronto Maple Leafs Stanley Cup-winning squad. At 93 years old today, the outspoken Meeker is living in Parksville, British Colombia on beautiful Vancouver Island. Howie was a great admirer of Thomson as a player, having high praise for his former teammate and friend. "Jimmy Thomson was our best defencemen by a country mile. He's a Hall of Fame calibre player 100%. He's not in there, but he should be," Meeker said sternly. "Jimmy was the most underrated defenceman in the league by far."

"Thomson had the ability to put his stick in between a player's legs very well," recalled Leafs teammate Wally Stanowski. "That's how he used to always stop opposing players."

A 1950's *Ottawa Citizen* newspaper once ran a player profile on Thomson. "It has been said that when scouts all over the league face the question from worried parents, 'But would a pro career be good for my boy?' they point to Thomson. At St. Michael's fabulous factory of so many hockey greats—Red Kelly, Ted Lindsay, Joe Primeau, Tod Sloan, Ed Sandford, Fleming Mackell, to name a few—Thomson was rated as one of the most brilliant scholars ever to attend. He chose hockey as a career. Today, at 28, he had no regrets.

"Personable and prosperous, with a good business on the side, his picture tells that Jim is still doing what he loves best."

Jimmy Thomson was born in Winnipeg on February 22, 1927. Growing up during The Great Depression, the young Thomson spent most of his childhood playing on the outdoor rinks of Winnipeg. Thomson attended Gordon Bell High School. He was his class historian at graduation, earned a sports letter and sang in the school's production of *HMS Pinafore*. During this time, he played hockey for Vince Leah's Excelsior Bantam B and A teams that won the provincial championship in 1941 and 1942. In 1942, he was brought up to the midget Excelsiors that won the provincial midget championship. He played with the midget team the next season.

It was on the outdoor rink at a local community club that a fourteen-year-old Thomson was discovered by Toronto Maple Leafs scout "Squib" Walker. A few years later, Leafs boss Frank Selke instructed "Squib" to bring Thomson, now a sixteen-year-old, to southern Ontario to play for one of the Leafs sponsored junior teams.

He joined the St. Michaels Majors for the 1943-44 season, and his play as a strong defensive defenceman did not go unnoticed with the Leafs brass. In his second year with the team he played a vital role in helping his team win the 1945 Memorial Cup. After that triumph, it was decided that the eighteen-year-old Thomson would get a shot at playing in the National Hockey League. He was paired with fellow Manitoba hockey great Babe Pratt on defence. It was a big jump from playing juniors and after five games he was sent down to the Pittsburgh Hornets of the AHL for grooming.

After a season of honing his craft and learning about the pro game in Pittsburgh, Thomson was ready for the NHL and promptly won a spot on the Maple Leafs roster out of training camp for the 1946-47 season. Right away he became one of the best defensive defencemen in the NHL.

With Thomson acting as a stabilizing force on the Leafs blueline alongside defensive partner Gus Mortson, the duo was coined "The Gold Dust Twins" by the media and fans in Toronto. Very few goals against happened when Thomson and Mortson were out on the ice defending. Early on in Thomson's time with the Leafs he earned himself high praise from Conn Smythe, the Leafs notorious general manager. "Thomson's record of goals-against is the best of any defencemen we have ever had," said Smythe. "He has many of the attributes of Hap Day; he can hurt attackers—although not so seriously as Red Horner. He can get that puck out of his own end like King Clancy—not in as dashing but just as decisively. He'll be one of the all-time greats of hockey if he keeps his head and continues to give his best."

Thanks in part to the strong play of Thomson night in and night out, The Toronto Maple Leafs won the Stanley Cup in 1947, 1948, 1949 and 1951. Howie Meeker, who claims that Thomson was the Leafs best defencemen during his tenure with the club, said that, "The team that gets along best in the National Hockey League wins ninety percent of the time. We won four Stanley Cups and only once were we the best team on paper. We just had the best coach and the best group of fifteen guys that played really hard for each other."

Jimmy's role on the Leafs was that of protecting his own zone and preventing the opposition from scoring goals. In those days, it was extremely rare for the defencemen to come up and join the offensive attack. Thomson was quite the physical player on the ice, but also a clean player. It has to be mentioned that he never had over 100 penalties minutes in one season.

The 1956-57 NHL season might have been the year that Thomson is best remembered for today by fans, if remembered at all. After battling long-time rival Ted Lindsay on the ice for years, the two joined up off the ice in the battle for player rights. It was move that didn't sit well with the higher ups of the National Hockey League, notably Leafs president Conn Smythe.

To start the year, Thomson was named team captain prior to the first game, succeeding veteran Sid Smith who gave up the captaincy after one season because of his plummeting offensive production since being named captain. Thomson himself didn't have the captaincy for too long as it was given back to former captain Ted Kennedy when he came out of retirement after initially hanging up his skates after the 1954-55 season.

During that same 1956-57 campaign, Thomson became one of the strong forces in Ted Lindsay's attempt to have a players' association formed, which was done to help improve players' conditions and especially improve their pensions. Jimmy's role with the association was secretary-treasurer and he led the drive within his Toronto Maple Leafs. In the end, he ended up getting every Leafs player besides Ted Kennedy to join the players' association.

In Kelly McParland's book *The Lives of Conn Smythe*, the author says that, "Smythe was especially aggravated to find Jimmy Thomson on the association's list of vice-presidents. It convinced him he'd been right to oppose making him captain. If he'd had his way, Thomson wouldn't even be on the team, yet now here he was joining up with that ingrate Lindsay—who had played at St. Michael's and by all rights should have been a Leaf himself—to challenge the authority of the man who'd been signing his paycheques the past ten years.

"Smythe knew exactly what that amounted to. With his customary thoroughness, he had a report compiled of Thomson's earnings, going back to the laundry and spending money he'd received as a junior at St. Mike's (where he'd played at the same time as Lindsay). It amounted to $127,563 over fourteen years. In addition, Smythe had a second report prepared on the pensions due Lindsay and his five cohorts on the association executive; Thomson topped the list, due $3,415 a year at age sixty-five."

It should be noted that the demands that this players' association had been extremely reasonable. They wanted better compensation for exhibition games and a limit of the number of exhibition games they had to play, travelling expenses, moving costs and injuries. They also wanted the owner to contribute to the pension fund and set limits on the owners' ability to transfer contracts. Finally, they wanted a copy of their own contracts without having to beg the owners to see one.

The owners at this time were very greedy and had no intentions of giving in to the players. It got to the point where Conn Smythe had basically kicked Thomson off the Leafs. Pretty crazy stuff since Jimmy started the season as the Leafs captain.

Eventually Thomson was fed up enough to the point where he left the team for good. "I will never again play for the Leafs," Jimmy said. "It would be impossible for me to play for a team has questioned my loyalty."

Thomson and Lindsay were both shipped from their teams during the offseason to the last-place Chicago Blackhawks. They were martyred for their roles in trying to rally players to combat the owner's dictatorial style of running the league.

Thomson spent just one season in Chicago before retiring at the conclusion of the 1957-58 season at the age of 31. He finished with 19 goals and 215 assists for 234 points in 787 career NHL games. His four Stanley Cups were the pinnacle of his career. Jimmy also played in seven NHL All-Star Games and was named to the NHL Second All-Star Team on two occasions (1951 and 1952).

An induction into the Hockey Hall of Fame was very much warranted for Thomson after his career was over with, but it never happened. Despite being one of the best defencemen of his era, because of his falling out with Conn Smythe, he never got in. Smythe sat on the Hall's selection committee until

1971 and blocked any chance of Thomson getting inducted. Jimmy wasn't the only former Leafs player that Smythe vetoed from of the Hall of Fame. Busher Jackson was another Leafs star of the past that Smythe had blocked for years due to personal conflicts. Smythe quit the committee in 1971 in protest after they finally elected Jackson to the Hockey Hall of Fame.

Jimmy had started a coal and oil company when he was playing for the Maple Leafs, so when his hockey career was over he returned to Toronto and went into the business full-time. Thomson died of a heart attack on May 18, 1991 at the age of 64.

In 1984, legendary hockey author and broadcaster Stan Fischler ranked Thomson as the ninth best defensive defenceman of all-time in his book *Hockey's 100: A Personal Ranking of the Best Players in Hockey History*. Unfortunately, that little anecdote is about all the recognition that Thomson has received from his hockey playing days, besides being a member of the Manitoba Hockey Hall of Fame.

One of the big reasons I did this book was to recognize underrated players like Jimmy Thomson who have been long since forgotten over the years. If I can put the spotlight on Thomson and shed some light on him to hockey fans who have never even heard the name Jimmy Thomson, and have no idea just how incredible he was in the National Hockey League, then in my mind I think I have done a good job with this book.

27
TOM JOHNSON

Cigars and bow ties. If you didn't know Tom Johnson for his hockey prowess you might have known him for his "bling".

Following in Frank Frederickson and Slim Halderson's footsteps, when the six-foot, one-hundred-and-eighty-pound Tom Johnson broke into the NHL he was the only player in the league at the time that was of Icelandic descent. "I was classified as a defensive defenceman. I stayed back and minded the store," Johnson said. "With the high-powered scoring teams I was with, I just had to get them the puck and let them do the rest."

"If we all are allowed an ultimate friend, mentor, confidant and teacher, Tom Johnson was all of those to me," said Harry Sinden, Boston's former coach and general manager.

Overshadowed on the Habs blueline by the legendary Doug Harvey, Tom quietly went about his business and had an exceptional career that won him six Stanley Cups as a stalwart defender on the Canadiens' blueline. And here's a crazy stat for you: Tom's the only true Manitoban that has ever won the Norris Trophy as the league's top defenceman.

Tom "Tomcat" Johnson was born on February 18th, 1928 in Baldur, a town of five hundred or so in the south-western portion of the province between Portage la Prairie and Brandon. The community was founded in 1890 when the Northern Pacific Railway built a line through the area and a town was soon formed. Baldur was named after Odin's son from Norse mythology by Icelandic homesteaders who were the first to settle in the area.

One of Baldur's earliest businessman was Tom's grandfather, Kristjan Johnson who owned a farm machinery outlet in town. One of Kristjan's brothers served as the province's attorney-general. Kristjan's son, Tom, was a great athlete and one of the best curlers in Manitoba for his time. Tom Johnson gave his son his name as well as his athletic genes.

The young Tom Johnson had his hockey beginnings in the confines of his home, shooting at his sister who played goalie in the broom cupboard. When Tom later started skating, he played at the frozen Baldur Creek with friends and at the local rink.

A sign that Tom was going to have hockey in his future came in the third grade when his teacher asked the class to write down what they wanted to do for a living when they grew up. Tom wrote "professional hockey player."

Hockey wasn't the only sport that Tom enjoyed however. Like his father, Tom was a talented curler in his own right. In his junior year of high school, he skipped his Baldur team to a Manitoba High School Curling Championship.

After Tom was finished with high school, his family moved to St. Vital. And that's when Tom's hockey career took off. The Winnipeg Monarchs asked him to play for them and when Tom played his first game for the Monarchs, it was the first time that he had played in an indoor rink. Such luxury was nonexistent in Baldur and the towns nearby so it was a big eye-opener when Johnson started playing in the city.

While living in Winnipeg, Tomcat began attending classes at the University of Manitoba and played a little for their hockey team in addition to playing with the Monarchs. Montreal general manager Frank Selke caught a glimpse of Johnson while playing for the Monarchs in Winnipeg. In the game Selke watched, Johnson scored two end-to-end goals (the tying and game-winning goals) and that was enough for him to sneak Tom away from the Toronto Maple Leafs, who were sponsoring the Monarchs then. At the time, Leafs management thought that Johnson had too many rough edges and wasn't a skilled enough skater so they didn't bother putting him on their protection list. Frank Selke swooped in after seeing Johnson score those goals and promptly acquired his rights for the sum of five hundred dollars.

Tom came over to Montreal the following year and transferred his schooling from the University of Manitoba to Montreal's McGill University. Frank

Selke was unable to gain a transfer from the Canadian Amateur Hockey Association (CAHA) so Johnson spent a year playing mainly informal hockey and taking classes at McGill University, while at the same time spending plenty of time around the Habs' locker room at the Forum, learning the ins and outs of most dominant franchise in hockey history.

He later played with the senior Montreal Royals team. The *Montreal Gazette* reported that, "Tom was no ball of fire with the Royals. He wasn't a very good skater then and every time (coach) Frank Carlin put him on the ice, the crowd raked him with raspberries. The fans even took to yelling insults at Frank Selke, knowing Johnson was his protégé. It got so bad one day that mild-mannered Frank started to go after one fan and had to be restrained by Dick Irvin."

Johnson eventually moved on to the AHL's Buffalo Bisons team and it was there that his real development started. He got attention throughout the league for his play, and Bruins scout Harold (Baldy) Cotton liked him so much that he asked the Canadiens how much money it would take to part with Tom Johnson. Montreal didn't bite.

Tom Johnson joined the Canadiens full-time for the 1950-51 season. He showed up to training camp that year in a brand-new Thunderbird convertible with a bow tie and a cigar. It left quite the impression on his coach and teammates. Maybe they thought it was a little cocky, but it was just who Tom Johnson was.

Early on in Johnson's rookie season with the Habs he endured a memorable intermission rant from coach Dick Irvin one night. "Johnson, you remind me of that convertible you drive," Irvin said. "When the sun is out, your top is down. When the rain comes, up goes the top. You run for cover as soon as things go bad."

By the end of the season it appeared that Johnson had improved considerably to Irvin's liking and had made a believer out of him. Author D'Arcy Jenish wrote that, "Tom was a stronger, faster skater than he appeared to be. He was tough and fearless. He moved the puck well and was one of the best at stealing it from attacking forwards."

Montreal Canadiens coach Dick Irvin told a newspaper in February of 1951 that "Tom Johnson is the steadiest defenceman in the league today. He's one of the main reasons why we're still in the battle. And, what's more, he's a future all-star."

Tomcat's first year in the NHL proved to be a big success. He finished second in Calder Trophy voting, just behind Red Wings phenom Terry Sawchuk. And in the playoffs, Montreal got to the Stanley Cup finals, but fell in five games to the Toronto Maple Leafs on Bill Barilko's famous overtime goal on Gerry McNeil.

Johnson's success in his first full season in the league was just a sign of things to come. With Doug Harvey and Tom Johnson stabilizing the Canadiens defence, the Habs would win Stanley Cups in 1953, 1956, 1957, 1958, 1959 and 1960.

Despite their success, Johnson and Harvey were never really paired together on the blueline. Coach Toe Blake basically rotated the other three (sometimes four) defencemen around Harvey and Johnson. There was rarely a moment where the Canadiens didn't have either Harvey and Johnson on the ice.

Johnson's fortunes took a turn for the worse in 1962-63 when he suffered a horrific facial injury that damaged his eye muscles to the point that his career was in jeopardy. In a difficult business decision, the Canadiens left him unprotected in the Waiver Draft for the sole reason that it was unclear whether he could fully recover his vision. Boston took a chance and claimed him, a decision that would quickly help improve their fortunes, which had sagged in recent years.

An extremely durable player in his 979 games with Montreal and Boston, Tom likely would have played longer had he not suffered a serious leg injury in the 1964-65 season while playing with Boston. Chicago's Chico Maki's skate slashed a nerve in Johnson's left leg. The gash ended Johnson's playing career despite a feverish attempt to comeback by Johnson. Tomcat also suffered two serious eye injuries and was left with a permanent limp.

Tom retired after the 1964-65 NHL season. His career totals were 264 points in 979 games. Tom won six Stanley Cups (1953, 1956, 1957, 1958, 1959 and 1960) with Montreal during his seventeen-year NHL career. His big individual achievement was of course winning the Norris Trophy in 1959, but Tom was also a First Team All-Star that season and was a Second Team All-Star in 1956.

The very modest Tom Johnson simply said, "That was the year Doug Harvey was hurt" when asked about his 1959 Norris Trophy.

Tom likely would have won more Norris Trophy throughout his career if it wasn't for the fact that he played on the same team as Doug Harvey, who was an all-star for ten straight seasons (1952-62) and won the Norris Trophy seven times in eight seasons starting in 1955.

After retiring, Johnson immediately started working in the Bruins front office. "For him the transition seemed pretty easy," recalled Johnson's son, who is also named Tom, "because after he got injured, he wanted to stay with the team and that's how he became the assistant manager. He was hands on with the team, going in the locker room after every game and practice. Things of that nature. And then finally when they moved on from the coach they had, Tom was already in the front office so they thought it would be a good idea to see what Dad could do behind the bench."

Tom won his seventh Stanley Cup as assistant general manager of the Bruins in 1970. He then became the team's head coach later that year and was very successful behind the bench, winning his eighth Stanley Cup in 1972. To this day, Tom holds a .738 regular season win percentage which is the highest in the history of the NHL for coaches who have been behind the bench for at least 200 games.

When Tom was inducted into the Hockey Hall of Fame in 1970, veteran Hall of Famer Eddie Shore was so upset by it that he actually demanded to buy back his own acceptance. He didn't appreciate Tom's alleged cheap shots and questionable stick work apparently. At 42 years of age, Tom was one of the youngest people ever to be enshrined in the Hall.

After his tenure of coaching the Bruins, Johnson spent many years as general manager Harry Sinden's bow-tied assistant. Tom spent nearly forty years with the Bruins in one capacity or another before finally retiring in 1998 to Cape Cod where he lived for the rest of his life, golfing lots and still attending nearly every Bruins home game, watching from team owner Jeremy Jacobs' private box.

He didn't get back to Manitoba a whole lot after his career ended. Johnson's father passed away early in his hockey career, but he would still come home to Winnipeg and Baldur while his mother was alive.

In regard to the whole being underrated during his career tag that he seemed to have, Tomcat's son said that, "I think he preferred the underrated tag. I know he did later in life as far as the fame goes. He didn't wear his Cup rings and wasn't flashy about it. If people didn't know what he did, it didn't matter to him. He was very quiet about the successes that he had."

On November 21, 2007, Tom passed away from congestive heart failure at his home in Falmouth, Massachusetts. He was 79 years old.

"Tom Johnson did it all," recalled Don Cherry. "He played and won six Stanley Cups, he coached Stanley Cups, he won a Norris Trophy, he's in the Hall of Fame—what else can you do in hockey?"

Former Rangers coach Emile Francis added, "Johnson's trouble was playing on the most colourful team in hockey history. But he was the real worker on the team."

"He was very well-respected and modest," Tom's son recalled. "He was no nicer to the President of the United States than he was to the guy who ran the fruit stand by the train station outside the Boston Garden. He treated everyone the same and he taught me that."

26
ART COULTER

Few were better at playing tough on the blueline than Art Coulter. The second captain in the history of the New York Rangers, Coulter played the game the way it was supposed to be played in his age, combining toughness with skill in the heyday of the Original Six. He's the first player on this Top 50 list that has been inducted into the Hockey Hall of Fame in Toronto.

MANITOBA HOCKEY HALL OF FAME

"He was a superb ice general," said his Rangers coach and teammate Frank Boucher. "He lent strength to our smaller players, always on the spot if opposing players tried to intimidate them, responding beautifully to new responsibilities. He was a well set up fellow, quite tall, very muscular without an ounce of fat."

"Art Coulter was our best player," Clint Smith, a center on the 1940 team and a fellow Hall of Famer, recalled. "He was a leader, like what the Rangers later had in Mark Messier. He could really carry the puck, but he had to head-man the puck. That's the way we played."

Art Coulter was born in Winnipeg on May 31, 1909. The middle boy of three brothers, Art learned to play hockey at The Forks, located at the junction of the Red and Assiniboine Rivers, an experience he later described as "300 kids and one puck". He grew up around Church Avenue and went to St. John's College for a few years and played a lot of hockey at the old tiny indoor St. John's Rink. Art also played junior hockey in the Winnipeg and District League for the Pilgrims club where he began to make a name for himself in local hockey circles.

Art's older brother David won many titles in amateur boxing and wrestling and was the runner-up in qualifying for the 1928 Summer Olympics in heavyweight boxing. David had moved to Pittsburgh and then convinced his father that more opportunities existed for the family's automotive and hardware business in the United States, so the entire Coulter family moved to Pittsburgh in 1927.

In the United States now, Art got back into hockey with the Philadelphia Arrows of the Can-Am League in 1929. He spent two and a half seasons in Philadelphia before the NHL's Chicago Blackhawks got wind of the talented defenceman and signed him on the spot. Right from the get-go, Coulter's physical play and ability to handle the puck at a high pace made him the perfect defence partner for the burly veteran Taffy Abel.

Art's younger brother, Tom, played hockey back in Winnipeg growing up, winning the Senior School Series Hockey Championship with St. John's College in 1927. He was also a notable track athlete. Tom came back to Manitoba in 1932 where he won the 400-meter hurdles event at the Canadian Championships which qualified him for the 1932 Summer Olympics in Los Angeles. Later, Tom wanted to attend the University of Chicago to pursue a master's degree in economics, but he didn't have the funds to pay for his tuition. Art suggested his brother play professional hockey to pay for his schooling. After a season in the minors, Art and Tom became not only teammates, but a defence pairing in Chicago. That is until Tom got injured as a result of a freak collision with the great Howie Morenz, who was playing for the Blackhawks at the time, that broke his fibula bone. That was pretty much the end of Tom's hockey career.

Led by the heroic Charlie "Chuck" Gardiner in goal, the Chicago Blackhawks defeated the Detroit Red Wings three games to one to win the 1934 Stanley Cup. For Art, it was the first big success he had in the league and it gave him lots of confidence going forward. The next season (1934-35) he was named to a Second Team All-Star at the end of the year. The 5'11" Art Coulter was quickly becoming one of the most sturdy and dependable defencemen in the National Hockey League.

It should be said that Art meant a great deal to the Chicago Blackhawks organization when they surprisingly dealt him to the New York Rangers on January 15, 1936 for Earl Seibert. Coulter later said the trade came in the aftermath of sassing the Blackhawks owner when he came to the locker room after a game to scold some of his teammates.

Coming into New York would prove to be a really good thing for Coulter. Early on he thrived under the influence of star forward Bill Cook, who had been the captain since the team came into the league in 1926. "If you stepped out of line, he put you back," Coulter would recall.

Cook retired from hockey at the age of forty partway during the 1936-37 season which left the captain slot open for the time being. It just so happened that at the time there was a rift going on between Rangers coach Lester Patrick and Art Coulter. "I asked Lester what was wrong between him and Art," teammate Frank Boucher recalled, "and he said he didn't seem to be able to get through to him. I suggested that Art, being a man of tall pride, should be made captain of the team. If Lester did this and took Art into his confidence, I was convinced the change would benefit Coulter psychologically."

Coach Lester Patrick agreed and the change seemed to do wonders for Art and the Rangers. With Coulter as captain, the Rangers won the Stanley Cup in 1940. Every Rangers player on that Cup winning team will tell you right away how amazing of a captain Art was. In fact, one tidbit stands out when I was researching his time as captain. Prior to a game against the Boston Bruins in the 1940 Stanley Cup semis, Art put a message in every player's dressing room stall: "Determination was the predominating factor in last year's Stanley Cup Champions. We have it too. Let's Go. Art Coulter."

In the 1940 Stanley Cup playoffs, the Rangers first defeated the top seeded Boston Bruins in six games, which put them in the Stanley Cup Final against the Toronto Maple Leafs. Tied two games apiece, New York won game five in double overtime and then followed it up with another overtime win in game six for their first Stanley Cup in seven years. It would also be the last Cup the Rangers would win until 1994. For Art, it was the pinnacle of his NHL career.

In Stan Fischler's 2015 book *New York Rangers: Greatest Moments and Players*, he tells a humorous story of Coulter during his Rangers heyday: "Tall and muscular and without a trace of fat, Coulter was teamed on defence with Lester Patrick's bruising son, Murray, also known as Muzz. Any forward who attempted to bisect that defence was guaranteed a surplus of black and blue marks.

"As tough as Coulter and Patrick were on the ice, they were sweethearts in civilized clothes. Both enjoyed the good life on Broadway, and Art in particular had a reputation as a free spender. During the Great Depression, the Rangers players were to travel in groups of four in taxis. One of them was named 'cab captain' and in charge of the fares. Coulter was one of those captains.

"One day, after the Rangers had completed a road trip, Patrick invited all his cab captains into his office so that he could review the various receipts that the players were required to obtain from the taxi drivers. Patrick was unmoved as he noted receipts ranging from six to eight dollars, but he did a double take when Coulter handed him a chit that totalled $12.75.

"'Art,' Patrick inquired, 'why is your bill so much large than the others?' 'Well, Lester,' Coulter replied, 'you've told us that we're in the big leagues now, so I tip like a big leaguer.' Patrick didn't bat an eyelash. 'That's very commendable, Art,' he shot back. 'but I don't know if the Rangers can afford big tippers like you.'

Art chuckled, 'Okay, Lester, you have nothing to worry about. I resign my cab captaincy.'"

Everything seemed to be going really well in New York for Coulter and the Rangers, but eventually all good things have to come to an end. With the breakout of World War II, Coulter joined the Coast Guard after the 1941-42 NHL season ended. Little did Art know that would be the end of his career in the National Hockey League. He played two seasons for the Coast Guard Cutters of the Eastern Amateur Hockey League (EAHL) and was nearly a point-per-game player in his time there. Those days with the Cutters would be the last form of competitive hockey that Art would play.

Coulter's last recorded hockey game was in 1944, but he formally retired after World War II ended. He finished with 112 points in 465 career NHL games. Over his eleven seasons in the National Hockey League he won two Stanley Cups and was an All-Star on four occasions.

After he retired from hockey, Art owned and operated the Coulter White's hardware store in Coral Gables, Florida for a number of years as well as his family's importing business in Miami. It took awhile but Coulter was inducted into the Hockey Hall of Fame in 1974, thirty years after he retired from the game. In his later years, Art settled in Georgia and later Birmingham, Alabama, far away from the sport of hockey that he excelled at for many years. Art passed away in Mobile, Alabama on October 14, 2000 at the age of 91.

When Art was elected into the Hall of Fame in 1974, his Rangers teammate Muzz Patrick had this to say at the induction ceremony, "He was a real smart player. He hardly ever made a bad play or a mistake. And he had leadership abilities that made him a good captain. The rest of the guys respected him and looked up to him."

Always very opinionated throughout his life, Coulter found no one to praise among the hockey players of the newer NHL in the 1990's, saying they "just shoot the puck and chase it around like headless chickens." Later, when his old Ranger jersey had crumbled, he tossed it away and never asked the club to replace it. He also found nothing good to say about the 1994 Stanley Cup-winning New York Rangers, instead giving praise to the Rangers of his time.

"All of 'em are in the Hall of Fame," Art said sternly. "They had brains, stick-handling and passing. They played the game like it should be played. Our old team that won the Stanley Cup could skate backwards blindfolded and whoop the Rangers they've got today."

25
HERB GARDINER

Have you ever seen that classic baseball movie called *The Rookie* starring Dennis Quaid? Well, Herb Gardiner's life is hockey's version of that incredible story.

A stellar two-way defenceman, Herb didn't make the jump to the NHL until he was at the advanced hockey age of 35 years old. Despite being at least a decade older than most players in the league, Gardiner quickly established himself as one of the NHL's most skilled and consistent blueliners.

Herb's rookie season was so tremendous that he was awarded the Hart Memorial Trophy as the league's most valuable player. Gardiner was the first of twelve Montreal Canadiens players to win the Hart Memorial Trophy throughout the league's history. He was the first defenceman to win the award, and he is one of two players to ever win the Hart in their rookie year. The other being none other than Wayne Gretzky.

The *Montreal Canadiens* website wrote that, "The 5-foot-10, 190-pound blueliner was one of the bigger men in the game and among the strongest. Playing in an era that featured a far more brutal form of play than is accepted today, Gardiner was in his element when the going got tough."

Herb Gardiner was born in Winnipeg on May 8th, 1891. The grandson of a British military general, Herb grew up on a Winnipeg military base in the 1890's and would skate along a series of frozen rivers and waterways to school every morning. Skating became a mode of transportation for young Herb so maybe that's why he took to hockey early on in life, playing with his friends on corner ice lots.

Herb lost his father very early in life when he perished in the Second Boer War around the turn of the century. Herb ended up sticking with hockey throughout his youth and by fifteen he was playing in a local bankers' league and was on the Northern Crowns Bank team that won the league. A few years later at age seventeen he was already playing senior hockey for the historic Winnipeg Victorias club, winning a senior championship with the club.

Despite being an exceptional young hockey player, Herb didn't think that hockey was going to pan out as a potential career for him so he quit the game at the age of nineteen and decided to go to school to become a civil engineer, while also working as a surveyor for the Canadian Pacific Railway in Calgary.

A few years later, Gardiner enlisted in the Canadian Army for the First World War and was sent overseas in 1915 where he was on the front lines as a lieutenant, fighting in Flanders (Belgium) and France. In 1918, while fighting in France, Herb was severely wounded, taking shrapnel to the face and chest. Ironically, a piece of shrapnel hit him in his chest pocket where he was carrying his civil engineer training book. He lost part of his lung, but because the shrapnel got embedded in his training book, it ended up saving his life.

Gardiner returned to Calgary with medical discharge from the army and resumed his surveying job. He also decided to try and get back into hockey. Despite not skating for nearly nine years, Herb tried out for the Calgary Wanderers and then later turned pro at the age of 29 with the Calgary Tigers of the Western Canada Hockey League (WCHL).

In 1924, Gardiner helped Calgary win the WCHL championships in a hard-fought series with Regina. Herb and future NHLer and league president Red Dutton were stellar as defence partners against the likes of superstars George Hay, Dick Irvin and Barney Stanley on the Regina team. On the road for game one, Herb scored the tying goal in a 2-2 tie. The teams met back in Calgary for the final game of the two-game total-goals series and Herb's Tigers were victorious, winning 2-0 on home ice.

That put Calgary in the Stanley Cup finals where they went up against Howie Morenz, Aurel Joliat and the powerhouse Montreal Canadiens. Although Calgary lost to Montreal in the 1924 Stanley Cup final by a 6-1 and 3-0 scoreline, Herb's strong and sturdy play, culminated with a thunderous Gardiner hip check that sent Howie Morenz over the boards, convinced the Canadiens to try and sign the unknown surveyor. Canadiens general man-ager Leo Dandurand approached Herb on the ice after Montreal had won the Cup and offered him a playing and off-season job if he'd move to Montreal. Herb declined. As his great nephew Brian Costello of *The Hockey News* once wrote, "Herb was a stay-at-home defenceman, right to the core."

At the time, Herb was 33 years old, married, and expecting his first child. It simply didn't make sense to pack up and move across the country for hockey. Costello writes that, "For hockey players in the 1920s, making the NHL wasn't the be-all, end-all it is today. If you were from the west and excelled at the game, you probably played in the Western Canada Hockey League. Teams in Calgary, Edmonton, Victoria, Vancouver, Regina and Saskatoon had all-world stars such as Newsy Lalonde, Red Dutton, Frank Boucher, Dick Irvin, Bill and Bun Cook skating for them. The calibre of play was on par with the National Hockey League. For a few seasons, WCHL champs played the NHL winners for the Stanley Cup. Players of that era generally had other paying jobs outside hockey, especially in the offseason. So, it didn't make a lot of sense for WCHLers to pack up and go play in the NHL, unless there was an offer just too good to turn down."

Everything changed two years later when the WCHL folded and Herb was without a hockey team. That's when he was approached by Dandurand again and asked if he would play for the Canadiens, a team that was in a deep struggle after their goaltender, Georges Vezina, passed away from tuberculo-sis. Without a team and still feeling like he could play at a high level, the now 35-year-old Gardiner decided to quit his surveying job and moved his family to Montreal. The Canadiens did their due diligence by buying his rights from Calgary for the sum of one dollar. At the time, the Canadiens were having trouble signing a fourth defenceman for the 1926-27 season, so Gardiner simply told the Habs boss, "If you pay me his salary, I'll play his position."

Montreal signed him and the rest is history.

The 35-year-old rookie didn't leave the ice for the entire season. Playing on the point with Sylvio Mantha as his defensive partner, Herb played every second of every game during the Habs 44 regular season contests and four playoff games. He was awarded the Hart Memorial Trophy for his efforts at year's end (the second oldest to ever win the award after Eddie Shore) and was appropriately named the "Ironman of Hockey" by his peers.

It was nothing short of remarkable what Gardiner did as a veteran 35-year-old rookie. The *Montreal Gazette* wrote in the days after Herb received the

Hart that, "Gardiner's selection as the winner of the Hart Trophy comes as no surprise. This veteran from the prairie, who came up to the Canadiens this season from Calgary, has been credited with much of the success that the team attained. He not only has proved a star at left defence, but he has travelled practically 60 minutes in all games; has taken few penalties, but above all, has been the inspiration to the team from the first. He generals them on the ice and when they show signs of crumbling, he always cuts loose with speedy hockey which serves to rally his teammates. His generalship has been the big factor in Canadiens' triumphs and his example as a clean player has been a benefit to the club."

After another season with Montreal, Gardiner was loaned to the Chicago Blackhawks to serve as their player-coach. Montreal recalled him to the squad later in the season where he retired at the end of the 1928-29 season. Herb's NHL stats were 19 points in 109 games and in the WCHL he had 51 points in 130 games. The Hart Trophy in 1927 was the highlight of his career and it was nothing short of remarkable given his advanced age. He could not only play with the best players in the world, but he did so without ever needing a breather.

When he retired from hockey, Herb settled in Philadelphia where he became coach of their minor league team. Herb knew Lester Patrick (coach of the New York Rangers) from his playing days, and Patrick offered him the job of coaching the Philadelphia Arrows, an affiliate of the Rangers. Herb didn't get back to Winnipeg all that much after his playing days were over. He had some brothers and sisters there but for the most part he stayed in the Philadelphia area.

Herb became the father of hockey in Philadelphia, coaching the city's minor league teams that were called the Quakers, Arrows, Ramblers, Rockets and Falcons continuously for eighteen years until 1947. During his tenure, he mentored plenty of future Hall of Famers, including Bryan Hextall, Babe Pratt and Art Coulter. Gardiner's biggest coaching success came in 1936 when he led the Philadelphia Ramblers to the Canadian-American Hockey League (CAHL) championship. It was the first pro championship that the city of Philadelphia ever won in hockey and it stayed that way until the NHL's Philadelphia Flyers won back-to-back Stanley Cups in 1974 and 1975.

In 1947, when there was talk about the NHL's Montreal Maroons moving to Philadelphia, Herb was named the GM of the future Philadelphia NHL team. Unfortunately, the move never happened and it would be another twenty years before Philadelphia received an NHL franchise.

Herb received the highest honour a hockey player could achieve when he was inducted into the Hockey Hall of Fame in 1958. And when the Philadelphia Flyers came into the NHL in 1967, owner Ed Snider sought out Herb and had him fill out the first application for season tickets. He was considered Philadelphia's "Mr. Hockey" for all he did for the sport there so Mr. Snider gave him the tickets for free and he attended virtually every home game for the rest of his life.

Herb's nephew Barry Costello recalls that, "On one of the many train trips our family took to Philadelphia, I told Uncle Herb and Aunt Carrie that the previous winter (1950/51) I had played defence on the Pee-Wee Canadiens in the old Calgary Buffalo Athletic Association Pee-Wee, Midget, Juvenile and Juniors Hockey Leagues. Uncle Herb immediately wanted to know how many games I played in but, thankfully, never asked me if I scored any goals or got any penalties—because I hadn't! He did, however, give me the tip to 'always stand your ground on the blueline'."

Herb Gardiner passed away on January 11, 1972 at the age of 80. He was buried in his Hockey Hall of Fame blazer.

"He was a very tough man," recalled Herb's grandson Jim Rhodes. "When he was eighty years old, he had a heart attack, and actually drove himself the twenty minutes it took to get to the hospital. He got there and they admitted him and he was in the hospital for six weeks because his health continued to decline after the heart attack. They couldn't figure out why. Eventually he passed away so they performed an autopsy and it turns out that he died from the ulcers he had from coaching hockey. Once he stopped coaching, they subsided, but once he entered the hospital, all the stress your body is going through, the ulcers came back with a vengeance and killed him."

"He was such a fascinating person because of all the things that happened to him," said Rhodes. "He didn't think he could make a career out of hockey so he stopped playing. He went to school and then went to war. He got injured in the war, losing part of his lung and was lucky to be alive, and then starts up hockey career again. He married a woman who understood completely when he decided to move the family to Montreal as a 35-year-old rookie. He played every second of every game for the Canadiens becoming the Iron Man of hockey. He coached the Philadelphia team for eighteen years and had many players on his team go on to play in the NHL. I've been wearing his Hall of Fame ring since 1972 when he died and I'll always be so proud of what he accomplished in hockey and in life."

24
HARRY OLIVER

For all you trivia buffs out there, if you want to sound smart the next time you're watching an NHL playoff game, mention that the first Manitoban to ever score a Stanley Cup playoff goal was none other than Selkirk native Harry Oliver.

It's safe to say that Harry Oliver had a gift. That gift was a strong skating stride that was described as being "smooth as silk" and he possessed great stick-handling abilities and an accurate shot. He was a gentleman on and off the ice. Being a humble man, Harry was a silent leader who spoke with his performance on and off the ice.

<blockquote>MANITOBA SPORTS HALL OF FAME</blockquote>

Being only 5'8" and 150 pounds, Oliver was appropriately named "Pee-Wee" during his career. The book *Ultimate Hockey* wrote that, "In an era when a small man could finesse his way to professional hockey, Oliver was considered to be in a class by himself. He moved with the speed and grace of a greyhound. Always the perfect gentleman on and off the ice, Oliver never smoked or drank and was always dressed to the nines. As a skills player, he let the likes of Red Dutton, Eddie Shore, Billy Coutu and Sprague Cleghorn do the fighting."

The first player to score at the Boston Garden and the first to score 100 goals in a Boston Bruins uniform, Oliver carved out a remarkable sixteen season Hall of Fame career for himself that saw him play professional hockey in Calgary, Boston and New York.

Harry Oliver was born in Selkirk on October 26, 1898. A self-taught hockey player, Harry perfected his shooting and skating technique on the frozen Red River near his home messing around with friends. "When I was a kid, there was no organized hockey," Oliver recalled. "We just went out and played, sometimes on an outdoor rink, but mostly on the river."

Oliver didn't even play organized hockey until he joined the Selkirk Fishermen junior club as a seventeen-year-old. The son of a single mother, Harry's mom was vital in Oliver's career early on and encouraged her son to reach new heights and play hockey as a way to explore North America.

Playing junior as well as senior hockey with the Selkirk Fishermen, Oliver was busy during the winter months. In 1919, the Fishermen won the Manitoba Senior Hockey League title and challenged the Hamilton Tigers for the Allan Cup. Harry scored a goal in the second game but it wasn't enough as the Selkirk Fishermen lost the two-game total goals series by a 7-6 scoreline.

Oliver's talent was evident enough that by the next season he was playing hockey for the Calgary Canadians in the Alberta Big-4 senior league and then later joined the Calgary Tigers of the Western Canada Hockey League (WCHL) for the 1921-22 season. It was the speedy right winger's first taste of professional hockey, but Harry sure didn't show it as his speed and grace quickly made him one of the league's best players. Oliver spent five seasons with the Tigers and was well over a point-per-game player during his time in Calgary and was always one of the league's top scorers. He was twice named to the WCHL First All-Star Team (1924, 1925) and his time in Calgary was highlighted with an appearance in the 1924 Stanley Cup finals where his squad eventually fell to a more powerful Montreal Canadiens team.

Eyeing a chance to play in the National Hockey League, Harry was sold to the Boston Bruins on September 4, 1926. He enjoyed playing with the likes of fellow Winnipegger Frank Frederickson and the very tough Eddie Shore. "I left the rough stuff to others, especially to Eddie Shore when I played for Boston," recalled Oliver.

Harry was put on the team's first line with Frank Fredrickson and Percy Galbraith. They were called The Boston Fog Line and they always seemed to put the puck in the net while they were on the ice. Bruins coach Art Ross, who was not known to praise his own team too much, called them the smoothest-working forward line he had ever seen.

The 1928-29 season would be the pinnacle of Harry's hockey career. It would be an interesting campaign as star player Frank Frederickson was traded to the Pittsburgh Pirates mid-season and Bill Carson joined Harry and Percy Galbraith on the Bruins' top line. During the season, Harry set an NHL record for fastest goal at the start of the game when he scored just ten seconds into a contest against the Toronto Maple Leafs that ended 5-2 in his Bruins favour.

In the playoffs, Boston was pitted against the Montreal Canadiens in the semi-finals. Montreal, the best team in the NHL during the regular season, was considered to be the overwhelming favourite. Well, Oliver and the Bruins swept aside the supposedly favourite Canadiens in three straight games. This put them in the Stanley Cup final where they went toe-to-toe with the New York Rangers. It marked the first time in National Hockey League history that two American teams played each other for the Stanley Cup.

The final series was reduced to a best-of-three, while the previous round was best-of-five. Apparently, this was designed to theoretically reduce the chance of an upset. Game one was at the Boston Garden and the Bruins rolled to a 2-0 victory. Bruins goalie Tiny Thompson was terrific and earned the shutout.

Game two went back to Madison Square Garden in Manhattan, but there was nothing stopping the Bruins. They were on a mission. Harry scored the game's opening goal early in the second period when he split the Rangers defence and fooled goalie John Ross Roach on a shot from in close. Oliver later assisted on teammate Bill Carson's Stanley Cup-winning goal with just 118 seconds left in the game, giving the Bruins a 2-1 win and more importantly, the team's first Stanley Cup championship.

Harry recalled the Cup-winning goal many years later and how they were a lot more stoic than what you'd see today after such an important goal. "I was going down the right side. I saw Bill Carson loose on the right side. I passed him the puck and wingo! It was in on the left side," Oliver said. "Today, they make a big fuss about a goal, hugging each other and jumping up and down. We just gave a tap on the shoulder, nice going, and that was all. Today, they're more emotional after a goal."

After eight seasons in a Bruins uniform, Harry was traded to the New York Americans on November 2, 1934 and played with the New York club until the conclusion of the 1936-37 season. On a line with Art Chapman and Lorne Carr, Oliver continued to be a productive scorer until the day he retired.

When Harry left the game in 1937, he had played nearly 600 professional hockey games over a sixteen-year career. During his eleven seasons that were played in the National Hockey League, he scored 212 points in 463 NHL games. One of the most gentlemanly players of his time, Oliver was always in the running for the Lady Byng trophy and never took more than 24 penalty minutes a season during his entire professional career.

Oliver is the All-Time top scorer, assist and goal-scorer of the Calgary Tigers WCHL franchise. He was his team's top point-getter for seven straight seasons with the Calgary Tigers and then the Boston Bruins. A terrific career that was highlighted by the 1929 Stanley Cup, Oliver was one of the quiet superstars of his era.

Harry came back to Selkirk following his hockey career and lived at a house on Reid Avenue. He worked as a self-employed electrician by trade. He then moved to Winnipeg where he worked for the Weights and Measures Department of the Canadian Government and was the head electrician for an airplane repair depot. While he was living in Winnipeg, Harry's house on Borebank Avenue was broken into and all of his old hockey memorabilia was stolen. To this day, none of his trophies and Stanley Cup items have turned up. He soon after moved to a condo in the Osborne Village area.

It should also be noted that Harry was a very religious man. Whether that's why he was such a gentlemanly player remains to be seen, but he had a strong faith in God which seemed to carry him through life. Harry and his wife were proud members of the United Church in Selkirk throughout their lives.

"Harry and his wife Lottie were very generous people," recalled grand-nephew Bill Martin. "They didn't have any kids of their own so they kind of inherited my dad and his two brothers. He came from a single family, his mother raised him, there was no dad, so he wanted to make sure he did his part as a family man despite not having any children of his own."

Oliver received the honour of being inducted into the Hockey Hall of Fame in 1967. For Harry, it was an amazing experience because he and his wife Lottie got to go to Toronto for the ceremony and he got visit with old friends like Eddie Shore that he had lost contact with once he retired from hockey and moved to Manitoba.

In his later years, Oliver moved back to Selkirk and passed away there in June 16th, 1985 at the age of 86.

"Very soft spoken and modest, he wasn't all that outgoing and led by example," recalled Bill Martin. "He didn't really talk about being a professional hockey player a whole lot."

Andrew Podnieks' 2003 book *Honoured Members* is a piece that looks at every person that has ever been inducted into the Hockey Hall of Fame. For Harry, he wrote that, "Oliver played like a gentleman on the ice and behaved like one off it as well. He skated like the wind and moved with balletic grace. His career was marked by an effortless on-ice grace."

23
JOE HALL

Joe Hall was the misunderstood bully of the hockey world during his time playing professional hockey. An absolute mercenary on the ice, teammates and also opponents swear that he was the nicest guy in the world once you got him off the ice, refuting the "Bad Joe" moniker he'd once been given by a journalist looking to sell some newspapers.

"He wasn't mean," said friend and teammate Joe Malone, "despite what a lot of people said about him. He certainly liked to deal out a heavy check and he was always ready to take it as well as dish it out. That in itself was remarkable when you consider that Joe weighed in at a hundred fifty pounds. As far as I'm concerned, he should have been known as 'Plain' Joe Hall and not 'Bad' Joe Hall. That always was a bum rap."

A little-known fact about Hall is how he had a role in the invention of the modern hockey skate. While living in Brandon his neighbour was a man by the name of George Tackaberry and Joe would often complain to him about his hockey boots not being able to last for an entire season without collapsing. Being a good neighbour, Tackaberry worked on making a new, more durable pair of hockey boots for Joe. He combined the natural strength of kangaroo leather with a reinforced toe and the result was a home-run. Joe loved the skates and so did everyone on his hockey team and Tackaberry soon became flooded with orders. The business took off from there and became the top brand of hockey skates on the market for years.

Eventually when Tackaberry passed away in 1937, the patent for the skates was sold to CCM—the same CCM business that is still making hockey skates to this day.

So when you're lacing up a pair of skates for now on you can think of the name Joe Hall.

Joe Hall was born on May 3, 1881 in Milwich, England. When he was two years old his family emigrated to Canada, settling first in Winnipeg and then later in Brandon. Joe went to school and had his hockey beginnings on the river rinks of Winnipeg. It wasn't until his family moved to Brandon that Hall's hockey playing abilities were noticed.

Clint Bennest, one of Hall's oldest pals recalled that, "Joe's hockey career started in the season of 1898-99. It was in the fall of 1898 before the rink opened that the boys of the Brandon hockey teams went out to Lake Percy to practice. While there they noticed a new boy on the ice who was some skater. They asked him to come and practice with them. The boy was Joe Hall, who had shortly before come to Brandon to make cigars."

Joe quickly joined on and played intermediate hockey for the Brandon Wheat Cities to kick-start his hockey career and in 1901-02 his team won the intermediate championship and earned their promotion into the senior ranks the following year. A cushy off-ice job lured Hall to play for the Winnipeg Rowing Club in 1903-04. The Winnipeg Rowing Club would take Joe with them to the nation's capital when they challenged the famous Ottawa Silver Seven for the 1904 Stanley Cup. Although his team wasn't successful in their Cup challenge, Hall scored a goal in his team's lone victory in the best-of-three series.

It was during his time with the Winnipeg club that his rough and tumble antics first came into the newspaper spotlight. In a January 1904 game at the Winnipeg Auditorium, members of the crowd were taunting Joe with cat-calls of "butcher" and "lobster" for his dirty play and were egged-on more after Hall made "an alleged breach of etiquette towards the audience."

Hall returned to Brandon the following season but the word was out on his rough play. He quickly became an outlaw of the Manitoba senior ranks, often suspended and having to watch his team's games from the stands. Finally, the league had enough and kicked him out at the end of the season.

Not really having much of a choice, Hall turned pro in the 1905-06 season with the Portage Lakes club in Houghton, Michigan of the International Professional Hockey League. When he left for Houghton, friends and fans gathered for a farewell party at the Brandon CPR station. It just goes to show you how well liked Joe was as a person off the ice. "A number of boys lifted him shoulder high and bounced him about in the air, during which proceeding Joe blushed and smiled," read the news report. "He has always been a valuable member of the local puck-chasing septette, a straight, honest hockeyist, who played the game with a vigour that sometimes laid him open to criticism. But when the season gets into swing, it is pretty safe to predict that Houghton will show no more valuable defencemen on its lineup than Joe Hall."

Joe made the IPHL's First All-Star Team in what was a spectacular professional debut, scoring 33 goals in just 20 games. His rowdiness as a tough enforcer certainly didn't go unnoticed in that year. One opposing team's management even went as far as not letting Joe Hall enter its rink anymore.

Portage Lake challenged for the Stanley Cup but their request was denied because the team was openly professional. After one season in Houghton, Hall returned to Canada and played once again for Brandon and then the next year in Montreal. He was able to play in the Manitoba league because it was now considered professional, but when he went to Montreal he had to be let in by the league to rejoin the amateur ranks.

"I have been reinstated," Hall said, "and I am going to show the Montreal people that I am not half as bad as I have been painted in the matter of rough play. I had two tickets waiting for me from Pittsburgh, but I thought I would rather stay in Canada and take a hand in the struggle in this part of the country."

Around the time that Joe was reinstated, teammate Art Ross (Yes, the same Art Ross that the trophy is named after) talked to a local newsman to try and give Hall some positive PR: "He is a fast, clever player, and all right when he is left alone. Unfortunately for himself, he has earned the reputation of being rough, and when he steps on the ice for a game he is a marked man for every player on the other side. I have heard 'Dirty Hall' called out by a crowd for a piece of work which happened at the other end of the rink from where Hall was at the moment. His temper, I suppose, gave under repeated provocations in the Winnipeg match, but to show you that he put up with a lot himself, I can say that he came out of the game with two cuts on his head, each of which required four stitches. He was told by Winnipeg players that they would get to him. He is a gentlemanly fellow off the ice, and he played good, clean hockey against us in our two matches. I would like to see him playing in the east, and I am sure it would not take long for him to wipe out the impression that he is a rough player, and to build up a reputation for what he is—a fast and clever one!"

The *Winnipeg Tribune* replied to Ross saying, "Hall's one drawback as a hockey player is his temper, which, on the ice, he appears to be unable to control. Joe possesses the qualities of a great hockey player and if he could only dampen this feature, his worth would be doubled."

Hall went on to play for Montreal AAA's and Shamrocks clubs in the Canadian Amateur Hockey Association and was on the Kenora Thistles team that won the Stanley Cup in 1907. Eventually he joined the National Hockey Association which served as the forerunner to the NHL and skated for the Quebec Bulldogs. He made a lot of enemies while with the Bulldogs, including a long-time feud with Montreal Canadiens superstar Newsy Lalonde.

"One night, Joe Hall nearly crushed my windpipe and I came back and almost broke his collarbone," Newsy Lalonde recalled. Another night Joe drove Lalonde's head into the fence at the end of the rink. On another occasion, Hall beat up Lalonde pretty bad and was chagrined after the game to discover that Lalonde's wife had delivered a baby, a daughter, that morning. Hall went to the hospital and apologized to Mrs. Lalonde for injuring the father of her child on such an important day.

It wasn't just Newsy Lalonde that Joe went after. In fact, Lalonde got off easy compared to some of the other players that got in Hall's way on the ice. After one game, he was charged by police for disorderly conduct for an on-ice fight in Toronto. Another night he attacked an official and was ordered to pay a $100 fine and a further $27 for ruining the man's suit. Joe refused to pay either fine, claiming that he was trying to get back at an opposing player. What really happened is that in a span of about two minutes Hall cut Lester Patrick with his stick, knocked out Fred Whitcroft's tooth, slugged the referee, tearing the official's trousers pants in the process after Hall kicked him while he was down on the ice. This of course only added to his "Bad Joe" label that he'd be given. What the papers at the time didn't tell you, however, is that Hall's good nature prevailed as he went to visit the referee at home, apologized for any wrongdoing and offered to pay for his trousers to get fixed.

I know you'd think after reading those last few paragraphs that Hall was nothing but a goon that could only wreak havoc but that actually couldn't be farther from the truth. Despite all the heads he bashed in, he really was one of the great scoring defencemen of his time if you simply look at his stats alone. Perhaps Hall's in-your-face toughness threw off opponents and gave him more space on the ice which led to scoring. Be that as it may, it worked. That being said, referees and officials never liked Hall much and were often quite biased against him during games. One scribe agreed with Joe and wrote, "The whole trouble is that no referee thinks he is doing his duty unless he registers a major or a minor penalty against the Brandon man. There are far dirtier players in the NHA (National Hockey Association) today but they get away with it, though the referees know that they are handing out the rough stuff, even though the crowd does not always tumble to it right away."

With Joe leading the Bulldogs blueline, they won back-to-back Stanley Cups in 1912 and 1913. He was very well liked by his fans in Quebec as they went as far as voting him as the most popular player in hockey. Hall really enjoyed playing with the Bulldogs but when the National Hockey League formed in 1917, the Quebec team had to take a sabbatical for financial reasons and their players were offered up in a dispersal draft for the four inaugural NHL teams. Joe ended up being picked by the Montreal Canadiens and in the process, became one of the first English-speaking players in team history. His feud with Newsy Lalonde was thrown out the window and the pair became really good friends and roommates while on the road.

"I never really had anything against Newsy," Hall recalled. "He began the whole thing by keeping up a running fire of insulting and sarcastic remarks to me once during a game. I became sore and always handed back the same line of conversation. I bodied him hard on every occasion and literally goaded him on to hitting me—and I struck back."

Hall led the newly-formed league in penalty minutes during its first two seasons of operation and was one of the top-scoring defencemen in the NHL's primitive years. Joe's contract for the 1918-1919 season paid him $600, plus a $100 signing bonus and a further $100 bonus if the team finished first. The Canadiens did finish first but Hall never got to enjoy his bonus.

Despite everything that Joe achieved as a hockey player he'll always solely be remembered for the 1919 Stanley Cup Finals and what transpired when Joe and the Canadiens (NHL champions) travelled to the west coast to take on the Pacific Coast Hockey Association (PCHA) champion Seattle Metropolitans for Lord Stanley's Cup. The series became a wild, intense affair that eventually got taken over by the Spanish influenza epidemic that caused many of the players on both teams to fall ill, including Hall. In the last hockey game that Joe ever played he was reportedly in a state of exhaustion, doing everything he could to keep playing but eventually was too sick to continue. He was taken to the hospital where his temperature was recorded in the dangerously high range of 105 degrees F.

With most of Montreal's team and a lot of Seattle's players in the hospital, the series was cancelled on April 1, the morning of the final game that would have decided the Cup. When it was clear that Hall might not recover, his wife was summoned from Brandon to be by Joe's bedside. She, along with Hall's mother and sister, left immediately but they didn't make it in time. A telegram came while en-route stating that he had died.

Joe Hall succumbed to his pneumonia on April 5, 1919 at the age of 38. Once in a bitter feud, now best friend Newsy Lalonde was at Hall's bedside when he passed away. Joe was the only player in the series that failed to recover from the flu.

The rest of the Canadiens team quickly recovered and travelled to Vancouver where they met up with Joe's family and attended his funeral there. Joe was interred at Mountain View Cemetery in Vancouver and had hockey greats such as Lester Patrick, Cyclone Taylor, Si Griffis, Newsy Lalonde, Billy Coutu and Louis Berlinguette serve as his pallbearers. The team then travelled by train across Canada back to Montreal with a stopover in Brandon for another service for Hall. The flu that killed Joe would kill up to one hundred million people before the epidemic finally ended.

Hall's teammate and good pal Joe Malone was especially upset about Joe's passing because it meant that he wouldn't have any more chances to erase the "Bad Joe" name he was given. "There were plenty of huge, rough characters on the ice in Joe's time," recalled Malone, "and he was able to stay in there with them for more than eighteen years. His death was a tragic and shocking climax to one of the most surprising of all Stanley Cup series."

"One of the real veterans of hockey," Pacific League president Frank Patrick said at the time of Joe's death. "The game suffered a loss by his passing. Off the ice he was one of the jolliest, best-hearted, most popular men who ever played."

Joe's obituary stated, "Hall played the game for all there was in it, and although he checked hard and close, he was never known to take a mean advantage of a weaker opponent. He was popular with his club mates, and made many friends in the cities in which he played hockey."

In the years that followed Joe's death, the hockey world rallied around his family. A trust fund was set up for his widow and their children and "Joe Hall Memorial Week" games were played throughout Manitoba to raise funds, with the biggest one in Winnipeg at the old Amphitheatre. There was a game in Montreal as well. The Winnipeg game featured all-stars from various Winnipeg-based teams playing against the same from other teams in Manitoba.

Hall was a journeyman professional hockey player ever since he was nineteen years old. His longevity in the sport was incredible for his time, especially with the way he played the game.

Throughout his whole life he never once forgot his Manitoba roots, coming home to Brandon every offseason to work as a brakeman for the railway. He made a decent wage with his hockey and rail work that he was able to purchase a nice home in town for his family. He also invested in other land around Brandon and its surrounding area. His wife, two sons and one daughter lived quite comfortably while Joe was away playing hockey all winter.

In 1961, Hall's family had the chance to celebrate Joe's hockey career one final time when he had the great honour of being posthumously inducted into the Hockey Hall of Fame.

Hall wasn't just known for being "Bad Joe" or the answer to the trivia question "Which Montreal Canadiens defenceman passed away tragically during the 1919 Stanley Cup finals?" He should better be known for the fact that he was one of the best early defencemen in the game of hockey.

22
REGGIE LEACH

He was known as simply "The Riverton Rifle" in his heyday with the Philadelphia Flyers. Possessing one of the hardest shots in the National Hockey League, Reggie Leach was a goaltender's nightmare, firing bullet shots from all angles and scoring almost at will it seemed sometimes. Without a doubt, you could make the claim that Reggie Leach is one of the best pure goal scorers and best Indigenous player to ever come out of Manitoba.

"I would feed him the puck in the slot, knowing that he would unleash a killer shot. It was powerful and accurate enough to terrify goalies, first in Junior A and then in the NHL," recalled teammate and best friend Bobby Clarke. "He was stronger and faster than most of us, but it wasn't his natural gifts alone that accounted for his phenomenal success as a goal scorer. Reggie spent hours on end working on his shot."

"The only person who could have stopped Reggie Leach from being remembered as one of the greatest snipers ever to lace up a pair of skates was Reggie himself," wrote Philadelphia Flyers beat writer Bill Meltzer. "Arguably the most naturally gifted member of the famous LCB line, Leach had a hat trick of devastating shots in his arsenal. He had a wicked 100 mph slapshot that intimidated defenders and goaltenders alike, a wrist shot that could pick any corner or find the tiniest five-hole opening, and a tricky backhander that made many a goalie look foolish. Leach was dangerous any time he got the puck over the blueline. He could score from any angle and was a good enough stickhandler to elude would-be shotblockers and poke-check attempts. He also had underrated speed and was lethal in transition."

Reggie Leach was born on April 23, 1950 in Winnipeg to a pair of young unmarried parents. When he was just a few weeks old he was sent to live with his paternal grandparents in Riverton, a small community about an hour and a half north of Winnipeg.

Although Reggie lived a fairly happy childhood, it was marred with tragedy and death that would certainly have a deep effect on any young kid growing up. His father figure died of a heart attack; a brother wrapped his car around a telephone pole and passed away, while another brother drank himself to death. And his sister fell asleep in a car with her boyfriend and they both died from carbon monoxide poisoning.

Reggie had his hockey beginnings in Riverton, playing road hockey as youngster with his chums. "There were a lot of kids in town, so when we played we divided ourselves into four teams, one from each quadrant of the town," recalled Leach in his 2015 autobiography called *The Riverton Rifle: My Story— Straight Shooting on Hockey and on Life.* "I was a goalie back then because I was too short and chubby to be anything else. We played for hours on end."

It's not often you hear that an NHL great didn't start skating until he was in the double digits, but for Reggie that was the case: "I didn't put on skates until I was ten years old. The first pair I tried on had belonged to one of my brothers and was about twice as big as my feet. I had to stuff them with newspapers so I could use them."

He excelled at hockey right from the start and did everything in his power to get on the ice at the Riverton Memorial Arena. "I was on the ice at the Riverton Memorial Arena playing hockey about five days a week, but I wanted to be out there every day of the week, so I also signed up for figure skating and joined the girls on Wednesdays and Saturdays. I took part in some figure skating carnivals—no word of a lie. I loved being on the ice in front of a crowd, showing off my bunny hop jump or camel spin. I'm certain those lessons helped make me a strong skater.

"But even that wasn't enough ice time for me. After the arena closed for the night, I would sneak into the building, which was essentially a barn, and spend hours on the ice by myself, skating in circles and firing pucks at the net. I would pick a target and shoot at it until I hit it, again and again. In time, I could fire the puck from the top of the face-off circle and hit the exact spot where the crossbar and post intersected. The arena was completely dark at that hour except for the beams of moonlight that shone through knotholes in the slats of wood. Most people in town knew that I was there because they could hear the puck ringing off the crossbar in the middle of the night. It didn't seem to bother them because no one ever asked me to leave. I guess they figured no harm was being done."

All of that shooting late at night is a very good reason why Reggie ended up having one of the most lethal shots of his era. Despite being on the ice at the arena virtually every day, Reggie felt that he still needed more hockey in his life, so he went ahead and built his own backyard rink.

"When our family moved into a bigger home, I created a small patch of ice in the backyard by hauling buckets of water from an outside well. I spent two or three hours at a time shooting the puck at a plywood board propped up against the shed. I had marked targets on the wood to shoot at. I was determined to have the best shot around. Friends would sometimes join me out there and we held friendly competitions."

Playing hockey as much as Reggie did it's no wonder that he became one of the top players in his area. By the time he was fourteen he was representing Riverton in the bantam, midget, and juvenile ranks. He even suited up a couple of games for the senior Riverton Lions squad which was a big deal for Reggie since he grew up idolizing the local senior team.

When Reggie was fifteen, he went to Weyburn and tried out for their junior team at the request of a Detroit Red Wings scout. He ended up being the last player cut at training camp, but that didn't discourage Leach as he ended up playing until Christmas that year for a Junior B team in Lashburn, Saskatchewan.

Reggie was homesick so once he returned for Christmas he stayed in Riverton and played for his old teams the rest of the season. The next season he made the big jump to the Flin Flon Bombers of the MJHL. He arrived in Flin Flon with seven dollars in his pocket and a dream to make the Bombers team out of training camp.

Shortly after he arrived in Flin Flon, Reggie met Bobby Clarke, the son of a local miner who would of course go on to be one of the game's all-time greats. "He was so good I had heard about him back in Riverton," Reggie recalled. "We met a few weeks after I arrived in Flin Flon when he spotted me at the arena practicing my shot. There was no ice there in the summer, so I stood on the concrete firing the puck at a net. It wasn't long before we became fast friends. We shared a great bond: our love of hockey."

Reggie and Bobby both made the Bombers team and the rest, as they say, is history. The pair's chemistry was simply incredible on and off the ice. When they weren't playing hockey, they were working together in the mines for the Hudson Bay Mining and Smelting company. They were inseparable and it showed in their strong play. In his first year with the Bombers they won the MJHL championship and Reggie had scored 67 goals and 113 points in just 45 games.

The following season the Bombers moved into the stronger Western Canada Hockey League (WCHL) and Reggie continued finding the back of the net at a rapid pace, scoring a league record 87 goals. It was around this time that Reggie started to get the idea that he might be able to play in the NHL one day. "I was a pretty good hockey player in Riverton but it was a small community so I didn't know how my career was going to go from there," recalled Leach. "Once I went to Flin Flon and played there, I had a rough idea in my fourth year of junior there after Bobby Clarke came back. He was a year older than me so he turned pro a year before me and encouraged me to keep going at it because he said that I shouldn't have any problems making it."

While with the Bombers, Reggie won league championships in three of the four years he was up in Flin Flon and averaged nearly two goals a game during his junior career. NHL scouts loved the quick release that he possessed which led Reggie to being drafted by the Boston Bruins with the third overall pick of the 1970 NHL Amateur Draft.

Reggie made the Bruins out of training camp, but he was joining a club that had just won the Stanley Cup the year prior so they were loaded with talent up front and as a result, Leach was relegated to the bench more than he would have liked.

"You're very excited at first being right there with the defending Stanley Cup champions. I thought at the time that these guys were so much better than I was as a hockey player because of what they had accomplished the previous year and here I am sitting in the same room and not getting a chance to play. The first year was okay, but by the second year you start to get frustrated. I thought I was better than at least four or five of the guys they had but they never gave me a full chance."

Eventually Reggie voiced some frustrations to his coach and it led to him being traded at the 1972 trade deadline to the California Golden Seals in a deal that sent Carol Vadnais back to the Bruins to bolster their roster. Although playing in Oakland, California was a chance for Reggie to get plenty of ice time, they were a last-place team for most of the three years he spent there and there weren't many high points.

"California was a chance for me to play on a regular basis. I just wanted to play the game at the highest level," said Leach. "But the team was run horribly. Junior teams were better run than the California NHL team. One of the few good things about playing in Oakland was the fact our owner, Charlie Finley, also owned the Oakland Athletics and we got free tickets to all of the big games including the World Series."

One week after the Philadelphia Flyers won the 1974 Stanley Cup, they traded a promising young player named Al MacAdam, Larry Wright, and a first round pick to the Seals for Leach. Word has it that Bobby Clarke had pushed for the Flyers to make the trade, telling owner Ed Snider that Reggie could score forty goals in his sleep.

"I came from a last place club and then all of the sudden I got a break and came on the defending Stanley Cup champs team once again. I know Clarkie said in the press that I would score 40 goals on a bad year, but I sure didn't look very good at Christmastime with only four or five goals. I wasn't used to playing in a system and being disciplined on the ice. In California, we just did what we wanted and tried to keep the games as close as possible and go from there. My attitude and love for the game certainly came back when I went to Philadelphia and things changed as I ended up having a pretty good finish to the year."

Pretty good finish indeed as Leach pumped 42 goals in the last 60 games of the year. He added eight more in the playoffs as the Flyers won their second straight Stanley Cup. The following 1975-76 season would be Reggie's best in the NHL as he scored 61 goals during the regular season which would have won him a Rocket Richard Trophy as the league's top goal scorer if it wasn't for the fact that the trophy didn't come about until 1999. He also played in the inaugural 1976 Canada Cup and was on the Team Canada squad that was victorious, defeating Czechoslovakia in the final by 6-0 and 5-4 score lines.

In the playoffs that year, Reggie continued his scoring ways and potted 19 goals during the postseason. He even had a five-goal game during his team's playoff run that saw the Flyers bid for a three straight Stanley Cup falter in the finals when they were swept by Ken Dryden and the Montreal Canadiens.

For his efforts, Leach won the Conn Smythe Trophy as playoff MVP. He's one of five players ever that have won the award despite losing the Cup final. Reggie's 80 combined goals (regular season and playoffs) became a league record until the 1980-81 season when New York Islanders sniper Mike Bossy scored 85.

Reggie is the first to credit Bobby Clarke for a lot of his success with the Flyers. "Well Clarkie and I have been friends all our lives," said Leach. "We grew up in Flin Flon together working in the mines. He went to Philly while I was in Boston and California so it was really nice to get back together since we knew each other so well. We had Billy Barber on the left side and together we had amazing chemistry and played together as a unit which led to us being one of the top lines in the NHL at that time."

All in all, Reggie spent eight years with the Flyers and then finished off his NHL career with a one-year stint in Detroit. He was a part of the Flyers' 35-game unbeaten streak in 1980, which is a record that still stands to this day, which also includes his team's 22-game unbeaten streak on home ice that same season. Leach retired with 381 goals and 666 points in 934 NHL games over thirteen seasons. Twice surpassing the 50-goal plateau, Reggie's hockey career is highlighted by his 1975 Stanley Cup and Conn Smythe Trophy. He played in two NHL All-Star Games (1976, 1980) and was named an NHL Second Team All-Star in 1976.

When his career ended, Leach got into the landscaping business. He started off as just a regular worker but soon came to own the company and grew it into quite a profitable business for a number of years. Reggie had a son named Jamie that played parts of five seasons in the NHL, mainly with the Pittsburgh Penguins, winning the Stanley Cup in 1992. Reggie and Jamie became one of the rare father and son combinations in NHL history to both win the Stanley Cup.

Today, Leach and his wife live in Aundeck Omni Kaning First Nation on beautiful Manitoulin Island in northern Ontario. Reggie was named to the Order of Manitoba in 2016 and continues to be a role model for Aboriginal kids by delivering speeches at First Nation schools all across Canada about the dangers of drugs and alcohol. His speeches come right from the heart because he himself overcame alcoholism and has been sober now for over thirty years. Reggie's life has truly been an inspiring story.

If you want to read Reggie's whole story then I highly recommend going out and getting a copy of his book. It's quite the fascinating read.

CHICO RESCH SAYS

Reggie was another Manitoba guy who was really funny and would make you chuckle. You had Bobby Clarke and Bill Barber on the Flyers who were both extremely intense, and then you had Reggie, a lovable guy who was just kind of rolling with the punches.

I can still see that little blade he had on his stick and my goodness he could rip that puck. The players who could really shoot well in the top corners, they did really well, and he was one of the first high shooters. Players like Dennis Hull would deliberately try to shoot high just to scare you. Reggie didn't have that malicious side to him, but he was the one guy I didn't want to see coming down the wings with his stick raised.

One of the big reasons why we didn't go into the butterfly back then has to do with if you had gone down into a butterfly and someone shot it at your face, even with those fibreglass masks, serious damage is going to happen—so you tried to stand up and protect your face. Reggie was a guy that it took a little more courage to stand in the net and not close your eyes when he's shooting at you. When he got in the zone and found his spot, he'd shoot it so hard that you wouldn't get it.

I remember a couple of times he'd hit me high and then say, "Hey sorry Chico!" as he was skating by me after. He was just a pure shooter and a pretty darn good skater. He was different than Mike Bossy who could shoot the puck all over—five hole, low, all corners. Reggie was a little more predictable where his shot was going, but he shot it so hard that even though you might know where it's going, you're not going to get it. It's like knowing that Roger Clemens is going throw a fastball at you, you're still not going to hit it.

Everybody loved Reggie with that big smile. He's always been one of my favourite players except for when he had the puck and his stick was over his head.

21
KEN REARDON

*"I couldn't skate, I couldn't shoot, and I wasn't very intelligent.
But I was spectacular."*—Ken Reardon

Nicknamed "Beans" from his army days, Reardon used to drink penicillin for breakfast and bath daily in pickling brine. It was quite the different regimen than what you might see an NHL player partake in today, but back then it worked for Ken.

Reardon was a top-flight defenceman known for his headlong rushes and all-out intense, physical game that left opposing players in his wake and himself often injured; though he showed extraordinary toughness in playing while he was in pain.

The fact that Ken Reardon was the player that Don Cherry idolized as a kid should tell you all you need to know. Cherry admired Reardon so much because he stood for all the right things. Reardon fought in World War II and was this incredibly brute and tough player on the ice, but deep down was a very compassionate person who was admired by a lot of people.

"He did some scouting right after he retired from hockey and if he went and scouted you up in Winnipeg and you came out of the arena without a coat on, he would literally give you the coat off his back—no questions asked," recalled Reardon's son who is also named Ken. "As much as he terrorized the league, he was this incredibly kind, passionate human being."

Ken Reardon was born in Winnipeg on April 1, 1921. He grew up in the city's West End and played his hockey at nearby Clifton Community Club, winning the city playground championship in 1931 and 1932. He then helped the East Kildonan Bisons win the Bantam Championship in 1933 and 1934 and also won a Midget City crown for them in 1935. The following year he won another city championship, this time in juvenile hockey with the Winnipeg Monarchs.

It should be said that despite all the success that Ken accomplished early on in hockey, he'd be the first to tell you that it was his brother Terry Reardon, two years his senior, who was the real hockey star in the family. Terry was quickly rising through the ranks of junior hockey in Winnipeg, and was a prolific goal scorer for the East Kildonan North Stars and later the St. Boniface Seals. For Ken, his claim to fame at school was that he was Terry Reardon's younger brother.

At the age of thirteen, Ken experienced the worst kind of tragedy when he lost both of his parents in an automobile accident. Ken, his two brothers and one sister were orphaned and eventually the family, still overwhelmed from what happened to their parents, moved to northern British Columbia to live with an uncle.

Back in those days, youth hockey in British Columbia wasn't up to the same level as it was in Winnipeg, but Ken wanted to continue playing hockey so he was encouraged by his uncle to play for the Blue River Rebels of the British Columbia Junior Hockey League for the 1937-38 season.

Now, Ken's brother Terry, was the star player of the Brandon Wheat Kings, scoring 45 points in just 16 games. The next season he would make his NHL debut with the Boston Bruins. Inspired by his big brother, Ken wrote a letter to a junior team in Edmonton requesting a chance to try out. He made the team, but mostly watched the games from the bench as he rarely found playing time, even though his team made it all the way to the Memorial Cup final.

In the fall of 1939, Ken attended a New York Rangers camp in Winnipeg but was let go because of his "poor" skating. During the 1939-40 season, Reardon worked extremely hard to improve his skating and all the work he put into it showed on the score sheet. In that year's Memorial Cup playdowns, Ken exploded for 31 points in 14 games, as his Edmonton Athletic Club lost a hard-fought Western final to the Kenora Thistles.

Paul Haynes, a Montreal Canadiens forward who was injured and out of action, was sent by the team out west to scout junior hockey. On his trip, he discovered Elmer Lach and Ken Reardon. "One look was enough," recalled Haynes. "From the first time I saw him, Ken was a tough, hell bent-for-rubber kid who electrified the stands. I slapped him on the Canadiens' list pronto and the following autumn he was brought east to the Canadiens' training camp at St. Hyacinthe, Quebec. Dick Irvin had the rookies working a week before we old-timers reported. Reardon looked good and I was plenty proud of my scouting. Naturally, too, a rather intimate friendship had grown between us.

"The very first day we old-timers put on skates, Irvin lined up a team against the rookies. I snaffled the face-off, passed to Toe Blake who carried it over the blueline and whipped it back to me. At that identical moment, an earthquake hit. I found myself dazedly staring up at the roof lights. Players were looking down in wondering sympathy. Reardon had hit me with the most blistering check I ever received in ten seasons in the National Hockey League. I was sore as a boil but when I cooled down I realized the guy just doesn't mix sentiment with business—he plays for keeps all the time."

Most hockey players have to play in the minors before they play in the NHL to get used to the pro game—not Ken Reardon though. The Canadiens liked him so much that the 5'11", 180-pound defenceman made the 1940-41 Canadiens squad out of training camp and debuted for the team as a nineteen-year-old rookie. Reardon signed his first pro contract on October 26, 1940 for $4,000 a season, plus a $1,000 signing bonus. He played his first NHL game a few nights later as he was one of the half-dozen rookies who suited up for new coach Dick Irvin on opening night and immediately the Canadiens coach Irvin realized he had something special in front of him. Ken was fierce and fearless right from the get-go and was a rock on defence. Any opposing forward that tried to get around Ken was met with a crunching body-check.

After a very strong rookie campaign, the Canadiens decided to bring in Ken's brother Terry for the 1941-42 season and the two brothers became teammates in Montreal. Ken and Terry seemed to have a really good thing going in Montreal, but that's exactly when World War II broke out, and of course the Irish brothers enlisted in the Canadian Army.

Call it fate or whatever you want to call it, but the future president of the National Hockey League Clarence Campbell and Ken were privates together early in the war at an Edmonton base, sharing the same tent. Since Ken used to enjoy a few extra winks of sleep in the mornings after reveille, Campbell would shine up his buttons to keep him from having trouble with the sergeant.

Before Ken was shipped overseas, he kept up with his hockey and helped the Ottawa Commandos win the Allan Cup in 1943. During the war, Ken got up to corporal and was personally presented with a Certificate of Gallantry by Field Marshall Montgomery for work under fire with a heavy bridging group of the Canadian Army in Belgium. Ken's brother Terry survived being shot in the back on the battlefield, but his hockey career was never the same once he returned from war.

When Ken returned home, he rejoined his Canadiens club and picked up right where he left off as one of the league's most prominent and toughest defencemen. In the 1946 Stanley Cup final, Ken and his Canadiens went up against brother Terry and the Boston Bruins. The series was so intense that the two brothers even fought each other during one of the games. Ken's Canadiens ended up winning the series in five games, but it was one of those series that really could have gone either way. For Ken, it was also a matter of personal triumph as that 1946 Cup win would be his one and only he would win as a player.

Ken had some more stellar years in the late 1940's but just couldn't get the job done against the powerful Toronto Maple Leafs teams of that era. Still though, Reardon's intense play on the ice certainly made him a lot of enemies, but it also garnered a lot of respect from other members of the National Hockey League.

"He's a wild, crazy guy out there on the ice," said Rangers star Frank Boucher, "but he's the most inspired player in the league today. He can rally a team when it needs it and lift it all by himself."

Toronto Maple Leafs coach Hap Day added that, "Reardon is the most demoralizing player in the game. He can knock a whole National Hockey League team off balance—get them thinking of everything but hockey."

"He was a no good rotten son of a bitch, but he was a nice guy too!" recalled former Leafs player Howie Meeker with a chuckle. "I got to know him very well over the years and he was a really great guy. Reardon ran on skates, was tough as nails, and on the ice, you never knew what he was going to do. But get him off the ice and he was full of shit and vinegar. He was definitely the English-speaking heart on those late 1940's Montreal Canadiens when they had good years. Ken certainly got by with less skill than any defenceman that ever played in the National Hockey League. I mean on a scale of one to ten, he was probably a six, but he was an incredibly smart player at the same time. I've always had a ton of respect for Reardon as a player and person."

In New York, the fans at Madison Square Garden's despised Ken's play so much that the upper gallery of the arena formed an anti-Reardon hate club. Shortly before Christmas one year, they threw an unplucked turkey at Ken during a game that missed his head by mere inches. Ken looked up to the fans and saw a banner that they unravelled from the railing that read: "Merry Christmas, Reardon!"

On an off-day one year, Ken visited Mont Tremblant, a famed ski resort and went skiing for the first time in his life. After a mere ten minutes of instruction, he went up the first chair lift and actually negotiated the rapid descent without falling. That's what can happen I guess when you have absolutely no fear, a solid sense of balance and the ability to absorb coaching instantly. Astounded ski instructors saw Ken the following afternoon skiing with several members of the Canadian Olympic team, which is crazy because he'd only been skiing for a day. It just goes to show you what kind of a natural athlete Reardon really was that he could take on a totally different sport and excel almost instantly.

As mentioned earlier, Reardon often found himself injured and playing through great deals of pain. It's the result you can expect from throwing your body out there on a nightly basis. One shoulder injury was supposed to keep him out of the lineup and in the press box for three weeks but he returned to the Canadiens' lineup after just ten days. He attempted to hit an opponent in the first few minutes of his first game, missed, and slammed the tender shoulder into the boards. Ken completed the game and then asked the team doctor to look at the throbbing arm. "It's your head I should be examining, not your shoulder," replied the doctor.

Through all the success that Ken had during his short but stellar NHL career, he is likely best known today for his longstanding feud with Cal Gardner.

The Ken Reardon/Cal Gardner feud started on March 16, 1947 during a late-season game that featured what hockey historian Stan Fischler calls, "the greatest fight in Rangers' history; no questions asked." The radio play-by-play man Bert Lee was yelling hysterically, "It's a riot! It's a riot! It's a riot!" as the two teams were having an old-fashioned donnybrook that featured endless bouts and stick fights.

It all started with just thirty seconds remaining in the game as the Canadiens were nursing a 4-3 lead. Reardon took the puck up the ice and as he skated across the blueline, Bryan Hextall of the Rangers checked him, bouncing Ken towards the Rangers' Cal Gardner, who in turn cross-checked Ken in the mouth. Reardon would later recall how his upper lip felt as if it'd been sawed off his face. "There was quite a bit of blood on the ice," said Reardon. "My chewing gum was on the ice and I could see a couple of teeth sticking in it."

That's the moment when all hell broke loose. A bench-clearing brawl ignited which also involved some fans too. One fan took a shot at the bloodied Reardon as the police struggled to keep the Canadiens team from attacking the crowd.

After the game, Reardon promised to the media that he would get revenge on Gardner every time they met again. He even told a magazine that he was going to break Cal Gardner's jaw. Well in their next couple of meetings nothing really happened that was noteworthy, but that all changed in November of 1949 when Gardner, who was now a member of the Toronto Maple Leafs, had his jaw broken by Ken in a game at the Montreal Forum.

"I wanted to get even, I make no bones about it," recalled Reardon. "The week the magazine came out I ran into Cal Gardner accidentally. I never got a penalty for it and unfortunately he broke his jaw off both sides."

Reardon had to go in front of league president Clarence Campbell, his former bunk-mate in the Canadian Army and was given a strict talking to. He even forced Reardon while he was on the ice to post a $1,000 bond against future violence.

Ken, who retired after the 1949-50 season before the on-ice war with Gardner continued any further, said with a chuckle, "If I'd have played one more year I would have had one more go (at Gardiner) I think because $1000 is not that much money."

That old saying that time heals all wounds doesn't apply here as Reardon and Gardner would remain enemies for their entire lives.

Ironically, November of 1949 was also when Reardon and teammate Leo Gravelle were arrested and put in jail for a few hours in Chicago after another wild melee. Fans had claimed that Leo and Ken had attacked them with their "deadly sticks" and one of the fans even needed seven stitches after Ken supposedly slashed him in the head with his stick. Reardon and Gravelle faced charges of assault with a deadly weapon and it was all over the news across North America. Fortunately, all charges were cleared very quickly and the pair could switch their full focus back to hockey.

Ken ended up retiring from hockey when he was just 29 years old, which is no doubt a testament to the rugged style of play he endorsed. Ken said that his body could no longer withstand his violent style of game, but that his heart and mind would never let him tone down his game. He retired with 26 goals and 122 points in 341 NHL games over seven seasons in a Montreal Canadiens uniform. Among the defencemen of his time, he ranked second in points over his seven NHL seasons. Ken was also a First Team All-Star twice (1947, 1950) and was a Second Team All-Star (1946, 1948, 1949) on three occasions.

After his retirement, Ken stayed in the Canadiens organization and was their Director of Public Relations until 1956 when he became the assistant and right-hand man to Canadiens general manager Frank Selke. Reardon led the team's scouting system in western Canada for years and helped the Habs find plenty of players that eventually suited up for the Canadiens.

Reardon was also instrumental in the Canadiens decision to hire Toe Blake at the beginning of the 1955-56 season. In Dick Irvin Jr's book, *The Habs*, Reardon recalled how the coaching decision was made.

"Frank Selke didn't want to bring Toe Blake back. He never wanted Toe as coach. He said he did, but he didn't. Selke wanted to bring in Joe Primeau. The French press wanted Roger Leger. My father-in-law (Senator Donat Raymond, the team's owner) wanted Billy Reay. And I held out for Toe Blake.

"When Blake was coaching in the Quebec Senior League, he would go the league meetings and cause Selke untold grief. That's why he never wanted him as coach.

"So, I said, 'If he gives you that much trouble working against you, imagine how it would be with him working for you.'"

Selke finally relented and history was made since Toe Blake would go on to coach the Canadiens to eight Stanley Cup championships, including five in a row from the 1956 through 1960.

Eventually, Ken was named the team's vice president and he held the position until 1965. In 1964 when Selke retired as the club's general manager, Reardon was one of the final two candidates to fill the job along with Sam Pollock. Although the Habs ended up going with Pollock, Ken never felt any bitterness towards him.

"Sam Pollock is the most intelligent man I've ever met," recalled Reardon, "not just in hockey, but in life."

In addition to his 1946 Stanley Cup as a player, Ken also won Cups in 1956 as assistant manager, and then in 1957, 1958, 1959 and 1960 as vice president. Reardon's stellar career as a player was honoured in 1966 with his induction into the Hockey Hall of Fame.

In his later years, Reardon stayed out of the spotlight but remained best friends with hockey legends such as Bobby Orr and Maurice Richard. He followed the game all through his life, but claimed that the invention of the jet airplane was the worst thing to happen to hockey. In his day, players would travel by train and they did everything together. In the modern game, there is too much time apart and he felt that teams aren't as close-knit as they once were.

Ken Reardon passed away in Saint-Saveur, Quebec at the age of 86 on March 15, 2008 after a lengthy battle with Alzheimer's.

The final word on Reardon comes from Jacques Plante's biographer Todd Denault, who wrote, "Ken Reardon was not the most gifted or talented player to ever play for the Montreal Canadiens. But his level of determination and toughness was rarely if ever matched by any future members of the team. His battling style and willingness to play all out, regardless of injury or the opponent endeared him to Canadiens fans."

20
RON HEXTALL

MANITOBA HOCKEY HALL OF FAME

Not many NHL players can say that they were best at their position from the moment they stepped into the league. Ron Hextall can. He came into the league in 1986-87 and was elite right from day one. He had one of the greatest rookie seasons a goalie could have, winning the Vezina Trophy and Conn Smythe. It was an unbelievable run that ended in game seven of the Stanley Cup finals to the high-flying Edmonton Oilers. Although injuries later hampered his career, Hextall will always be regarded as one of the top netminders of his time.

You could definitely make the argument that Hextall revolutionized the game. One of the great puckhandlers for a goalie, Ron acted as a third defenceman for his team in that he often become a lot more involved with the play than just stopping pucks. Hexy obviously wasn't the first goalie to handle the puck, but he was so good at it, and at shooting the puck that opposing teams couldn't dump and chase against the Flyers because Ron would roam behind the net to stop the puck and then lift it over everybody into the neutral zone. He even scored a goal while firing the puck out of his zone on two occasions!

That's just one side of Ron's game, however. Most hockey fans know Hextall best for his wild antics in the crease. New York Islanders great Billy Smith was tame compared to Hexy, who was considered by most to be just flat-out crazy. He would come out behind the net and along the boards, hitting opposing players at will. Try to imagine a goalie in today's NHL doing that.

Hextall might be the one and only goalie in NHL history to be the policeman on his team, most notably when he jumped Chris Chelios and then slashed Kent Nilsson in the Cup finals. For a long time, he was the biggest goon in hockey, but at the same time this terrific, athletic goaltender who stopped barrage after barrage of shots and often carried his Flyers teams to victories over teams that were thought to have been superior to them.

Ron even earned high praise from the greatest scorer the game has ever seen. "Hextall is probably the best goaltender I've ever played against in the NHL," said Wayne Gretzky. "Just when you think you'll bombard him, he comes up with the big saves. We always seem to get a 2-0 lead, then he tightens up, plays really well and doesn't give us anything."

Ron Hextall was born on May 3, 1964 in Brandon. Coming from the legendary Hextall family that started with his grandfather Bryan Hextall, a Hall of Fame forward of the New York Rangers in 1940. Bryan's sons Dennis and Bryan Jr. also played over ten seasons in the NHL. Ron is the son of Bryan Jr and became the first grandson of a former player to play in the NHL.

"The thing I'll always remember," Ron said, "is visiting the Hall of Fame and seeing my grandfather's name on the Stanley Cup. I thought, 'Wow.' My dream is that one day my name will be on there, too."

Because his dad played in the NHL, Ron would start each school year in Brandon, but then in October he'd move to a school where his dad was playing hockey and stay until the season was over. He'd then come back and split his summers in Brandon and Poplar Point, where his grandpa Bryan lived.

Goaltending seemed like a natural fit for Ron early on in life. "I was real young and my mom said I used to throw a sock up the stairs when I was two or three years old and catch it when it came down," recalled Ron, "so there was something wired in there from a young age."

"When I played in Vancouver in 1968, all the neighbourhood kids would be playing street hockey when I came home from practice," Bryan recalled, "and the kid in goal was always Ron. He was only four. It was the funniest looking sight."

The younger Hextall would go to his dad's NHL games on a nightly basis and simply watch the two goalies the whole time. Ron first played organized hockey at the age of eight while living in Pittsburgh. His dad, who played for the Penguins at the time, wanted him to start out at defence in peewee hockey and learn how to skate before trying the goaltender's position. In fact, Ron's world-class puckhandling skills might have very well come from his father's advice. "When he was going to hockey schools, I encouraged him to play out," Bryan said. "He was a big, aggressive kid so I advised him to play defence. I told him improving his skating and puck handling wouldn't do him any harm as a goaltender. But the next day, he'd be back playing goal."

"I played forward for the first half of the year," Ron said. "Then one day our goalie, who was the coach's son, got sick. I remember Mom taking my brother (Rod) and me to the rink. We were behind the coach's car, and I could see that his son wasn't in the car."

Ron took to the net and stayed there ever since.

He was eight years old as well when he watched the dramatic 1972 Summit Series between Canada and the Soviet Union at the height of the Cold War. It's one of the all-time moments in Canadian hockey history since the series was ultimately won on a late goal by Paul Henderson in the final game. For most Canadians, it had a lasting impact and for Ron it was no different. "I remember sitting in a classroom watching a game thinking that I was going to die if Canada didn't win," Hextall said. "That's pretty extreme thoughts for a young fellow and I guess silly on one hand. But it just felt that important to me that Canada won that series."

Growing up as the son of an NHLer gave Ron a big advantage over most kids his age as he got to learn the trade of goaltending from many of the game's greats. He would watch his dad's team practice and then after it was over, Ron always wanted to stay at the arena and watch the other team (their goalies) practice. He was particularly fond of Rangers netminder Eddie Giacomin.

"We'd hang around his practices in Detroit and Minnesota," Ron recalled, "and we'd skate when the team was finished. Some players would stay and work with us."

Ron got his first mask from Jim Rutherford when Bryan played in Pittsburgh. Dan Bouchard offered advice on playing the angles when he was Bryan's teammate in Atlanta. Glen Sather would fire pucks at a nine-year-old Ron Hextall. After practice, he would go up and talk to the opposing goalies and pick their brain about goaltending. From an outsider's point-of-view it seems like the perfect upbringing for a young netminder.

When Bryan Jr. retired from the NHL in 1976 the family was able to stay in Brandon full-time and as for Ron, he was finally able to experience playing minor hockey in Canada. "I grew up in Brandon but my dad was playing until, I think it was eleven was my last year that we travelled down to the States," Ron said. "I think my first year of hockey in Brandon I was twelve years old. It was important at that age to get that level of hockey. Some of the places I played in, like Atlanta at the time, it was not great hockey. It was time to ramp up the level and I think getting back to Brandon and playing, it was great hockey now and great hockey then. It was a level I hadn't played at yet so it was important."

Just a few years later, at age fifteen, Ron helped lead his midget Brandon AAA team to the provincial championship. The next year he joined the Melville Millionaires of the SJHL and stood in goal night after night for the worst team in the league. One game against the Prince Albert Raiders he faced an astronomical 105 shots and made 84 saves in a 21-2 loss. Ron was praised by local newspapers after the game who called it one of the most brilliant goaltending performances in junior hockey history and had any other goalie in Canada been in net for Melville that night the score would have been at least double what it was.

Ron returned to Brandon the following season and suited up for his hometown Brandon Wheat Kings of the WHL. It was a big moment in his young career as the Wheat Kings were huge hockey heroes to him growing up. Ron was at every home game in 1979 selling programs when the Wheat Kings got all the way to the Memorial Cup finals.

"For me it was an absolute dream come true," Hextall recalled. "Watching the big teams, (Bill) Derlago, (Ray) Allison, (Laurie) Boschman, (Brian) Propp, the McCrimmon boys (Brad and Kelly), I always wanted to play in the NHL but I was more focused on, at that point, playing for the Wheat Kings just because I knew it came first. That was a huge deal for me."

Once again, Ron didn't play for the strongest team, but he battled hard and still managed to put up decent numbers in each of his three seasons as a Wheat King. Hextall knew that he was on the cusp of being a pro hockey player. It was his dream and he was soon to make it a reality. "I'd like to say that I had other interests besides hockey, but I can't," Ron said. "I put it (hockey) in front of school, in front of everything, and when I was sixteen, I really felt like I had a shot at making a career of it."

Brandon is where Hexy's repressed anger really came out. He would break his sticks over the crossbar like there was no tomorrow and had an out-of-control temper. During one season in Brandon he accumulated a grand total of 117 penalty minutes in a 46-game season. That year, Ron was suspended eight games for instigating a free-for-all against the Regina Pats when he struck their goalie with his stick and punched out another player with his blocker.

Despite his antics, Flyers scout Gerry Melnyk became very interested in getting his team to draft Ron. Other NHL scouts thought that Ron should be in a loony bin somewhere, but to Melnyk, Ron's demeanor was music to his ears and he thought that with Ron's certain attributes he would fit right into the Philadelphia Flyers organization.

Ron was the 119th overall (6th round) draft pick of the Philadelphia Flyers at the 1982 NHL Entry Draft. At the time Philadelphia was set in the goaltending department with arguably the game's best puck-stopper in Pelle Lindbergh. That all quickly changed on November 11, 1985 when Pelle died suddenly and tragically in a car accident, crashing his Porsche into an elementary school wall in the middle of the night while intoxicated. Instead of immediately calling up Hextall to fill the void, the Flyers decided to wait and let him continue to grow as a professional in the minors with the AHL's Hershey Bears.

Hextall always had a bad reputation in juniors and it would carry over to his early pro days in the minor leagues. His junior team in Brandon was poor at best and his team afforded little protection, so he fought back. He swung his stick freely at opposing players and it ended up hurting the team more than helping it. When he turned pro, he tried his best to calm it down a bit as referees knew about his junior exploits and gave him penalties for the lightest of incidents. Hextall calmed it down from his standards, but to an outsider he still would have been seen as the craziest goaltender of all time.

Ron also received advice from his Hockey Hall of Fame grandfather Bryan Hextall Sr. on a regular basis. Ron always listened to his grandpa and carried his guidance into the pro hockey ranks when Bryan Sr. passed away in 1984. "He told me to quit taking dumb penalties," Ron recalled. "He told me to leave the fighting to the other players. I had a pretty short temper back then."

Ron wasn't really expected to make the Flyers team out of the 1986-87 training camp since he was up against last year's Vezina Trophy finalist Bob Froese and veteran Chico Resch. From his performance in the team's preseason, Flyers coach Mike Keenan gave the reigns to Hexy on opening night and he promptly made his coach look like a genius when he backstopped his team to a win past the powerhouse Edmonton Oilers 2-1.

To Hextall, playing in the NHL with the Flyers was something that he certainly never dreamed of. He of course dreamed of playing in the NHL, just not for Philadelphia. You see, Ron hated the Flyers growing up because they always beat up on his dad's teams. The Broad Street Bullies were enemy number one to Ron, but it's sure funny how that all changes in a hurry once you put on that team sweater and play your first NHL game with them.

Hextall became a fan favourite in Philadelphia instantly and his play quickly backed him up as the best goalie in hockey. His puckhandling skills were unprecedented and he stopped the game's top shooters with ease on a nightly basis. When all was said and done, Hexy won the Vezina Trophy as the league's top goaltender and was runner-up for the Calder Memorial Trophy to Luc Robitaille. In the playoffs, Ron was world-class, backstopping the Flyers to the Prince of Wales Trophy and a date with the Edmonton Oilers in the 1987 Stanley Cup finals. It went down to Game 7, and although the Flyers lost, Ron was awarded the Conn Smythe Trophy for most valuable player in the playoffs. He's one of five players ever to win the award despite losing the Cup finals.

The next season Ron became the first goaltender to shoot at goal and score in the NHL when he potted an empty net goal in the final minutes of a regular season game against the Boston Bruins. He scored a goal a few years later in the playoffs versus Washington, becoming the first goalie to score in the playoffs. His two career NHL goals rank him number one all-time amongst netminders.

Unfortunately for Hextall, he was never able to get back to the level he was at in his rookie season. He was constantly hampered by a nagging hamstring and groin injury that never fully healed. It hurt his game and forced him to change goaltending styles to keep himself in the league. Hextall was still a solid goalie for many years, but injuries likely kept him out of the Hockey Hall of Fame.

In the 1992 offseason, Hextall was one of the pieces involved in the major trade that brought Eric Lindros to the Flyers from Quebec. Ron went to the Nordiques and had a good season by all accounts there before being traded the following offseason to the New York Islanders. After one season on Long Island, Ron was once again on the move, but this time to a familiar place.

Hextall returned to the Philadelphia Flyers and played out the rest of his career in the city of brotherly love. He retired in September of 1999 after thirteen NHL seasons and finished with a record of 296-214-69 with 23 shutouts. Although he had a couple of other deep playoff runs over the course of his career, the year 1987 will always be the highlight of his career. Despite being on the losing end of game seven in the Stanley Cup finals, Ron won the Conn Smythe Trophy as playoff MVP, and later the Vezina Trophy. Hexy was named to the NHL's First Team All-Star that season and was on Team Canada when they won the 1987 Canada Cup. He also played in the 1988 All-Star Game.

Hextall joined the Flyers' front office in 1999 as a pro scout and was later promoted to Director of Pro Player Personnel in 2002. Hextall later served as the Assistant General Manager of the Los Angeles Kings and won a Stanley Cup with them in 2012. Just a few years later in 2014, he was named General Manager of the Philadelphia Flyers, the position he currently holds, and is doing everything in his power to bring a Stanley Cup back to Philadelphia.

Through it all Ron's never forgotten his Manitoba roots. He still tries to get back to his hometown once during every summer. His parents have a cabin near Clear Lake and his wife still has family in the Minnedosa area.

CHICO RESCH SAYS

One of my all time favourite goalie partners was Ronnie Hextall. I got to know him very well during his rookie year where he won the Conn Smythe. I was his backup that year. Ron's always been a terrific Manitoba ambassador. He's still got land north of Brandon and goes back in the summer I believe.

I loved Ronnie's attitude, he was so competitive. He was a Gordie Lane in goalie pads. You didn't mess with him, ever. With the history of his dad, uncle, and grandfather in the NHL, Ronnie felt the weight of being the consummate player, the goalie of his era, and part of that was standing up for his team. Stopping the puck was always his first priority, but a close second was that if someone messed with a teammate, he was on it.

I remember one time he went out a long ways to give Chris Chelios quite the crosscheck. Chelios had given a cheap shot to Brian Propp so Hextall went after Chelios. I think sometimes Ronnie thought it was hard for a forward to get back at someone who cheapshotted a teammate, but as a goalie, he could get away with it. And he did.

He got a lot of criticism and that was when the game was changing too. I remember Ronnie saying to me, "I'm not going to do it anymore. If the winds are changing and now I get criticized for standing up for my teammates." So, I think he mellowed out a little bit. He would have been a Hall of Fame goalie and one of the all-time greats had it not been for a chronic groin injury that never really healed, so because of that he had to change his style a little bit.

Goalies now are very predictable, they come out and drop in a butterfly, move on their pads. I'm not knocking it, but with Hexy, oh my goodness he was exciting to watch. He was in the last group of stand-up goalies who were not only innovative, but was very good with his stick, moving the puck up and even scoring goals on a couple of occasions.

Martin Brodeur said that he would get up really early to watch the sports highlights and watch Hextall moving the puck up. So, Marty was motivated by Ronnie's puck moving. Hexy was the last of the goalies that incorporated every aspect of goaltending up until the butterfly era. Some of the saves he made with his legs looked like Terry Sawchuk a little bit. He had a very good glove and that was exciting to people watching him make a glove save.

That rookie year he had when we lost to Edmonton in Game 7 of the Stanley Cup Final, but he was still awarded the Conn Smythe for his efforts. There's only two guys I think that played at the highest level of goaltending that was astounding to me as a goalie. It was Ronnie and then Timmy Thomas when Boston won the Cup in 2011. Those two displayed the best string of playoff goaltending in my 45 years of watching the National Hockey League.

19
BUTCH GORING

Butch Goring was probably the first Manitoba hockey legend that I became aware of in life. Being a St. Vital boy, I played a lot of minor hockey at Glenwood Community Centre and I recall it as being one of the coldest indoor arenas I've ever played in. I can't even begin to imagine how cold my parents must have been sitting down in the arena and watching one of my 8am games. In the lobby of the arena I remember there being a Butch Goring jersey, hung up and framed on the wall. Being six years old, I had no clue who this person was, but my dad filled me in that this Goring person won four Stanley Cups with the New York Islanders in the 1980's and grew up playing at Glenwood. So, every time I played at Glenwood after that I thought it was the coolest thing that I was playing in the same arena that Goring started at.

When you think of the Lady Byng Trophy, Butch Goring should be the first thing that pops into your head. Tough and hard-working but at the same time also clean and fair, Butch only had 102 penalty minutes over a 1107 game NHL career, which is just insane to put it simply.

"What I like about Butch the best is that he's a hockey player," said former Islanders general manager Bill Torrey. "He's a real throwback, a guy who loves to play, who's happy in his career, and to whom hockey is very, very important. He's the classic professional who works his butt off and knows what he is."

Robert "Butch" Goring was born on October 22, 1949 in Winnipeg. Growing up in St. Boniface, he started playing hockey at a young age on the outdoor rinks of the local community clubs Winakwa, Glenwood and Glenlee.

"It was common to freeze your hands, feet, ears and nose," recalled Goring. "We had no option but to brave the weather. It's not like there were any indoor rinks around."

Butch was a hockey prodigy from an early age. Just by going through the *Winnipeg Free Press* archives, you can see Butch's photo in their sports section plenty of times from the time he was a mere ten years old. In the minor hockey ranks he put up Gretzky-like numbers, scoring 150 goals in a 40-game season as a twelve-year-old with the Glenwood Bears. In one particular game that year he scored 15 goals and 5 assists in a 21-1 blowout. "I'm not sure what I was doing when we scored that other goal," joked Goring. "I was robbed."

Although the NHL seemed extremely far away at the time, Butch just played the game that he loved and let the rest fall into place. "Growing up when I did there wasn't as much exposure to the National Hockey League as there is today," recalled Goring. "I was a big Gordie Howe fan and a huge supporter of the Detroit Red Wings so of course I had dreams of playing for them and winning a Stanley Cup. When I was nine or ten I would watch them on television or listen on the radio and I became very focussed on that possibility. But at the time I was just playing the game that I loved because it was a lot of fun."

It was when Butch was twelve years old that his dad bought him the famous Snaps brand helmet that he would go on to wear for the rest of his hockey career. He would wear one for home games and one for away games for the next twenty-five years.

"You know for myself in Winnipeg, it's always been about the minor hockey program. That's my fondest memories of hockey there in my hometown," recalled Goring. "Back in the 1960's they had a suburban city championship for eleven, twelve and thirteen years old in Winnipeg called 'Booster Night'. If you got to the final then you played at the Winnipeg Arena which was a big deal because not only did you get to play indoors, but you played in front of 10,000 people. I was lucky enough to get to play in that on three occasions and it was a great memory for me, a very exciting time in my early life, and it's something looking back on that I think they should bring back in Winnipeg."

Goring kept getting better and better every year and was playing as much hockey as humanly possible. As a sixteen- and seventeen-year-old, Butch was playing for the Winnipeg Rangers in the MJHL in addition to attending classes at Windsor Park Collegiate. When he was eighteen he headed to Quebec and played senior hockey for the Hull Nationals and also the Canadian Junior National Team. Butch then came back to Winnipeg and played in the MJHL playoffs for the Winnipeg Junior Jets and then joined the St. Boniface Mohawks for the Allan Cup playoffs.

Never playing enough junior hockey it seemed, Butch spent the next season with the Winnipeg Junior Jets and then joined the Dauphin Kings and later the Regina Pats in the Memorial Cup playdowns at the end of the season. During the offseason that followed, Goring was drafted by the Los Angeles Kings (5th round/51st overall) at the 1969 NHL Amateur Draft and suddenly his NHL dream looked like it was about to become a reality.

"Things have changed so dramatically now with the draft. I didn't even know I was drafted and I hadn't been paying any attention because there was no television coverage back then. I don't even remember how I found out because it was just a minor event. I spent a couple of months with Springfield in the AHL and got off to a terrific start there. Myself and a guy named Mike Corrigan led the team in scoring after about the first twenty games and the Kings weren't very good at the time so that helped give me the opportunity to get called up and make my NHL debut. Winnipeg was a pretty big city growing up in, but Los Angeles was huge! It was a little scary at first, but once you're in the building, hockey is hockey. So, I really enjoyed it and was excited about the opportunity of playing in the NHL."

Butch became a consistent two-way player for the Kings almost instantly. He was mentored in his rookie season by none-other than legendary defencemen Doug Harvey, then an assistant coach who taught him the finer points of goalmouth deflections among other key things.

After splitting the first couple of seasons with Los Angeles and in Springfield, the Kings' AHL affiliate where he won a Calder Cup in 1971, Goring became a full time NHLer in the 1971-72 season when he scored his first of eleven consecutive 20+ goal seasons. Included in that streak are four straight 30+ goal seasons.

He was also known for being one of the poorer dressers in the league, a fact confirmed by a robber. On a road trip with the Kings, a burglar sneaked into his hotel room and took everything that belonged to his roommate but left all of Goring's clothes hanging in the closet untouched.

What's surprising is the fact that Butch even had clothes hanging in a closet. Most of the time when he was away on road trips, he only brought with him the clothes he was wearing and a toothbrush.

Once called the worst-dressed player in pro hockey, a famous tale is told by broadcaster Bob Miller. According to Miller, Goring spilled spaghetti sauce on a white turtleneck sweater during a trip, and his teammates bet on whether he'd get it cleaned. When Goring came down to the hotel lobby the next day, he was wearing the same sweater and there was no sign of a stain. After his teammates commended him for his unexpected fastidiousness, Goring removed his jacket and turned around. The stain was still there, but Goring had turned the sweater around and was wearing it with the back to the front.

In 1977-78, Butch won both the Lady Byng Trophy as the NHL's most gentlemanly player and the Bill Masterton Memorial Trophy for perseverance and dedication to hockey. Unfortunately, during the time period that Butch played with the Los Angeles Kings, they were never a very successful team.

Montreal Canadiens defenceman Larry Robinson had a lot of battles with the Kings in the 1970's and said that, "Butch was a gentleman when he played the game. He could be tough. I could challenge him, but there could be a good trade-off. He was a good guy, too. It was a lot of fun to play against him."

Eventually after eleven seasons in a Kings uniform, Goring was given a chance to shine when Islanders general manager Bill Torrey made what is now considered one of the greatest deals ever at the 1980 trade deadline when he shipped Billy Harris and Dave Lewis to Los Angeles in exchange for Goring.

"I was actually supposed to get traded to Denver back in training camp that year and Barry Beck's name had come up since the Kings were looking for a defenceman and he was available," recalled Goring. "There were rumours about it but it didn't happen so everything got real quiet and I never gave it much thought. When I did get traded however, I was really angry because I was on the second year of a long-term contract and I had really made peace with myself that I may not win a Stanley Cup, but I'm going to play sixteen years with the Los Angeles Kings, which would have been great because I loved Los Angeles. So initially I was very angry, but then after the initial shock I sort of analyzed what was going on and realized I was going to a team that was very good and could win the Stanley Cup."

Butch Goring was the final piece of the puzzle that put the Islanders over the top. At that time, the belief was that the team needed both a second line center to take the pressure off the top line and a shot of confidence for a play-off run. When Goring first came to Long Island his teammates later recalled how much they gained from Goring's sharing with them how good the rest of the league thought they were.

With Goring's insertion into the lineup the New York Islanders went on to win four consecutive Stanley Cup championships between 1980 and 1983 and are the last true dynasty that the hockey world has seen. They were very close to winning a fifth straight Cup if it wasn't for those pesky Edmonton Oilers that beat them in the 1984 Stanley Cup Finals in five games. Still though, the Islanders' nineteen consecutive playoff series wins between 1980 and 1984 is a feat that remains unparalleled in the history of professional sports.

Although Butch was playing behind the elite scorers in Mike Bossy and Bryan Trottier, his role on the team was extremely vital to the Isles' success that they had. This can be confirmed when he was awarded the 1981 Conn Smythe Trophy as Playoff MVP despite not being close to leading in playoff points. His contributions on the ice other than just offence were highly valued on the dynasty team. His Isles teammates Mike Bossy and Denis Potvin both have said that the likely originator of the playoff beard that is now common with every playoff team today was none other than Goring.

"It was an incredibly talented hockey team with so many weapons and so many styles of play that it was fun and was really easy, not to brag in any way shape or form," said Butch. "The first Stanley Cup took a lot out of the hockey club because it was a battle to win every series, but after that we really did just breeze. We had a lot of confidence and knew what we had to do to win so we really took it to the Edmonton Oilers who proved how good of a team they were with all of their Cups after us. It was an amazing time in my life and it all went by really quickly."

Midway through the 1984-85 season, Butch was claimed off waivers by the Boston Bruins and played his final NHL season. At the time of his retirement he was the last player that was still around that had played in the 1960's. After sixteen NHL seasons, Goring retired with 375 goals and 513 assists for 888 points over a 1109 career games.

In May of 1985, just five months after picking him up on waivers, the Bruins named Butch Goring their sixteenth head coach in team history. General Manager Harry Sinden had held the post during the previous season after firing Gerry Cheevers as coach. Sinden wanted to promote from within the team and liked what he saw in Goring.

Butch ended up coaching the Bruins for a year and a half before moving on and coaching all across North America and Europe in the AHL, IHL and German League over the next twenty years. He even returned to the NHL and had a two-year stint as the Islanders' head coach around the turn of the millennium.

"I loved the game, I loved the challenge, and when it was time for me not to play anymore, I had an opportunity to get right into coaching with the Boston Bruins. I always had this passion and being a student of the game, the next step after being a player in professional hockey is being the coach. I didn't have the success in the NHL as a coach that I would have liked to have, but I was successful at the coaching level in the IHL and over in Germany so it was fun, I enjoyed it and coached for over twenty years so I certainly have no regrets."

Butch later got into broadcasting and is now the full-time New York Islanders television analyst for the MSG Networks. Despite living in New York for most of the year, he still comes back to Manitoba every summer for at least a few weeks as he has a cabin up at Dauphin Lake.

Through all the highlights of Butch's career, he has a couple that still to this day stand out for him a great deal: "Well I think I had two moments that stand out for me. Certainly, winning the Stanley Cups—you're hoping to win one in your career and I won four so that was the icing on the cake for my career. As an individual though I think scoring a game six overtime goal against the Boston Bruins in the 1976 playoffs and being carried off the ice in Los Angeles was a huge and very memorable moment for me. And then of course winning the Conn Smythe Trophy which was something I never dreamed of or thought at any point in time was possible with all the good players we had on our team like Billy Smith, Trottier, Potvin and Bossy who are all Hall of Famers. For me to have that kind of playoff and win a major award like that was really special to me so those two moments really stand out in my career."

The Hall of Fame debate is certainly one that comes up for Butch a lot with hockey folks. You really have to think that if his Islanders teammate Clark Gillies got in with a less impressive resume, then Butch should certainly be a lock. That's not the case however, as the selection committee has other ideas and Goring still remains on the outside looking in.

A lot of fellow Top 50 Manitoba players that I talked to for this book weighed in and all had a lot of positive things to say about Butch's career in the National Hockey League and all felt that he should one day be enshrined in the Hall of Fame.

"Butch Goring's such a great player. He won four Stanley Cups and played a very long career," said James Patrick. "He was a fantastic two-way player and was one of the best penalty killers for probably fifteen years in the NHL. I certainly believe he should be mentioned in that breath as one of the best Manitoba players of all-time."

Gord Lane added that, "He should be in the Hockey Hall of Fame. Simple as that."

"The first time I ever met Butch was at a Windsor Park high school reunion a few years back in 2011," recalled Mike Ridley, "but I knew of him from the time I was in high school and before that even everyone knew of him at Winakwa Community Club. My teachers at Windsor Park would mention how they taught Butch Goring so that was a pretty cool thing growing up and having someone before me from my area make the NHL."

Goring relishes the idea of one day being inducted into the Hockey Hall of Fame and has certainly plead his case over the years, but if it's not to be, he promises not to be too disappointed.

"With the Hall of Fame, you don't know what the committee is thinking and what credentials you need to have. There's no criteria. It's not that you have to do this or that so it's a very hard thing to try to understand why or why not you should be inducted," said Butch. "The people that are in are very fortunate individuals, and those like me who'd love the opportunity, we have to wait and see what happens. I'm not losing any sleep over it though. If I never get in, I know what kind of career I had and I don't need to be in the Hall of Fame to make it any better."

CHICO RESCH SAYS

I think his name lives up to his personality. He was a pretty unique, diverse individual when you think about it. You think about his looks on the ice with that old helmet with his blonde hair coming out the back. He wasn't very big, but he was really creative on the ice and a real top competitor. He was a much smarter person than people realize because hockey players didn't go to college back then so they didn't get a chance to get a title that people think, "Oh, a college degree makes them smart." Well Butchie was very bright and intuitive. He figured things out well which made him such a smart centreman. The other thing with Butch is that he was centreman that wingers would love to play with because not only could he beat defenders individually, he wasn't a puck hog. He knew how and when to dish it off, and how to play as a three-man or five-man unit.

As a player, he was much better than he got credit for—especially playing for Los Angeles, who never did much when he was there so he didn't get the attention that he deserved. But he was the one that propelled us to being the team that was just about impossible to stop once we found out how to win. He was underrated but I'd say that Trottier and Goring were right up there with Gretzky and Messier as the top 1-2 punch at the centre position. Butchie was much more than people realize.

18
CHING JOHNSON

C hing Johnson is regarded as one of the hardest bodycheckers to ever play the game. In his time, he was up there with Eddie Shore as the top defenceman in hockey. He was built so much like a brute at 5'11" and 210 pounds, that when Ching connected with an unsuspecting target, it was like being hit by a train. Ching wasn't a dirty player like so many were at his time, he was just a terrifically hard hitter.

Possibly the best defensive-defenceman the game had seen up until that point, the *Hockey Hall of Fame* website writes that, "It was his physical play and his charismatic leadership that made Ching one of the most valuable rearguards of his time."

Johnson was a fierce competitor who ignored the pain and didn't let injuries stand in his way. One of the most colourful players of his generation, he always had a wide grin on his face whenever he went to crunch an opposing player to the ice. More significantly, he perfected the technique of nullifying the opposition by clutching and grabbing them as discreetly as possible—a pragmatic defensive strategy for the wily but slow-footed rearguard.

Fellow Hockey Hall of Famer and Rangers teammate Bill Cook once claimed that Johnson was the greatest hockey player he'd ever seen.

"Prematurely bald, Ching was the kindest, most gentle man you would ever meet off the ice," wrote long-time *Winnipeg Tribune* writer Vince Leah.

MANITOBA HOCKEY HALL OF FAME

"He had a marvelous smile that captivated people. He had time for everybody, young and old. But when he clobbered incoming attackers, he would turn an impish grin as if he had snatched the last cookie out of the jar."

A two-time Stanley Cup winner (1928 and 1933), Johnson was a fan favourite in the Big Apple, but also a late bloomer of sorts as he didn't play his first NHL game until he was nearly 28 years old.

"Ching was not what you'd call a 'picture player'—he wasn't a beautiful passer or stickhandler—but he was one of the hardest hitters in the history of the game, a great leader, and an absolute bulwark on defence," recalled former teammate Babe Pratt. "He'd hit a man and grin from ear to ear and he'd be that way in the dressing room, too. There was never a time when Ching didn't have itching powder in his pocket, ready for a practical joke. One time he gave Lester Patrick a hotfoot and Lester's shoe caught on fire; Lester was half-asleep at the time and after they put out the fire he couldn't walk for a week. It took a lot of nerve to do that to Lester Patrick."

Ivan "Ching" Johnson was born in Winnipeg on December 7th, 1897. Growing up in a house at 287 Stradbrook Avenue in Fort Rouge, Ivan played hockey recreationally with his brother Ade (Adrian) from a young age, but throughout his youth he was more focused on other sports like lacrosse and football as he excelled at both.

When Ching was just eighteen years old he joined the Canadian Expeditionary Force for World War I and fought for three years in the trenches of France as part of a mortar outfit. Johnson returned to Winnipeg after the war and worked for an electric light company, in addition to attending classes at the University of Manitoba. It wasn't until Johnson got home from the war that he really decided to get into hockey. He played his first competitive hockey game when he joined the Winnipeg Monarchs senior team in 1919 as a twenty-one-year-old.

In the early 1920's, the town of Eveleth on the Mesabi Iron Range of northern Minnesota sought to improve hockey in the area by bringing in players and giving them mining jobs. Ching and his brother Ade joined the Eveleth Reds team in 1920 and spent three seasons playing amateur hockey on the Iron Range. In 1923, the brothers were picked up by the Minneapolis Millers of the same league and they played a few more seasons of amateur hockey.

It was while playing in the minors where Ching earned his nickname. First, he was known as "Ivan the Terrible," but fans quickly took notice of the fact that when he smiled, his eyes made him look Asian despite him being of Irish descent. Fans would shout "Ching-a-ling Chinaman!" and that eventually got shortened to just "Ching." The nickname would stick for the rest of his life.

Ching caught his big break in 1926 when he was first discovered by Conn Smythe during a scouting trip to Minnesota. Smythe had been hired to recruit a team for the expansion New York Rangers team and was supposed to manage the club for their inaugural season. He really liked both Ching and his defence partner Taffy Abel, but found Johnson to be a tougher negotiator than anything he'd ever seen before.

"I must have reached an agreement with Ching forty times," recalled Smythe. "Each time, when I gave him my pen to sign, he'd say, 'I just want to phone my wife.' Then there'd be a hitch, and he wouldn't sign. In my final meeting with him, I said before we started, 'Ching, I want you to promise that if we make a deal, you will sign, and then you'll phone your wife.' He promised. We made a deal. He said, 'I've got to phone my wife,' I said, 'You promised!' He said, 'Okay, Connie,' and signed."

Johnson was apparently adamant on signing a three-year deal because he thought it would be the only one he would ever get. He had no idea how well he would fare joining the fray of what is the National Hockey League. Conn Smythe never got to enjoy Johnson on his club as he was dumped before the season even started by the Rangers owner and replaced with Lester Patrick.

Ching made his NHL debut just before his 28th birthday. A late bloomer some would say, but for Ching, he came in at the right time and was a force in the National Hockey League from game one. He quickly became the team's leader, both for his enthusiasm on the ice and his take-charge, rah-rah manner in the dressing room.

A fan-favourite from his booming body-checks and physical play, sports writer Al Laney of the old New York Herald-Tribune claimed that only Babe Ruth equaled Ching Johnson in winning the hearts of fans in New York City.

"Ching loved to deliver a good hoist early in a game because he knew his victim would probably retaliate, and Ching loved body contact," recalled Frank Boucher. "I remember once against the Maroons, Ching caught Hooley Smith with a terrific check right at the start of the game. Hooley's stick flew from his hands and disappeared above the rink lights. He was lifted clean off the ice, and seemed to stay suspended five or six feet above the surface for seconds before finally crashing down on his back. No one could accuse Hooley of lacking guts. From then on, whenever he got the puck, he drove straight for Ching, trying to out-match him, but every time Ching flattened poor Hooley.

Afterwards, grinning in the shower, Ching said he couldn't remember a game he'd enjoyed more."

Throwing his body at every player, of course, had its consequences. Throughout his career he spent over thirty weeks recovering in a hospital bed from his hockey injuries. A broken collarbone, damaged ribs, broken jaw, and a cut-open forehead was just a small portion of what he endured. In total, he had 27 broken bones and close to 400 stitches over the course of his career.

On one occasion while he was at the Montreal General Hospital recovering from a broken ankle, a fire broke out and he had to escape. Luckily, Ching had a visitor at the time (goaltender Lorne Chabot's brother) and with the help of orderlies, Ching was carried from his second-floor room down a fire escape, outside, and to a friend's nearby apartment. When Johnson returned after the fire ceased, a newspaper wrote that, "on the shoulders of his stalwart supporters, greeting the staff with a typical good-natured wave and an announcement that he had returned."

In his third year in the NHL, Johnson helped the New York Rangers win their first Stanley Cup in team history. He won a second Stanley Cup in 1933 and by that time he was widely regarded as one of, if not the best defencemen in hockey. Without Ching manning the blueline, it's very unlikely that the Rangers would have won either Stanley Cup.

While playing in New York, Ching had a place in Yonkers that his kids grew up in. His son Jim remembered that during the season his dad would have these grotesquely swollen knuckles all winter long and usually a broken bone to go with it. Jim recalled that, "One time he had broken his jaw and I had broken my jaw at the same time playing college basketball at Marshall University. Both of us had our jaws wired shut and I remember sitting across the table from him, both of us dribbling baby food down our shirts."

Johnson finished as the 1932 Hart Trophy (NHL's Most Valuable Player) runner-up by one vote to Howie Morenz. He finished his NHL career after the 1937-38 season with the New York Americans and "retired" at age 41. He continued as a player-coach until he was 46 for minor-league teams based in Minneapolis, Marquette, Washington and Hollywood.

In twelve NHL seasons, Johnson finished with 86 points in 436 games. His two Stanley Cups in 1928 and 1933 were his best accomplishments, but he was also an NHL First Team All-Star three times (1928, 1932, 1933) and a Second Team All-Star on two occasions (1931, 1934). He played in the inaugural 1934 All-Star Game in benefit of Ace Bailey and was voted as the most outstanding player on both Rangers Cup teams that he was a part of. Ching also led the Rangers in penalty minutes in eight of the eleven seasons he played with them.

After he retired, he coached in the minors and then later officiated. During one Eastern Hockey League game in Washington D.C. that he was officiating, fans saw the hard-hitting Ching Johnson one more time. "I was calling this game," recalled Ching, "when some young forward broke out and raced solo against the goalie. Instinctively, I took this player down with a jarring body check. Following the game, I apologized to his team. I don't know what made me do it, but I did it. I guess it was just the old defenceman's instinct."

After his stint in Washington, Ching decided to move to California, where promoters were trying to get hockey started in The Golden State. One day he was spotted skating on a local rink in Hollywood and was asked to play for their minor league team. Ching was on a championship team in 1944 at the age of 46 when the Hollywood Wolves won the league and national title.

After he finally left the game of hockey for good after putting in his twenty-five years, he became a general contractor in the construction business in Washington D.C. and later ventured in the plumbing, heating and air conditioning business. He attended Washington Capitals games periodically when they came into the league in 1974 up until his death. Ching's passion for the game never died as he was still skating well into his seventies.

During his career Johnson always had great pleasure coming back to Winnipeg every year for the New York Rangers training camp at the old Amphitheatre since that's where his games were when he first started out in competitive hockey with the senior Winnipeg Monarchs. Ching never lived in Winnipeg after he made the NHL, but he still made a point in coming back home throughout his life to visit family and friends.

Ching's career was honoured in 1958 when he was inducted to the Hockey Hall of Fame.

In his later years, Johnson and his wife resided in Takoma Park, Maryland. He passed away in nearby Silver Spring on June 16, 1979 at the age of 81.

"He always wore a grin," recalled teammate Frank Boucher, "even when heaving some poor soul six feet in the air. He was one of those rare warm people who would break into a smile just saying hello or telling you the time."

17
RED DUTTON

Red Dutton's life consisted of hockey, war, and tragedy. A rugged, strong-skating defenceman with the all-around ability to do just about everything that was required in a hockey player of his time, Red played his entire ten-year NHL career with teams that aren't around anymore.

"I wasn't a good hockey player," once said Dutton, "but I was a good competitor." What Red was is an extremely smart player. He could pitch in on the scoresheet and was also very sturdy in his own end. He wasn't necessarily a dirty player, but he had no problem dealing out a big hit when it was needed to help his team.

"I never saw anyone who could flatten an enemy player or pinwheel him into the promenade seats as deftly as he could," wrote journalist Frank Graham.

Hockey aside, Dutton was one of the most fascinating people I came across when doing research for this book. The only NHL president that Manitoba has ever produced, it's surprising that Dutton has never been honoured with having an NHL award named after him or something along those lines. Hockey Hall of Fame player, coach, manager, league president, trustee of the Stanley Cup, there's not much that Red failed to do in hockey, except for his goal of winning a Stanley Cup.

Ultimate Hockey wrote, "An incident that best symbolizes Dutton's approach to hockey took place at the Forum in Montreal. The Maroons and

Canadiens had become archrivals, and they were lined up, on this night, preparing for the opening face-off. For some reason, the referee was unable to find a puck with which to launch the game. The official skated over to the timekeeper's table, but there was none there so he asked someone to obtain a puck from the dressing room. Dutton was so frustrated and so anxious to get the fray going that he shouted: 'Never mind the damn puck. Let's start the game!'"

Norman Alexander Dutton was born on July 23, 1897 in Russell, Manitoba. His father, Bill, was a very successful contractor who helped build Canada's transcontinental railway system. He operated one of the biggest railway and road construction companies in western Canada and had its headquarters in Russell and Winnipeg. As a kid, the younger Dutton would help his father at work, becoming very interested in building things, which would become such a big part of his later life.

Early on in his childhood, Dutton's birth names were ignored. A family friend stopped calling him Norman as the name had a negative connotation for her, so she started calling him "Mervyn," which soon stuck. His nickname "Red" came about because of his copper-coloured hair and he became known as Mervyn "Red" Dutton.

Dutton's family eventually moved to Winnipeg and resided at 47 Cornish Avenue, across the street from where the Misericordia Hospital presently sits. He started playing hockey with his friends and siblings on the nearby Assiniboine River, which was only a stone's throw from his family home.

Red attended St. John's College (now St. John's-Ravenscourt) as a youth and in 1914 he was captain of the St. John's hockey team. When he was seventeen he joined the Army for the First World War. It was during a time when thousands of under-aged kids in Canada went to the armories and to recruiting sergeants and presented themselves as soldiers. Red was one of them when he joined in May of 1915, two months before he turned eighteen—the minimum age to enlist. Just by simply looking at his forms, you can see that Red lied about his age, claiming to be born a year earlier, so that they would let him enlist.

After a few years overseas, Red was on the frontline battling with his comrades in the Princess Patricia's Canadian Light Infantry at Vimy Ridge on April 9th, 1917 (Easter Monday). Vimy Ridge in northeastern France is a commanding ridge, roughly seven kilometers long. The Germans captured it in October 1914 and fortified for two and a half years. Red and his fellow Canadian soldiers knew that they were likely walking into a deathtrap.

During the battle, Red caught pieces of shrapnel in his right leg, hip and buttocks. His leg was torn open and bleeding profusely. He was left lying for three days in a chalk pit with a dozen pieces of shrapnel in his body. He laid there and survived until it was safe for his fellow troops to pull him out. As he was being carried away to the hospital, Red could hear the medics discussing whether his right leg needed to be amputated.

Red sat up and screamed, "Doc, you can't do that to me!" He told the surgeon that he was a hockey player and that there would be no amputation.

"I felt that a young soldier who had played hockey all his life would find things rather empty in western Canada if the game were to have denied him when he was discharged from the service," Dutton later recalled.

The surgeons followed Red's orders. Instead of taking the leg, they merely removed what shrapnel was accessible to them. The doctor told him "Keep punching," which would go on to be a common catchphrase for the rest of his life. Dutton was discharged from the army in 1919 with pieces of shrapnel still in his leg. He thought that the best way to recover his body was to play a lot of commercial hockey. He joined about seven or eight leagues and played for hours every day, sometimes three or four games a night. Most nights he was at the local rink past midnight, but as he once wrote, "I was determined to be a hockey player again even if I died in the attempt."

Playing so much, he got pretty good at hockey very quickly and was rising through the local ranks as his leg continued to get better and stronger. He played senior hockey for the Winnipegs in 1919-20 and scored well over a point-a-game for the club. It's beyond remarkable that Red was even able to play hockey, let alone succeed, after having his leg literally torn apart.

The Dutton family moved after the war from 27 Cornish Avenue to a place on Wellington Crescent. When Red returned from the war, he started a contracting business, but the economic depression of 1920 forced it to shut down. He then started working for a packing plant in Winnipeg, but that, too, quickly went belly-up.

Red was soon to be penniless, but instead of going to his dad for financial help, he was met by the owner of a hockey team in Calgary who had seen him play and was interested in acquiring Dutton's services. Red signed for $2,500 and headed to Calgary, where he played for the Calgary Canadians of the Big Four Hockey League for the 1920-21 season. The next year he joined the WCHL's Calgary Tigers and that's where Red's pro hockey career really took off. He spent the next five years with the Tigers and was partnered up on defence with fellow Manitoba Top 50 player Herb Gardiner. The pair were called the wildest checking defencemen of their time by one newspaper.

In his five seasons with the Tigers, Red was named a First Team All-Star twice (1922, 1924). His time in Calgary being highlighted with a WCHL championship that led to an appearance in the 1924 Stanley Cup finals against the Montreal Canadiens.

Ultimate Hockey wrote that, "Red repeatedly tangled with the cold-eyed bad man of the NHL, Sprague Cleghorn. The Canadiens beat the westerners in two straight games, but eastern papers glowed with accounts of Dutton's fearless retaliation when Cleghorn jabbed him with his stick, elbowed his head, tripped him up and butt-ended him. Cleghorn is renowned to this day as one of the meanest men who ever played the game, overt and covert, but there was nothing surreptitious about Dutton's responses; he simply threw down his stick, tossed off his gloves and sailed into Cleghorn. Blood flowed like wine."

When the WCHL folded a few years later, Dutton declared himself a free agent. He first turned down a $3,500 offer from a Cleveland minor league team, and then later accepted six grand a year from the NHL's Montreal Maroons. Dutton joined the Maroons and spent the next four seasons rough-housing the NHL and potting the occasional goal.

Red's strong, tough play was noticed as soon as he stepped foot in the National Hockey League. "Dutton bashed all comers with fine disregard for reputations. He loved nothing better than to leave an opponent lying on the ice gasping for breath," wrote *Montreal Star* journalist Baz O'Meara.

Dutton's physicality was proven when he checked Chicago's Dick Irvin so hard that Dick suffered a fractured skull and was forced to retire from hockey and join the coaching ranks.

At one time, Red held the NHL record for penalties with 139 minutes in a forty-four game schedule—and was taking so many that Maroons coach Eddie Gerard benched him for three games. Dutton was shocked. He stormed into Gerard's office and demanded he be reinstated or be traded.

"If I put you back in the line-up, do you think you can control your temper?" Gerard asked.

"Temper," Dutton cried. "There's nothing wrong with my temper. It's my enthusiasm I can't control."

His physical play night after night took a toll on his body, but he still did everything in his power to play through the pain. During one game against the Rangers at Madison Square Garden, Red cracked three ribs and simply wrapped tape around his abdomen and returned to the ice. It was only when another hit jarred the bones loose that Dutton finally took a seat.

In 1931, Red was traded to the New York Americans in exchange for "The Big Train" himself, Lionel Conacher, who would later be named Canada's Athlete-of-the-Half-Century. Hockey maven Stan Fischler writes that, "Red was one of the leading badmen of the day, but the Americans were a hapless bunch of skaters with no real leadership to speak of."

Red soon earned a piece of the team when he bailed out owner and bootlegger Bill Dwyer for $20,000 worth of player salaries. He had some money from the summer months when he'd go off to build highways and railways all over western Canada. He formed a successful partnership with a businessman by the name of Reg Jennings and they did quite a few projects together. They built the Estevan, SK to Minton, SK and Reston, MB to Wolseley, SK rail lines among many others.

It wasn't until 1935-36, when Red became player-manager of the Americans, that they began to approach respectability. Dutton's leadership got the Amerks unto the playoffs, but he suffered a painful back injury and was forced to watch from the sidelines as the Toronto Maple Leafs bounced the Americans in the league semifinals.

Dutton retired from the sport in the offseason that followed and stayed on as the Americans coach and manager. Red finished with 96 points in 426 NHL games over ten seasons and added 871 penalty minutes.

He kept managing the team for the rest of the team's existence. The New York Americans played out of the Madison Square Garden, but Red thought that to help promote his team, they needed to separate themselves from the rival New York Rangers as much as possible. He renamed the team the Brooklyn Americans and urged his troops to live in Brooklyn. The team practised in Brooklyn and Red began planning a new arena to be built at Fort Greene Place in Brooklyn.

His colourful nature made him a favourite of fans and sportswriters. He was the first NHL manager to fly his team to games when he did so with the Americans in 1938. Unfortunately, the Americans were forced to disband in 1942 with the outbreak of World War II. They simply ran out of players as most had enlisted in the Canadian Army and were headed overseas.

In 1943, when NHL president Frank Calder died, Dutton agreed to take over on an interim basis with the condition that his Americans be reinstated when the war ended. During the war, Dutton's company, called the "Standard Gravel and Surfacing Company," built numerous airports across Canada as part of the British Commonwealth Air Training Plan. Heartbreak fell on Red during the war as two of his sons, Joseph and Alex, members of the Royal Canadian Air Force (RCAF), perished overseas within months of each other.

At the end of the 1945-46 season, after the war had ended, Dutton handed over the league presidency to Clarence Campbell at a board meeting. After handing over the reins, Dutton was betrayed. The NHL's board of governors reneged on their previous agreement with Dutton as they were under great pressure from the New York Rangers, who claimed the Amerks were in their franchise territory. Just like that the Brooklyn Americans team was no more.

Dutton was shocked and furious as he had already secured $7 million in financing for a new arena in Brooklyn.

"Gentlemen," Red said. "You can stick your franchise up your ass." And with that he left the room and declared that as long as he was alive, the Rangers would never win another Cup. The curse worked as the Rangers didn't win another Cup until 1994, seven years after Dutton passed away.

He stayed out of the sport for pretty much his whole life after that. The betrayal he suffered from the league's owners, and also the success of his several businesses are the main reasons why he stayed away. Despite this, he accepted a nomination in 1950 to become one of two Stanley Cup trustees, and held the position until his death.

Red was inducted into the Hockey Hall of Fame for his terrific career as a player in 1958. He got in despite never winning a Stanley Cup or putting up big offensive numbers, which just goes to show how valued he was as a defensive-defenceman. Red later served on the Hall of Fame's selection committee for fifteen years.

Dutton kept himself very busy in his post-hockey days as he owned and operated several successful businesses across Canada. He kept up his road construction, building the MacKenzie Highway from Grimshaw, AB to Yellowknife, NWT in the late 1940's. Later on, in 1960, he put up the McMahon Stadium (home of the Calgary Stampeders) and made a $1000 bet with George McMahon, the stadium's benefactor, that he could have the 19,000-seat facility completed in 100 days. He won the bet with three days to spare. On the 100th day was the Stampeders home opener and McMahon paid Dutton the bet right on the field with $1000 worth of pennies.

In the early 1960's, it was clear that the Canadian National Hockey Team was at a disadvantage to the Europeans as international hockey was played on a larger ice surface. With Russia becoming a powerhouse in the hockey world, something had to be done to help the National Team. Red was a major contributor to the building of the Dutton Memorial Arena at St. Johns-Ravenscourt school in suburban Fort Garry. The one and only arena in Manitoba that is built to international dimensions, the Dutton Memorial Arena was named after Red's sons Joseph and Alex. It became a place where Canada's National Team could train for events and also for St. John's-Ravenscourt teams and other local minor hockey teams to play.

Although he didn't attend any games, Red kept close tabs on the NHL in the years he was away from it through television and newspapers. "One of the reasons I stayed away was because it (hockey) was in my blood," said Dutton. "I couldn't sleep at night."

After turning the presidency over to Clarence Campbell in 1946, Red never entered an NHL arena until October 9, 1980. On that night, he dropped the puck at the Calgary Flames home debut. That same year he received the Order of Canada.

Red's last public appearance was prior to the opening game of the 1986 Stanley Cup finals when he dropped the puck in a ceremonial faceoff before Calgary and the Montreal Canadiens.

"One day while visiting his sister, he fell and broke his hip. He never really recovered from that," recalled Red's nephew, Bill Dutton, who just so happens to be a minority share owner of the Arizona Coyotes.

Mervyn "Red" Dutton passed away on March 15, 1987 at the age of 89.

In addition to his family's Dutton Memorial Arena, there is also an arena in Red's name in Calgary. Red was posthumously awarded the Lester Patrick Trophy in 1993 for his dedicated service to the sport in the United States.

One of the biggest wrongdoings in National Hockey League history has to be the fact that Red Dutton to this day continues to get shunned despite all he did for the league. He was the second-ever NHL president. Many executives of Original Six franchises who had worked beside Red at one point or another at the NHL headquarters in Montreal (Frank J. Selke and Conn Smythe of Toronto; Jack Adams and James Norris of Detroit; Art Ross of Boston) and the presidents who preceded and succeeded him (Frank Calder and Clarence Campbell) all had NHL awards named after them. So, the question is simply, why does Dutton have nothing named in his honour?

The way things went down with his departure from the league in 1946 might have something to do with it, but I strongly urge the NHL to make right on this and honour Red with an award legacy that he so richly deserves.

16
BILL MOSIENKO

lthough being a St. Vital kid, I was often in the North End for hockey games or just visiting relatives. As a result, I'd be in the car lots while driving northbound on Main Street and my eyes would always be glued to the mural on the side-wall of Billy Mosienko Lanes near the junction of Redwood Avenue. Depicted in the mural is a Chicago Blackhawks player holding up three pucks in his one hand. I would ask my parents about its significance and they'd tell me the story of Bill Mosienko's record.

Mosienko is famous for scoring the fastest hat-trick in NHL history, three goals in twenty-one seconds on March 23, 1952. A record that has stood the test of time and will likely never be broken— unless perhaps they double the size of the nets. "Like they say," Bill recalled, "I caught lightning in a beer bottle."

He was one of the smaller guys out there at 5'8", 160 pounds, but he was extremely quick on his feet. Bill's strong strides gave him the extra time and space needed to get that pass off or fire a shot without much hindrance.

A poll of sportswriters and sportscasters across in the NHL in March of 1953 declared that Mosienko was the fastest skater in hockey. He quickly became a target of Toronto's star defenceman Babe Pratt on the ice, but because Bill was a smaller guy and got low while he skated, he frustrated Babe a lot with how difficult he was to check.

Mosienko spent his entire fourteen-year NHL career in a Chicago Blackhawks uniform. What I learned most in my research for this book is how well-liked Mosienko was by everybody. You'd think that playing so many years in the NHL would gain you some enemies, but nope, not for Bill. Even opposing players liked him a great deal!

"He was just a beautiful skater. He wasn't very tall but he was extremely strong," recalled former teammate Ed Mazur. "The thing that stands out with Billy is that while being such a great hockey player, he was such a wonderful person, too. He cared about other people."

Bill Mosienko was born on November 2, 1921 in Winnipeg. He came into the world shortly after his parents had emigrated from Ukraine. One of the younger children of the thirteen kids his parents had, two of Bill's siblings died on the trek to Canada, with one of the babies passing away on the train ride from the east over to Manitoba.

Bill's parents faced many difficulties upon arriving in Canada. This included learning a new language and adapting to a new culture, but they also faced great economic hardship as his father did his best to make ends meet working hard as a boilermaker with the Canadian Pacific Railway.

Growing up at a house on Selkirk Avenue in Winnipeg's tough work-ing-class North End, Bill had his hockey beginnings at the rink right across the street from his house. It's long since been demolished and replaced with houses, but Tobans Rink was a community club on Shaughnessy Street between Selkirk and Pritchard Avenue. The community club was initially built out of old wooden boxcars by the fathers of Bill and fellow hockey great Fred Shero.

Bill later recalled, "We used to drag barrels of water over the field to flood it for making ice."

Because of the close proximity of the rink to his home, Mosienko got into hockey from a very young age and spent all of his free time in the winter months out on the ice. He started from the age of ten with the Tobans Athletic Club and promptly won the "Paperweight" playground city championship. Bill's first hockey pants were strips of wood or bamboo sewed into a pair of cut-down trousers, which is certainly a testament to what the Great Depression was like. Bill later joined the nearby Sherburn Athletic Club where he played Flyweight, Midget, and Juvenile hockey.

In 1939, Bill joined the Winnipeg Monarchs hockey club. Initially he had requested to try out for the MJHL's St. James Canadiens, but they turned him down, claiming that he was too young and inexperienced.

As an eighteen-year-old, Bill scored 21 goals in 24 games for the Monarchs, but he decided to leave the Monarchs after one season due to money issues despite having three years of junior eligibility left. "I lived in the North End and the Monarchs wouldn't give me $5 a week for car fare (street cars)," Mosienko recalled. "I needed that money to get to games and practice. Our family was poor and I knew darn well Paul Platz and Bill Benson (his Monarchs linemates) were getting it. That made me mad. I left the first chance I got."

He had signed a paper to go to a New York Rangers tryout camp, but right before he was about to do that, Chicago Blackhawks defenceman Joe Cooper (a Winnipegger) spotted Mosienko playing at the Old Exhibition Grounds outdoor rink, which was also extremely close to Bill's home, and was intrigued with how good Mosienko was. So much so that he followed Bill home and convinced him to sign with the Chicago Blackhawks. What no one could have predicted at the time is how Cooper and Mosienko would later go into business together.

The Blackhawks assigned the eighteen-year-old Mosienko to the minors where he spent time over the course of the next two seasons with farm clubs in Kansas City and Providence, developing his skills, while at the same time playing professional hockey.

"I wanted to get ahead, really wanted to get ahead in hockey. That was my one ambition. I wanted to succeed so badly," recalled Mosienko. "I had to sacrifice a lot of things. I could have gone out and had a good time, but I stuck to hockey and worked hard because it was the only way I knew where I could make what I wanted out of my life."

Mosienko was first called up to the Blackhawks in 1942, replacing players who had left to fight in World War II. He scored his first NHL goals in a game on February 9th, 1942 on fellow Top 50 Manitoban Sugar Jim Henry. The pair of goals came in a span of 21 seconds. Go figure.

Bill was medically exempt from the army because of his smaller size, but there were travel restrictions and he couldn't cross the US border during the war. As a result, Bill spent most of the 1942-43 season playing with the Quebec Aces senior team, while working during the day for a shipyard. He would only play games for the Blackhawks on a few occasions when they were in Canada to face the Toronto Maple Leafs.

He finally established himself as a full-time NHL player in a big way during the 1943-44 season as he scored seventy points, the most he would ever score in his career, and it was good for eighth in the league. In the postseason, Bill got as close as he ever would to winning a Stanley Cup in his career, but it wasn't meant to be as his Blackhawks were swept in four straight games at the hands of the Montreal Canadiens in the 1944 Stanley Cup final.

After the war ended, everyone returned to their respective clubs and Bill played on a line with the high-flying Bentley brothers, Max and Doug. Known as the "Pony Line," together they formed one of the most dynamic offensive units of the 1940's despite only playing together for a couple seasons. They were called the fastest line in the league at the time, which was a big compliment in itself since Montreal boasted the famed Punch Line of Toe Blake, Elmer Lach and Maurice "Rocket" Richard.

The line was broken up after Mosienko broke his leg while playing in the first ever NHL All-Star Game at the beginning of the 1947-48 campaign. When he returned a few years later, Max Bentley had been traded to the Toronto Maple Leafs so the "Pony Line" was done for good.

Throughout his career, Mosienko was the key offensive contributor on some pretty poor Chicago Blackhawks teams. It was the last game of the 1951-52 season between two last-place teams, however, that is the sole reason why even the most random of hockey fans know the name Bill Mosienko.

On that historic night—March 23, 1952, Bill told his troops before the final game of the season, "We've had another disastrous season. Let's try hard to win our final game."

The stage was set at Madison Square Garden with about four thousand New York Rangers fans in the crowd, many of whom disguised by dressing up as seats.

The first two periods were not Chicago's finest in terms of effort and they found themselves trailing heading into the final period. Mosienko refused to quit. Down by a 6-2 scoreline, Bill did something incredible.

Chicago centreman Gus Bodnar picked up a loose puck at center ice and fed it Mosienko's way near the Rangers blueline. Mosienko went around an off-balance Hy Buller on the Rangers defence and cut straight in on goaltender Lorne Anderson. Mosienko faked to the left and shot the puck flat along the ice and into the right side of the net. "Chicago goal by Bill Mosienko, assisted by Gus Bodnar. Time: 6:09," said the public address announcer.

Just seconds later, Bodnar got control of the puck off the face-off and once again spotted Mosienko at the Rangers blueline. Despite falling backwards a bit in grabbing the pass, Mosienko took the puck and skated through the defence. In a mirror image of his previous goal, he slapped the puck flat along the ice and into the right side of the cage. Time: 6:20.

"I'm sure Anderson was expecting high shots," Mosienko recalled. "Twice before during the game he had stopped high ones and I thought that he'd fall for the low shot. He did—a lucky thing for me."

Blackhawks coach Ebbie Goodfellow motioned for Mosienko's line to stay on the ice, and, just as the fans finished cheering in appreciation of Mosienko's two quick goals, the referee dropped the puck. Again, Bodnar won the draw, but this time he dished the puck to left winger George Gee, who then relayed it to Mosienko at the Rangers blueline, his usual spot. Bill skated halfway in toward the goal and then slowed down. His hesitation drew Anderson out of the net to challenge the shooter, and just as the netminder was coming out, Mosienko rifled the puck high into the right side of the goal. Bill said, "I figured Anderson would be looking for another low shot." Time: 6:30.

For a moment the entire crowd was dead quiet. Finally, when Mosienko skated to his team's bench, the stunned crowd rose as one and burst into great applause. "I wasn't quite sure what to do," said Mosienko, "until one of our forwards, Jimmy Peters, told me to get the puck. 'That's a record, Mosie,' he kept yelling."

Bill had scored a natural hat-trick on Rangers goalie Lorne Anderson at 6:09, 6:20, 6:30 of the third period. A little-known fact is that less than a minute after scoring the third goal, Mosienko had a glorious opportunity to score a fourth. Somehow, he hit the post of the gaping open net staring him in the face. When he returned to the bench, Chicago coach Ebbie Goodfellow commented jokingly how he must be slowing down!

The scoring flurry rattled Lorne Anderson and the Rangers. Before the game ended, the Blackhawks added two more goals to their total to complete a remarkable comeback. The final score was 7-6 in Chicago's favour. For poor Anderson, it would mark the last time that he was ever spotted inside of an NHL arena.

After the game and in his team's dressing room, Bill took the iconic photo of holding the three pucks he scored with. He swiped the puck from the net after each goal because scoring his 29th, 30th, and 31st goal of the season was a big deal at the time. This was an era when just twenty goals in a seventy-game schedule made you an elite player.

"We were thumbing through the NHL record book," Mosienko recalled a few days later, "and I remarked how nice it would be to have my name in there with some of the hockey greats. But I just figured it would never happen—and then it did, 48 hours later."

"That record will never be broken. Never," said Hall of Fame teammate Bill Gadsby. "It was just fantastic, it was damn near the same play off the face-off each one. He could really skate and could fly out there. He scored those three goals and I mean, it was unbelievable just to watch it!"

"When I think back to those days and how I wanted to leave some sort of a mark in hockey, I never dreamed it would be by scoring the three fastest goals," recalled Mosienko. "It seems everybody remembers me for that. Hardly a day goes by without somebody wanting to talk about it. And I'm sorry I helped end the career of the kid goalie, Anderson. He never played another game."

After a few more seasons in the NHL, Chicago decided to release Bill to the WHL's Winnipeg Warriors for the 1955-56 season. Bill still had some hockey years left in him as he was only 33 years old. He could have continued playing in the NHL if he wanted to, but he was at that point in his life where he'd rather be around his family all year. He spent the final five years of his pro career with the Warriors, acting as the player-coach for the final year. The Warriors team was the first tenant of the brand-new Winnipeg Arena. Considered to be good enough to not only play in the NHL, but make the playoffs on a yearly basis, the Winnipeg Warriors won the Edinburgh Trophy in 1956, which gave them bragging rights as the winner of the World's Minor Professional Hockey Championship.

One night when playing for the Warriors, Bill was on the bench when teammate Cecil Hoekstra scored two goals in under twenty seconds. Coach Alf Pike was about to change line when Mosienko shouted, "Leave him on! He's got a chance to break my record." Hoekstra stayed on the ice and nearly scored a few seconds later but hit the goal post.

"That told you what kind of a guy Bill Mosienko was," said Fred Shero, who was the legendary coach of the Philadelphia Flyers in the 1970's.

Mosienko retired from hockey in 1960. In fourteen NHL seasons that were all with the Chicago Blackhawks, Bill finished with 258 goals and 282 assists for 540 points in 710 NHL games. Mosienko was a two-time Second Team All-Star (1945, 1946) and was the 1945 recipient of the Lady Byng Memorial Trophy, as he went the whole 1944-45 season without taking a single penalty. He appeared in five NHL All-Star Games throughout his career and in 1957 he had the great honour of being named Manitoba's athlete of the year. A few years after he retired in 1965, Mosienko was rightfully inducted into the Hockey Hall of Fame. One of the most talented players of his era, Bill often challenged for the NHL scoring title and finished among the top ten scorers in five seasons. When Mosienko retired from the NHL, he was ranked seventh in the all-time goals department.

Another sport became a big part of Bill's life when he retired from hockey. In the late 1940's, Mosienko was looking for something to invest money in during his career. He opened Cooper-Mosienko Lanes in Winnipeg with Chicago teammate Joe Cooper in 1947. Cooper retired from hockey soon after the alley opened and would run the business while Mosienko was away playing hockey in the winter. Bill would then come back in the spring and work at the alley all summer. He eventually bought out Cooper once his own hockey career was over and the alleys became known as Billy Mosienko Lanes. Bill's son Brian later went into a partnership with him and owned the bowling alley well after his own dad's death. Seventy years since it was first opened, Billy Mosienko Lanes are still open today (albeit under new ownership) at the same Main Street location that its always been at.

Throughout his later life, Bill was active with the Manitoba Oldtimers and Manitoba Hockey Foundation. He was also a big part of the annual hockey-golf tournament. He lived at a house on Cathedral Avenue, which was a quick drive from both his bowling alley, and where he first learned how to play hockey.

Mosienko continued to skate well into his later years, playing in every old-timers game he could. "When I was about nineteen, he was still playing old-timers hockey," Bill Mosienko Jr. recalled. "We'd go to the outdoor rinks in the evening and skate and I couldn't keep up with him. He was well into retirement and he still skated circles around me.

"Charles Schulz, the creator of the Peanuts comic strip used to hold an old-timers hockey tournament down in San Francisco that my father would attend," said Bill Jr, "and I guess one day a fellow died on the ice and that was when Bill figured it was time to hang up the skates."

In his later years, Bill had perhaps the biggest battle of his life when he was diagnosed with bowel cancer. The doctors operated on him and he later took chemotherapy and everything appeared to look good. He was almost at the critical five-year stage when they did a spinal tap on Bill and discovered precancerous cells. He was soon diagnosed with terminal brain cancer and went deaf and blind near the end of his life.

Bill Mosienko passed away in Winnipeg on July 9, 1994. A few years before he died in 1991, the Keewatin Arena was renamed to the Billy Mosienko Arena. The arena continues to live on in his name today and is home to all kinds of minor hockey, just how Mosienko would have wanted.

15
BABE PRATT

Babe Pratt was one of the game's first offensive defencemen. He was one of the few in the NHL's early days that would take the puck from behind his own net and go for rushes, similar to what Bobby Orr would do many years later with the Boston Bruins. Pratt would always be the first one to tell you that good defence makes a good offence. He kept the puck deep in the offensive zone, because as we all know, the other team can't score if the puck is in their end.

Pratt was a big man at 6'3", 210 pounds and had a really big personality to go with it. He was called "larger than life", and was very similar in a lot of ways with his namesake Babe Ruth in baseball. He had this certain flair and flamboyancy about him that made him a very popular man with fans and the press. He was a consistent winner at every level of his career, winning a remarkable fifteen championships over twenty-six years in hockey. His best moment coming in 1945 while as a member of the Toronto Maple Leafs, Pratt scored the Stanley Cup winning goal in game seven of the Cup finals against Detroit.

Babe Pratt could always be counted on in the dressing room for some form of raillery. Once Pratt was playing in a game being refereed by an official well-fortified with brandy. Whenever there was a face-off in Babe's defensive zone, he would take the draw; and whenever Pratt prepared to take the draw the referee leaned over Babe's shoulder to drop the puck.

"Sir," said Pratt politely to the referee. "Would you mind leaning over my opponent's shoulder when you drop the puck? You're making me drunk."

Walter Pratt was born on January 7, 1916 in Stony Mountain. Shortly after he was born, his family moved to the north end of Winnipeg. Pratt learned to skate when he was six at the old Atlantic Avenue Rink, using a pair of his dad's old skates that had heels on them. It wasn't until the following winter that Pratt's dad bought him his first pair of skates. Growing up in a neighbourhood that revolved solely around sports, it was hard not to be into hockey from a young age. His hockey hero was Winnipeg Falcons legend Frank Frederickson, who lived not too far from Pratt's childhood home.

"Winnipeg was such a hotbed of hockey," said Pratt, "that when I was a kid they had a saying: no matter where you were in the world you could find a Swedish match, an English sailor, a German whore, and a hockey player from Winnipeg."

It was in his early sporting years that Pratt got his famous nickname. His older brother took him to play baseball one day and after the younger Pratt connected with a couple of fastballs, his friends started saying "he's a regular Babe Ruth!" The next day, they started calling him "Babe" for short, and it stuck with him the rest of his life.

Winning championships would be a common theme of Pratt's hockey career. In 1926, he won the first ever Winnipeg Playground Championships (under-12 division) for his local Atlantic Avenue Rink team as a ten-year-old. He won a provincial juvenile title shortly after with the Elmwood Maple Leafs and led the league in scoring.

In 1933, he played for five teams in his area of town—high school, church league, juvenile, senior, and commercial. What's crazy is that all five of those teams won a championship that year with Babe on their team.

"There wasn't enough hockey around for me to play. That's how much I loved it," recalled Pratt. "Once, I played four games in one day. Between noon and 1:00 pm, I played for the high school; then at 4:30, I had a game at another high school; at 7:00 that night, I played in the church league; and there was a taxi waiting to take me to an 8:30 game, played in 30 below zero weather. I think I won every game that day."

On the nights when there weren't league games, Babe and his pals would have to wait until the public skating sessions were done for the night at around 10 pm before they could get on the ice.

Later in that 1933-34 season, Pratt joined the Kenora Thistles of the MJHL as a seventeen-year-old and although Pratt was a defenceman, he led the league in scoring—something he'd been doing for years previously. Pratt carried his Kenora Thistles to within a game of the Memorial Cup final, when they fell in the midnight hour to the Winnipeg Monarchs.

While playing in Kenora, Pratt was scouted by New York Rangers scout Al Ritchie. Rangers boss Lester Patrick had friends all across western Canada and whenever they saw someone that had potential, Lester would send out his head scout, Al Ritchie, to see and evaluate. Well, Al told Lester that Pratt was the best prospect he'd ever scouted, and so he was promptly invited to the team's training camp in 1934.

Babe attended the camp and stayed a little longer because a pair of the team's defencemen, Ching Johnson and Earl Seibert, were holding out for more money. As a result, Babe stayed on and worked out with the Rangers for ten days.

Pratt returned to Kenora for the 1934-35 campaign and had another dominant season, scoring 42 points in 18 games, which was once again tops for the league. Babe was destined to be an NHL star it seemed like. After getting a letter in the mail from the Canadian Olympic Team asking if he wanted to try out with them in 1935, he knew that at his young age they wouldn't give him any ice time, so he made the decision to sign with the New York Rangers and join the professional ranks.

After a stint with the minor league Philadelphia Ramblers, Pratt was called up a few months into the season and made his Rangers debut. There were a lot of jokers on the team when Pratt was a rookie. One of them was Ching Johnson, who took Babe under his wing and worked a lot with him on what it took to be an NHL player.

Pratt later replaced Johnson the following spring during the 1937 Stanley Cup playoffs against the Toronto Maple Leafs and scored the series-winning goal. In the Cup finals, Pratt's Rangers took the Red Wings to the fifth and deciding game, but it was not meant to be as they fell 3-0.

It would only be a few short years later in 1940 when Pratt won his first Stanley Cup. Bryan Hextall's overtime winner in game six of the Cup finals lifted the Rangers past Toronto. Pratt was known as one of the hardest-hitting as well as stingiest defencemen in the league. During the championship season of 1939-40, Pratt and defence partner Ott Heller allowed just seventeen goals against through the forty-eight game schedule.

The following Rangers training camp, Pratt stayed out till 3 am one night. Lester Patrick fined him $1,000 but promised to return the money to Babe if he didn't drink again until the end of the season. Pratt agreed, but soon after, the team went on a losing skid which made Patrick reconsider. It's been said that Pratt played better half-drunk than completely dry, so Lester went back on his previous demand and told Babe it was all right if he had the odd drink.

Pratt likely would have been a New York Ranger for his whole career had it not been for his off-ice antics that drove Lester Patrick to the point where he felt he was forced to trade his star defenceman. Leafs manager Conn Smythe was a long-time fan of Pratt's game and made the deal for him as soon as he heard that Babe was on the market during the 1942-43 season.

"I remember once when Pratt was with the Rangers and we were tied late in the game," recalled Smythe. "A good Rangers forward got hurt and Pratt was moved up to wing. I thought, 'Aha, here's our chance to win.' Who got the winning goal? Pratt, playing forward."

Pratt became an instant star at Maple Leaf Gardens. He brought with him his larger than life personality, but cooled down on his off-ice antics during the season as he roomed with none-other than coach Hap Day. Pratt's probably the only player in NHL history to have had his coach as a roommate while on the road. He later recalled how he often took ribbings from players around the league that he was under his coach's thumb, but to Babe, he simply thought that Hap was a lonely person and wanted to keep him company.

Babe won the Hart Memorial Trophy in 1944 after scoring 57 points in 50 games, which was practically unheard of for a defenceman in those days. The pinnacle of his career came in the 1944-45 season when Pratt won his second Stanley Cup. He scored the game-winning goal in game seven of the Stanley Cup finals, so you can see why he lists that as his greatest thrill in the sport.

Pratt recalled game seven of the 1945 Stanley Cup finals: "It was in Detroit and whenever we played there we usually left for the rink at about 7:30 pm. I was rooming with Hap Day as usual and was snoring away when Hap came in and kicked me right out of bed. I woke up on the floor, looked up, and said, 'What the hells with you, Hap?'

'How can you sleep when the final Cup game is going to start in less than an hour,' he demanded. 'How can you do it?'

'Well, Hap,' I said, 'it's simply because the game doesn't start until 8:30. That's when I'll go to work.'

The coach wasn't upset anymore. 'Well, Babe,' he replied, 'I'll tell you one thing, you were never short on building yourself up, so I'll look forward to a good game from you.'"

Pratt continued: "The score was tied in the third period when Detroit had a man off with a penalty. I started toward the Red Wings net and took a pass from Nick Metz, a great but underrated player. Harry Lumley was the goalie for Detroit and Earl Siebert and Flash Hollett were on defence. When I got the puck, I skated in from the point, made a double-pass with Metz, and received it back on my stick. I slid a long one into the corner of the net—it turned out to be the winning goal.

"I always felt that if any one person could have been given the Stanley Cup to keep for himself that year, Hap Day should have gotten it for the way he handled our club. We had great goaltending from Frank McCool plus some good players like Wally Stanowski, Elwin Morris, Gus Bodnar, Teeder Kennedy, and Mel Hill. But, to me, Hap Day was the man who made it all work."

Pratt was on top of the world and one of the league's big-name players, but his time in the NHL almost came to an abrupt halt in January of 1946 when NHL president Red Dutton suspended him for betting on games. Pratt claimed that he never bet on games involving his own team and the league eventually reinstated him later that season after making him promise never to bet on games again.

During the following offseason, Pratt was traded to the Boston Bruins and played his final NHL season with them. He spent some time in the minors after that with the Hershey Bears and later out on the west coast where he finished off his career as player-coach of the New Westminster Royals.

Pratt retired after the 1951-52 season. He left the game with 292 points in 517 career NHL games over twelve seasons. One of the game's great offensive defencemen, Pratt has his two Stanley Cups (1940, 1945) and the Hart Memorial Trophy as league MVP in 1944. He was named an NHL First Team All-Star in 1944 as well and was a Second Team All-Star in 1945.

"If he'd looked after himself, he could have played until he was fifty," said Conn Smythe. "But he was as big a drinker and all-around playboy as he was a hockey player."

Pratt heartily agreed in his later years saying that, "I got it all backwards in my life. When I played hockey, I stayed up late at night and drank a large amount of beer. As soon as I quit playing, I stopped drinking and kept regular hours. If I had done it the other way around, I could have played hockey until I was fifty."

After retiring from hockey, Pratt stayed out in the Vancouver area and entered the lumber business. He was a foreman in a sawmill for three years and then was a log buyer for seventeen years.

He was inducted into the Hockey Hall of Fame in 1966. It was a very special moment for Babe as it affirmed what he always thought about his playing abilities. "Being inducted into the Hockey Hall of Fame was the greatest thing for me," said Pratt. "I was on two Stanley Cup-winning teams, won the Hart Memorial Trophy, yet to be inducted by your peers into the Hall of Fame and being with all those great players, having your picture among them is the frosting on the cake you might say. It's the sweetest thing that can happen to athlete to be inducted into the Hall of Fame."

Babe became the first employee of the Vancouver Canucks when they entered the National Hockey League in 1970. Towards the end of his life he served as the team's goodwill ambassador, appearing at conventions, dinners and minor hockey games across British Colombia. He later worked as an analyst for CBC's *Hockey Night in Canada* during their telecasts from Vancouver.

Pratt followed the NHL all his life and although he was always a fan of the game, he also felt that the game was better back in his golden days. "When I played, we were taught not to shoot the puck until we saw the whites of the goaltender's eyes," Pratt recalled. "Now they blast them from anywhere, hoping the puck will hit somebody's skates or ankles and bounce into the net."

Babe Pratt passed away on December 16, 1988 at the age of 72. He suffered a fatal heart attack while sitting in the media lounge of the Pacific Coliseum during the first intermission of a Canucks game. The Canucks honored Pratt by stitching "BABE" into their sweaters for the remainder of that 1988-89 season.

Being the gambling man that he was, Pratt won the final gamble of his life on the night that he died. During every Canucks home game, members of the press box would place money in a pool to guess the correct attendance of that night's game. On the evening that he died, Babe was the closest to the correct total and won the $16 prize.

14
THEO FLEURY

Theo Fleury was arguably the best "small" player in the history of the game. At only 5'6", he played with the heart and grit necessary to reach the highest levels of the sport. Being constantly told that he would never make it, Theo became a Stanley Cup champion, two-time Olympian, and one of the most dynamic forwards of his time.

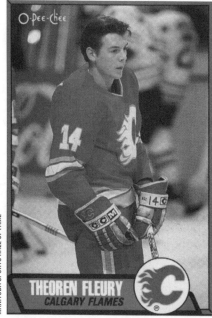

"When you use the word 'little' to describe Theo Fleury, you're not talking about his heart," said Wayne Gretzky. "This is a 50-goal scorer who could play for any team in the NHL. He's a small man who has the ability to make the big play at any time. He's living proof that size is not an insurmountable hurdle in making it to the NHL. I thoroughly enjoyed playing with Theo in the 1991 Canada Cup. His quickness in going to the net often catches defencemen and goaltenders asleep. When his arms are raised after scoring a goal, then he doesn't look so small."

Theo overcame so much to get to the top of the hockey world. He was very pesky and annoying to play against, but Fleury had the speed and skills to score in bunches too in addition to his tough play. There's no doubt about it that Fleury was one of the defining players of his era. With tons of star quality, he was one of the most popular and exciting players in the game. During a time where the focus on size was at its peak, he redefined what was possible from a "small" player. Theo won the Stanley

Cup in his rookie season with Calgary. They won the deciding game at the Montreal Forum, becoming the only visiting team in NHL history to win the Stanley Cup on Montreal's home ice.

Former teammate James Patrick had some great words on Theo: "The one thing I want to get out there for this book is that I played four and a half years with Theo Fleury and played against him for a long time. I know he had some personal demons, but when push comes to shove, Theo was one of the most talented players I ever played with. He's a world-class player, simply world-class. Theo could play on the Canadian World Cup team or the Stanley Cup-winning Calgary Flames team and be the best player on the ice. He could do everything: score goals, set up goals, win face-offs, be physical, block shots, be an antagonist and a pest... I know he had demons and it affected him and I'll be frank and say that his off-ice troubles often affected his on-ice game. His issues really hurt him at times and led to some behavioral issues, but one on one with Theo, I admired and really enjoyed being around him. He's a fantastic guy. I think that there's no chance in the world he can't be in the top five Manitobans of all-time. I can argue from the length of his career to the numbers he put up. He was just a really great player who deserves to be up there with the best."

Theoren Fleury was born on June 29, 1968 in Oxbow, Saskatchewan. Coming from a family that moved around a bit in his early years, Theo's father Wally was a decent hockey player himself whose dreams of playing in the pros ended when he broke his leg playing baseball one summer. The injury fuelled a drinking problem that would go on for many years. Theo lived in Williams Lake, British Colombia for four years and then came to Manitoba—first to Binscarth, and soon after Russell.

Theo hit the ice for the first time as a five-year-old while living in Binscarth, Manitoba. He was walking home from kindergarten one day when one of his buddies asked him if he'd like to come play hockey that night. "Sure, why not?" was Theo's reply. He went home and asked his mom if they had any hockey equipment he could use. She found a rusty pair of old skates that young Theo's dad used to wear and a broken hockey stick and shoved them into a pillowcase.

"I walked down to the rink by myself. It was an old barn with two sheets of curling ice on the sides and a tiny skating surface in the middle." Fleury recalled. "And you know what? I don't recall falling down. I just laced 'em up, stepped out onto the ice and zoom. It was like I belonged somewhere for the first time. Three hours later, when the game was long over, they had to force me to go home."

Fleury was hooked on the sport instantly.

Growing up in nearby Russell, Theo's dad did all the ice maintenance at the arena for a few years so basically Theo had unlimited ice time. He would spend six hours a day skating and stickhandling through phantom defence-men and then shooting pucks from all angles of the ice.

From the time Theo was six, he played with the same group of guys in Russell on a minor hockey team called the Russell Rams until he left town to play for the Moose Jaw Warriors at the age of fourteen. "We travelled all over Manitoba and Saskatchewan and killed everybody," said Fleury.

Although he knew right away that he was going to be an NHL player and was doing all the necessary steps to make that dream a reality, his chances were nearly squashed altogether when he suffered a deep cut under his arm during a game in Portage la Prairie that severed his brachial artery. Theo missed nearly a year of contact hockey as a result of the injury, and the only hockey he really played in that time was when the community of Russell raised enough money to send him to the Andy Murray Hockey School in Brandon.

Fleury was finally cleared by doctors near the end of the following season during the bantam provincial championships that was held that year in his hometown rink, Russell Memorial Auditorium. In his first game back, Fleury won the opening face-off and scored about five seconds later. He was back and he led his Russell Rams to a provincial championship.

Fleury joined the junior ranks as a fifteen-year-old with the St. James Canadiens of the MJHL. He burst onto the scene and scored 64 points in 22 games, nearly an average of three points per game. The next year he moved on to the Moose Jaw Warriors, who had just relocated from Winnipeg and starred there for three seasons. His last season in Moose Jaw he won the Bob Clarke Trophy as the WHL's top scorer.

Fleury was selected for Team Canada's 1987 World Junior champion-ship and was front and centre for the infamous Punch-up in Piestany, a bench-clearing bloody brawl between Canada and the Soviet Union that was finally broken up when the arenas lights were turned off so the players couldn't see who they were hitting anymore. Both teams were disqualified from the tournament because of the brawl.

Although he was a big-time scorer in juniors, NHL teams worried that due to his size he wouldn't be able to compete in the league. The Calgary Flames drafted him in the eighth round (166th overall) of the 1987 NHL Entry Draft with even themselves thinking that he was a minor league player.

Fleury would go on to prove everybody wrong when he went on to become the best player out of the draft class and arguably the greatest Calgary Flames player of all time.

After starting his pro career in the minors with the Salt Lake Golden Eagles, Fleury was called up midway through the 1988-89 season and joined the Flames in a big way. He scored 34 points in 36 games in his rookie season and then added 11 points in the playoffs, playing a vital role in the Calgary Flames Stanley Cup triumph, their first and only that they've won in team history.

Fleury spent eleven seasons in a Flames uniform, including two as team captain. He had two 100-point seasons and one fifty-goal season in 1990-91. In the 1991 playoffs, he scored the memorable game six overtime winner against the Edmonton Oilers that saw him sliding across the ice, pumping his fists and crashing into the boards into the arms of his teammates in celebration. The goal and celebration still gets played all the time by CBC come playoff time every year.

After many seasons in Calgary, Theo was part of a six-player deal on February 28th, 1999 that sent him to Colorado. He finished the year with the Avalanche and then signed on the following summer with the New York Rangers. Despite his wild off-ice antics, Fleury was a star player on Broadway, averaging well over a point-per-game in his three seasons there.

When Wayne Gretzky was selected to manage Team Canada at the 2002 Winter Olympics in Salt Lake City, he made it very clear early on that the one player he really wanted on his team was Theo Fleury. People considered the selection questionable but Wayne felt there was no better big game player in the NHL at the time than Fleury and Wayne needed him on Team Canada to make them the best they could possibly be. Wayne's hunch on Fleury turned out to be right as despite overcoming a lot of adversity throughout the tournament, Team Canada rallied to win the gold medal.

In Team Canada's post-game press conference after their gold medal triumph, Theo was the one player that Wayne Gretzky singled out when making his address. "I can't tell you how proud I am of Theo," said Gretzky. "He's gone through so much. But the way he played, that's exactly why we picked him, to grind it out and play hard every shift."

Fleury played his last season in the NHL in 2002-03 with the Chicago Blackhawks. At the end of the year he was suspended by the league for violations of its substance abuse program. Still having some hockey left in him, Theo went and played in Northern Ireland for a season and also played senior hockey for teams in Horse Lake and Steinbach for their respective Allan Cup playdowns.

Upset with how his NHL career ended, Fleury decided in 2009 to try and make a comeback to the NHL. League commissioner Gary Bettman lifted his suspension and he joined the Calgary Flames as a walk-on at their team's training camp. Theo later said that he wanted to prove to himself that he could still play at the NHL level. He played in four exhibition games that fall, scoring four points in those contests. The highlight of his comeback being a pretty shootout-winning goal in a game against the Islanders.

He was released by the team after coach Darryl Sutter decided that he wasn't a top-six winger in the training camp, a pre-requisite of both Theo's and Darryl to have the try-out continue. Just a few days later, Fleury announced his retirement at the Saddledome on September 28, 2009. In his retirement speech, he noted that he always wanted to retire as a Calgary Flame and had no interest trying to carry on a career with another team at that stage in his life.

Theo retired as one of the best players of his era. He scored 1088 points in 1084 NHL games over fifteen seasons. Consistently amongst the league's top ten scorers, Theo was named a Second Team All-Star in 1995 and played in seven NHL All-Star games between 1991 and 2001. In addition to his Stanley Cup and all his other NHL accolades, Theo also has quite the impressive international resume. He won gold for Canada at the 1988 World Juniors, 1991 Canada Cup and 2002 Salt Lake City Olympics. Theo also picked up silver medals at the 1991 World Championships and 1996 World Cup of Hockey.

Fleury stayed in Calgary after hockey and ran a concrete business for a number of years. He used to run a hockey school back in Russell and still gets back to Manitoba over the course of any given year. These days he keeps himself very busy as one of the leading advocates in Canada for sexual abuse victims.

As of 2017, Theo Fleury has not yet been inducted into the Hall of Fame. That's not to say that he's not deserving of it. He had a career that was definitely deserving of enshrinement, winning just about everything you could possibly win in the sport. Add that up with the fact that he was over a point-per-game player over his career and one of the big stars of the 1990's, you'd think he'd be a no-brainer to get in, right? Maybe his off-ice stuff has a bit to do with being snubbed, but I think you have to look at the case of Busher Jackson (a former star player with the Leafs back in the 1930's), who had similar off-ice problems. It took a while, but the Hall eventually inducted Jackson and I believe the Hall of Fame will do the right thing and induct Theo as well. The question is just how much longer does we have to wait until the greatest Calgary Flames player of all time gets his induction.

If you'd like to read more about Theo's incredible story, please check out both of his books: *Playing With Fire* and *Confessions With A Rattlesnake*. They are simply amazing reads.

CHICO RESCH SAYS

Obviously he had a heart as big as any tiny player ever to play hockey. Theo was ferocious and relentless, and knew how to take care of himself as a smaller player. He was incredibly skilled and had world-class puck handling, he could really do it all on the ice. The energy he exuded, he just wouldn't let you not choose him.

I can still remember when he came to New York to play with the Rangers, and there were all of these billboards of him. He had such a big impact on the hockey world. When he came to New York he was considered the top free agent available at the time so that kind of shows what kind of respect he had.

He's one of those few guys that gave every ounce of energy he had on every shift he played. If you go really hard for 65 out of 82 games, that was impressive. No one went hard for 82. But Theo did. He was an overachiever and never left much on the ice.

Later on in his career I think that hurt him a little bit because he had spent so much energy in his earlier years. One of the things I noticed with him is if you're playing against Fleury as a skater, it didn't matter how big the other guy was, Theo always felt equal at the very least, but usually he had an edge in the puck battling. I think most people forget about things like that.

When Theo got the puck, he knew what to do with it. He made the high percentage play all the time and really used his speed to his advantage. People all the time talk about potential and it drives me crazy because thousands of players have potential. Theo used all of his and was a guy that goes down as one of the elite smaller players in the history of the game.

13
JACK STEWART

Black Jack Stewart was the name, throwing crushing body-checks was his game. An absolutely amazing defensive defenceman and one of the most punishing body-checkers of his time, Stewart hardly gets recognized among the Orrs, Potvins, Shores as one of the league's all-time best defencemen, but he no doubt should be right up there.

Stewart took charge of the Red Wings blueline and was the team's on-ice general. In past interviews, fellow Red Wings legends such as Gordie Howe, Sid Abel and Ted Lindsay have all gone on record in saying that Black Jack was the biggest reason why the team became a winner in such a short order.

The only defenceman in NHL history to be named an All Star both before and after the Red Line was introduced, Stewart wasn't very big for a man who could throw such a thunderous bodycheck at 5'11", 185 pounds, but he was all bone and muscle. He was so tough that he once played an entire season with a broken hand!

And just how did he get the nickname Black Jack? "I bodychecked some fellow one night," recalled Stewart, "and when he woke up the next day in the hospital he asked who'd hit him with a blackjack."

"As a defenceman he did everything on the ice you're supposed to do, stop the other people and knock them around," recalled Sid Abel. "He was one of the most easy-going guys off the ice but one of the strongest and most intense on it."

It took 201 stitches to close the 48 wounds on his body over the course of his career, but Black Jack always fought through his injuries and played on until his body eventually gave out.

John Sherratt (Jack) Stewart was born in Pilot Mound on May 6, 1917. Growing up on his family wheat farm, Jack learned how to play hockey on the local outdoor rinks in his hometown. He loved hockey, horses, and curling in that order, and he also played some softball in the summer months. He moved to Portage la Prairie for high school in 1935 and attended Portage Collegiate Institute, playing for the school team, as well as the Portage Terriers junior club.

Stewart starred for the Terriers for a couple of seasons before catching his big break. A Winnipeg businessman by the name of Gene Houghton thought highly of Stewart, enough that he recommended him to his friend, James Norris Sr., the owner of the Detroit Red Wings. The Red Wings signed Stewart and assigned him to their minor league affiliate, the Pittsburgh Hornets of the International-American Hockey League (IAHL). After one and a half seasons with Pittsburgh, Detroit called up the 21-year-old Stewart to bolster their defence and that's exactly what he did.

Stewart joined the Red Wings midway through the 1938-39 season. His reputation for delivering huge hits quickly spread around the league and soon enough, he became one of the more feared men in the league. He earned high praise from pundits, including his boss Jack Adams. "He's one of the strongest guys I've ever seen in a hockey uniform. He works hard on his farm all summer and he's outdoors all the time. That probably accounts for it," said Adams. "He's a manager's dream. "He's a very deceptive skater. He packs a terrific shot. He's an uncanny judge of a forward's play. He's one of the greatest of the game."

With Stewart manning the Red Wings blueline, the club got to both the 1941 and 1942 Stanley Cup finals, but fell to the Boston Bruins and Toronto Maple Leafs, respectively. The 1942-43 campaign was possibly the best of Stewart's career. He was named to the NHL First All-Star Team and helped lead his team to the NHL regular season title. The Red Wings advanced to their third straight Stanley Cup final, and this time they were victorious as they swept the Boston Bruins in four games.

Jack's hockey was interrupted by the Second World War just as he was getting into the prime of his career. He enlisted in 1943 and served as a Leading Aircraftman in the Royal Canadian Air Force. He played some hockey the next two years, albeit a lot more recreationally than he was used to with the Montreal and Winnipeg RCAF teams.

When the war ended, Stewart was discharged and quickly returned to the Red Wings lineup, where he picked up right where he left off, playing strong defensive hockey and leaving opposing players in his wake. He spoke softly and carried a big stick, that's basically how you can summarize Stewart's postwar playing days.

"Others called him Black Jack but we on the team used to call him Silent Jack," said Red Wings teammate Sid Abel. "He was a man of actions, not words."

Despite being one of the quieter players on a dynamite Red Wings team, Black Jack played a key role in one heck of a prank on teammate Red Kelly that was told for the first time in David Dupuis and Waxy Gregoire's recent biography on Kelly: "Early on in Red's career, he was charged with making an improper left turn while driving in Detroit. He innocently mentioned the incident to Jack Adams. At traffic court the next morning, Judge John Watts ordered a trial for that same afternoon.

When the case reconvened, Adams and the whole team showed up for moral support and to act as character witnesses; Black Jack Stewart even offered his services as defence counsel. Red was honestly worried when 12 older women were ushered in as the jury.

The proceedings got underway: 'The State of Michigan versus one Leonard Kelly.'

When Red briefly smiled, the judge chastised him: 'Young man, this charge is serious!'

His smile evaporated as his teammates, all in on the gag, tried to suppress their laughter. Stewart had a key role, and was serious, defending his client with all the legal terms he knew. Judge Watts kept cutting Stewart off on technicalities. Red was increasingly worried. The judge looked at Red and said, 'You'd better get yourself another attorney. This guy is more like a prosecutor!'

Ignoring the slight, Stewart kept on talking. Finally, Judge Watts had seen enough. He banged his gavel and asked Red and his counsel to stand.

'Leonard P. Kelly, the court hereby finds you ... guilty of the said charge,' Watts boomed. The court room quieted. Red gulped. 'I hereby fine you ... two goals! And you'd better deliver them against the Rangers tonight, or I'll have you back in my court!'

The court erupted in laughter, howling and foot-stomping. Red could only smile and shake his head. He knew he'd been had, again. When he showed up for the game that night, a fake newspaper was posted on the dressing room wall with the headline declaring 'Kelly—Sentenced! Stewart's Defence Fails!'"

"I had a front row seat in the classroom—Defence 101," said Red Kelly. "Adams called him the strongest hockey player he had ever seen. There was security in having Black Jack around."

"I called him 'Dad' because he always looked after me," recalled Marty Pavelich. "I remember one night against the Rangers, I got into a scuffle with a guy by the name of Pat 'Boxcar' Egan. Egan fell on top of me and was about to really hit me when Stewart skated in close and said, 'Egan, if you lay a hand on that kid, I'll put you into the balcony.' Egan looked up and instantly backed right off. With Stewart around, we all thought we were eight feet tall."

Stewart was a man of habit. He tried to go walking as much as he could to stay conditioned throughout the season, over and above the regular amount of skating he did. "I eat foods," he said, "that my system has been used to and at regular hours. I go easy on pickles and pastries. A steak dinner is the thing not less than three hours before playing a game. I aim at eight hours' sleep nightly. As for alcoholic drinks, leave them strictly alone—the best they can do for you is ruin your health."

Jack won a second Stanley Cup with Detroit in 1950 off a Pete Babando overtime goal in game seven of the Stanley Cup finals against the New York Rangers. In the offseason that followed, Stewart was traded to the Chicago Blackhawks in a nine-player trade, which was at the time the largest in NHL history. The Blackhawks quickly made Stewart their team captain and assistant coach and he played the first half of the year before suffering a serious spinal injury in a game against Toronto. Doctors diagnosed his injury as a ruptured disc and pleaded that he retire from hockey. Jack was lucky he could still walk without a cane, and shouldn't risk losing that privilege by continuing to play. The rugged defenceman returned to Chicago for the 1951-52 season and suffered another big injury when he fractured his skull. His injuries led Jack to walk into the Blackhawks front office and ask for outright release so he could retire from hockey and seek a minor league coaching job.

Jack Stewart retired after twelve NHL seasons with 115 points in 565 games. He won two Stanley Cups (1943, 1950) and played in four All-Star games (1947, 1948, 1949, 1950) over the course of his career. He was named a First Team All-Star three times (1943, 1948, 1949) and a Second Team All-Star twice (1946, 1947).

Stewart got into coaching when he stopped playing and was behind the bench for teams such as the Chatham Maroons, Kitchener-Waterloo Dutchmen, Windsor Bulldogs, Sault Ste. Marie Thunderbirds, and then coached his final year (1963) with the Pittsburgh Hornets, who were otherwise known as the Red Wings AHL affiliate.

In 1964, Stewart was honoured for his amazing career by being inducted into the Hockey Hall of Fame. He remembered being inducted years later by saying, "That was a great thrill to have my name placed up there with all those great players."

After leaving the game of hockey for good, Stewart turned his attention into another great love of his: harness racing. His father had built a track on the family farm while he was growing up and would hold a horse racing meet every year to entertain the people of Pilot Mound. Jack would follow his dad and help when the elder Stewart worked as a race judge at various fairs across Manitoba. Black Jack got back into it once hockey was behind him, serving as a race-timer and as a judge with the Ontario Racing Commission for nearly thirty years.

Stewart always had his farm in Pilot Mound, but mainly resided in Troy, Michigan. He eventually retired to Florida, but had to return to Michigan when he was diagnosed with cancer and underwent various treatments.

Jack Stewart died in Troy on May 25, 1983 at the age of 66 after a lengthy battle with cancer. His body was promptly returned to Manitoba and he was buried in his hometown of Pilot Mound. Black Jack is forever immortalized in Pilot Mound to this day with the town's arena being named after him.

"He was one of the greatest defencemen of his era," recalled Canadiens legendary coach Dick Irvin. "He didn't have a great deal of colour, but he was a very sound player. The only rearguard who could be compared with him was Butch Bouchard when he was at his peak and they were somewhat the same type. You had to respect Stewart. He was the kind of a player you like to have on your side."

12
JOE SIMPSON

Bullet Joe Simpson has to be one of the best hockey names of all time. He was also one of the best defencemen ever. The nickname "Bullet Joe" comes from being such a fantastic, fast skater who regularly made incredible end-to-end rushes, and was known for firing bullet shots from centre-ice at opposing goaltenders. It was also a reference to the wounds he suffered during the First World War.

In the early 1920's, while Simpson was playing for the Western League's Edmonton Eskimos, Newsy Lalonde called him the best player alive, which is a huge compliment since most hockey historians of the first quarter century of the 1900s consider Lalonde himself to be the game's best player.

Simpson wasn't the biggest player on the ice, but "Bullet Joe" as his nickname suggests was remarkably fast and afraid of nobody. His "corkscrew rushes" as you'll read about shortly made him very popular with fans and sportswriters. Bill Corum, a columnist with the *New York Journal-American*, referred to Bullet Joe Simpson as "a rollicking, rocking man, flashing down the rink with the puck on the end of his stick."

The first player signed by the New York Americans when they joined the National Hockey League in 1925, it wasn't long after he started playing in New York that the press dubbed Simpson as the Babe Ruth of hockey. It's just a shame that when Simpson finally started playing in the NHL at the veteran age of 32, he played for the worst team in the league. In six NHL seasons, Joe only got to skate in two playoff games.

Harold Edward Joseph Simpson was born in Selkirk on August 13, 1893. The youngest boy in his family, Simpson skated on the frozen pond from the time he could walk and spent close to six months of the year playing hockey every day after school with his chums. "We started to play hockey about as soon as we could walk in those days. The hockey I know was started by skating on the slough which was just down from our house where I was born," Simpson later recalled. "In those days, there were only two schools in Selkirk, public school and high school. The boys living in the north end were the North team and south of Manitoba Avenue was the South team."

Joe began his hockey career with the Selkirk Prep School team, and later played with the University of Manitoba club. He played intermediate amateur hockey with the Winnipeg Strathconas and Selkirk Fishermen before joining the Winnipeg Victorias of the senior ranks in 1914-15. He first started with the Victorias as a rover, but then soon after made the switch to defence.

When World War I came about, Simpson was quick to enlist in the army. Before being sent overseas, Simpson was Captain of the Allan Cup-winning team from the 61st Battalion Canadian Expeditionary Force (CEF). He then served in France with the 43rd Cameron Highlanders and his unit held a part of the British front alongside a battalion commanded by none other than Major Winston Churchill. Simpson was twice wounded in the war at the battles of Somme and Amiens. "Once [it was later reported] by machine gun bullets in his legs," though "good surgery kept him from lameness." Joe survived and was decorated with the Military Medal for Valour, and reached the rank of Lieutenant during the war.

The 5'10", 175-pound Simpson got back from the war in time for the final four games of the 1918-19 season for his Selkirk Fishermen. Removed from the game for nearly three years, Simpson came back stronger than ever and helped lead his team to the 1919 Allan Cup where they fell to Hamilton by one goal on a two-game total-goals series. He had a strong season the following year with Selkirk, scoring nineteen goals in ten games, which was virtually unheard of for a defenceman in those days.

Joe was in a Winnipeg poolroom in the fall of 1920 when Kenny Mackenzie of the Big-4 league Edmonton Eskimos offered him $3,000 to turn pro with his club. Upon hearing the offer, Simpson chalked his cue and replied that if Mackenzie could sell the deal to his father then Edmonton would have themselves a defenceman. The Eskimos got their player in the end and Joe was shipped off to Edmonton, playing his first game of professional hockey at the advanced age of 27.

In his second year with the Eskimos (1921-22) he was named a Western Hockey League First Team All-Star. He would win that award two more times and was also a Second Team All-Star once over his five years with the Eskimos. He earned high praise from everyone who saw him play over the course of this time, including Newsy Lalonde, who famously called him the "greatest living hockey player."

Joe's end-to-end rushes were legendary and without comparison. Known for his "corkscrew rushes" when he would dip and dodge through opposing players with plenty of dekes and feints as opposed to just skating in a straight line, no one brought the puck up the ice like he did, and the fact that he could also put the puck in the net seemingly at will was simply amazing.

It really was the wild, wild west as Simpson recalled vividly playing some of his games outdoors in Edmonton and Saskatoon even when the temperature fell to such extremes as minus 45: "We used to have snow shovelled into the dressing room to warm our feet when we came off the ice. We'd tramp around in the snow in our stockings. Thaw out gradually that way and avoid frozen feet. Sometimes a fellow would have to sit when his feet in a pail of snow for twenty or thirty minutes."

Simpson got as close as he would to winning a Stanley Cup in 1923 when his WCHL champion Edmonton Eskimos fell to the NHL champ Ottawa Senators by 2-1 and 1-0 scorelines in the Cup final. The games were played in Vancouver and it was the last Cup final that was played in its entirety at a neutral site. It also marked the last time that an Edmonton team contested for the Stanley Cup until 1983.

When the WHL was forced to cease operations at the conclusion of the 1924-25 season, Simpson's contract was purchased by the New York Americans of the NHL for the record sum at the time of $10,000. He was a big name and was a major gate attraction for fans in New York. You could say that he was partly responsible for making New York the strong hockey market it is today.

When he arrived, the Americans publicity team tried to portray him as a trap-liner from 450 miles north of Edmonton who travelled to New York City by dogsled and toboggan and was guarded by friendly Indians. They might have been exaggerating just a tinge.

Simpson was 32 years old when he first got to play in the NHL, so naturally, he had a lost a step or two from this Edmonton days. Baz O'Meary of the *Montreal Star* wrote that, "the Joe Simpson who played in the east was only a shadow of 'Bullet Joe' who thrilled western audiences. It's too bad so few sportswriters saw him at his best. They would have seen a player who could break faster than Eddie Shore, skate faster than King Clancy, handle a stick like Johnny Gottselig, and shoot like Sprague Cleghorn. But the east did something to him. He became a wobbly skater, put on about twenty pounds that he never seemed to be able to shed, and was always too amiable to be impressive."

George Mackintosh of the *Edmonton Journal* replied with, "Mr. O'Meara is right. Bullet Joe was past his best by the time he went east, but when he was with Edmonton the guy was the biggest attraction in hockey. There's been no player quite like him since, and it's doubtful if another like him ever will come along. From the strict defensive angle, there have been plenty of better performers than Simpson, but none his equal at serving up rushing thrills."

Playing for the Amerks was quite the experience for Joe as the club was run by bootlegger Bill Dwyer and because of that there were plenty of distractions for the players to deal with. One day, Simpson made a wrong turn in one of the arena hallways and walked straight into a room full of elephants and lions belonging to a circus, which was to take place at Madison Square Garden later that week. Simpson made the quickest U-turn imaginable and got the hell out of there. He fled back to his dressing room and found the team's trainer

"Where in the hell did that bad hooch come from?" Joe asked. "Christ! I could swear I saw a herd of wild elephants out there."

Bullet Joe Simpson retired from hockey after the 1930-31 campaign, his sixth season with the Americans. He finished with 40 points in 228 NHL games and 99 points in 113 WCHL games. When Joe retired, he stayed in the game, coaching the Americans for three years, before moving on to manage various minor league teams in New Haven, Minneapolis and Miami.

Bullet Joe moved to Florida in 1938 to promote ice hockey. He suffered a bad heart attack there in the late 1940's that kept him inactive for two years. He was down in the dumps until fellow Manitoba hockey legend Art Coulter hired him to work at the Coulter White's hardware store in Coral Gables, Florida, a position he held until 1965.

"He gave me a job selling skates in his hardware store, four hours a day," recalled Simpson. "It may sound funny, selling skates in Florida, but Coral Gables, at that time, had an arena."

In 1962, Simpson was inducted into the Hockey Hall of Fame. A little over a decade later, in 1975, he was inducted into Canada's Sports Hall of

Fame. In 1994, the Marine Museum of Manitoba in Selkirk restored a 1963 flat-bottomed freighter and renamed it the Harold Bullet Joe Simpson.

In his last few years he had a lot of health problems and was nearly blind towards the end of his life. Bullet Joe Simpson passed away in Coral Gables, Florida on December 25, 1973 at the age of 80.

11
BRYAN HEXTALL

Bryan Hextall was a strong and fearless power-forward on the ice. One of the best players of his time, there was a never a man in the league that could discourage Hex from going into corners. An iron-man of his day, Hextall rarely missed a game. In fact, he played in more than 340 straight NHL games before sitting one out. "He was the hardest bodychecking forward I have seen in more than 40 years of watching hockey," said long time *New York Sun* reporter Herb Goren.

Hockey historian Joe Pelletier writes that, "Bryan Hextall was one of the highest skilled and most respected players ever to grace a sheet of NHL ice. He was the dominant right winger of the era directly before the arrival of Rocket Richard and Gordie Howe."

"There wasn't anyone like Bryan," recalled Rangers teammate Max Labovitch. "He was just this strong and amazing hockey player. I consider him to be the Superman of those 1940's Rangers teams."

Hextall scored 20 or more goals in seven of his eleven career NHL seasons, which was during a time when scoring 20 goals in a season was a very big deal as they only played a 50-game schedule. He even won a retroactive Art Ross Trophy in 1942 and scored arguably the biggest goal in Rangers franchise history, the overtime winner to clinch the 1940 Stanley Cup.

Playing all eleven of his NHL seasons on Broadway, Hextall was a bullish winger who could skate right over any opposing defenceman that tried to stop him without breaking stride. He was a very tough player for such a big goal-scorer. Hextall always felt that you didn't need to drop the mitts to prove yourself on the ice.

Bryan Hextall was born in Grenfell, Saskatchewan on July 31, 1913. His family moved to the small hamlet of Poplar Point, Manitoba when he was just six. A few years later at the age of nine, he started playing hockey as a goalie because he couldn't skate. His uncle Jack Bend, the local hockey guru in Poplar Point. worked on Bryan a lot and moulded him into quite the outstanding defenceman. Bryan's first success in hockey came when his team got to the provincial midget final in 1929-30. The next year he won the Manitoba juvenile championship for Poplar Point.

The 5'10", 195-pound Hextall spent a few years playing junior hockey for the Winnipeg Monarchs and Portage Terriers before turning pro with the Vancouver Lions of the North West Hockey League in 1934. It was in Vancouver that Hextall first made the switch from defenceman to forward, playing on the left wing. Hextall helped Vancouver win a league championship in 1934-35.

After a few seasons in Vancouver, the New York Rangers signed Hextall as a free agent, and the Poplar Point native came over to the east coast for the first time in his life. Bryan spent most of the 1936-37 season with the IAHL's Philadelphia Ramblers before being called up to Broadway. When he was brought up, Rangers boss Lester Patrick quickly moved Hex over to right wing from the left side and it paid off immediately. He was 24 years old when he broke in with the Rangers.

A left-handed shot playing on the "off wing," Hextall was one of the first right-wingers to do what has become commonplace in today's NHL. Bryan and Lester Patrick both agreed that he had a much better shooting angle, as a left-handed shot, by cutting in on goal from the right wing.

It worked as Hextall scored 17 goals in his rookie season, and then followed that up with 20 in his sophomore year. The goals wouldn't stop there either as Bryan led the league in goals in back to back seasons (1939-40, 1940-41), and then led the league in points in 1941-42. It would have been good for two Rocket Richard Trophy's and one Art Ross Trophy had the awards been given out back then.

Hextall skated on the Rangers top line that also featured Phil Watson and

Lynn Patrick. Basically, Bryan was the best player on the best line in the NHL. In 1940, Hextall won his one and only Stanley Cup. His club dispatched the Boston Bruins in six games in the semifinals, which set them up for a battle against the Toronto Maple Leafs in the Cup finals.

The Rangers took the first two games at home, but then the circus forced the Rangers to vacate Madison Square Garden after game two, so the rest of the series had to be played in Toronto, and the Leafs proceeded to win the next two games. Game five was a double overtime thriller that ended in the Rangers favour, which set the stage for game six of the Stanley Cup Finals on April 13, 1940. The game was a back and forth affair that was tied 2-2 at the end of regulation. That's when Hextall's heroics happened at the 2:07 mark of the first overtime period to send New York into euphoria.

"I got the puck behind the net," recalled Phil Watson. "I passed it out blind. I didn't even see Hex."

Phil Watson was the centre on that line. Lynn Patrick was usually the left wing, but Dutch Hiller was skating at left wing instead and had sent the puck to Phil Watson behind the net. And when Phil Watson's pass skidded onto Bryan Hextall's stick, he backhanded a fifteen-foot shot into the Leafs net.

"I took a pass from Dutch Hiller and Phil Watson," Hextall fondly remembered years later. "The puck came out from behind the net and I took a backhand shot to put it past (Turk) Broda."

When Bryan talked about the goal in his later life, he claimed he just happened to be near the net and modestly managed to put it past the goal line. Who would have known at the time that it would take 54 years for the New York Rangers to hoist another Stanley Cup.

Also, that 1940 Rangers team could have probably been called the "Manitoba Rangers" because in addition to Hextall, the squad also featured Stony Mountain native Babe Pratt and Winnipeggers Art Coulter, Alf Pike, and Alex Shibicky.

Hextall would have continued being one of the best players in the game had his career not been interrupted by the outbreak of World War II. Hex had to miss the entire 1944-45 season after being refused entry into the US by the War Mobilization Command. When the war ended, he was forced to miss most of the 1945-46 season due to a serious stomach and liver disorder. Doctors said he'd never play hockey again and some even had doubts that he'd survive the ordeal. Bryan proved the doctors wrong and not only lived, but he came back to the Rangers and played in all sixty games during the 1946-46 season. His comeback was the big hockey news story of the year.

After a few more seasons, Bryan retired from pro hockey after the 1948-49 season. He finished with 187 goals and 175 assists for 362 points in 449 NHL games over eleven seasons. One of the greatest players of his time, Hextall led the league in goals twice, and points once. He was a three-time NHL First Team All-Star (1940, 1941, 1942) and a Second Team All-Star once (1943).

Once his NHL career ended, Bryan returned to Poplar Point and lived proudly on his wheat farm. He kept playing hockey in Poplar Point for their team (Poplar Point Memorials) and won four Manitoba Intermediate Championships. In addition to playing with Poplar Point, he also played senior hockey for teams based in Portage la Prairie and Minnedosa, before finally stopping when he was fifty. Bryan also did some coaching for the junior St. Boniface Canadiens and Portage Terriers. In 1953, he coached St. Boniface all the way to the Memorial Cup final against the Barrie Flyers.

Hextall operated a lumber mill in Poplar Point and also owned a white wooden hunting lodge that housed roughly twenty people in the marshes outside of his community. "He loved to shoot ducks and play poker," said his Rangers teammate Muzz Patrick. "I remember when we trained in Winnipeg, which wasn't far from Poplar Point, we would play poker late and then get up at 5 in the morning to shoot ducks in those cold marshes. Everybody else was freezing, but he loved it."

Bryan raised four sons and a daughter in Poplar Point. Two of his sons, Dennis and Bryan Jr., had great NHL careers of their own and they both played for their dad's New York Rangers at one time or another. And of course, Bryan's grandson is Ron Hextall, who you've already read about.

"Our father never talked about his career," said son Dennis Hextall. "He was a modest guy. If he had pushed himself (in the press) he could have been an NHL coach. But it wasn't his nature. He was low-key. He would come to our junior games and he'd curse us out if we fought. I had 20 goals and 20 major penalties (fighting) in one season. My father said, 'You'd have 30 (goals) if you didn't spend so much time in the box.'

"I told him, 'Dad, if something happens out there, I'm not gonna back away.' He understood, he just didn't like the cheap penalties. He said there was a difference between being tough and being dumb.

"Bryan and I would ask about his career and he'd pass it off. The only time we'd hear things was when other (former) players would drop by our house. We lived in Poplar Point, which was on the main highway through Manitoba. All the kids in the neighbourhood would gather around. These were legendary figures like Sid Abel. They'd tell stories and our eyes would be this wide.

I remember them talking about my father's goal in the Stanley Cup. "Phil Watson got the puck behind the net and passed it out front. My father put 'er in with his backhand. The goalie was Turk Broda, another Hall of Famer. I played it back in my mind a thousand times imagining what it must have looked like. I still never realized how great my father was until I got to the NHL. That's when I saw what it meant to be a first-team All-Star. He was the Gordie Howe of his era."

"My father never pushed us into hockey," Bryan Hextall Jr. said. "It was something we wanted, Dennis and myself. Dad said, 'If you want to play, fine. If not, that's fine, too.' I was only seven when dad retired from the NHL so I don't remember much about those days. I remember he'd put me on his shoulders and ride me around the rink after practice. I didn't know he was a star. Kids don't see their fathers that way.

"My grandfather was a quiet man, he was a humble man, he was unassuming," recalled Ron Hextall. "For me, we would talk about present-day more so. I think he was uncomfortable talking about himself."

Bryan Hextall was finally inducted into the Hockey Hall of Fame in 1969. It's very surprising that a player of Hextall's calibre had to wait over twenty years to get into the Hall, but the modest Hextall didn't seem to mind the wait. He was just happy to be mentioned in the same breath as all the other greats of our fine sport.

Unfortunately for Bryan, he battled circulation problems in his lower legs throughout his retirement. It got so bad that both of legs needed amputation below the knee in 1978. Even with his artificial legs however, he would still sit in a canoe and shoot ducks.

In 1979 when the Winnipeg Jets joined the NHL, the team honoured Manitobans who had been inducted into the Hockey Hall of Fame prior to their home opener. One by one, legends came onto the ice until finally it was Hextall's turn. Bryan stubbornly refused to be taken out to centre ice in a wheelchair and walked out proudly on his crutches as thousands stood and cheered, some even weeping openly with tears of admiration for the spectacular hockey warrior that is Bryan Hextall. Broadcasted on national television, it marked the last time that most hockey fans saw Hex.

Bryan Hextall died of a heart attack at his home in Portage la Prairie on July 25, 1984. He was 70 years old.

"I saw him play in a senior league game back home," recalled Bryan Hextall Jr. "He was strong even then. He never slapped the puck, everything was with the wrists. He'd come in, snap those wrists and boom!"

10
DAN BAIN

MANITOBA HOCKEY HALL OF FAME

Dan Bain is the one and only player on this Manitoba Top 50 list that was a part of the early primitive years of the sport. To this day, Dan and his Winnipeg Victorias are still the most successful hockey team in Manitoba history, winning three Stanley Cups in 1896, 1901 and 1902. The very muscular Bain was the star player for all three Cup wins, providing scoring, playmaking and a physical presence. Most importantly he was blessed with natural leadership qualities that helped guide his troops to the Cup.

Winnipeg played such a big role in hockey history, being the first Western city to have success in a sport that had previously been dominated solely by the east. And Dan Bain was at the centre of it all.

A hockey player, figure skater, roller skater, cyclist, gymnast, and trap shooter all rolled into one, Dan Bain is without a doubt one of Canada's greatest all-time athletes despite playing only as an amateur, never turning pro.

At 6'0", 185 pounds, Bain was considered a very big man for his day and it helped make him one of the finest playmakers of the pre-NHL era. Bain's out-of-this-world sporting career was recognized when he was selected as Canada's most outstanding athlete of the last half of the 19th century.

Donald Henderson (Dan) Bain was born in Belleville, Ontario on August 15, 1874. He moved to Winnipeg with his family at the age of six. The second-youngest of seven children, Bain grew up in a nice two-storey house at

168 Fort Street and attended a nearby public school. He later earned a bacca-laureate degree from Manitoba College, a Presbyterian institution that was situated near where the University of Winnipeg stands today.

Bain's athletic prowess was first put on display in 1887 at the age of thir-teen when he won the Manitoba provincial roller skating championship. Four years later, he was named Manitoba's all-around gymnastics champion. Dan cycled as well and won the provincial racing crown in three straight years (1894-1896). In 1903, Bain travelled to Toronto where he won the Canadian Trapshooting title. He was also an active lacrosse player and golfer, but Bain's best-known sporting achievements come from hockey.

When the sport of hockey was introduced from out east, Bain was eager to learn the game. He joined the Winnipeg Victorias after reading an ad in a local newspaper soliciting new players and ended up playing eight seasons for them, including three as team captain, becoming one of hockey's greatest early players in the process. Dan played centre for the Victorias' team that won Stanley Cups in 1896, 1901 and 1902.

It all started while Dan and his Winnipeg Victorias were touring Montreal, they visited the Montreal Victorias clubhouse and saw their trophy case that held this particular piece of silverware called the Stanley Cup. It caught everyone's eye. They hadn't heard of it before and when they found out that any team could challenge for the Cup, they became very interested.

On this eastern tour, Winnipeg was given the title "Champions of Canada," because they beat everybody they played. At the start of the 1895-96 season, there was talk of the Winnipeg team wanting to challenge for the Stanley Cup. This didn't go down well with most eastern folk, notably the Montreal contingent.

The success of the Victorias' eastern tour had shown that a Manitoba association team should have every right to compete for the Canadian cham-pionship. The Manitoba Hockey Association secretary, Mr. Code, sent a letter suggesting the winner of the eastern association should play the winner of the Manitoba association. They eagerly waited for a reply, but nothing came. The Vics' who were showered with praise during the previous season, were basic-ally being given the cold shoulder.

All this waiting only helped fuel the Winnipeg Victorias' passion to chal-lenge for the Cup. Eventually they sent an official challenge for the Stanley Cup to its trustees, Sheriff Sweetland and P.D. Ross. A western team had never challenged for the Cup before, so they were entering unchartered territory.

When the Victorias made the challenge, they had no idea if they would be given the chance to play for the Cup. The decision was solely given to the Cup trustees. The Winnipeg club had requested a best-of-three series against the champion Montreal Victorias because of the fact that if they were going to travel all the way to Montreal, they should at least play more than one game.

At that time, however, the Stanley Cup challenge was decided by one game, and when the trustees finally accepted Winnipeg's challenge, they sided with Montreal in having a one-game playoff for the Cup as opposed to the best-of-three series that Winnipeg had proposed.

"The Victorias of Winnipeg realize that they will have their work cut out to win the Cup," wrote the *Manitoba Free Press*, "but will be in fine condition by the date of the game."

February 14, 1896 was the date of the match at the Victoria Skating Rink and Winnipeg arrived in town by train. The game began and Winnipeg led 2-0 at the halfway point of the game thanks to goals by Dan Bain and Colin Campbell. They proceeded to play defensively all throughout the second half of the game and won 2-0, with Bain being credited with the Cup-winning goal.

"The battle was a fierce one, and the victory hovered long over the heads of the contestants before she decided to settle finally on the banners of the men from the west," wrote the *Winnipeg Tribune*. "This was the first time the eastern men had to submit to a defeat at the hands of comparative babies in the art of hockey, and yet it was not only a defeat, but a complete whitewash."

Winnipeg wasn't even viewed as a threat going into the match.

"(Montreal) acknowledged that the westerners would put up a very good game, but they would not take the Cup with them back to Winnipeg," wrote the *Tribune*. "The Montrealers went to bed lonely, sadder and wiser men."

Fellow hockey author Richard Brignall writes that, "Not only did the Montreal team lose the Stanley Cup, but people also lost all the bets they made on them. It was popular to gamble on sports at this time. The people of Montreal put their money on a hometown victory. They all went home with empty pocketbooks. The Winnipeg contingent on the other hand had enough money to start a private bank. They put all their money on the Winnipeg seven. Their gamble paid off. No less than $2,000 in Winnipeg winnings were passed over Montreal's Windsor Hotel counter after the Stanley Cup match."

Goaltender Whitey Merritt was the first to return home from Montreal and he had to bring with him a description of what the Cup looked like since Montreal wouldn't let the Victorias take it back with them. "The Stanley Cup is in the form of a punch bowl," said Merritt. "It is of sterling silver and has about a two-gallon capacity."

When the rest of the players returned to Winnipeg they were pulled on sleighs through the city by their adoring fans. The Stanley Cup victory was unfortunately short-lived as Montreal came to Winnipeg in December of 1896 and defeated Bain's Vics'.

In 1899, Winnipeg challenged Montreal again and this time they played a two-game total goals series. Montreal won game one 2-1. Bain injured his eye during the game and was forced to miss the second game due to haemorrhaging behind the eye.

The second game wasn't completed due to a major controversy that arose. Winnipeg had always maintained a strict level of professionalism and class at all times so when one of Montreal's players violently slashed Winnipeg's Tony Gingras and the Montreal player was only given a two-minute penalty despite Gingras being carried off the ice, Winnipeg left the ice in protest and headed to their dressing room. Referee Bill Findlay felt insulted and abruptly left the arena to go home, but returned after officials followed him on a sleigh and convinced him to come back. Once back at the rink, Findlay gave Winnipeg fifteen minutes to return to the ice to finish the game. Winnipeg refused and thus Findlay disqualified them and awarded Montreal as winners of the Stanley Cup.

Winnipeg got back in the winner's circle in 1901 when they challenged and defeated the powerhouse Montreal Shamrocks in two straight games. On January 31, 1901, the Winnipeg Victorias and Montreal Shamrocks played the first overtime game in Stanley Cup history. Despite wearing a rudimentary wooden mask to protect a broken nose, Bain scored the winning goal in overtime to give the Victorias a 2-1 win and more importantly the Stanley Cup. Bain scored three goals in the two games for Winnipeg.

The Victorias won their third Stanley Cup when they defended it in January of 1902 in a two-game series from the upstart Toronto Wellingtons. Just two months later, Winnipeg met the Montreal Athletic Amateur Association, winners of the first-ever Stanley Cup challenge in 1893 in a best-of-three series. Winnipeg won the first game, but fell in back-to-back games to give the Cup back to Montreal. In the newspapers, Bain was heralded as the best player on the ice throughout the series.

Bain retired shortly after losing the Cup in early 1902. He finished with 10 goals in 11 Stanley Cup challenge games and 66 goals in 27 Manitoba league games, leading the league on three occasions. He was only 28 years old so it's under speculation why he quit when entering what should have been the prime of his career. Gordon Goldsborough writes, "It is possible the demands of his growing business interests required greater attention, or he might have simply wanted to retire before the inevitable decline."

He stayed in the game as the Honorary President and Coach of the Winnipeg Victorias well into the 1910's. Bain stopped playing team sports, but continued to skate for many years. In 1930 at the age of 56 he won the Canadian figure skating championship in the pairs competition. He continued to appear in pairs exhibition performances until the age of 70.

Manitoba historian Gordon Goldsborough writes that, "Bain was a resolute amateur, and as he grew older, he was increasingly vocal that the quality of hockey play had deteriorated as the game was taken over by professionals lacking stamina and skill. Bain derided the use of protective equipment; in his day, players wore nothing but skates and a uniform. During Bain's playing career, the team played the entire game without substitution, in marked contrast to regular shift changes that characterize modern hockey."

After hockey, Bain became a prominent Winnipeg entrepreneur and businessman. As the President of Donald H. Bain Limited, a grocery brokerage firm with offices across Canada, Dan became very successful in his professional life and amassed a substantial fortune. In 1906, shortly after his father's death, Dan bought the three-storey Waghorn House at 69 East Gate in the exclusive Armstrong's Point neighbourhood of Winnipeg. In 1932, he constructed Mallard Lodge as a retreat for hunting and relaxation on his large property on the Delta Marsh at Lake Manitoba. He spent lots of time there over the years, surrounded by his cherished curly-coated retrievers. He also built a hunting lodge and farm at Grosse Isle.

Dan was one of the first automobile enthusiasts in western Canada, owning thirteen vehicles at one point, among which were a bunch of fancy British sports models. Bain also helped found the original Winnipeg Winter Club. A life-long bachelor, Dan used to tell people that to be successful in life, you needed to avoid three things women, liquor, and politics.

In 1948, Bain became the first amateur player and one of the first western Canadian players to be inducted into the Hockey Hall of Fame. He was elected posthumously to the Canadian Sports Hall of Fame in 1971.

Dan Bain died in his Winnipeg home at 69 East Gate on August 15, 1962. He was 88 years old and left behind an estate valued at just over one million dollars (eight million today). A lifelong bachelor as noted earlier, Bain left almost all his fortune to various charities and former employees, with the remainder being given to relatives and friends.

Throughout his later life, Bain always proclaimed that the time that he played hockey was the best the sport has ever been: "Those were the days of real athletes," Bain recalled. "When we passed, the puck never left the ice and if the wingman wasn't there to receive it, it was because he had a broken leg."

9
ED BELFOUR

Eddie Belfour was one of the game's elite goalies for a very long time. He was the fourth-best goalie from the top era of goaltending since the original six days, which is actually a pretty major accomplishment in itself. He was slightly below the Haseks, Roys and Brodeurs, but significantly ahead of netminders like Mike Richter, Curtis Joseph, John Vanbiesbrouck, Chris Osgood, Olaf Kolzig, and Tom Barrasso.

MANITOBA SPORTS HALL OF FAME

"Whatever the motivation was—the desire to prove people wrong, the desire to be loved or needed—Belfour focused all of his energies into preparing to win," said ESPN's Scott Burnside. "And though he was demanding of his teammates, he saved his greatest demands for himself."

Focus and preparation were everything to Eddie. "The bigger the game, the narrower the focus," recalled his Dallas Stars coach Ken Hitchcock. "The bigger stage the better he played all the time."

Eddie was a stand-up/butterfly hybrid style of goaltender in a time where the position was slowly evolving to what it's like today with virtually every goalie playing solely a butterfly style. The 6'0", 190-pound Belfour relied on his quickness, aggressiveness, and technical strength. He was excellent at controlling rebounds and had solid puckhandling skills to go with it. His only major flaw perhaps was his volatile temper that sometimes came out with his aggressiveness and determination.

A neat stat I found out when researching Belfour is that he is one of two people ever (along with Neal Broten) to win an NCAA championship, an Olympic gold medal, and a Stanley Cup over the course of his career.

Ed Belfour was born in Carman on April 21, 1965. He wanted to be a goalie at the age of four when his parents first took him to the local arena. He started skating by the time he was five, but didn't start playing goalie full-time until he was eleven or twelve.

Growing up, Ed, his sister Patricia, and parents Henry and Alma lived in a three-bedroom bungalow in Carman. His father was a maintenance worker for the town of Carman. Right from an early age, Eddie and his buddies spent hours at a time playing hockey on the outdoor rink. On days where it was super cold, Ed would take off his skates and have mom rub his feet until the feeling returned to his toes. He would then go back and play hockey for a few more hours.

His first job was having a paper route in town so he could help pay for his hockey in the winter.

"He's always been so competitive," recalled his mom Alma, "so when the paper ran a contest to see who could get the most subscriptions he canvassed the whole area and won the contest. He won a stereo and it's the one we used for many years."

Ed watched *Hockey Night in Canada* every Saturday night and idolized Chicago Blackhawks netminder Tony Esposito and Soviet legend Vladislav Tretiak, often emulating the two in daily street hockey games. He became a goalie after seeing the cool-looking masks and acrobatic saves that Esposito and Tretiak made on television.

Belfour had his fair share of obstacles in making it, but from the time he started playing hockey, he had a dream that he was going to make the NHL. A dream that seemed a bit farfetched at times, especially when he was cut from his Carman Cougars high school team. He eventually battled his way back onto the roster as a backup goalie, and then finally became the starter, playing two and a half years of high school hockey.

After he graduated from high school, Belfour joined the MJHL's Winkler Flyers for the 1983-84 season and spent three years there. He was 21 years old by the time he played his last game with Winkler. He went undrafted several times at the NHL Entry Draft, but managed to get a hold of a scholarship to play college hockey at the University of North Dakota.

In his freshman year, Belfour went 29-4 and led his Fighting Sioux to the

NCAA championship. It was finally after that great success that NHL teams came knocking at his door, and he signed with the Chicago Blackhawks as a free agent on September 25, 1987.

Legendary Soviet netminder Vladislav Tretiak was hired by Blackhawks bench boss Mike Keenan to be the team's goaltending coach and for years he worked extensively with Belfour, who later credited Tretiak with his maturation as a goalie and more importantly as a person. Eddie wore number 20 in tribute to Tretiak later in his career.

Belfour was sent by Chicago to their IHL affiliate in Saginaw, where he spent a season and a half learning the ins and outs of the professional game. The Blackhawks called him up during the 1988-89 season and he played his first 23 games of NHL action.

For the 1989-90 season, Belfour played for the Canadian Olympic development team, but was called up by Chicago during the 1990 Stanley Cup playoffs. Alternating with two other goalies, Eddie appeared in nine games for Chicago and went 4-2, but they ultimately fell in the conference final to the Edmonton Oilers in six games. Edmonton went on to win the Cup that year.

Belfour had a pretty interesting set-up in his early years in Chicago. Vladislav Tretiak was his goalie coach and the other goalie on the team was Dominik Hasek. Eddie's 1990-91 campaign was one of the greatest rookie seasons anyone's ever put together. He played in 74 of the team's 80 games and went 43-19-7, leading the league in wins, goals-against-average and save percentage. When the awards night came around at the end of the year, Belfour left with all of the hardware as he won the Calder, Vezina and William Jennings Trophy, and was runner-up for the Hart Memorial Trophy.

Eddie followed up his dream rookie season by leading the Blackhawks to the Stanley Cup finals in 1991-92 season where they ran into Mario Lemieux, Jaromir Jagr and the Pittsburgh Penguins who promptly swept them for their second straight Stanley Cup.

After five more years as Chicago's starter, Belfour was dealt to San Jose, and then from there, signed as a free agent with the Dallas Stars in time for the 1997-98 season. In his first season with Dallas, Belfour led his club to the conference finals.

The pinnacle of Eddie's career came the following year in the 1999 Stanley Cup playoffs when he carried Dallas to their lone Stanley Cup win in team history. For those who don't remember, Dallas won game six of the Cup finals over the Buffalo Sabres in triple overtime off a highly controversial Brett Hull goal that still gets talked about today. Nonetheless it was a huge personal triumph for Eddie as previously he had faced much criticism from the press on whether he could push a team all the way to the Cup, which is the likely reason why he was not invited to Canada's 1996 World Cup or 1998 Olympic squads. But in 1998-99 he was simply on fire the whole way through and you have to wonder if any Stanley Cup-winning goalie has gone through a more impressive line of opposing goalies than Eddie overcoming Tommy Salo, Grant Fuhr, Patrick Roy, and Dominik Hasek. Three of the four are Hall of Famers which pretty much says all that needs to be said.

Dallas coach Ken Hitchcock thought that Belfour was even more impressive in the 2000 Stanley Cup finals where they fell to the New Jersey Devils in game six of the Cup finals. "As good as he was in the Cup year (1999), he was better the next year in the finals," Hitchcock said. "Just check out the shot totals against New Jersey—we'd have something like 18 or 19 a night, and they were always over 40. We had no business being there but for him.

"I've never seen a person so oblivious to what's going on. If you ever want to see goaltending alone win a playoff, look at us in 2000. Eddie won two series all by himself—our team had nothing left, we were banged up and just done. He just refused to let us lose games."

"Eddie was a unique teammate. Socially, he probably wasn't real tight with anybody, but we all admired the seriousness he took at his position. He prepared himself. He was the first guy there and the last to leave," said teammate Joe Nieuwendyk. "There were a lot of things that went with that. Eddie needed his certain type of groceries; he needed a skate sharpener and all that kind of stuff. But we accepted it because we knew the type of goalie that we had. We knew the competitor he was. He was maybe the best biggest-game goaltender I ever played with."

After a few stints in Toronto and Florida, Belfour retired from hockey after the 2007-08 season. Belfour finished with a 484-320-125 record in 963 NHL games with 76 shutouts. He also had 88 wins in the playoffs. Currently, Eddie ranks 3rd in wins all-time and 5th in games played for a goaltender. In addition to his one Stanley Cup (1999) and 2002 Olympic gold medal, Belfour won the Calder Trophy (1991), two Vezina Trophies (1991, 1993), and four William Jennings Trophies (1991, 1993, 1995, 1999). He was named an NHL First Team All-Star twice (1991, 1993) and a Second Team All-Star once (1995). Ed also played in six NHL All-Star Games (1992, 1993, 1996, 1998, 1999, 2003). Belfour was inducted into the Hockey Hall of Fame in 2011.

Today, Eddie lives in Dallas where he and his son, Dayn, have started a distillery "Belfour Spirits". He still gets back to Carman a few times a year to see his parents and other family and friends.

When asked about how he made the big leagues and had such an amazing career despite being pegged as a long-shot, Belfour said, "growing up in a small town in Canada and watching *Hockey Night in Canada* and playing for the Stanley Cup every day on the street. We had a real competitive high school. I played a lot of sports and I was a pretty good athlete. Obviously, a God-given talent, never give up, never quit and always give 110%."

8
DICK IRVIN

D ick Irvin was one of the hockey world's top centremen of the 1920's. He was an exceptional stickhandler who possessed a wicked hard and accurate shot that made goalies look like fools.

Also one of the greatest NHL coaches of all time, most hockey fans don't realize that Dick Irvin was elected to the Hockey Hall of Fame as a player and not a coach. His playing career seems to

get forgotten as the years have gone by. In fact, if you're to think of the name Dick Irvin, the first thing that pops into your mind is his son, Dick Irvin Jr, who had a more well-known career as the long-time broadcaster for *Hockey Night in Canada*.

But don't be fooled, the 5'9", 162-pound Irvin was one of the game's all-time greats, and arguably the most prolific goal-scorer that our province has ever produced. He was always his team's star player and he constantly led his league in goals for a good portion of his career.

"Dick Irvin deserves a book of his own," says Vince Leah. "Many rate him as the finest hockey player ever developed in Manitoba, and his record in amateur and professional hockey as a player and a coach is indeed remarkable."

Irvin's best game came against the Toronto Rugby and Athletic Association, when he scored all nine of his team's goals in a 9-2 win. The feat was huge at the time and it even landed him a page in the first-ever *Ripley's Believe It or Not* book!

James Dickinson "Dick" Irvin was born in Limestone Ridge, Ontario (just outside of Hamilton) on July 19, 1892. His father was a butcher by trade and moved the family to Winnipeg when Dick was around six years old. Dick was one of ten children in the family, six boys and four girls. Two of his brothers died in infancy and all four sisters died of tuberculosis at an early age, so it was Dick and three brothers that were still left by the time the family moved to Winnipeg.

Irvin grew up in the North End at a house on 220 Atlantic Avenue. He went to nearby Machray School, which was located at the intersection of Mountain Avenue and Charles Street, but only up until grade six because that's when his father made him and his brothers work with him in the butcher shop.

Dick started playing hockey soon after the family moved to Winnipeg and followed in the footsteps of his brother Alex, who had started a few years earlier. Dick began playing on his street with a homemade wooden puck before moving on to the outdoor rinks on Selkirk and Atlantic Avenue. In 1902, Dick snuck in the back door of the old Winnipeg Auditorium with some friends to watch a Stanley Cup finals match between the Winnipeg Victorias and the Montreal hockey club. Seeing the game's best players up close like that inspired Irvin to become just like them.

Soon after that he started playing Sunday-school hockey and then later played for the Strathcona junior team. By the age of twelve he was playing for their senior team. Dick got in all the hockey he could, honing his craft by playing at home on the rink he made on his driveway, skating up and down, starting and stopping, and stickhandling on the narrow area. In the summer, he had a goal area chalked up on the garage door and practised shooting off a flat board imbedded in the ground. On rainy days, he would go up into the attic of his house and shoot pucks at the doorknob of an old door mounted sideways against a wall.

Hockey wasn't the only sport that Irvin played. He also enjoyed curling, bowling, and was a baseball player (shortstop and second base) for the Dominion Express team in the fastball Winnipeg League. Dick's brother, Alex, said that if he had taken up sprinting he would have been outstanding as he always beat the local neighbourhood kids in races.

"I remember he used to tell me how his father got mad at him once for not showing up to work one day because he was playing hockey," recalled Dick Irvin Jr. "and his father said, 'you'll never get anywhere chasing that little black thing!'"

Dick's father was actually really encouraging and a positive figure in his son's hockey career. He just wanted to make sure the work in the butcher shop got done too! Dick's father saw to it that his four sons were well-equipped with skates and even bought skates for other kids that were less fortunate in the neighbourhood. The craziest thing is that he would drive his son's hockey team via horse and sleigh to towns like Dugald, Niverville and St. Jean for games. Many times, they were lost in blizzards coming home from the games and only the horse's sense of direction got them back.

Irvin always considered the first big thrill he had in hockey to be when he was first called up from the Winnipeg Strathconas to play with the Winnipeg Monarchs in 1913-14. "My dad was playing in the church league and I guess he went to watch a Monarchs game one night, it was maybe their third game of the year," said Irvin Jr. "The Monarchs came out for the game with a couple of guys missing who were hurt or sick so they brought him out of the stands to play in the game. I guess they had seen my dad play in the church league and do well, so they brought him out to play and he ended up scoring a few goals that night and played for the Monarchs full-time after that."

"Never in the history of Winnipeg hockey has a player dominated the game as Dick Irvin was able to do during the 1913-14 season," wrote long-time *Winnipeg Tribune* writer Vince Leah. "Not even the great Dan Bain could compare to the impact Irvin would have on Winnipeg hockey."

Vince Leah made those remarks after Irvin scored 23 goals in an 8-game season.

In that 1913-14 season, the Monarchs made the Western final of the Allan Cup and were slated to play the Kenora Thistles. Dick had played a few games in the church league earlier in the season, so because of that the CAHA ruled him ineligible to play for the Allan Cup. There was a headline in the paper the next day proclaiming "NO ALLAN CUP GAME TONIGHT" and since the CAHA banned their best player, the Monarchs threatened to pull out of the series. It's unlikely they were going to win without Irvin's services.

"The guy who made the ruling for the CAHA," recalled Dick Irvin Jr., "was a guy named William Northey, who became a partner with the people who ran the Montreal Canadiens, and when my dad coached them years later, they were in the same office working together!"

The game was ultimately played with Irvin in the lineup and the Monarchs won 6-2. In a quick turnaround, they were then knocked out of Allan Cup contention just a few nights later when they fell to the Regina Victorias by a 5-4 scoreline.

Irvin got another crack at senior hockey supremacy the following year and made the most of it. His Monarchs won the 1915 Allan Cup and Dick was credited the cup-winning goal in the finals against the Melville Millionaires.

When Dick first turned pro, he signed with the PCHA's Portland Rosebuds for $750 and played his first season of professional hockey with them. Irvin's hockey career was really coming on until World War I happened and he was forced to put his hockey on hold for a few years.

Irvin joined the army back in Winnipeg with the Fort Garry Horse regiment of the British Expeditionary Force for World War I. He was a motorcycle dispatch rider in Belgium and France. When the war ended he was in a military hospital since he'd been involved in an accident with his motorcycle so he didn't get back to Winnipeg until April of 1919.

"The funny thing," recalled Dick Irvin Jr., "is when the Monarchs won the Allan Cup in 1915, the city of Winnipeg gave each player a motorcycle. Most of the guys sold it I'm sure for something like $25 or $50 bucks, but my dad learned how to ride his, and so when he joined the army a few years later, he joined as a motorcycle dispatch rider."

When Dick returned to Winnipeg after the war, he got back into hockey right away, and worked for the Dominion Express, which was the original express company of the CPR. It was the UPS, FedEx and Purolator of its time. Irvin was later convinced by the owner of the Regina Victorias to come and play for their senior team. He played two seasons of senior hockey before joining the Regina Capitals of the WCHL.

The closest that Dick ever came to winning a Stanley Cup during his playing career was with the Capitals in the 1921-22 season. The Regina Capitals won the WCHL championship that year and met up with the PCHA champion Vancouver Millionares in a two-game total goals series for the right to play in the Stanley Cup final. Irvin scored the game-winning goal in a 2-1 game one victory for Regina, but his Capitals fell 4-0 the following game to lose the series.

Dick was already 34 years old when he played his first NHL game so he was past his prime, but that didn't stop him from having one heck of a rookie year. Irvin was named the first captain in franchise history and promptly scored 36 points in 43 games, leading the league in assists and finishing second for points. He also finished fourth in league MVP voting.

For a time, Irvin had the league all-time record for most assists in a season. Back in those days, you only got an assist if you passed in a certain zone of the ice, so assists weren't nearly as common as they are today. It's amazing that even at such an advanced age, Irvin was one of the NHL's best players. Unfortunately, his career was suddenly ended by a vicious hit by Montreal Maroons defenceman Red Dutton that fractured Irvin's skull. He tried to return from the injury, but it wasn't happening. He retired during the 1928-29 season and instantly was named the team's head coach.

Dick retired as one of the most prolific goal-scorers the game had seen up until that point. He scored a whopping 207 goals in 70 senior hockey games in Manitoba and Saskatchewan. Dick also went on to score 152 goals in 250 pro games split between the WCHL and NHL. He won the Allan Cup in 1915 and was a four-time WCHL All-Star. He was inducted into the Hockey Hall of Fame for his impressive playing career in 1958.

Irvin got into coaching from the time he hung up his skates, and coached Chicago for a few seasons before being fired after the 1930-31 season despite taking his Black Hawks to the Stanley Cup final that year. Chicago's owner was an eccentric. He made something like thirteen coaching changes in eighteen years! Irvin wasn't out of work long as he soon answered a call from Conn Smythe to coach the Toronto Maple Leafs and won one Stanley Cup (1932) with them in his nine years as coach. He later joined the Montreal Canadiens and coached them for fifteen years and won another three Stanley Cups (1944, 1946, 1953). In his 26 years of coaching in the NHL, Irvin's teams made the playoffs on 24 occasions, and the Stanley Cup finals 16 times! That actually doesn't sound too great if you think about it, as he was 4-12 in Stanley Cup finals. The fact that he constantly iced contending teams, however, is extremely impressive. Add that with the fact that his 692 regular season wins is good for sixth all time and it's cemented that Irvin was one of the greatest coaches in NHL history.

How Dick Irvin got into coaching is an interesting story. During his playing career, he had no idea what he was going to do after he retired from hockey. He thought he would just go back to his offseason job at the Patrick Burns Meat Packing Company in Regina and do that throughout the year. That thought process all changed when he joined the Chicago Black Hawks. For a few days one year, the team did some land training in South Bend, Indiana at Notre Dame University. Irvin watched Knute Rockne, a famous American football coach, run a practice with the school's football team and he liked what he saw. He thought maybe he could do that, so when the chance to coach the Black Hawks came about, Irvin jumped at it.

Irvin commuted between Regina and wherever he was coaching for the last part of his life. He built a house on Angus Street in Regina and lived for many summers there. The hockey season was much shorter in those days (November to March) so he spent plenty of time on the Prairies in his later years. Dick suffered from bone cancer towards the end of his life and died on May 16th, 1957 at the age of 64.

"Ron MacLean and I went up to Winnipeg in 2000 after the Hall of Fame there picked an all-time all-star team for Manitoba hockey players," recalled Irvin Jr. "They put my dad as the top coach and Terry Sawchuk was picked as the number one player of all time for Winnipeg, which was a great choice. Some reporter wrote a column the next day that Irvin's choice was totally wrong and that he didn't didn't spend enough of his life in Winnipeg to qualify and he thought the top coach should have been Billy Reay. So, I did some research and found that my dad spent more of his life in Winnipeg than Sawchuk did. I wrote the guy a letter, but he never acknowledged it. That chicken bastard!"

7
CHUCK GARDINER

Chuck Gardiner is the only goaltender in NHL history to win a Stanley Cup as team captain. His hands, feet and mind were lightning quick. Rarely was he ever caught off guard by an opposing shooter. Gardiner's exceptional play was augmented by his ability to direct his teammates on the ice, a factor that led to his being chosen to serve as team captain in the Black Hawks' 1933-34 Cup year.

Howie Morenz put Gardiner on his personal all-star list. "He was the hardest man I ever had to beat," recalled Morenz. "We considered him 75 percent of the team. When I was able to get one single goal past Chuck in a game, I felt I had had a big night."

A good modern-day comparison to Gardiner would be Dominik Hasek. Both goalies carried sub-par teams that offered very little offensive support and eventually made them contenders all on their own. They were both considered to be the best goalie of their respective times and won many individual awards instead of team awards.

"Without Gardiner," praised Chicago Blackhawks coach Tommy Gorman, "we wouldn't have made it. He's the greatest goalie that ever donned the pads."

Chuck always seemed to be smiling and in a good mood even out on the ice. During one game against New York, his team was up by a goal late in the game when Rangers' star Bill Cook skated around the defence and had a breakaway on Chuck. He took his time but Gardiner waited him out and made the save. He chuckled and waved at Cook as he skated away. "Tough luck," said Chuck, "but be sure and come around again."

What's very notable about the 6'0", 175-pound Gardiner is his impeccable durability. He only missed four games over a seven-year NHL career, which you'll find downright miraculous after you read the health problems he had to suffer and play through. It's very easy for me to say that had Gardiner lived past the age of thirty, he no doubt would be looked upon today as one of the greatest netminders in hockey history, instead of being so overlooked when comparing the game's greats.

Charlie "Chuck" Gardiner was born in Edinburgh, Scotland on December 31, 1903. The fourth of five children, his family moved to Winnipeg when he was seven and lived first at a house on William Avenue, before moving to nearby Alexander Street. Both streets were south of the railways and full of fellow Scottish-Irish working-class families. Chuck attended Albert School, and soon befriended Wilf Cude, who himself had immigrated from Wales and would also go on to become an NHL netminder. In his teens, Chuck's parents moved and he lived at houses on Tache Avenue and Langside Street.

Charlie had two brothers who joined the army and were sent overseas during World War I. His father also enlisted but died in Winnipeg before he got the chance to fight in the war. Both brothers returned home after the war with one of his brothers, John, having been involved in a poison gas attack and was seriously ill, dying years later from his war injury. Chuck's other brother Alex came back healthy.

Around this time, Chuck began working at the J.H. Ashdown Hardware Company to help support his family. And it was while working at the hardware store that he got his first taste of playing organized sports as a member of the store's baseball team. But his attention would soon shift to hockey as he started to carry the same passion for the game as the children who were born in Canada.

"We used to flood the backyards of all the homes and improvise hockey teams. I couldn't skate very fast, so by unanimous consent I was shoved into the goal and told to stay there," Chuck recalled. "You see, I didn't learn to skate until after I was eight years old."

What Chuck would do is wrap the magazines around his legs for goalie pads and go in the makeshift crease marked by tree branches. "I remember the fellows using old magazines as shin pads, wrapping them around their legs, inside the stockings. Newspapers—bundles of 'em—would be converted into kidney pads for whatever purpose the individual needed them. We all wore stocking caps, or toques as we call them, for open air play. Sometimes it would get so cold that we could only stand to play ten minutes at a time. Then we'd go into a nearby shack and warm up by the heat of an old wood stove and go back and finish the period. It was the only way we could survive."

Since Charlie started playing as a goalie on the cold, harsh frozen ponds, he played an acrobatic style of goaltending to avoid having his hands and feet frozen, instead of the stand-up style that was most commonly used in that era.

When Gardiner was thirteen he joined the Victorias, a team in the Winnipeg City League. In his first game at the old St. Vital rink he recorded a shutout, but in the next game it was his own team that got shutout so Gardiner was cut. Being cut didn't discourage Chuck too much as the next season he made the intermediate team of the Selkirk Fishermen. He later played intermediate hockey for a Winnipeg Assiniboia team.

Gardiner played both junior and senior hockey with the Winnipeg Tammany Tigers of the MJHL and MSHL from 1921 to 1924. He then joined the Selkirk Fishermen senior team for the 1924-25 season and led them to the championship final where they fell to the Port Arthur Bobcats. After this, he decided to turn professional with the Winnipeg Maroons of the American Hockey Association. And it was around this time that he had to give up the other sports that he played competitively. He was a notable baseball player with a career batting average of .300 and played rugby as well for a team that reached two Western Canada Junior Finals. He also played in the 13th Grey Cup with the Winnipeg Tammany Tigers in 1925, and lost 24-1 to the Ottawa Senators.

Gardiner then joined the Winnipeg Maroons, the first pro hockey team to exist in Manitoba, playing in the American Hockey Association (AHA) from 1926 to 1928. While Gardiner was a member of the Maroons, he was reading the *Winnipeg Free Press* one morning and found out that Canadiens great Georges Vezina was so severely ill with tuberculosis that he was forced to retire. The news jolted Chuck and he was extremely saddened because Vezina was a big idol of his and he had a great deal of respect for the Habs netminder.

After two seasons with the Winnipeg Maroons, Gardiner joined the Chicago Black Hawks who were only playing their second season in the NHL. As a result, they were not very good. During his first year in the NHL, playing for such a terrible team who were often called "goalless wonders", Chuck was booed constantly by the Chicago fans despite Gardiner playing well every night. The Black Hawks fired their coach midway through the season and gave the job to Hugh Lehman, a retired netminder of less than a year. He replaced Gardiner in goal with himself. An experiment that went well for a few games (2-0 win, 1-1 tie), before being shelled for nine and ten goals the next two games. Gardiner became more determined once Lehman's experiment was over with, and he went back to playing solid night in and night out.

Maroon teammate Murray Murdoch, who later faced Gardiner as a New York Ranger left wing, noted, "When he went to the Black Hawks, his goaltending style changed. He developed a whole new goaltending style—coming out of the net to meet the attacker—very effective. It's all in the timing. If you go at someone's feet when they're being chased from behind it's very hard to change direction. No goalie was using that style at that time. Some people said it wouldn't work, but we knew. He was very hard to score on."

Gardiner was so good that despite having a 7-29-8 record, he managed a 1.85 goals against average. How that's even possible I'll never know.

By the 1929-30 season, Chicago wasn't the joke of the league anymore, qualifying for the playoffs with a 21-18-15 record, before falling to the Montreal Canadiens 3-2 in a two-game total-goals series. The next season would be one of Gardiner's best stats-wise, recording twelve shutouts and a 1.72 goals against average. In December of that season, the New York Americans offered $10,000 to Chicago in exchange for Chuck, but the Hawks refused. Gardiner was named to the NHL First All Star Team that year and in the playoffs, he carried his team to the fifth and decisive game of the Stanley Cup final, but once again lost to their old foe Montreal.

After the game, Gardiner skated over to Canadiens goalie George Hainsworth and shook hands with him. His teammates and coach followed suit and began to shake hands and congratulate the other Canadiens. To his great surprise, the Montreal Canadiens lifted up Charlie Gardiner on their shoulders in tribute to his tremendous effort. They carried him to their dressing room, where they offered their congratulations for having given them such a strong battle, and fed him champagne. He then slipped out and returned across the ice to his own teammates. The Montreal crowd, still in their seats with the joy of their victory, gave him a tremendous ovation for his stalwart performance.

During the offseasons in Winnipeg, Gardiner took flying lessons from former teammate Konrad Johannesson. He was a fast learner and quickly began flying all by himself. Chuck also purchased shares in the Winnipeg Flying Club which was founded by his friend Johannesson. He also had a passion for shooting rifles and was recognized for this when he was elected Field Secretary of the Winnipeg Gun Club.

Charlie was a regular at the Grace United Church in Winnipeg, the same Church he was married in. He was also a Freemason and a member of the St. John's Lodge. Because he was playing hockey most of the year, the only chance he had to go to school was during the summer. He earned a certificate in business administration and sales from the International Correspondence Schools. Shortly after, he was a partner in a sporting goods business and travelled across western Canada in the summer to sell various products to sports teams.

Some of the trips were closer to home, in southern and central Manitoba. A budding goalie by the name of Turk Broda, an eighteen-year-old who lived in Brandon, found out that Gardiner was in town selling baseball equipment and other sporting goods. "I asked him all kinds of questions about goaltending," Broda told his teammates, "and he was kind enough to answer."

Gardiner wasn't just cool on the ice. One time during the season, two men approached Gardiner in a deserted hotel lobby and asked to talk to him about a business deal. Gardiner asked them who they were. They told him certain "businessmen" were interested in making a deal with him, and wasn't he interested in making a little extra money, especially with a wife and child to support? The other man, who had been silent until now, opened his briefcase to reveal a pile of cash, and told Gardiner that there was more where that came from; all he had to do was let in a goal or two at crucial times in a couple of games so the other team would win, and make it look accidental, and nobody would ever know the difference.

"No!" said Gardiner, and angrily demanded how dare they think he would ever consider doing such a thing.

The man with the money smiled and said that anybody could be bought.

"Not me," said Gardiner. "Go to hell!"

The man with the briefcase looked at the other man, who shrugged. They left. A furious Gardiner called his coach and the police to tell them the mob had approached him to fix games.

In a December 1932 game against the Toronto Maple Leafs, Chuck's health problems first came to light. Gardiner heroically made 55 saves in a Chicago win. But what the public didn't know at the time was that Chuck was running a high fever and was sprawled out on the locker room floor to rest between periods. After the game, he was rushed to the hospital, but was released the following day.

Unfortunately, that was just the beginning for Chuck's health problems. He was later bothered by pains in his throat and kidneys. He often had pain shooting upward from his throat to his head and pain burning like liquid fire through his kidneys. He experienced vision problems and once while the Blackhawks were on a train back to Chicago, Chuck suddenly felt an intense pain in his throat that spread to the rest of his body, notably his kidneys. When questioned by the team's coaching staff about the issue, he lied and said it was only a minor headache. But when Charlie woke up on the train in the morning, he had trouble seeing as black spots obscured his vision. This was Gardiner's first uremic convulsion. He told his coach Tommy Gorman, "I can't see...there's black spots before my eyes." Gorman told Gardiner that those black spots were just pucks.

Still, Gardiner played, and played extremely well. His teammates unanimously elected him team captain to start the 1933-34 season. It was during this year that Charlie's heath really started deteriorating as he was playing with a tonsillar infection for most of the season. He was often seen slumping over his crossbar during stoppages in play, nearly blacking out. At intermissions and after games you would find him passed out on the floor of his team's dressing room.

Despite everything he was going through, Chuck had another amazing year, winning the Vezina Trophy for the second time in his career. When the playoffs rolled around, Chuck kept on with his goal of winning a Stanley Cup. During one playoff game against the Montreal Maroons, Charlie was in extreme pain with a fever of 102 degrees Fahrenheit.

Chicago won the series and went up against Detroit in the Stanley Cup finals. For Gardiner, it was a reunion of sorts with Red Wings netminder Wilf Cude. You see, Gardiner and Cude lived on William Street growing up and were great friends who walked to and from school every day for many years. To be now playing against each other in a best-of-five Stanley Cup final was really something.

To Gardiner, he wasn't really playing against the Red Wings. He was up against a much bigger opponent. He was playing against time and how much longer he could play before the game killed him. It became a race against the clock for Chuck to achieve his dream of winning a Stanley Cup as his health was deteriorating fast with the chronic tonsil infection spreading and causing more uremic convulsions. He won the first two games for his team 2-1 (2OT) and 4-1, but lost game three 5-2. Chuck was so ill and withdrawn after losing game three that management sent him to Milwaukee to unwind before game four at home.

Going into Game 4, Gardiner was nearly comatose, but told his teammates, "Look, all I need is one goal next game. Just give me one goal and I'll take care of the other guys."

Game 4 was a game of superb goaltending from both Gardiner and Cude. While the crowd of 18,000 grew increasingly more anxious, the game remained scoreless through regulation. Then the first overtime period came and went without a goal. Gardiner was getting sicker as the game went longer, hardly being able to stand up in the net, but he held his word and was rewarded in the second overtime when teammate Mush March fired a wrist shot past Cude to give Chicago their first Stanley Cup in franchise history. Gardiner raised his stick in the air and then proceeded to stumble off the ice and pass out in the dressing room.

The next day during the Blackhawk's Stanley Cup parade, Gardiner collected on an early-season bet when he was carted around Chicago's business district in a wheelbarrow by defenceman Roger Jenkins while teammates and fans cheered their goalie. This would be the last time that Chuck would hear the roaring fans of Chicago.

Chuck was still extremely sick when he returned to Winnipeg. Doctors told him to just rest, but Charlie was a celebrity and soon found the strain of inaction too much and resumed doing activities around his hometown. Soon after, Gardiner fell into a coma. He was treated at home for three days before Charlie was rushed to the St. Boniface Hospital. He died soon after on June 13, 1934 after complications arose when he underwent brain surgery to remove a tumour. He was only 30 years old. A series of uremic convulsions brought about the brain haemorrhage that killed him, and it all started with a tonsillar infection.

Looking back, it's beyond crazy how Chuck kept playing and didn't miss a single minute despite going through what he went through. Coaches and teammates came out after his death and remarked how Gardiner was seriously ill for months but wouldn't take himself out of the game. Chuck actually played more determinedly even as his symptoms became more ominous.

Black Hawks manager Tommy Gorman used to say that Chuck Gardiner was the sole reason that Chicago won the Cup in 1934 and weren't an embarrassment in the league. "He was one of the most colourful figures that ice hockey has ever produced. Chuck Gardiner was taken away at the peak of his career. Never in the history of hockey has a better exhibition of goalkeeping been given than that which 'Gardiner the Great' put up against Detroit in the championship final. He was a born showman. Every move was a picture. He made bad games look good. Dull matches he transformed into fascinating ones."

"To me Chuck Gardiner was the essence of manhood and sportsmanship," recalled Frank Frederickson, who served as a pallbearer at Chuck's funeral. "His personality and character was a dominant factor in forging a chain of friendship, wherever he went, both in sport and business. In hockey, he had the respect and admiration of friend and foe alike, for his was ever 'generous in victory and glorious in defeat.' His untimely passing in the heyday of life, at the zenith of his career seems to me the saddest blow of all."

It was absolutely no surprise to anyone when Chuck was inducted into the 1945 inaugural class of the Hockey Hall of Fame. He was just an incredible goalie, the best of his generation, and without a doubt the best the game had seen up until that point. The end of the year all-star teams only existed for his final four NHL seasons and he was named a First Team All-Star three times (1931, 1932, 1934) and a Second Team All-Star once (1933). He won two Vezina Trophies in 1932 and 1934 and played in the original NHL All Star Game in Ace Bailey's benefit in 1934. His 2.02 lifetime goals against average and 42 shutouts over seven seasons are a testament to his out-of-this-world play since his career record was 112-152-52 in 316 NHL games.

If you want to learn more about Chuck then I highly recommend trying to get your hands on a copy of Antonia Chambers book, *Before the Echoes Fade*. Fellow Manitoba Top 50 player Art Coulter didn't do a lot of interviews in his later years, but did one for Chambers to talk about Chuck. "I wouldn't do this for everyone," said Coulter, "but Charlie Gardiner was a superior human being."

One thing I'd like for Chuck is have him remembered more in our province. In Winnipeg, there are arenas named after Billy Mosienko, Terry Sawchuk, and now Jonathan Toews, but nothing for Gardiner. I know that Chuck's nephew Ted Poulter made a proposal a few years back that the St. Vital Arena be renamed the Gardiner Arena, but he never even received a reply for his request, which is just absurd considering what a hero Chuck Gardiner was. I think that it would definitely make sense that the St. Vital Arena be named after Chuck since he first played junior hockey at a rink in St. Vital. Hopefully some progress on that front can be made soon and an arena can one day bear the name Charlie Gardiner, one of the best goaltenders ever to strap on a pair of pads.

6
ANDY BATHGATE

Andy Bathgate was the model hockey player. On top of his God-given talent, he was a tough but clean player. NHL.com writes that he was "a modest man of great integrity, a leader and something of a matinee idol." There weren't many better offensive players than Bathgate in his time. The 6'0" right winger was a smooth skater, skilled puck-handler, and possessed one of the hardest shots in hockey.

I find myself very fortunate to have gotten the chance to interview Bathgate a few years before he passed away in 2016. He was simply an artist on the ice, a real gentleman that was the first player to speak out against overt violence in hockey.

"Hockey players are entertainers," said Bathgate. "I always felt that I gotta make some good plays and good passes. Every time I'd go on the ice I'd say 'Create.' The smoother I skated and had my head up, the better I could handle the puck."

Andy had a fantastic seventeen-year NHL career and is still considered today as one of the greatest New York Rangers of all time. One of his biggest accomplishments is that he led the NHL in points from 1957 to 1964, outscoring fellow NHL greats such as Gordie Howe, Jean Beliveau, Maurice Richard, Henri Richard, and Bobby Hull.

Bathgate was a notable playmaker who was also known for his blistering shot that was comparable to Bobby Hull's. Andy's shot was known to have "curved," making it harder for goaltenders to stop. "Yes, sometimes there was spin on my shots," Andy said. "I picked it up from curling. Talking to curlers in Winnipeg, I was told that a curling rock delivered straight doesn't go true because of the irregularities on the ice. So, by twisting the rock, it goes true and is under control."

"His mother was my school teacher in Winnipeg," recalled Ted Harris. "I didn't really know him personally, but he could sure shoot that damn puck I'll never forget that."

Andy Bathgate was born on August 28, 1932 in Winnipeg and grew up in West Kildonan. The youngest of three hockey-playing brothers (he also had two sisters), Andy started his hockey on the outdoor rinks of his neighbourhood. "My father built a rink right by our house and that's where I started," recalled Bathgate. "It didn't have boards or anything on it but it was good enough for me and my friends to practice. Growing up, I played on quite a few junior and minor hockey teams that were quite successful and I guess I really enjoyed it because it was outdoors. I basically would play on any team that wanted me!"

"I played in the Knights of Columbus league at the age of twelve because all the other boys were battling for our country in World War II. The St. Joseph's Church invited me so I played in it with the people that didn't go to war who had a handicap of some sort or stayed here while working with the military. They were good players too. It taught me a lot about playing indoors because it was at the old Olympic Rink and it was that or the Amphitheatre for indoor rinks in Winnipeg. It wasn't much of a rink for today's standards but it was a good for me since I was always playing outdoors in the wind so it was a great experience."

In his early years, Andy was always around the hockey rink trying to get in as much playing time as humanly possible. His Sunday morning routine usually looked like this:

- Wake up at 4:30 AM.
- Change into multiple pairs of trousers, sweaters, socks, boots, and a parka.
- Walk five miles with his friends through -25 weather to the Olympic Rink (The trolley has yet to begin its rounds).
- Skate at the Olympic Rink from 6-8am because that's the only time Andy and his friends could scrimmage on indoor ice.
- At 8am, take the trolley back to West Kildonan.

+ Thaw out in the glow of the stove in the Bathgate's kitchen.
+ Eat a quick breakfast.
+ Go to the 10 o'clock Mass with family.
+ More hockey, this time on the outdoor rinks for the remainder of the day before coming home at night to tune in to an NHL game on the radio.

Bathgate recalls his childhood: "As a kid, you'd be listening to Foster Hewitt every Saturday night and I always tried to follow the game as much as I could. I also played the sport as much as possible, playing for six teams at a time even. Sometimes I'd have to walk a couple of miles for certain games because the streetcars wouldn't work when I needed to get to a game. My father then passed away when I was thirteen which was tough, but you could say it all made me appreciate the game more."

It was lucky for Bathgate that he had another father figure in his life named Vince Leah, the legendary Winnipeg sportswriter, who lived next door and basically took him under his wing. Andy later called him the "most important person in my life," and when Andy was later inducted into the Hockey Hall of Fame, he had Vince introduce him.

"I have to give him all the credit in the world," Bathgate recalled. "Vince was there before my father passed away and after my father passed away when I was thirteen. Vince really encouraged me an awful lot to get really involved in hockey. I couldn't thank Vince enough."

The New York Rangers regularly held camps in Winnipeg and when Bathgate was fifteen, they signed him to a C-form which made him Rangers property. When Andy was seventeen, his family decided to escape the cold and move to Guelph where his older brother was already playing. Andy ended up playing junior hockey for the Guelph Biltmore Madhatters and in one game, he received a check that severely damaged his left knee. A steel plate was fixed beneath the kneecap yet it plagued him throughout his career. The injury didn't stop him from being the star player and captain for his Guelph team that ultimately won the coveted Memorial Cup in 1952. It also didn't stop him from playing in the NHL as he only missed five games during his entire tenure with the New York Rangers.

Andy made his debut with the Rangers the very next season and would go on to play there for the next twelve years. Back in the 50's and 60's, New York was arguably the worst team in the league. They only made the playoffs four times in Andy's tenure with the franchise and didn't even make a single Stanley Cup final. For a long time, Bathgate was one of the few bright spots on the team as he was still considered among the league's elite players, despite playing for a very poor franchise. In 1959, he won the Hart Memorial Trophy (League MVP) after scoring 40 goals and 48 assists, beating out Dickie Moore, Jean Beliveau, and Gordie Howe for the award. What's more impressive is that he won the award even though his team failed to make the postseason. That year he also became the first Ranger to appear on the cover of *Sports Illustrated*.

On November 1, 1959, Bathgate became famous for being the man who struck innovative goaltender, Jacques Plante, in the face with a shot that made Plante first don the goalie mask that quickly became a trend in the league. Andy remembered that night vividly, "Jacques used to wander quite a bit and this one night we were playing against him, and he used to go behind the net to stop the puck and shoot it to the corner, normally circling the net. But this time he came out the same way he went to stop the puck and he gave me a poke check while I was skating hard around the net and I fell hard into the boards. Anyways, I went to my bench and the trainer said I needed stitches, but I told him I'd get them at the end of the period because I was really cheesed off at Plante. So, I went back out on the ice and tried to hit [him]on the cheek with a wrist shot but he turned his face and it cut his lip very badly, so off he went to get it stitched up and when he came back out he was wearing a mask. I remember we were all like, 'what the hell is this?' It was the first time I saw a goalie with a mask on. But for the record, I was never trying to do what happened. I just wanted to give him a warning because he tried to hurt me and I was trying to retaliate."

Andy's career was frustrated by the mediocrity of the Rangers and a nagging knee injury that stuck around since his junior days. He was eventually traded to the Toronto Maple Leafs during the 1963-64 season and was a major factor for Toronto as they went on a run in the playoffs, winning the only Stanley Cup of Andy's career. In the semi-finals, they knocked out Montreal in seven games, and in the Cup Final, Toronto defeated Detroit in a gruelling seven-game slugfest that saw Bathgate score the Stanley Cup-winning goal in Game 7.

"Punch Imlach had traded for me late in the season and I scored the first goal of the game in a 4-0 Game 7 win," recalled Bathgate. "The puck was shot around the boards and I tipped it over the defenceman, going in on a breakaway, I put it high on the short side past Terry Sawchuk. I saw the replay later and the defenceman was actually right on my tail but at the time I hadn't even noticed anyone was near me. It was one of those goals you remember your whole life. I knew Punch put a lot of faith in me and I didn't want to let him down so when I got the chance, I scored a nice clean goal and we went on to win the Stanley Cup. It ended up good for me because I was with New York for twelve years and never won a Cup. I also never practiced in Madison Square Garden in all in my years there so that might have contributed to why we weren't a very successful team. We had to go upstairs to a small rink on the fourth floor of MSG to practice. The rink had aluminum boards and was only maybe 60 feet wide and 160 feet long. It was a very primitive-looking rink and our goalie, Gump Worsley, used to swear at me when I'd practice my slap shot in that rink."

Pete Stemkowski was a rookie when Andy was traded to the Maple Leafs and the two became friends thanks in part to the both of them being Winnipeggers: "Andy had come to Toronto from New York and he was a bit of an outcast when he joined us because back then with the Leafs they had Carl Brewer, Bob Pulford, Frank Mahovlich, Dave Keon, who had all come up through the St. Michael's College and Toronto Marlboros system. They had been together since they were fifteen years old and they all progressed enough to be playing for the Leafs, so when Andy Bathgate joined the team, he was an outsider. The team took him in, but he was a bit of an outcast since he didn't know everybody. He talked with me because I was the young rookie who had to prove myself, so we talked a lot and we became good friends. I always remember how he didn't drink. Most guys would often go out for a cold one, but he didn't. He was always a real gentleman. One story about Andy I have is he dabbled a little on the stock market and when Ron Ellis and myself were young guys on the team, he got us to buy a stock called Pere Marquette, which was an oil stock if I recall right. We put some money in it and it didn't do too well. He eventually bought the stock back from us, but that was my first venture in the stock market and it was with Andy Bathgate. We talked and hung out together while we played together. We were both from Winnipeg so we talked about stuff from our old town. He was a great guy, a real gentleman. I liked him a lot."

After spending one more season in Toronto, Bathgate was traded once again, this time to Detroit, and he would go on to play two years in a Red Wings uniform. When the NHL's 1967 Expansion came around, Bathgate was selected in the Expansion Draft by the Pittsburgh Penguins. Andy closed out his NHL career with the Penguins, but not before leading the club in points in their inaugural season.

Bathgate's 973 career NHL regular season points is still the most all time by a Winnipegger. In addition to his Hart Memorial Trophy, Andy played in eight NHL All-Star Games and was also an NHL First Team All-Star twice (1959, 1962) and a Second Team All-Star twice (1958, 1963). He was elected to the Hockey Hall of Fame in 1978 and his number "9" was finally retired into the rafters at MSG on February 29, 2009 before a regular season game against the Toronto Maple Leafs. In 2017, the NHL commemorated its 100th anniversary with a list of the 100 Greatest NHL Players and Bathgate was named to the list.

Bathgate lived in southern Ontario for the rest of his life after he left hockey. He soon became very passionate about golf and ended up running a golf facility in Mississauga for a number of years. Andy Bathgate died on February 26, 2016 at the age of 83 in Brampton, Ontario. At the time of his death, he had both Alzheimer's and Parkinson's disease.

Through it all, Andy Bathgate was one of the best showmen in hockey. "Wherever you play, you've got to give it your best," said Bathgate. "The people pay, you're out there for basically 20 minutes every game, and if I can't exert myself for 20 minutes then I shouldn't be there."

CHICO RESCH SAYS

What an ambassador for hockey and the province of Manitoba. He's kind of like Jean Ratelle, who I played against, in that he had an absurd amount of class. He had great skill obviously, and was the key figure on those Rangers teams. Unfortunately, he didn't get to play on a lot of great teams except for his one Stanley Cup with Toronto.

He was never a mean player on the ice. He said "Let's just play the game within the rules. I won't cheap shot you, you don't cheap shot me." But he was thick, really thick with the puck. Andy did good to make it in Winnipeg and New York. If you can make it in those two places, you can make it anywhere because those places are polar opposites.

The biggest thing about Bathgate is how highly respected he was. Even to this day when I'm up in New York, everyone talks about Andy Bathgate. My wife loves Andy Bathgate—his smile and his looks. He's like the Manitoba version of Jean Beliveau where he was just all about class and playing within the rules, but he also had this tremendous skill and competitiveness.

He just had this drive deep beneath the surface that is so hard to understand unless you also have it. Year after year in New York and Toronto, Andy was just this engine that was going all the time, never stopping. He had some really nice hands, could pass great, had an amazing forehand or backhand. He was just so slick on the ice. It's too bad he didn't get a chance to play for a great team for any prolonged period of time. He was always having to play against the opponent's top defender, never having that great second line centreman to back him up.

I compared Bathgate and Beliveau to each other when I was around those guys because they were royal hockey players and royal representatives of the game. There's only a few guys in the history of the league that were kind of like royalty. You looked at them as not just hockey players, but something bigger. Andy Bathgate was one of those few guys. He was royalty.

5
FRANK FREDRICKSON

F rank Fredrickson is one of the most interesting people that ever played the sport of hockey, let alone be successful at it. Famous sportswriter Jim Coleman calls him "one of the most brilliant players ever to don skates". And when I say that Frank was one of the most interesting people I've ever come across, I'm talking about him also being a very accomplished violinist and pianist, and the fact that for a while he was best buddies with Albert Einstein!

MANITOBA HOCKEY HALL OF FAME

I'd say that Frank is definitely the player I learned the most about in my research for this book. I had some knowledge of him beforehand as I knew of the Winnipeg Falcons and their accomplishments and that Frank was their star player. What I didn't realize is how he's in the conversation as one of the all-time greats of the sport. Early on in making this list he was probably slotted around the #15 spot, but after doing my due diligence he quickly moved up into the top ten, and from there into the top five.

Fredrickson had perhaps the biggest impact on the game of any player from his generation. His play totally changed the way hockey was played. Hockey historian Helen Edwards says that, "To me, he was the Pavel Bure of his generation as he could bring people to their feet when he picked up the puck."

Many hockey writers peg Montreal Canadiens centre Howie Morenz as the superstar of that era, but a lot of the players that played in that era commented on how they would rather have Fredrickson steering their team's ship.

"Morenz is faster than Fredrickson," said Slim Halderson, "but I really do not think that he has the finish that Frank possesses." Cyclone Taylor added that Frederickson was "as fine a player I've ever seen. He is fast, shifty and smart and has a wonderfully quick shot."

Frank Fredrickson was the legendary centreman and captain of the great Winnipeg Falcons, who won the first Olympic gold medal in men's hockey. As you've already read in Slim Halderson's chapter, it can't be stated enough how the Falcons went from being called "goolies" to national heroes within such a short time span.

Frank Fredrickson was born in Winnipeg on June 3, 1895. The son of Icelandic immigrants who only spoke Icelandic in the house, Frank couldn't speak a word of English until he was six years old and was starting school. You could say that learning hockey came easier to Frank than learning English. He started playing hockey on the family's backyard rink at age five and flourished from there.

Frank grew up in a house at 739 Elgin Avenue in the West End. He first attended Wellington School as a kid and then later went to Kelvin Technical High School and Central Collegiate, before enrolling at the University of Manitoba's law school.

Being of Icelandic descent was difficult because of the attitude some of his neighbours had. They looked down on his family and other Icelandic families, as "those white-haired Icelanders" and would make fun of him in various ways. Coming home from school frequently turned into a battle for young Frank. The kids would gang up on him and start fighting for the sole reason that he was Icelandic.

"My best outlet was hockey. I got my first pair of skates when I was five and had a great time learning to play," recalled Fredrickson. "School came easy for me. After finishing grade eight I decided I ought to earn a living and got a job as an office boy in a law firm. This turned out to be an excellent move since the firms all sponsored hockey teams then so naturally we had one too.

"I played well and captured the attention of two of our attorneys. They took a great deal of personal interest in me, not just as a hockey player, and urged me to go back to school. So, in 1914 I enrolled at the University of Manitoba, took liberal arts courses, and a year later was named captain of the hockey team."

This was also the time when he first joined the Winnipeg Falcons. Prior to that he had been playing hockey for the Lutheran Sunday-school team in his church league and his Central Collegiate high school team. Frank quickly became the offensive dynamo of the Falcons as about half of his team's goals during Frank's time with the Falcons came from his stick. He averaged roughly two goals a game.

As we all know when World War I came about, Frank and his Falcons teammates enlisted in the Canadian Army. Frank joined the 223rd Scandinavian Battalion, but when he arrived in England, he switched to the Royal Flying Corps along with his Falcons teammate Konrad Johannesson.

Frank's life nearly ended during World War I. He was being transferred from Egypt to Italy when the transport he was on was hit by a German torpedo. Fredrickson, who was wearing only pajamas, searched for an empty lifeboat but found none.

"Suddenly, I realized that I had left my violin in my bunk," Fredrickson recalled years later to Stan Fischler. "My violin was very important to me. So, I ran back, got hold of it and gave it to one of the captains of another lifeboat and told him to take good care of it."

Before the ship sank, Frank found space on another lifeboat, and was saved from perishing at sea. He spent the next few days in a collapsible lifeboat in the Mediterranean Sea clutching only his violin before being rescued and returned to Alexandria, Egypt. He eventually got to Gullane, Scotland in 1918 and served as a flight instructor and test pilot until the war ended. Frank recalled how every morning at 7am he would get in his plane and fly around and do all sorts of crazy maneuvers.

When Frank returned home from the war he was eager to get back into the hockey ranks, but there would be challenges in doing so. "It took a year from the time the war ended before I could get back to Winnipeg," Frank recalled. "When I returned in 1919, a bunch of us, led by Mike Goodman, the speed-skating champion of North America, and Slim Halderson, a great big, gangling six-footer who was a beautiful stickhandler, organized the Falcons and applied for admission to the senior league.

"The leaders of that league wouldn't let us in because they claimed we weren't good enough to compete with teams like the Monarchs and Winnipegs. So, we did the next best thing and organized our own league composed of teams such as Selkirk, which had Bullet Joe Simpson as captain. We later found out the reason we couldn't get in the senior league was because the players were from well-to-do families and wanted no part of us. But they couldn't quite get away from us that easily. We finished in first place, then played the winners of the big league in a two-game series. In a terrific upset, we beat them in two games straight, 14-2. We then defeated Lake-of-the-Woods, Head-of-the-Lakes and Fort William and went on to Toronto, where we won the Allan Cup for the senior championship of Canada, beating the famed University of Toronto."

The Winnipeg Falcons would go on to represent Canada at the 1920 Winter Olympics in Antwerp, Belgium and coast to the gold medal. Frederickson exploded for twelve goals in three games during the tournament and was by all accounts the Olympic MVP for Team Canada.

"Winning the Olympic championship was quite a feather in our cap and gave us all a lot of publicity. I had the world at my feet, but instead of returning immediately to Canada, I was asked by the Icelandic government to go there to do some experimental flying. As it turned out, I became the first pilot of Icelandic extraction to fly in Iceland.

"Then I went to England to try and get some of the English concerns interested in flying to Iceland but I failed in that and returned to Canada, making a stop in Toronto. When I got there, Mayor Church entertained me and asked, 'Now that you're back, Frank, what do you want to do?' I told him I wanted to join the Canadian Air Force but didn't think I could get in because there were many senior officers ahead of me. Church was a wonderful guy and a very influential man; when I got home to Winnipeg there was a telegram advising me to report to camp for duty. So, in 1920 I joined the Canadian Air Force."

Unfortunately, working for the Canadian Air Force didn't pay that well. Especially since he was newly married and raising a young family in a new home on Dominion Street. Frank would supplement his income by playing the violin in a dance orchestra at the Fort Garry Hotel on Saturday nights.

"Out of the blue [in 1920] I received a letter from Lester Patrick, the old Silver Fox of hockey, who was in Victoria, British Columbia, where he had a team in the old Pacific Coast League. It was top-notch hockey and Lester offered me what was a substantial contract in those days—$2,500 for 24 games. I call it substantial because the rest of the boys were playing for $800 and $900. I couldn't resist the offer and so found myself right back in the middle of hockey again."

Frank joined the PCHA's Victoria Aristocrats (later the Cougars) and spent six years with the club, leading the league in scoring twice. One of the notable games he played in early on with Victoria was a 1921 New Year's Day tilt with their rival Vancouver Millionaires. It was billed as the battle of the

World's Greatest Professional (Cyclone Taylor) versus the World's Greatest Amateur (Frank Fredrickson). Victoria won the game 3-1 and Frank scored twice for his side.

Frank was a PCHA First Team All-Star for four consecutive years from 1921 to 1924. He was also named to the WCHL All-Star Team in 1926. Frank won the Stanley Cup with Victoria in 1925, defeating the Montreal Canadiens in the Cup final. At that time, Howie Morenz was the star player of the Montreal Canadiens. He was most outstanding forward in the NHL, and the Cougars manager Lester Patrick put Fredrickson on Morenz to try and stop him. Frank blanketed Howie and ended up outscoring him in the series, leading his club to the Stanley Cup. They became the first western team to win the Cup in ten years, and in doing so, Frank became the first player (along with Slim Halderson) to win both an Olympic gold medal and Stanley Cup.

In 1926, the Cougars were purchased and moved to Detroit, joining the National Hockey League. Frank moved east with the team, but made his own deal that saw him earn $6,000 per season, making him the highest-paid hockey player in the world.

Though his Victoria glory days were behind him, Frank Fredrickson was still a powerhouse at age 31 in his first year in the National Hockey League. The highest-paid player in all of pro hockey, at $6,000, he was the league's fourth-highest scorer with 18 goals and 31 points in a 44-game schedule. A third of the way into the season he was traded with Harry Meeking to Boston for Duke Keats and Archie Briden.

"As things turned out I didn't do well in Detroit. Previously I had been first, second or third in scoring, but now was 24th and getting nowhere at all. The problem was dissension on the team, but I didn't last too long and was traded to Boston for two good hockey players. As soon as I arrived with my new team, Art Ross scheduled a meeting with me. At first, I thought he'd give me the business but instead he said, 'I'm taking Dick Ferguson off the first line and I want you to take it with Harry Oliver and Perk Galbraith and work with them.' At that time Boston was the second tail-end team in the American Division, but after I got there we took the lead. Now, I don't say that this good fortune was due to their acquiring Frank Fredrickson; it resulted from fellows working together in a collective effort. I learned one thing: by cooperation and joint effort you can do an awful lot more than when you're by yourself.

"My first game as a Bruin was against the New York Rangers who were now managed by my old boss, Lester Patrick. We beat New York 3-2 and I got three goals. Those days with Boston were outstanding from the viewpoint of competition because there were great players all over the place. New York had Frank Boucher and the Cook Brothers, Bill and Bun. Frank was as sweet a hockey player as you could find, and that line, well, there was nothing like it. But on our club, we had Eddie Shore and he was really something."

Frank helped the Bruins reach the Stanley Cup final in 1927, but they lost to the Ottawa Senators. During the offseason that followed, Fredrickson would fly friends, including the baseball hall-of-famer Jimmy Foxx, to Winnipeg to play golf. All in all, he spent the better part of three seasons in Boston, with his best year coming in 1927-28 when he scored 14 goals in 28 games. He was traded to the Pittsburgh Pirates midway during the 1927-28 season and when Boston won the Cup at the end of the year, Fredrickson's name was engraved.

After two seasons with the Pirates, Frank signed as a free agent with the Detroit. His career ended prematurely in 1931 after suffering torn-knee cartilage that required surgery. Frank retired as arguably the best player of his generation. He was the big-scoring centreman that every team wanted to have, usually leading his team, if not the league, in scoring throughout his career from his Winnipeg Falcons days all the way up to the National Hockey League. A two-time Stanley Cup champ and 1920 Olympic gold medal winner, Fredrickson scored 193 points in 163 games with Victoria of the PCHA/WCHL. He then scored 73 points in 161 NHL games.

After his playing career Frank Fredrickson turned to coaching. He coached and managed the Pittsburgh NHL team in 1930-31 before returning to his home in Vancouver. He then coached some senior teams in Manitoba until he took a job coaching the Princeton University hockey team from 1933 to 1935. At Princeton one of the people he befriended was Albert Einstein. Fredrickson regularly walked to campus with the great man, who, he said, was charming and unassuming. They both enjoyed the violin and would play together on many occasions.

Frank eventually moved back to the west coast and coached the RCAF Flyers to the Allan Cup in 1942. You'd think that after serving in the First World War that Frank would be let off the hook for the next one, but at age 45, he served as a flight school commanding officer at Sea Island near Vancouver until his discharge from the RCAF in 1945. He then coached the University of British Colombia Thunderbirds for seven seasons.

After his coaching days were behind him, he was elected an Alderman of the City of Vancouver and even served a short stint as the Acting Mayor of Vancouver. He was inducted into the Hockey Hall of Fame in 1958. In his later years, Frank and his wife moved to Toronto, where he lived out his remaining years. He was nearly blind towards the end.

Frank Fredrickson passed away on May 28, 1979 at the age of 83 in Toronto.

From the UBC Sports Hall of Fame website: "He could do anything" relates one of his former UBC players, Hugh Berry. "He was a master bridge player, musician, pilot, magician...he was also modest, never said a bad word about anybody." Clare Drake, another of Fredrickson's players at this time and a Hall of Fame coach in his own right, opines "Frank was years ahead of his time."

What else can you expect from the most interesting man in hockey?

4
TURK BRODA

Turk Broda was one of the best money goaltenders of all time, and by that, I mean he played his best when it really mattered most. With five Stanley Cups and a pair of Vezina Trophies, he's certainly the greatest netminder the Toronto Maple Leafs franchise has ever seen.

"When the playoff bucks were on the line," noted *Toronto Star* writer Gary Lautens, "the Turk could catch lint in a hurricane."

"For one thing, I always needed the money from the playoffs," Turk said. "But it probably was a case of me being too dumb to realize how serious it was and never letting the pressure get to me."

It's hard to make a case for many goalies being better than Broda was. This is a man who won the Cup in 1942 and then missed two years of his prime because he was serving in the Second World War. When he returned, he played better than before the war and won four more Stanley Cups, which is truly incredible stuff.

"He won me four Stanley Cups," recalls Maple Leafs teammate Howie Meeker. "Without Broda, we win maybe only one Cup because out of those four playoff runs, we only had the best team in one of those years. Broda led us. We had no reason to win the goddamn thing but he did it for us because he was so excellent in the net, that's why he's in the Hall of Fame. In my playing era and broadcasting era, he was by the far the best goalie I'd ever seen."

Broda always had this happy-go-lucky, jolly nature about him and used to say that "the Maple Leafs pay me for my work in practices. I throw in the games for free."

Walter "Turk" Broda was born on May 14, 1914 in Brandon to a Ukrainian family. He got the nickname "Turk" as a result of an English history lesson and his mass of freckles. His school teacher had been telling them about an English king who, behind his back, was called "Turkey Egg" by his intimates because of the huge freckles that dotted his round face. The class was no sooner out than one of Broda's school chums laughed and said, "Hey, look at Broda. He looks like a turkey egg, too." From that day on they called him "Turkey-Egg" or "Turkey" until eventually, as he grew older, he became just plain "Turk."

Broda got into hockey from the time he attended his elementary school, playing on the outdoor rink with his chums. He was a pudgy young man and a poor skater, yet he contained an incredible enthusiasm for playing the game, so he was always stuck in net because of his poor skating. Turk would cover his legs with paper to help pad his legs and then let his friends fire pucks on him for hours at a time.

The principal of the school Broda attended in Brandon was a hockey fan and when Turk showed an interest in playing goal, the school head decided to help him. Almost daily until the cold weather set in they would head to the basement of the school and engage in a half-hour hockey drill. Turk would don the goal pads and stand guard on a six-foot section of the wall while the school principal would fire the puck at him from all angles or stickhandle, as well as possible on the concrete floor, to Broda's faux net and then try to fool him with a quick deke.

From that modest beginning, Broda progressed rapidly and soon became a standout in Brandon juvenile hockey with a team known as the North Stars. He was so good that commercial and intermediate teams lured him from the age-limit ranks but so much fuss was made by Brandon junior officials that Turk was ordered to return to junior hockey.

Broda gained recognition as a top prospect when he performed remarkable feats of netminding for Brandon Native Sons against the Regina Pats in the 1932-33 Western Canadian junior finals. The Pats won the series, despite Broda standing on his head, but Turk's puck-stopping was the talk of the West. The next year he moved to Winnipeg to play for the Monarchs and the quality of his goal work attracted the attention of Gene Houghton, a scout with the Detroit Red Wings, who passed on his recommendations to the big club, who soon signed Broda to a C-form.

How Broda got to joining the Toronto Maple Leafs from Detroit is a good story in itself. The Leafs had wanted to replace George Hainsworth, who was nearly forty years old. Earl Robertson and Turk Broda were both property of the Detroit Red Wings, and it seemed like Robertson was going to be the likely replacement for Hainsworth.

Detroit GM Jack Adams had a soft spot for Broda from the beginning. They met after one season when the Red Wings were eliminated from the play-offs early, and were touring western Canada and the Pacific Coast with the Toronto Maple Leafs, playing a series of exhibition games. In Winnipeg, the Detroit manager was sitting in his hotel room when someone rapped on the door. He opened the door and gazed upon two young fellows wearing sweaters with big letters in the front. They looked like high school kids.

"Mr. Adams?" one of the boys queried, nervously.

"That's right," Jack said, heartily. "What can I do for you?"

"I'm Turk Broda," the young fellow said. "And this is Mud Bruneteau."

He said the names as if they should be of high importance to the manager of the Detroit Red Wings. That was Turk's introduction to pro hockey. Adams knew then that Turk and Mud were Red Wings property and they all chatted for a bit, and Jack introduced them to some of Detroit's players, and then gave the boys tickets for that night's game. That's all that Turk and Mud wanted after all was free tickets. Jack Adams later invited Turk and Mud to the club's training camp.

The Red Wings were set in goal at the time with Normie Smith and John Ross Roach in the system so Turk started playing for the minor league Detroit Olympics. Broda was sensational in a three-game battle with the Detroit Red Wings called the City Series. Thanks to Broda, the Olympics won the series in the final game and he was lifted out of the Red Wings dressing room after the game was done. When Turk was then sold soon after to the Toronto Maple Leafs for the then record sum of $8,000, he didn't even believe it when he first heard the news from his teammate and roommate Wilf Starr. Turk thought he was the victim of another prank as many teammates had had laughs at Broda's expense since he joined the Red Wings organization. All in good fun of course because of Turk's jovial nature. But this time it was for real, and it was here that Conn Smythe made his choice of Broda over Earl Robertson.

Broda went to Leafs training camp with the legendary George Hainsworth there and enjoyed the experience of getting to compete with an all-time great. "He's really great," Broda remarked. "I'd sure like to be as good as George one day. I've been studying him every chance I get, and I'm learning plenty."

Hainsworth and Broda had a legendary battle in training camp, and when it was all said and done, Conn Smythe decided to carry two goaltenders for the start of the season. They rotated starts but it was Turk who played best, while Hainsworth struggled. Within the first ten games of the season, Smythe made his choice and released Hainsworth outright from the Leafs, meaning that Turk had won the goaltending job.

Conn Smythe later recalled that, "I always believed in Broda. George Hainsworth started that 1937 season for us, but in Broda's first start he beat Detroit and I made up my mind. I released Hainsworth outright and said Broda is my goalie. He was the best I ever had with the Leafs."

Reporters loved Broda right from the start. They found his talkative, laughing self a good source of copy. The result of this is that Turk received an awful amount of publicity, both written and photographic. Broda lost the Stanley Cup final in his first three seasons with the team and began to think he'd never win one. To help improve his hand-eye coordination, he played handball until he became an expert at the game and would spot teammates ten points and still beat them.

"Broda knew that he could play goal and rise to heights," remarked Smythe, "but the past never worried him, not like some players who would have a bad night and then go all to pieces. He was also as decent and loyal as a man could be... decency and loyalty go a long way with me. So does great goalkeeping, and both were a part of Turk Broda."

Broda finally won his first Stanley Cup in 1942. In perhaps the most incredible comeback in playoff history, Toronto was down three games to none in the Cup finals against Detroit and rallied, winning four straight games.

Turk joined the Army in 1943 and went off to do his military duty in the Second World War, which mainly consisted of playing hockey in England. When he was discharged from the Army during the 1945-46, Broda immediately rejoined his team at Maple Leaf Gardens for practice. By the time he returned, however, there were new rules in place that changed the game. Installing the red line permitted forward passes into the neutral zone, which in turn opened up the ice and sped up play. Some returning veterans couldn't make the transition, and things got especially tough for goalies as defences backed off from the neutral zone, resulting in more crowds in front of the net.

Broda's solution was to move higher in the crease to see the puck around the traffic. He played as if he had never been gone.

Broda's second tour of duty with the Leafs proved to be more successful than the first. The Leafs emerged as one of the greatest teams of all time. Broda would be the puck stopper in each of the Leafs Stanley Cup wins in 1947, 1948, 1949 and 1951. He was very good during those regular seasons, but come playoff time he somehow was able to take his game to a new level— he led the entire league in wins and shutouts in each of those Stanley Cup years, and in goals against average in 3 of the 4.

"The key to Broda's great success as a playoff goalie was his unflappable disposition," wrote Toronto columnist Jim Hunt. "On the afternoon of a Stanley Cup Final, his teammates would be pacing the floor and chain-smoking cigarettes in an effort to calm their nerves. Meanwhile, Broda would be in his hotel room sleeping. Once, as Conn Smythe delivered an impassioned plea to his team just before they took the ice for an important game, he looked over and saw Broda sitting on a stool in front of his locker sound asleep."

Known during his career to let in the odd weak goal during the regular season, Broda was as stingy as a netminder you could find once the playoffs rolled around. In one three-season stretch of 24 playoff games, he surrendered only 34 goals. In losing a 1950 semifinal to the Detroit Red Wings, the Turk had three shutouts in Leaf wins and lost the seventh game, 1-0, in overtime.

Despite everything that Broda did on the ice, he will forever be known for the famous "Battle of the Bulge" incident that occurred during the 1949-50 season.

"Broda is off the team," declared Smythe. "I'm taking him out of the nets and he's not going back until he shows some common-sense. I've never had to do a thing like this before but it seems I'm running a fat man's team. Two years ago, Turk weighed 185 when he won the Vezina. Last season he went up to 190—and now this! A goalie has to have fast reflexes—and you can't move fast when you're overweight."

It wasn't just a ruse Broda quickly found out, as Smythe announced that a young goalie out of Pittsburgh named Gil Mayer would be replacing Broda for Thursday night's game with Detroit. As for the Saturday game, Smythe snapped, "That's up to Broda. If he gets down from 197 to 190, he'll play. Not before."

Smythe even went as far as making a trade with the Cleveland Barons to acquire a tall, slim goalie by the name of Al Rollins. The whole thing ended up becoming the hockey story of the year. Journalists had a field day with it, dubbing it "Broda's Battle of the Bulge." Newspapers were assigning sportswriters, feature writers, and photographers to cover Turk's effort to get down to the required weight. It was really quite the spectacle. Every day in the paper there would be pictures of Turk doing various exercises, or eating healthy foods.

It was a three-day sensation. On November 30, he was down to 193 and the next day he was weighed in at 189 meaning that he made the cut, and would be guarding the Leafs goal the following game. He shut out the Rangers 2-0 in his first game back, even the Rangers congratulated him. As a reward, Broda treated himself to pancakes on the ice after the game.

Broda commented years later how the scales had been rigged in his favor and he never lost a pound during the ordeal.

Turk's career came to an end at the beginning of his fourteenth NHL season with the Leafs. He was planning on playing one more year, but as he readied himself for the 1951-52 campaign, he realized that he was done so he retired after one game. On December 22, 1951, the Toronto Maple Leafs staged a Turk Broda Night at Maple Leaf Gardens. The immensely popular Broda was given gifts and accolades from around the National Hockey League.

Broda retired with a 302-224-101 record in 629 career NHL games (all with the Maple Leafs) with 62 shutouts. In addition to five Stanley Cups, Broda was a two-time Vezina Trophy winner (1941, 1948). He was named to the NHL's First All-Star Team twice (1941, 1948) and the Second Team All-Star once (1942). At the time of his retirement, Broda was the career leader in regular season wins with 302. He was the first goalie to play in 100 NHL playoff games. Broda was recently named one of the 100 Greatest NHL Players in history in 2017 for the NHL 100 event.

Broda went on to a tremendous junior coaching career. He coached the Toronto Marlboros to back-to-back Memorial Cups in 1955 and 1956. Turk spent his later life coaching plenty, but also found time to golf and go to the racetrack. He was inducted into the Hockey Hall of Fame in 1967.

"He used to go back to Manitoba every year," recalled Turk's daughter Barbara Tushingham. "In those days, you'd have to ask Mr. Smythe if you could take a holiday so he would ask and then come out to Brandon for three weeks in the summer to see his mom, aunt, sister and four brothers. He did that for quite a few years until his mom passed away. His last trip was probably in 1970."

Turk Broda died of a heart attack on October 17, 1972 at the age of 58.

He passed just two weeks before the death of his long-time netminding rival Bill Durnan. "He had a massive heart attack at our home and passed away soon after," said Barbara. "When it was all over with, I talked with his doctor and apparently, he had the veins of an 85-year-old person and he said it was from the adrenaline and stress of playing and coaching hockey for so long."

Broda still remains atop Toronto's all-time regular-season goaltending lists in games played (629), wins (302), shutouts (62) and minutes played (38,167). During the 2016-17 season, the Toronto Maple Leafs honoured Broda by having his #1 retired to the rafters of the Air Canada Centre.

"He never blamed the forwards or defencemen when he gave up a goal," recalled teammate Harry Watson. "It was always his fault." Watson once accidentally shot the puck past Broda and Turk told him, "Don't worry about it, Harry. I should have stopped that shot."

3
JONATHAN TOEWS

Jonathan Toews was the kid in my neighbourhood who went on to become a big star in the National Hockey League. He lived just a few streets over from me in River Park South and even though he was five years older, I remember him playing a few times in some big street hockey games with me and my friends when I was seven or eight. I'll also confess that my buddies and I probably snuck onto his backyard rink a few times in the winter when we didn't have a ride to Dakota Community Centre.

Nicknamed "Captain Serious," the 6'2" centreman was the leader of a Blackhawks team that won three Stanley Cups in six years. There is nothing in the sport of hockey that Toews hasn't won, and, as of writing, he hasn't even reached the age of thirty. In addition to his three Stanley Cups, he's a two-time Olympic gold medalist with Team Canada in Vancouver 2010 and Sochi 2014 and has won two World Juniors, along with one World Championship. He's the youngest player ever to join the Triple Gold Club, which is exclusive to those who have won the Stanley Cup, Olympic gold medal and World Championship.

"Jonathan is the ultimate leader. He's the engine that makes our team go," says Blackhawks general manager Stan Bowman. "He leads by example and you watch the way that he battles and competes every shift."

MANITOBA SPORTS HALL OF FAME

"Toews is just a fantastic player, he's the complete package," says James Patrick. "I think when it's all said and done, he will be the greatest Manitoba player ever. He's certainly accomplished everything from World Juniors, College, Stanley Cup captain, Olympics. At times, he's the best all around player in the world. I certainly think the world of him as a leader, and I'd put him right up there as one of the all-time greats from our province."

Jonathan Toews was born on April 29, 1988 in Winnipeg to Bryan, an electrician for the University of Manitoba, and Andree, who came from Quebec and was the director of marketing for a financial institution. Jonathan grew up in a house in the extreme southern point of River Park South in St. Vital. And by extreme, I mean you could literally throw a rock and hit the Perimeter Highway from his house.

Jonathan grew up bilingual and attended French immersion schools such as Ecole Lavalee and then Ecole Christine-Lesperance for Grade 8 when it was built right near his home in 2001.

Hockey was a very natural thing for Jonathan as his dad had him on the ice from the age of three and he took the game instantly. From the time he was five years old his goal was to make the National Hockey League, and everything he did after that was to make that goal a reality.

"Jonathan could see things you'd show him and then go right out there and do them much better than I'd describe them," recalled his dad Bryan. "I remember I had him on the lake when he was four. He had such a natural stride. I remember several parents coming up to me and asking, 'How old is that kid?'"

To which Jonathan added: "It wasn't that natural for me. I never was one of the biggest kids, but I kind of found myself thinking of ways in my mind to beat them," he said. "I'd use my skating, my stickhandling, my wits to visualize ways to win."

Jonathan idolized his hometown Winnipeg Jets, and was especially fond of their strong scorers Teemu Selanne and Keith Tkachuk. He started playing for the Dakota Lazers out of the Dakota Community Club at the age of five.

"My first memory of Dakota Community Club is when I was five," Jonathan recalled, "before the actual arena was built there were outdoor rinks there. That's where it all started. When I was eight they built the two indoor sheets and that's the first year my team won the Winnipeg city championship."

There's no doubting the competitiveness that Jonathan had from the time he started playing. "If he lost a game or something didn't go right, I would make an excuse. He would look at me like I was crazy," said Bryan. "In his mind at a young age, there was no excuse."

"No one really had to push me to work hard and find that determination," said Jonathan. "That's one of the things that came naturally."

Jonathan would be at Dakota for practices and games, but the great majority of his hours playing hockey were out on the rink his dad built behind their home, horsing around and working on their skills.

The backyard rink was where Jonathan and his younger brother David (by two years) honed their craft. The rink was located behind their backyard fence in the large field that backed onto the Perimeter Highway. It had lights so they could play all night and small boards around it to block the puck from getting lost in the snow. Jonathan's dad Bryan started it as a little piece of ice for the kids to skate on, but made it bigger every year as his kids got older. Bryan would stay up all night and carefully move around an elevated sprinkler to get the ice surface as pristine as possible.

The family kitchen would serve as the kids "locker room" and a trail of rubber mats led to the rink from the kitchen. Jonathan and David would play one on one all night. "My dad built lights for the rink and you could turn them on and off from inside the house," recalls David, "so when it'd be time for dinner or we'd have to go to bed, he'd just flash the lights. We'd try to stay out as long as we could—until we could hear them yelling from the house for us to come in."

Jonathan would practice on the backyard rink in the middle of the night, often waking up his parents. "I didn't mind being out there alone," Toews said. "When a lot of kids wanted to be with their friends inside playing video games, doing different social things, I really didn't mind the silence and embracing being alone and trying to master something. I really loved that. I was addicted to that."

All of the time that Toews put into the game paid off in a big way as he was a prodigy in Winnipeg from an early age. He always played the top level of hockey possible from the Dakota Lazers to the Winnipeg Junior Jets, to the St. Vital Victorias, and to the Winnipeg Warriors. He won five straight city championships over that stretch and got used to winning.

In his bantam year, Jonathan scored 115 points in 30 games for the Winnipeg Warriors and was drafted first overall in the WHL Draft by the Tri-City Americans. He chose instead to play high school at the illustrious Shattuck-St. Mary's school in Faribault, Minnesota that has a history of churning out quality NHL players. He completed Grade 10 through Grade 12 in only two years and by the time he graduated he had a scholarship waiting for him at the University of North Dakota. In two years at UND, Jonathan amassed 85 points in 76 games and led the Fighting Sioux to the Frozen Four in both 2006 and 2007.

In those two years, he also represented Canada at the World Juniors and won the gold medal both times. In 2006, he was the youngest player to make the team and had two assists during the tournament. A year later, in 2007, he was the team's star player, known for his shootout heroics against the United States in the semi-final where he scored on three straight shots to propel his team into the gold medal game, where they dispatched Russia to win gold. Jonathan led Canada in scoring and was named to the tournament All-Star Team alongside his netminder Carey Price.

Going into the 2006 NHL Entry Draft, the Blackhawks were in a state of desperation. The team had only made the playoffs once since 1997, with not much sign of going up. That all changed when Jonathan Toews slipped to Chicago's number three overall pick and without hesitation, Chicago scooped him up. The next year, they took Patrick Kane with the first overall pick and all of the sudden they had two franchise players who would shape the team for the foreseeable future.

Chicago knew they had something special in Toews as soon as he fired his first shot in his first game, because it went in. He scored a point in each of his first ten NHL games to start his career and finished his rookie campaign with 54 points in 64 games. At the end of the year he was named a finalist for the Calder Trophy. Before the following season started, the Blackhawks named him team captain, making him one of the youngest captains in NHL history.

In 2010, at age 22, he became the second-youngest player to win the Conn Smythe Trophy as playoff MVP after scoring 29 points in the Blackhawks 22 games during their run to their first Stanley Cup since 1961. In 2013, Jonathan won his second Stanley Cup and took home the Selke Trophy, which is the award for the NHL's best defensive forward. In 2015, the Blackhawks won their third Stanley Cup in six years, and in doing so are now known as the first "dynasty" since the New York Islanders and Edmonton Oilers ruled the 1980's.

Jonathan Toews has a reputation as not only being one of the great leaders in hockey, but one of the best two-way players in the league. He's everything you want in a hockey player, and at only 29 years of age, it's crazy to think that he still has another ten years left in his career since there's nothing that he hasn't won in the sport. When he does eventually retire, he's likely going to be a first-ballot Hall of Famer.

Going into the 2017-18 season, Toews has 622 points in 717 career NHL games. In 2017, he was named one of the 100 Greatest NHL Players of All-Time for the NHL 100 event.

The Dakota Community Centre that Jonathan first started playing at as a child has since been named after him. A lake north of Flin Flon has also been named after him and he's been given the Keys to the City of Winnipeg for his achievements on the ice in addition to his hard work ethic.

Toews spends a lot of his offseason at his cabin in Lake of the Woods. That's where his family stays mostly these days as his brother David is a fishing guide out there.

Throughout his career, Toews has always been very involved in the grassroots efforts in the game. In regard to advice he has for the younger generation of players growing up in Manitoba, Jonathan says, "You become what you think about and focus on the most. See yourself attracting the things you want to accomplish. Thoughts and desires in your mind can become a reality."

2
BOBBY CLARKE

MANITOBA SPORTS HALL OF FAME

When compiling a list of the greatest leaders in sports history, Bobby Clarke's name has to be up there. Overcoming diabetes, Clarke led the Philadelphia Flyers to the only two Stanley Cups that they've won in franchise history. Although he was never the most skilled player, Clarke's tireless work ethic made him the NHL's most valuable player.

"Depending on who you ask, Bobby Clarke is one of hockey's greatest players or one of hockey's greatest villains. The truth is he was both," says historian Joe Pelletier.

Love him or hate him, Bobby Clarke was one of the all-time greats and in most people's minds the best two-way player the game has ever seen. During his prime he was the NHL's best defensive centre, playmaking centre, and cheap-shot artist all at the same time. It was neat to find out too that Wayne Gretzky modelled his behind the net play after Clarke when he was a junior.

Clarke may have better intangibles than any Hall of Fame player, ever. He was routinely regarded as one of the league's smartest and hardest working players. He was an outstanding playmaker, face-off winner, checker and penalty killer. He's been the face of the franchise since the day the club drafted him and still is to this day.

The thing about Bobby Clarke is that he would do anything to win. Not all players would do "anything" to win, but Clarke held absolutely nothing back, and in doing so he was one of the great leaders in all of sports and the perfect captain for a team that was dubbed the Broad Street Bullies. He was named captain of the Flyers at 23 years old and became the ringleader, leading by example with his work ethic.

No hockey player has ever worked harder than Clarke did. "You gotta work and produce if you want your teammates to do the same," said Clarke. "You can't demand of others what you don't do yourself."

In 1975 when the Flyers were battling the Buffalo Sabres for the Cup, a reporter asked Sabres GM Punch Imlach which player in the league he'd like to have most. He replied, "If you want to put fans in the stands, I'd take Gilbert Perreault. But if you want to win, take Clarke."

Bobby Clarke was born on August 13, 1949 in Flin Flon. He was the first and only son of Cliff and Yvonne Clarke (they later had a daughter, Roxanne) and he began to play hockey immediately upon abandoning his highchair, give or take a year. The Clarke family originally lived at 59 Hill Street when Bobby was born, but when he was four years old, they moved to 120 Riverside Drive, where the family was still living well into Clarke's heyday as a member of the Philadelphia Flyers. Cliff Clarke worked for the Hudson's Bay Mining & Smelting as a driller in a dynamite crew in the mines under Flin Flon. For 32 years, he held a drill on his shoulder while standing in dirty water. He also served as the town's fire chief.

"Bobby learned to skate at Lakeside Park," his mother said. "It was an open-air rink and he lived there, morning, noon, and night. As long as there was ice, he'd be out there practicing. Of course, that still wasn't enough hockey for him so we had another rink out in the garden. Many times, he'd shoot the puck off the side of our house—and a few times through the windows."

Almost all the kids in Flin Flon were playing hockey three or four nights a week. But not Bobby—he played every night. The mine did a lot of sponsoring for the hockey in Flin Flon back then and allowed every kid to play one game a week at the indoor arena, but the rest of the minor hockey was played outdoors.

When Bobby was still very young, his father took him on a trip to Winnipeg, the metropolis of Manitoba. "I figured he'd get a kick going down to Winnipeg," said Cliff, "and seeing all those bright lights. But when we got there he walked down the street, found an outdoor rink with a kids' hockey game, and spent the night watching them bat the puck around. That was Bobby's idea of a good time in the big city!"

Cliff Clarke never formally coached a hockey team but he was always around to help his eager son and, occasionally, father and son would play in the men-against-the-boys contests. Bobby's first big thrill in organized hockey didn't really come until 1957 when he saw the Flin Flon Bombers defeat the Hull-Ottawa Canadiens in the Memorial Cup final.

Bobby Clarke immersed himself in hockey at the expense of everything else, including his schooling. "I used to tell my parents that I was going to school," he says, "but I'd go to the rink instead." His mother confirms the report. "Bobby and his friend were always full of the dickens in school," she says, "and a lot of times they would be sent home by the teacher. They never came home, of course. No. They'd always go play hockey down at the playground. I'd look out the window and say, 'Gosh, that looks like Bobby down there,' and right then the principal would call to say he was sending Bobby home for three days for bad behavior."

It was clear that Bobby's first hockey goal was climbing the local minor hockey ladder to eventually play with his hometown Bombers. His first coach, Earl Garinger, had doubts about the kid's potential. Bobby was on the skinny side and wasn't a particularly good skater.

"He was a strange skater," Garinger recalled. "Most kids who start out have trouble with their ankles bending in, but only one of Bobby's ankles bent out! This worried his dad a great deal. I told Cliff not to worry about it; the ankle would straighten itself out in time. And it did."

Garinger taught Bobby at three different phases in his early hockey education: at the very beginning; then when he was eight years old; and, again, when young Clarke was 11. "At first," said Garinger, "he'd come to the rink in the back of my house. That's where he first learned how to stickhandle because we'd have a solid mass of boys on a 30 by 40-foot rink, not to mention a few girls who came on the ice to do some figure skating."

He'd worn only hand-me-down skates during his entire youth hockey career. But at 16, weeks before his tryout with the junior Flin Flon Bombers, he took the money he saved from working all summer at the town's only gas station and hitchhiked south to Brandon and back, having found a shoemaker who custom-made skates. The round trip took four days, but those skates, he believed, would help him get a spot on the roster.

He made the team and played for the Bombers out of the fabled Whitney Forum, Flin Flon's 2000-seat arena. Flin Flon's nearest opponent was 500 miles away in Winnipeg, which meant a nine-hour bus ride that went all day and all night. If you played junior hockey for the Bombers, the high school wouldn't let you be enrolled because you'd be away and on the bus most of the time.

Bombers head coach Pat Ginnell wasn't sure that Bobby was a champion the first time he saw him, but he didn't send the kid home either. "He was wearing glasses," recalls Ginnell, "and looked kind of thin when he got on the ice. But once he started moving, there was no doubt in my mind that this was going to be one of the best kids I ever coached."

Clarke recalls, "In Flin Flon you were so far away from the NHL that you dreamed of playing there but you weren't close enough to ever have any idea what it was about."

Bobby scored 51 goals in 59 games for the Bombers during the 1967-68 season. Add that with 117 assists for a league-leading 168 points. Based on those numbers alone people got the idea that Clarke was going to be a very high draft pick at the NHL draft at the end of the next season.

Unfortunately for Bobby's reputation, word had gone up and down the NHL's scouting grapevine that he was a diabetic and certainly could not be counted on to absorb the rigors of the NHL without suffering serious side effects. "Forget about Bobby Clarke!" they whispered often enough for Ginnell to finally hear and take affirmative action.

"I knew that Bobby wanted to be a professional hockey player," said Ginnell, "and I knew he'd never get there as long as he had the diabetes rap against him. I figured that there was only one thing to do and that was to have the best doctors determine just how bad, or good, his health really was and what kind of future he might have as a big-league player."

What Ginnell did is he arranged to have Bobby visit the world-renowned Mayo Clinic in Rochester, Minnesota. His coach personally drove him down before the 1968-69 season. Following a battery of tests, the doctors agreed that there was absolutely no reason why Bobby could not play professional hockey provided he took good care of himself. What's more, the doctor put it in writing.

"That was all I needed," Ginnell said. "We went home and when scouts came around the following season I showed them the letter. I wanted everyone from any NHL team who came to Flin Flon to know about Bobby exactly what the doctors at the Mayo Clinic knew."

Once on the ice that 1968-69 season, Clarke looked liked the healthiest 19-year-old in Canadian junior hockey circles. A neutral observer might question his decision to quit school at seventeen, but Flin Flon is a world of its own.

Bobby Clarke and his best buddy Reggie Leach worked at the mine for four hours a day while playing hockey the rest of the time. It was a pretty sweet set-up for living in a small northern Manitoba town, but Flin Flon wanted a team so the mine made certain that it had one. "Reggie was 16 and I was 17. You had to be 18 to work inside, so we shovelled sidewalks outside and cut the lawn and stuff," recalled Clarke. "At 18 I went inside and worked the crusher. They would bring in ore on trains and dump it in this huge gyrator to get crushed. That was my job. I never went underground. I was too small. If you were on the junior club, you would work from 8-12 in the mine and practice in the afternoon, but they would pay you for eight hours."

Through it all, Clarke just loved the game. It never crossed his mind that it was a means of getting out of Flin Flon. In the 1968-69 season, Bobby's last year of junior hockey, he scored 137 points in 58 games which was good for the league lead for the second straight year. "He never played a bad game for me," says Ginnell. "Never. Once Bobby started to fill out there was no stopping him."

Clarke was easily the best player available at the 1969 NHL Amateur Draft but dropped to the second round because of the diabetes. Looking back, it's crazy to think that some teams passed on Clarke twice.

There were two teams that really wanted Clarke at the draft: Montreal and Philadelphia. Sam Pollock, managing director of the 1969 Stanley Cup champion Montreal Canadiens was very high on Clarke and some of his scouts had him ranked as high as number three on their lists. Pollock knew he wasn't going to draft the diabetic in the first round but he definitely wanted him the second time around.

Gerry Melnyk of the Flyers wanted Clarke a little more than Pollock and made his views known to general manager Bud Poile. He also advised Poile that Clarke was a diabetic, so in knowing that, Poile decided that no matter how enthused Melnyk might be about the Flin Flon native, he wasn't going to draft a questionable young player unless the team doctor flashed the green light. Without hesitation, Poile went to a phone booth and dialed up a doctor in Philadelphia.

Poile asked the doctor what the chances of a diabetic making it in the National Hockey League, and the doctor pointed out other diabetics who had solid pro sports careers and told him that as long as Bobby was a cooperative individual, then there was no reason not to take him.

Now the draft was on and Melnyk continued lobbying for the Flyers to pick Clarke in the first round. Melnyk was overruled and Philadelphia selected Robert "Bob" Currier, a 6'6" forward who ended up being a major flop in the Flyers' farm system. Melnyk was furious. "I'd like to forget that we picked Currier first," Melnyk recalls. "But let's say there was some voices raised at our table."

"If you don't draft Bobby," Melnyk warned his colleagues, "my judgment isn't worth a damn."

The Flyers eventually picked Bobby with the 17th pick and the rest, as they say, is history. Bobby went on to have an immediate impact on the Flyers. He had a fantastic rookie season with the club and soon after became the youngest captain in the National Hockey League. Very early on you could see the kind of strong leadership qualities he had.

To cope with his diabetes, Clarke would drink a bottle of Coca-Cola with three spoonsful of dissolved sugar before a game. Between periods he downed half a glass of orange juice with sugar added, and after the game a whole glass. He always had several chocolate bars and a tube of 100% glucose in his bag, just in case it was needed.

Playing against the Russians in the 1972 Summit Series also really helped with Clarke's confidence as a leader. He knew by the time that the series was over and Canada had won that he had the ability to play with and defeat the best players in the world. Clarke earned the respect of many in the series for his determined play, his near-flawless face-off ability and his solid two-way play. Clarke will forever be known for his infamous slash in game six on Russia's top forward Valeri Kharlamov that fractured a bone in his ankle, making him ineffective for the remainder of the series. "There were guys on Team Canada who took their game to new heights in that series. A perfect example would be Bobby Clarke," stated Wayne Cashman.

Clarke returned to the Flyers after the Summit Series and put up a career year in the 1972-73. He finished with 104 points (second in the league) and was named the league's most valuable player, winning his first Hart Trophies. He also won the Lester B. Pearson Award as the most valuable player as judged by his peers.

Bobby went on to lead the Broad Street Bullies to back-to-back Stanley Cup championships in 1974 and 1975, becoming the first expansion team to win a championship. The Flyers got close to a third straight Stanley Cup, but lost in the 1976 Cup finals to the Montreal Canadiens. Clarke earned more praise as the most complete player in hockey by winning two more Hart Trophies in 1975 and 1976.

You really can't say enough about how much Clarke worked at the game to get to where he did. In his mind, every shift he took was game 7 overtime of the Stanley Cup finals. Teammate Paul Holmgren said, "His work ethic embarrassed everybody else on the team to work hard like him." Holmgren was a rookie on the Flyers in 1976 and learned about one of the unwritten rules of the Flyers pretty early on in that nobody dressed for the morning skates before Bobby Clarke did. "At first, I couldn't figure out what everybody was waiting for, then I realized they were watching him," said Holmgren. "Freddie (Shero) made it our choice but nobody wanted to be in sweats if Bob was in full equipment. That was my first lesson in the silent leadership of Bobby Clarke."

Defenceman Joe Watson said, "He means as much to us as Bobby Orr and Phil Esposito mean to the Bruins. The guts he shows. Everybody else has to give 100 percent. Him, he gives 150." Dave Schultz called him the "heart and soul of our club," while Flyers head coach Fred Shero said there would be no championships in Philadelphia without Bobby Clarke. Clarke played with so much determination that he demanded the same from every single one of his teammates.

Bobby Clarke retired after the 1983-84 season and immediately headed up to the team's front office to become their general manager. He finished with 1210 points in 1144 NHL games over fifteen seasons, all with Philadelphia. Clarke still has the record for most NHL points ever for a Manitoba-born player. Bobby Clarke won three Hart Trophies (1973, 1975, 1976) over his career and won the Bill Masterton Trophy in 1972 for overcoming diabetes. He won the Selke Trophy in 1983 as the league's top defensive forward. He likely would have won a lot more Selkes throughout his career, but the award wasn't even around until 1978. He won the Lou Marsh Award in 1975 as Canada's top athlete of the year. Bobby captained the Flyers to two Stanley Cups and was a part of Team Canada for their 1972 Summit Series triumph and 1976 Canada Cup. He was named to NHL First All-Star team twice (1975, 1976) and Second All-Star team twice as well (1973, 1974). He skated in nine NHL All-Star Games during the 1970's. When he retired he stood 4th all-time in NHL assists and 11th all-time in NHL points. His career plus-minus of +506 is still fifth all-time.

The Flyers retired Clarke's #16 jersey and named the Bobby Clarke Trophy after him, which is awarded annually to the Flyers' Most Valuable Player. He still holds eleven Flyers team records. He also won the WHL MVP his final year of junior in 1969 and now the WHL scoring trophy has been renamed the Bob Clarke Trophy in his honour. He won the Lester Pearson and Lester Patrick trophies, Lionel Conacher award, and was appointed an Officer of the Order of Canada.

Bobby Clarke was inducted in the Hockey Hall of Fame in 1987. He was named one of the 100 Greatest NHL Players of All-Time in 2017 for the NHL 100 event.

Following his retirement as a player, Clarke's first stint as the GM of the Flyers lasted six years and included two trips to the Stanley Cup finals in 1985 and 1987, both times falling to the mighty Edmonton Oilers. Clarke then spent two years as the GM of the Minnesota North Stars, one of which was a miraculous run to the Cup finals in 1991. He became the general manager of the Florida Panthers for their expansion season, before returning to Philadelphia as their GM for a second tenure. The Flyers made the playoffs for eleven straight years (one Finals appearance in 1997) during Clarke's second run as GM. He resigned from the GM position at the start of the 2006-07 to become the club's Senior Vice President, the role that he has to this day.

Clarke still gets back to Flin Flon every few years or so, but resides year-round at his home in Ocean City, New Jersey.

The last word on Bobby comes from legendary coach Scotty Bowman who remarked that, "He's the dirtiest player in hockey, but if I had Clarke on the Montreal Canadiens, we would have won six or seven Cups in a row."

CHICO RESCH SAYS

I'm going to choose my words carefully about Bobby. Most opponents hated him. They respected some parts of Bobby Clarke and detested most other parts of him, and I would probably fall under that category of people.

No one tried harder, prepared more, wanted to win more, took care of his hockey business on the ice than Bobby Clarke. He was ferocious and determined as anyone could ever be, and was an exceptional player in his day. His skill of course was nowhere near Andy Bathgate or Jonathan Toews, but Bobby knew who he was and knew how to function within the parameters of the team he played on.

Bobby knew he wasn't going to have to pay any consequences for his meanness, his chippiness and his dirty play. He knew he was a protected individual who could play freely every night. If he hadn't played on such a tough team, he could have never played the way that he did. That being said, he would have adjusted and would have been a great player regardless. But he knew that he had the liberties to get away with stuff and play his game.

Barry Cummins played for the Regina Pats with me in juniors and Bobby was playing with the Flin Flon Bombers. Cummins was a tough player and wouldn't take any of Clarke's crap, so he took it to Bobby in juniors. Later he got called up to the NHL's California Golden Seals and he didn't know his role. I saw him when we were in the NHL and he had a big bruise on his face, so I asked him what had happened, if he got into a fight in his last game. He said, "Oh no, this is from ten days ago. My old buddy Clarkie speared me in front of the net." I'm sure that went back to juniors with the shoe on the other foot now. So, Cummins started throwing Clarke around like in juniors, and then the whole Flyers bench jumps off and pounded him pretty good.

Then of course you have the two-hander on Valeri Kharlamov in the 1972 Summit Series. I had heard of it, but when I later saw the new footage years later. It was vicious. I'd seen two-handers plenty in my day, but in the annals of hockey, I'd never seen a two-hander like that. But again, Clarkie would just do anything and everything to win. And in that instance, John Ferguson had told him that someone has to take Kharlamov out of the equation, and Bobby did it.

He was kind of like Billy Smith in that he would leave his conscience at the door when he went and played hockey. Most guys wouldn't do "anything" to win. Most players had limits. Clarkie and Smitty were similar in that they would literally do anything to win, and worry about the conscience later. I'm not knocking it, it's just what they did. And you wanted Clarkie on your team.

He was a really smart player in close areas, making good tight passes with his forehand or backhand. He learned how to be a very smart player in that era. He wasn't like Jonathan Toews and go up the ice, swooping through the neutral zone and beating defenders one on one. Instead he knew how to chip the puck by a player and that kind of thing. I would say that Clarkie knew the game very well, knew how penalties would be called and took advantage of it. More power to him.

In the annals of impact players from Manitoba on your list, he's right where he should be. He had a tremendous impact on the game of hockey, and still does today. I'll just leave it at that.

1

TERRY SAWCHUK

"We are the sort of people that make health insurance popular."
—Terry Sawchuk

Terry Sawchuk is widely regarded as the greatest goaltender that's ever lived. So frankly it was a pretty easy decision to put him here as the number one Manitoba hockey player of all time. It's tough to top four Stanley Cups and four Vezina Trophies. A sportswriter who knew Terry well said, "He was the greatest goalie I ever saw, and the most troubled athlete I ever knew."

MANITOBA HOCKEY HALL OF FAME

The legendary Emile "The Cat" Francis told me personally that no better goaltender has ever come around in all of years he followed the sport and that Terry Sawchuk is still the greatest. Gordie Howe claimed throughout his later life that Sawchuk was the best goalie he ever saw. Don Cherry also says he's the greatest goalie he's ever seen. Basically, everyone that was around to watch Sawchuk play will tell you that he's the top netminder of all time.

The perfect goalie living in an imperfect world, shouldering the blame for every puck that slipped by him. The only thing that satisfied Sawchuck at game's end was a shutout. Terry dealt with clinical depression that went untreated his entire life. One can only imagine the severe mental anguish and trauma that went hand-in-hand with the physical sufferings of all the injuries he endured. He was a tormented soul there's no doubt about that, but he was put on earth if for no other reason than to be the greatest netminder in hockey history. "I don't think people understood the suffering he went through," said son Jerry Sawchuk. "He shouldn't have been an athlete. He was a freak of nature and was driven by two things—fear and adrenaline." His fear was "of losing his job because he didn't know how he was going to feed his family if he did. He was always insecure about it. That's why, despite horrible injuries, he hung on."

"A chain-smoking nervous wreck who seemed bent on self-destruction," wrote *The Hockey News* columnist Ken Campbell. "He was perceived as a moody, aloof cuss who seemed to be dogged by the dark clouds of insecurity."

I'm not going to go too much into Terry's personal problems in this chapter. Terry's full life story is very eye-opening and if you'd like to read more then I highly recommend checking out my colleague David Dupuis' tremendous book called *Sawchuk: The Troubles and Triumphs of the World's Greatest Goalie*. It's a truly fascinating read.

Terry Sawchuk was born in Winnipeg on December 28, 1929 to a Ukrainian family. He was the third of four sons (and one adopted daughter) born to his parents, Louis and Anne. Louis had fled Ukraine as a child and made a living as a tinsmith in a factory. Legend has it that Louis had once settled an argument with a former Canadian boxing champion by knocking him out with a single punch.

Tragedy became a common thing for Terry early on in his life. Louis and Anne's second son died of pneumonia when Terry was a baby and then when Terry was ten, his older brother Mitch died suddenly of a heart attack at the age of seventeen. Mitch was an up and coming goaltender that Terry idolized and his death scarred him for the rest of his life.

Terry was born and grew up in a house at 620 Aberdeen Avenue in the North End. Terry was put on skates for the first time at the age of three. His Uncle Nick played a big role in getting the Sawchuk boys started in hockey, "Louis (Terry's dad) had a nice big yard so we made a bob ski run. We had a larger, wider yard so we made the hockey rink there. Then, when Terry was getting better, we made one big rink, about the length of six houses, right to the sidewalk. It was as slick as you could make it. And we used to play with our shoes, just fooling around. All of the guys in the neighbourhood would come out, too, and we'd play around."

Terry went to nearby Strathcona School on McGregor Street and soon after started playing pick-up hockey with his chums at an outdoor rink on

Cathedral Avenue. It was his older brother Mitch who taught him how to play goalie and showed him the "Sawchuk Crouch" that would later set Terry apart from the rest of the game's top goalies once he got to the National Hockey League.

Mitch was a high school goaltender and Terry's role model. Him and George Hainsworth, Terry's favourite goalie in the NHL growing up. Mitch and Terry would listen to Foster Hewitt on Saturday nights and Terry would be in awe of the great Hainsworth's netminding. He even went as far as trading four hockey cards for one of Hainsworth. Terry would pretend he was Hainsworth when he was playing on the outdoor rinks when he wasn't emulating his brother. Mitch died at the age of seventeen. Terry was only ten at the time and his world as he had known had crumbled with Mitch's untimely death.

Shortly after Mitch passed away, the family moved to a modest two-storey home at 257 Bowman Avenue in East Kildonan. Living his teen years in East Kildonan where NHLers Wally Stanowski and Alf Pike had grown up, the writing was on the wall that you could make the NHL one day if you put in the time and effort. Terry played his hockey at nearby Morse Place and Chalmers Community Club.

When Terry was twelve he dislocated his right elbow very badly playing rugby, and not wanting to be punished by his parents, he hid the injury, which resulted in the arm not healing properly and it ended up being two inches shorter than his left arm and had limited range of motion. It's an injury that hindered him for the rest of his life.

At around this time the Esquire Restaurant in Winnipeg, owned by a man named Max Fanstein, sponsored a boys' Midget hockey club called the Esquire Red Wings. The coach, Bob Kinnear, a western scout for the Detroit Red Wings, helped sponsor Fanstein's outdoor rink and ran a minor hockey program because Detroit was always looking for talent in western Canada. Kinnear was looking for a goalie and recalled that, "Terry was about eleven or twelve, husky and chubby. He was a defenceman with his school team. He was one of a hundred or so kids who hung around my outdoor rink. We always needed equipment and I recall him saying he had a pair of pads at home so I told him to bring them down." Kinnear encouraged Terry to try the pads on and see how he fared stopping pucks. To his amazement, Terry was a natural. After consulting with his scouting partner, they both agreed that the young Sawchuk had massive potential in goal.

Under Kinnear's tutelage, it was apparent after only a short while that Terry was the best young goalie around. Remembering Mitch's tutoring about the importance of balance to a goaltender, Terry began to develop his unique "Sawchuk Crouch" that became one of the most innovative things to happen in goaltending until the mask. Placing his hands out in front of him and bending his waist so that his center of gravity seemed always to be perfectly above his feet, his stance allowed him to have excellent lateral movement as well as balance.

Terry went to Prince Edward School at 649 Brazier Street and briefly attended East Kildonan High School (now Lord Wolseley School), before dropping out at fourteen to acquire his working papers so that he could help out his family by earning a wage. His father helped get him a job at a sheet-metal company, installing, among other things, huge vents over bakery ovens.

Kinnear eventually got the Sawchuk family to sign Terry with Detroit when he was fourteen, after Baldy Northcott, a Chicago scout, unsuccessfully tried to get Terry to sign a C-Form. When Terry left a little while later for Ontario to play for the junior Galt Red Wings, his mother slipped him a ten-dollar bill to help him on his journey. "It was one of the few ten-dollar bills she ever had!" Terry later said.

"Terry was kind of my idol because he lived on Bowman Avenue which was one street over from me when I was growing up," recalled Ted Harris. "I knew his younger brother real well but of course Terry was gone all the time playing hockey. I used to chum a little bit with his brother."

It should be noted that Sawchuk was also quite the baseball prospect around the same time. After his first season in Galt, he came home and led his Morse Park Monarchs to the 1947 junior provincial baseball championships. His .500 batting average attracted attention from baseball scouts for the St. Louis Cardinals, Pittsburgh Pirates, and Cleveland Indians. The next year, Sawchuk had a tryout with the Cleveland Indians' Indianapolis farm team of the American Association. After taking his swings, he was offered a chance to go to the minors in New Orleans for conditioning. Terry was very pleased with the offer but respectfully declined and returned home to Winnipeg.

He played first base for the Elmwood Giants of the Manitoba Senior League. The two-hundred-pound goalie with a right elbow that was permanently disfigured and painful, led the league in batting after twelve games with a batting average of .418. He went on to win the league batting championship with an average of .376, His Giants team won the Manitoba baseball championships. He also played that summer again with the Morse Park Monarchs but the playoff schedule conflicted with Red Wings training camp, so Terry had to miss it, and his Monarchs didn't fare so well without Sawchuk in the post-season.

The Red Wings signed the 6'0", 200-pound Sawchuk to a professional contract in 1947 when he was just seventeen years old. The Red Wings assigned him to the Omaha Knights of the USHL and he quickly learned what it took to be a pro hockey player. On Terry's 18th birthday in a game with Omaha, he was hit in the eye by a bullet slap shot. He lucked out that a surgeon happened to be passing through town and ended up saving Sawchuk's vision and hockey career with a successful operation.

He won Top Goaltender and Top Rookie honors with Omaha in 1947-48 before spending two seasons with the AHL's Indianapolis Capitals, which was culminated by a Calder Cup win in 1950. He even had a solid seven-game stint with the Red Wings in the 1949-50 season and soon after the Red Wings were confident enough about Terry to trade away incumbent starter Harry Lumley so Sawchuk could play full time in the NHL.

Sawchuk made general manager Jack Adams look like a genius when he won the Calder Trophy in 1950-51 (winning the Rookie of the Year award in three pro leagues—a record), playing in all of the club's 70 games with 44 wins and 11 shutouts, leading his Detroit side to a first-place finish in the regular season. Ultimately, they were knocked out of the playoffs by the Montreal Canadiens.

"Terry was the best goalie I ever saw," said CBC Hockey Night in Canada broadcaster Dick Irvin Jr. "I remember in 1951, the year I moved out east. The Montreal Canadiens outshot Detroit 48-12 and Detroit won the game 3-1. I've never seen a guy in my life play goal like Terry did that night. If I could ever see that game again I'd say the same thing because it was really something."

The next season was even better for Terry as he led the NHL in games played and wins for the second straight year, winning the Vezina Trophy in the process. In the playoffs, Terry was literally unbeatable going 8-0 with four shutouts and he didn't allow a single goal on home ice en-route to his first Stanley Cup. At 22 years old, he was already considered by most of the press as the greatest goalie in the history of the sport.

This was only the beginning for Terry. In the three seasons that followed, he won two more Stanley Cups and two more Vezinas to add to his already impressive trophy collection. Everything seemed to be going great for the Winnipeg native until June of 1955 when the Red Wings shocked the hockey world by trading Sawchuk to Boston in order to stake their future on young netminder Glenn Hall, who had been excelling in the minors. Terry felt betrayed. He had just won his team a Stanley Cup and all of the sudden they were trading him like he was used goods.

It was obvious that Terry didn't like his time in Boston. During his second season with the club, he contracted mononucleosis, and although he only missed two weeks of action, he was still very physically weak when he returned and was playing poorly. To top it off he was on the edge of a nervous breakdown, so he announced his retirement from the game in early 1957.

It turned out to be a very short retirement as by the time the next season rolled around, he was back stopping pucks in a familiar Detroit Red Wings uniform. Times had changed in the National Hockey League, however, and the Montreal Canadiens and Toronto Maple Leafs were now the teams to beat, and Detroit was only average so Sawchuk didn't have the same team success as he did in the beginning of his career.

With Sawchuk carrying the Red Wings workload, he led them to the Stanley Cup Finals in 1961, 1963 and 1964. And it was during that 1963-64 season that Terry broke his idol George Hainsworth's record for most career shutouts at 94. Sawchuk would eventually finish at 103 shutouts which was a record for 45 years until Martin Brodeur surpassed that mark.

In 1964, Sawchuk was claimed in an intra-league waiver draft by the Toronto Maple Leafs and for the next three seasons he would join forces in goal with Johnny Bower and the pair formed one of the greatest goaltending tandems the game has ever seen. In their first season together, they shared the Vezina Trophy even though their club finished in fourth in the league standings.

Leafs teammate Ron Ellis recalled Sawchuk in the *Legends of Hockey* documentary saying, "He hated practices. He would stand beside one post in practice and he'd hope that you didn't hit him, and he'd wave his stick once in a while at the other side of the net to see if he could stop the puck. That was the way he approached practices."

"Sometimes at the end of practice we'd have a shoot-off and there was money on the line," added Dave Keon. "Then he would play. And he usually won. But if there was nothing to the practice, his net looked like a coal bin there was so many pucks in it that it used to drive coach Punch Imlach nuts. But when it came time for the game to start, his record speaks for itself, he's the best that ever played."

"People don't want to give him credit for it, but he had a lot of class. Don't forget now he played for the Detroit Red Wings with the big stars. They got all the headlines, and they forget about the man back in the net, Terry Sawchuk," recalled Rangers teammate Eddie Giacomin. "We're in a unique position as goaltenders. In order for us to be good we have to be shot at. Remember that. We have to be shot at. And Terry used to say, 'Well you don't have to kill me.' What Terry used to get mad about is in practice the guys would come in and give it their all and blast that puck, and he would get furious at them and say, 'Why don't you do that in the game to the opposing goaltender? What are you trying to kill me for?'"

Sawchuk is perhaps best known today for his heroics in the 1967 playoffs. Saying that Terry "carried" the Leafs to the Cup would still be a massive understatement so I'll just say that he played out of this world in such a big moment during the twilight of his career. "He played so well," recalled Ron Ellis. "I can still see him standing on his head, I can still see him challenging Bobby Hull shot after shot after shot."

Sawchuk played the role of a miracle worker in a six-game semifinal victory against Bobby Hull and the Chicago Blackhawks. He then did so again throughout a long and tiring six-game series victory over Montreal in the finals. After making several miraculous saves in the dying moments of Game 6, Terry retreated to the dressing room while his teammates celebrated with the Cup.

"I don't like champagne and I'm too tired to dance, but this has to be the thrill of my life," said Sawchuk. "I've had a lot of wonderful moments in hockey and other Stanley Cups but nothing equal to this."

Leafs teammate Pete Stemkowski had some great stories about Terry during their time together in Toronto: "I used to have funny hair, didn't know whether to have a crew cut or to let it grow and Terry would tease me a lot about it. He used to tell me 'why don't you just shave it all off and start over again?' He was really banged up with that bad elbow and was physically damaged so he walked kind of hunched. When he used to walk across the dressing room he'd walk with that hunch with the elbows sticking out and sometimes I'd walk behind him and imitate him. He'd turn around right away and yell at me!

"I remember I had a penalty shot once against Roger Crozier and I hit the post. In practice the next day, he'd move out of the way when I would come in to shoot on him and say, 'can you put it in now?' He could definitely be moody and grouchy, but he was always friendly to me. Sometimes when I used to imitate his walk through the dressing room, he'd turn around and I'd see a little smile on his face. "

When the NHL expanded from six to twelve teams for the 1967-68 season, Terry became the first overall pick in the Expansion Draft and went out west to the Los Angeles Kings to be the face of the franchise in their inaugural season.

Jiggs McDonald, the first play-by-play announcer for the Kings, tells a story about how Sawchuk was able to add to his earnings at the expense of his rookie teammates. " GM Larry Regan had a rule that no player was to have a car at training camp, but Terry did," recalled McDonald. "Because I was the advance man, Cooke had wanted me to find food and lodging for $9 a man. I was able to bring it in at $9.25 a man, much to Cooke's disdain, but we had to eat by this golf course out near Kitchener, and Sawchuk, with the only car, charged each player taxi fare. He really made some money. And Regan didn't try and stop him, explaining that Terry had been a pro a long time and was the Kings' number one man."

The Kings' eccentric owner Jack Kent Cooke predicted that Sawchuk would lead the Kings to the Stanley Cup in their first season, which I guess wasn't all that unrealistic since the six new teams were placed in the same division, with the winner facing the best of the Original Six teams in the Stanley Cup final. Unfortunately, the Kings' were bounced in the first round of the playoffs.

"I don't know what it was," Kings goaltending partner Wayne Rutledge recalled, "but the guys seemed to try harder when I was in net. I don't know if they relaxed in games with Terry behind them because they figured, 'Ah, we've got the best in net. If we screw up, he'll stop them,' and the guys figured I needed more protection, but that seemed to be an early pattern."

The team's trainer in Los Angeles Danny Wood recalls Sawchuk during that season: "As a physical specimen, he was a disaster! His shoulder looked like it had been broken and never set right. His bad arm was three or four inches shorter than the other. He'd walk around all stooped over, hobbling in and out of the rink. Yet as soon as he got on the ice, he'd skate around like he was just a kid. I used to think it's too bad Terry couldn't be on his skates twenty-four hours a day. He seemed to be in less pain."

It's no doubt that Terry's body could have been used as a medical textbook. Just some of the injuries that Sawchuk endured over the course of his career include: punctured lung in a car accident, torn tendons in his hand, an emergency appendectomy, ruptured spinal discs, mononucleosis, multiple nervous breakdowns, more than 600 stitches, a swayed back brought on by his style of playing goal that resulted in not being able to sleep for more than two hours at a time, insomnia, and migraine headaches.

On October 10, 1968, the Kings were in Winnipeg for an exhibition game against the Canadian National Team. Long-time Detroit teammate and now Los Angeles coach Red Kelly called Sawchuk aside to tell him he'd been traded to Detroit. "He cried," Red recalled. "I tried to explain to him that he would be better off, going back to a more established team like the Wings, that he would have a better shot at a Stanley Cup. It was a sad day for the both of us."

Terry played the last two years of his career with Detroit and then the New York Rangers as a backup. He died May 31, 1970 in the aftermath of a tragic accident that occurred just a few weeks after the 1969-70 season ended. He was only forty years old.

In one of my past books, *Hockey Hotbeds*, Emile "The Cat" Francis told me his firsthand account of Sawchuk's untimely death: "Identifying Terry's body at the morgue was the worst thing I ever had to do in my life. At the beginning of his career he had played for Indianapolis in the AHL and I was playing for New Haven so we had played against one another and that was when he was just breaking in. Well later in life, I was coaching the Rangers and I was looking for an experienced goalie to backup Eddie Giacomin, so I got Terry in a deal from Toronto and he was my backup goalie. I figured he could play 15 games and Giacomin could play the rest.

"Terry was living with teammate Ron Stewart. They were both split up with their wives and both had about five children. Stewart was from Calgary and Terry had married a girl from Detroit so he was living there. The season ended after we were knocked out of the playoffs and I was in Quebec. I answered the phone one afternoon and on the other line is a doctor from Long Island saying that a player of mine is in the hospital and he might not make it through the night. It was surprising to hear because the season had been over for three weeks already. He told me it was Terry Sawchuk, and I asked if he was in a car accident. The doctor said no and that he couldn't tell me what happened because he was sworn to secrecy by Terry. I told him I was on my way and the next morning I flew out to Long Island. I had my wife pick me up from the airport and got her to drive me right to the hospital. I quickly found out where the emergency ward was and went right in there and as I looked on, Terry was way down near the end of the hall and he saw me and said, 'What are you doing here?' I said 'What am I doing here? Better I should ask you that.' He said, 'Well it's a long story, I'll tell you the whole thing that happened but don't blame Ron Stewart'.

"So, he proceeded to tell me that they had been in an argument and had a couple drinks, and were fighting. They were smart enough to get out of there and go home but Sawchuk followed Stewart home because they were living together! The arguing started again at the house and Stewart was smart, he left. He was starting to go down the stairs to get to the ground floor and Sawchuk came from behind him and took a swing at him. And they both rolled over down the stairs with Sawchuk falling into a barbecue pit. Terry said that as soon as he fell in the pit he knew something was wrong. He said, 'My whole stomach feels like I got shot', so they called an ambulance and he'd been in the hospital for ten days already when I got there! I asked him how he felt now and he said that he keeps passing out so what I did was I called the Rangers' doctors in New York and they sent an ambulance to bring him right over. This was right at the beginning of Memorial Day Weekend and our doctors were about to go home before they got my call. Terry got to the New York hospital at about 1pm on the Friday, and three hours later they called me into the room where Terry was at and they said that they had found out what the problem is—Terry was bleeding internally and it was stopping and starting again. One of these times he's going to pass out and not come back. They said it's going to be a very difficult operation but it has to be done right away. Terry asked me for a priest and I got him one to give him his last rites. After that, as they were taking him in for the operation, he had a Detroit Red Wings Stanley Cup ring on and I'll never forget this. He took it off, handed it to me and said 'Emile, in case I don't come out of this will you be sure my son gets this ring.' I said 'You're going to come out of it don't worry. You'll come out of it.'

"The doctors started operating at 5pm and finally finished at midnight—that's how difficult of an operation it was. When they were through they said there was no sense in waiting here and to go home because the next 24 hours are going to decide whether he's going to make it or not. And that if they needed anything they would call me. Well, at 6am the phone rang telling me that Terry had died overnight.

"I now had to go to the morgue on 2nd Avenue in New York, told them who I was and that I was there to identify a body. Christ, they took me down through winding steps, opened a door and there was about 25 people all in bags that looked like the ones you'd carry hockey sticks in. All you can see is the head of the different people with a tag on them. The man asked which is the body that you're here to claim for and I said right over there and pointed to Terry. He had no idea who I was or who Terry was. He didn't know Terry Sawchuk from the man on the moon. I couldn't even sleep that night or for a few nights until we got things straightened out with Ron (Stewart). But I'll always remember looking at Terry in that morgue and thinking to myself, there's the best goaltender I'd ever seen and I still stand by that statement to this day."

When Terry passed away he left the game with a 447-330-172 career record in 971 NHL games over 21 seasons. At the time of his death he was the all-time leader amongst goaltenders for NHL wins and was the first netminder to ever reach the 100-shutout plateau. His 103 shutouts stood as an NHL record for 39 years until Martin Brodeur broke it in 2009 and he still remains the all-time leader in wins for goalies who played in the Original Six era.

Terry won four Stanley Cups (1952, 1953, 1955, 1967), four Vezina trophies (1952, 1953, 1955, 1965), and was selected to play in the NHL All-Star Game on eleven occasions. He was also named to the NHL First All-Star Team three times (1951, 1952, 1953) and the NHL Second All-Star team four times (1954, 1955, 1959, 1963). In 1971, just one year after he passed away, the Hall of Fame waived the usual mandatory waiting time and Terry was promptly inducted into the Hockey Hall of Fame. He was later inducted into the Canada Sports Hall of Fame in 1975. An arena near where he grew up in East Kildonan was renamed the Terry Sawchuk Memorial Arena in 1991. In 1994, his number "1" was retired by the Detroit Red Wings into the rafters at Joe Louis Arena. He was named to Manitoba's All-Century First All-Star Team and was selected to be Manitoba's Player of the Century in 2000. On January 1, 2017, Terry was named one of the 100 Greatest NHL Players for the NHL 100 event.

"I don't think Terry enjoyed his successes," recalled Ron Ellis. "That's what happens when you're depressed; you don't have the capacity to enjoy what you've accomplished. I just never saw that joy in him."

My good friend and fellow hockey historian Joe Pelletier has the final word on Sawchuk, saying poetically that, "Terry's hockey career began with a broken heart and an abandoned set of goalie pads. Just as tragically, his career and life ended the same way."

CHICO RESCH SAYS

Terry Sawchuk is a tragedy regarding how tormented he was. Playing goal in his day was a torment all by itself. The physical fear of getting hit in the face with the puck is something that all goalies had back then, and for Terry he had to deal with over 500 stitches during his career from pucks to the face. We've all seen that photo from *Time* magazine of Terry's face with his scars shown more clearly. I've shown that photo to people and it scares them!

It was always torment, trouble, and agony for him. Terry never loved the game really, it was always a love/hate relationship. The thing is he was just so darn good at it right from a young age, it became who he was. He defined himself as a great goalie and that's too bad. There's many more things that are more important in life like his family, he should have been more there for them.

I would say that Terry was one of the best of all time, and at the same time was a very tragic figure. But despite that, he could muster up whatever churned inside of him to be this incredible goalie. He was one of the best blocker save goalies to ever play the game, carrying that blocker high. Terry was the goalie's goalie, but the validity and the dial that he had when he moved in the crease, you were just mesmerized by the simple things that he did. When you were as great as Terry was, or any great artist, they think okay well that's awesome, but can you take it to another level. They're never satisfied.

I can still see him the way he came out of the door onto the ice. That look and how he would drop the puck for the guys in warm-up. It looked so cool. He wasn't trying to be cool, but he just had this style and grace that made you be in awe just watching him.

The other thing with Terry is that he came into a great situation when he first broke into the NHL with a fantastic Detroit Red Wings team which gave him the confidence and all that he needed as a goalie. One of his finest hours, however, is when he was beaten down and broken up in 1967 with the Leafs. They needed him and he rose to the occasion to win one more Stanley Cup.

I went down to the MET Centre when I was in college with the Minnesota-Duluth Bulldogs for a North Stars game against Terry's Los Angeles Kings. I got to meet him and honestly, he didn't respond the way I wanted an idol to respond. He didn't have the time for me and kind of gave me a mean look. I just don't think he enjoyed that part of the job, being an ambassador for the sport.

When you look at Terry Sawchuk, you see greatness and tremendous weakness. But through it all, somehow, he was one of the greatest goalies. He was a complex superstar so you have to look at it both ways. You can't cloud his problems, but at the same time I have so much respect for him because under the turmoil that he was dealing with and the way he could block it all out and play, and play at such a high level is nothing short of miraculous.

I talked to some guys that played with him and they all liked him. I talked to Johnny Bower and I'd ask him what he was like and he'd say, "Oh, he was good. He was a goalie's friend. But he didn't let you get very close, he was a bit aloof." With great artists, sometimes that's just the way they are.

Terry was very edgy and never at peace with himself and never comfortable inside his own skin except when he had the big pads on. I never had to deal with his demons so I don't know what it was like, but I think he was a great example of a dual personality. On the ice he got it together, and off the ice he never had it together. I think when you talk about him, you have to talk about both of his personalities so people really can understand the big picture, what he dealt with, and in some ways why he was so great.

You could compare him a little to Mickey Mantle. He was into the bottle like Mickey, tormented in some ways, and never was that comfortable with himself until later on in life. People say that Mickey made some dramatic changes after he got out of baseball. Terry died at a young age and never got the chance to do that, unfortunately.

ACKNOWLEDGMENTS

A book like this doesn't just get written by one person. So many people played a role in writing and getting this book finished that to be honest, I'm just the guy that compiled all of the information and compressed it into the book you're holding in your hands—if that makes sense.

I'd like to start off by thanking Great Plains Publications, and more specifically Gregg Shilliday, Mel Marginet and Stephanie Berrington for their help and guidance, and taking a chance on a young author like myself.

I'd of course like to thank my family and friends that supported me while writing this book. You know who you are.

A big heartfelt thanks goes out to historian Kent Morgan, who was instrumental in the early stages of this book. He went through the list of fifty players that I had and helped come up with the criteria and provided many books from his vast collection to help with my research.

There's been a lot of great Manitoba sportswriters that have come along over the years, but Vince Leah and Ed Sweeney are the two men that really helped pave the way for this book. The work that they did in their time was amazing and it's certainly sprinkled throughout this book.

Thanks to Glenn "Chico" Resch for giving his take on a lot of the players featured in this book. Chico was a great NHL netminder in his day and a fantastic colour commentator as well. He's a fantastic interview and he really told some awesome stories for the "Chico Resch Says" sidebars.

Thank you to my hockey writing mentors Joe Pelletier and Eric Zweig for always taking the time to be gracious and letting me pick their brain on a wide variety of topics at any given time. You guys are good pals and I look forward to meeting you at a future SIHR meeting perhaps!

Thank you to the Hockey Hall of Fame in Toronto.

Thanks to Don Kuryk, Jordy Douglas and Morris Mott of the Manitoba Hockey Hall of Fame for their support in this book.

A big thank you goes out to Rick Brownlee at the Manitoba Sports Hall of Fame for the use of the photos that you saw in this book. Thanks to Andrea Reichert for retrieving the photos from the Hall of Fame archives.

Thanks to fellow members of the Society for International Hockey Research for their help in coming up with the rankings of the players.

Lastly, I'd like to thank everyone who gave their time to be interviewed for this book. Without you, this book wouldn't have been possible and I'm truly so happy I got to spoke to each and every one of you.

SELECTED BIBLIOGRAPHY

Richard Brignall, *Forgotten Heroes Winnipeg's Hockey Heritage:* J. Gordon Shillingford, 2011

Antonia Chambers, *Before the Echoes Fade: the Story of Charlie Gardiner:* Lanark, 2005

David Dupuis, *Sawchuk: the Troubles and Triumphs of the World's Greatest Goalie:* Stoddart, 1998

Ed Fitkin, *Turk Broda of the Leafs:* Castle, 1950

Stan Fischler, *Bobby Clarke and the Ferocious Flyers:* Warner, 1974

Reggie Leach, *The Riverton Rifle: My Story—Straight Shooting on Hockey and on Life:* Greystone, 2015

Vince Leah, *Manitoba Hockey, a History:* Manitoba Hockey Players' Foundation, 1970

David Square, *When Falcons Fly:* Poppy Productions, 2007

Wes Wilson and Elma (Wilson) Kozub "Discovering Carol 'Cully' Wilson: An Icelandic hockey pioneer": *Lögberg-Heimskringla.* Online supplement to Issue 6, 2005